EIGHTH EDITION

CLINICAL GUIDELINES
FOR
SCHOOL NURSES

SCHOOL
HEALTH
ALERT

SCHOOL HEALTH ALERT
P.O. Box 150127
Nashville, TN 37215

Clinical Guidelines for School Nurses
Copyright © 2013 School Health Alert. Certain portions of this manual were originally published in *School Nurse Resource Manual: A Guide to Practice* Copyright © 2010.

NOTICES

Nursing, including school nursing, is a dynamic, constantly changing field. The publisher, editor and contributors have made a diligent effort to ensure any procedures or recommendations outlined in this manual are accurate and in accordance with accepted school nursing practices at the time of publication. It is, of course, necessary for readers to apply their professional judgment, experience and knowledge of the patient to determine the best treatment in a specific case.

Several websites are included in this manual to provide additional information and references on a particular topic. However, listing these websites does not imply endorsement. Note that with any internet site, addresses and content may change and information therein needs to be accuracy and the date the contents were updated.

ISBN-13: 978-0-9792497-4-7   ISBN-10: 0-9792497-4-0

Phone: 866-370-7899
Fax: 615-370-9993

ABOUT THIS MANUAL

"School nursing is a specialized practice of professional nursing that advances the well-being, academic success, and life-long achievement and health of students. To that end, school nurses facilitate positive student responses to normal development; promote health and safety including a healthy environment; intervene with actual and potential health problems; provide case management services; and actively collaborate with others to build student and family capacity for adaptation, self-management, self- advocacy, and learning" (NASN, 2010)[1]. School nursing services uniquely address health and safety needs of students individually but also in populations, and as a subspecialty of community/public health nursing.

School nurses' work focuses directly on three areas: health services, health education, and the school environment. Their services require diverse knowledge including, but not limited to, pediatric/adolescent health, infectious diseases, mental health, chronic diseases, and emergency care. They can influence health and safety aspects of schools and can provide leadership to a district's or campus' coordinated school health program that in addition to health services, health education, and the school environment addresses mental health and social services, nutrition services, physical activity, family and community involvement, and/or staff health promotion.

This resource serves as a quick reference for school nurses and can assist them, their administrators, and consulting physicians to develop policies and procedures for safe student care. This manual offers brief summaries of conditions that most school nurses encounter but is not intended to substitute for any comprehensive pediatric or emergency care textbook.

The *school nurse guidelines* were developed through cooperative efforts of school nurses and physicians. We strongly recommend a similar process at the district or system level with adaptations that account for state laws and regulations as well as the unique needs of students in a school district. The registered nurse plans student health services, but vocational/practical nurses, or unlicensed staff such as office personnel or clinic assistants may perform certain tasks within state nursing practice guidelines. The registered nurse is responsible for training persons assigned to perform a delegated nursing task, monitoring their performance, and ensuring their compliance with the procedures. State school nurse consultants are an invaluable resource regarding laws, regulations and nurse practice acts in each state.

---

[1] National Association of School Nurses. (2010). *Definition of school nursing*. Retrieved from http://www.nasn.org/RoleCareer

PHYSICIAN CONSULTATION

The availability of a physician's services to schools varies across communities. Some large districts have full-time medical directors or consultants, while others have part-time physician services. Small districts may engage a physician to consult for a set number of hours or on-call. Some physicians volunteer as a community service.

Regardless of the arrangement, it is sound medico-legal practice for the school nurse to have written guidelines to standardize assessment and management decisions. Such guidelines with physician consultation complement professional school nursing practice standards and the nursing process and should incorporate accepted injury and pediatric care recommendations.

We suggest that students who have conditions that are likely to require treatment or emergency care during school hours or activities, have individual written orders from their own healthcare provider. These orders should be reviewed and updated at least each school year or as necessary. The most common individual orders are for students with asthma or diabetes. Some students with seizure disorders, bee sting allergy, migraine headaches, or other chronic conditions need individual orders each school year.

DESCRIPTION OF SCHOOL NURSE GUIDELINES

We offer an outline format so that important features of each condition and guidelines for action can be seen at a glance. Each guideline includes a definition/etiology of the disease or condition, presenting signs and symptoms, management strategies and follow-up. This format provides the registered nurse a quick reference for student care and offers information to educate and train staff that may assist the school nurse.

Registered nurses apply their professional skills and judgment in the management of each individual case, but each school and district/system should provide care for all students in a consistent manner guided by local policies and procedures, e.g., criteria for referral or exclusion and return to class.

Usual procedures, such as Standard (Universal) Precautions, parent notification, record keeping, confidentiality, etc. may not be repeated in all guidelines but is understood to be a standard practice.

STANDING ORDERS

Although standing orders are not addressed in this edition, the distinction between the two types of orders should be understood.

General orders are written by a physician, often the school medical consultant, which apply to all students for whom the order may be applicable. They should be reviewed annually and updated when necessary. It is not necessary for the doctor to have previously examined the student. Dosage is based on weight or age. Common examples of general orders are acetaminophen for fever, ibuprofen for minor headache, etc. These orders are issued with the understanding that a registered nurse will administer these medications after an assessment of the child.

Some state boards of nursing do not allow general standing orders in school settings. Other boards may allow a "physician directed nursing protocol" which requires signatures of both a physician and a nurse (usually a nursing administrator or manager). If the administration of nonprescription products is permitted, the school's policy (for discretionary medications) should be in writing and parents must be informed. Parents should sign a written request for each school year indicating that their child may receive any of the named medications in the discretionary medication policy from school personnel according to the district's policy.

Specific orders are written and signed by a physician *for an individual child.* The parents should also sign a medication authorization form for school personnel to administer any medicine at school. These specific orders contain the drug or treatment, dose, route, time and duration of administration. Example for a child with diagnosed with ADHD: "Methylphenidate 20 mg (one tablet) by mouth daily between 11 A.M. and noon after lunch or with food through December 20, 2013". Most districts require that individualized orders be renewed annually.

Each school/district should have a medication policy that guides medication administration and documentation of both specific , individual orders for medication and for any discretionary medications that are allowed.

We welcome your suggestions for future editions and wish you success in caring for our nation's children. You may contact us on the Internet at *www.schoolnurse.com.*

ACKNOWLEDGMENTS

This 8th Edition was edited by Vicki Taliaferro, BSN, RN, NCSN. Clinical content revisions were prepared by:
Julia Lechtenberg RN, MSN, NCSN
Dona Roberts BSN, RN
Suzanne Levasseur MSN, APRN
Susan Zacharski, MEd, BSN, RN
Suzanne Putman, MEd, BSN, RN
Alicia L. Burrows-Mezu, MSN/ED, BSN, BSc, RN

This edition offers updated and new content since the 7th edition (2010) edited by Vicki Taliaferro and Jan Ozias, with major contributors, such as Suthatip Sirijunpen, M.D., and state school nurse consultants, including those in Georgia, Massachusetts, and Maryland.

Finally, the publisher acknowledges the *School Health Alert* co-editors, Jan Marie Ozias, PhD, RN and Howard Taras, MD, and Editorial Board members:
- Kathleen Johnston, MS ,RN,
- Larry Olsen, DrPH, CHES
- Phillip Nader, MD
- Martin Sklaire, MD

Robert Andrews, Publisher
School Health Alert
P.O. Box 150127
Nashville, TN 37215
(866) 370-7899
www.schoolnurse.com

Clinical Guidelines for School Nurses Eighth Edition Index

ABDOMEN: Blunt Injury

DEFINITION/ETIOLOGY:
Following a hard blow to abdomen (by rock, fist, bicycle handlebar, etc.) an internal organ may be ruptured and bleed into the abdominal cavity slowly but continuously. Injured abdominal organs may include the spleen, liver, retroperitoneum, small intestines, colorectal, bladder, kidney, diaphragm and/or pancreas.

SIGNS AND SYMPTOMS:
- History of blow to abdomen
- Possible bruise visible
- Pain and tenderness to mild pressure
- Abdominal distention
- Vomiting
- Rapid, weak pulse with low blood pressure
- If kidney is bruised or torn, there may be blood in urine shortly after trauma or next day (more likely if injury is to the lumbar area of the back)
- Shoulder pain (Kehr's sign). Kehr's sign is pain at the tip of the shoulder due to internal bleeding in the abdominal cavity. A positive Kehr's sign is a medical emergency. **Call 911 immediately!**
  - If spleen is ruptured there may be complaints of left shoulder pain
  - If liver is injured there may be complaints of right shoulder pain
- Gradual onset of shock and coma
- Symptoms may appear a day or two following the blow

MANAGEMENT/TREATMENT:
1. Identification of trauma may not be obvious with initial evaluation.
2. Notify parent. Tell what to watch for in the next 48 hours.
3. Keep in clinic for 15 minutes after blow to abdomen.
4. Allow to rest in position of comfort.
5. Monitor pulse and blood pressure.
6. If student has none of the above symptoms, may return to class. Send a note to the teacher to have the student return to clinic before close of school and sooner, if symptoms appear.
7. Reassess the student.
8. If any symptoms ensue, refer to emergency room or physician.
9. Record on injury report, including what parent/guardian was told.

FOLLOW-UP:
Check student again on following day.

1

ABDOMEN: Blunt Injury *(continued from previous page)*

POTENTIAL COMPLICATIONS:
- Ruptured spleen: can be life-threatening without immediate treatment.
- Hypovolemic shock: symptoms include rapid pulse, cold-moist-clammy skin, alteration of consciousness, low blood pressure.

NOTES:
Bicycle handlebar injury:
Abdominal injury may occur when handlebars are turned so they punch the abdomen with force. Bicycle handlebar injuries are often considered trivial; alarming symptoms may not develop for 24 hours. Symptoms of serious injury are severe pain, vomiting or collapse.

References

ACEP News. (2011). *ACEP clinical policy: Blunt abdominal trauma.* Retrieved from
     http://www.acep.org/News-/Publications/ACEP-News/ACEP-Clinical-Policy--Blunt-Abdominal-Trauma

Bodhit, A.N., Bhagra, A., & Ganti Stead, L. (2011). *Abdominal trauma: Never underestimate it.*
     Retrieved from http://www.hindawi.com/crim/em/2011/850625/

Emergency Medical Paramedic. (2013). *What is kehr's sign?* Retrieved from
     http://www.emergencymedicalparamedic.com/what-is-kehrs-sign/

Udeani, J. (2013). *Blunt abdominal trauma.* Retrieved from
     http://emedicine.medscape.com/article/1980980-overview

Udeani, J. & Steinberg, S. (2008). *Abdominal trauma, blunt.* Retrieved from
     http://emedicine.medscape.com/article/433404-overview

ABDOMINAL PAIN/APPENDICITIS

DEFINITION/ETIOLOGY:
Pain or discomfort located between the bottom of the diaphragm and the top of the pelvic region. Acute abdominal pain: less than 2 weeks' duration. Chronic recurrent abdominal pain: three or more episodes, severe enough to affect normal activities, occurring more than 12 weeks.

Abdominal pain may be due to a variety of conditions, including but not limited to:
Intra-abdominal causes:

Gastrointestinal tract
- Dietary (excessive or inappropriate intake, food-borne pathogens)
- Constipation
- Appendicitis
- Lactose intolerance (recurrent)
- Irritable bowel syndrome (discomfort for at least 12 weeks within past 12 months plus at least two of the following: altered frequency and/or appearance of bowel movements, pain relief with bowel movement)
- Peptic ulcer (recurrent)
- Incarcerated inguinal hernia
- Celiac disease (recurrent)

Liver/Gall Bladder/Spleen
- Hepatitis
- Pancreatitis
- Cholycystitis (inflammation of the gall bladder) and cholelithiasis (gall stones)
- Contusion/rupture spleen (trauma)
- Sickle cell anemia (recurrent)

Urinary tract
- Cystitis (inflammation or infection of the bladder)
- Glomerulonephritis
- Kidney stone

Ovaries, Fallopian Tubes and Uterus
- Dysmenorrhea (menstrual cramps) (recurrent)
- Rupture of ovarian follicle at ovulation (mittelschmerz)
- Pelvic inflammatory disease (PID)
- Complication of pregnancy (ectopic pregnancy/abortion)
- Sexual abuse

ABDOMINAL PAIN/APPENDICITIS *(continued from previous page)*

Extra-abdominal causes:
- Abdominal migraine
- Diabetic ketoacidosis
- Functional abdominal pain   (emotional or psychosocial)
- Group a streptococcal pharyngitis ("strep throat")
- Hypoglycemia
- Lead poisoning
- Leukemia
- Lower lobe pneumonia
- Rheumatic fever

Common causes considered by age of students:
1. <u>Preschool</u>: constipation, gastroenteritis, viral infection, urinary tract infection, pneumonia, trauma, lactose intolerance, sickle cell episode
2. <u>School age</u>: gastroenteritis, viral infection, constipation, appendicitis, trauma, urinary tract infection, pneumonia, lactose intolerance, sickle cell pain episode
3. <u>Adolescent</u>: appendicitis, in females: mittelschmerz (ovulation pain), pelvic inflammatory disease (PID), dysmenorrhea, complication of pregnancy

SIGNS AND SYMPTOMS:
Symptoms vary depending on the etiology of the pain. A good assessment will help to differentiate the cause of the abdominal pain.
- <u>Mildly ill</u>: pain interferes minimally with normal activities
- <u>Moderately ill</u>: interferes with normal routine or signs of infection or systemic illness
- <u>Severely ill</u>: signs of peritonitis or intestinal obstruction or mental change

ASSESSMENT:
History:
- Onset, location, duration, frequency, severity and pattern of the pain
- Associated symptoms such as fever, vomiting, diarrhea, red or dark red blood in stool, urinary symptoms, weight loss, jaundice, arthritis or cough and sore throat
- Precipitating factors including constipation, trauma, underlying diseases (sickle cell anemia), menstruation, medication and diet history

Physical examination:
- Check temperature; assess circulation and hydration status
- Note signs of emergency surgical conditions:
  - <u>peritonitis</u>: includes guarding and rigidity of the abdominal muscles, rebound tenderness, decreased bowel sound, abdominal distention or shock
  - <u>intestinal obstruction</u>: distention, decreased bowel sounds and persistent vomiting

4

ABDOMINAL PAIN/APPENDICITIS *(continued from previous page)*

- o <u>appendicitis</u>:
  - fever 99°-102° F (oral)
  - nausea, vomiting
  - anorexia
  - vague diffuse epigastric or periumbilical pain, over several hours pain becomes more intense and shifts to right lower quadrant , rebound tenderness, release of pressure on left lower quadrant of abdomen elicits pain in right lower quandrant of abdomen (Rovsing sign)
  - decreased bowel sounds
  - prefers to lie on left side/right knee flexed
  - **If suspect appendix, perform auscultation, percussion, followed by palpation**

  - o <u>complication of pregnancy </u>(female with history of delayed menstrual period) includes lower abdominal pain, pallor or shock, abnormal vaginal bleeding

- • Assess location and severity of the pain:
  Potential medical conditions according to pain location (list is not inclusive):
  - o <u>Diffuse abdominal pain:</u> associated with diabetic ketoacidosis, food poisoning, gastroenteritis, intestinal obstruction, pancreatic disease, peritonitis, pharyngitis and sickle cell anemia
  - o <u>Epigastric pain:</u> associated with duodenal/gastric/peptic ulcers, esophagitis, gastritis, gastroenteritis, GERD/hiatal hernia, myocardial infarction, irritable bowel disease, liver conditions and ulcerative colitis
  - o <u>Right lower quadrant:</u> associated with appendicitis, ectopic pregnancy, gastroenteritis, inguinal hernia, irritable bowel syndrome (IBS), kidney stone, ovarian conditions, pelvic inflammatory disease and testicular torsion
  - o <u>Right upper quadrant:</u> associated with acute pancreatitis, gallbladder conditions, kidney stone, duodenal ulcer, liver conditions and lower lobe pneumonia
  - o <u>Left upper quadrant:</u> associated with bowel obstruction, constipation, IBS, kidney stone, left lower lobe pneumonia, leukemia, pyelonephritis, spleenic conditions and ulcerative colitis
  - o <u>Left lower quadrant:</u> associated with constipation, ectopic pregnancy, inguinal hernia, irritable bowel syndrome (IBS), kidney stone, ovarian conditions, pelvic inflammatory disease, sigmoid colon and testicular torsion
  - o <u>Suprapubic region:</u> associated with dysmenorrhea, endometriosis, pelvic inflammatory disease, sexually transmitted disease, and urinary tract infection/ bladder infections

ABDOMINAL PAIN/APPENDICITIS *(continued from previous page)*

MANAGEMENT/TREATMENT:
1. If signs of appendicitis (the most common serious condition) or moderate-severe illness, notify the parent/guardian immediately and refer to the student's health care provider.
2. If mild, may rest for 15-30 minutes. If symptoms persist, refer for evaluation. If symptoms subside, return student to class.
3. No food or drink by mouth. May sip small amount of plain water.

FOLLOW-UP:
- If student returns to classroom, re-evaluate within 2-4 hours.
- If student requires surgery, upon the student's return, follow health care provider's instructions regarding athletic or PE participation.

References

Cosby, M., Miller, N.B., & Youngman, K. (2013). Acute measures for emergent problems. In J. Selekman (Ed.), *School nursing: A comprehensive text* (2nd ed.) (pp.516-577). Philadelphia, PA: F. A. Davis.

Higgins, R. (2009). Abdominal assessment and diagnosis of appendicitis. *Emergency Nurse, 9*, 22-24.

Mayo Clinic. (2010). *Abdominal pain.* Retrieved from http://www.mayoclinic.com/health/abdominal-pain/MY00390

Mayo Clinic. (2011). *Appendicitis symptoms.* Retrieved from http://www.mayoclinic.com/health/appendicitis/DS00274/DSECTION=symptoms

The Merck Manual Online. (2012). *Acute abdominal pain.* Retrieved from http://www.merck.com/mmpe/sec02/ch011/ch011b.html

ABRASIONS

DEFINITION/ETIOLOGY:
An abrasion is a denuded area of skin (epidermis) resulting from a scrape on a hard or rough surface. Abrasions can occur on any part of the body, but most often occur on bony areas, such as the hands, forearms, elbows, knees, shins, and face. Abrasions often result from falls or friction accidents.

SIGNS AND SYMPTOMS:
- Most abrasions are superficial.
- There is usually minimal bleeding and may ooze sero-sanguenous fluid. The amount of bleeding is greater when deeper layers of skin are scraped off.
- Abrasions can contain particles of dirt.

MANAGEMENT/TREATMENT:
1. Wash gently under running tap water with plain soap to remove foreign material. If feasible, allow a running stream of lukewarm water to pour over the wound.
2. During wash, if necessary, try to remove debris by gently rubbing with 4x4 gauze pads.
3. Do not scrub a wound imbedded with dirt. Instead refer to primary healthcare provider.
4. Assess Tetanus immunization status.
5. Solutions that should **not** be used for cleansing wounds include povidone-iodine, Dakin's solution and hydrogen peroxide. These can damage normal tissue and hinder neodermal development necessary for healing. Antibiotic creams and any topical medication should only be used if standing orders are on file.
6. Small abrasions may be left open to the air.
7. Cover larger abrasions with a sterile, non-adherent bandage.
8. After partial thickness abrasions are cleaned, a moist wound dressing can be applied within two hours of injury. This dressing can be a hydrogel or hydrocolloid dressing and can be any of a variety of brand-name products). This dressing must stay in place at least forty-eight hours and up to seven days to enhance optimal wound healing. Moist wound dressings allow rapid resurfacing or re-epithelialization of wound surfaces and allow for migration of proteins necessary for wound healing.
9. Notify parent/guardian if abrasion is not minor and enter on injury report.

FOLLOW-UP:
- Parent/guardian and student will be instructed that the dressing is to remain in place for seven days or until wound is healed. Dressing may be wrapped with plastic for bathing. The student may be given an extra dressing to take home in the event that his/her dressing falls off or is damaged and needs replaced.
- The student should have a daily wound and dressing recheck; replace dressing as needed.

ABRASIONS *(continued from previous page)*

- After seven days, the partial thickness abrasion will be re-evaluated by the registered nurse using the Bates-Jensen Wound Assessment Tool. If re-epithelialization has occurred at day 7, no further dressing or evaluation is needed.
- If after seven days, the laceration or abrasion is not healing, the student is referred to his/her primary health care provider.
- Repeat cleansing at least daily, more often if necessary to keep wound clean.
- This should be done at home, but school nurse may need to monitor or guide.

POTENTIAL COMPLICATIONS:

1. Infection:
    a. Pus on abrasion itself, usually located under crusts.
    b. Cellulitis: spreading redness immediately around the abrasion.
    c. Lymphangitis: red streaks radiating out from abrasion. (Sometimes this is mistakenly referred to as blood poisoning. It is actually an infection of the lymph channels.)
    d. Regional lymph nodes enlarged; if abrasion on arm, nodes will be in axilla; if on leg, nodes will be in groin.
2. Scarring:
    a. Minor abrasions: scar very superficial, usually regains pigmentation and blends with surrounding skin.
    b. Deep abrasions: scar usually deeper and permanent. (May require later management for
    cosmetic reasons).

NOTES:

- If no improvement in ONE day, refer to physician.
- For lymphangitis, refer to physician immediately.
- Nurse practitioners or other nurses with prescriptive authority may order amoxicillin or other antibiotics.

References

Ball, J., Binder, R., & Cowen, K. (Eds.). (2012). Alterations in skin integrity. *Principles of Pediatric Nursing: Caring for Children (5th ed.)* (p. 1033). Upper Saddle River, NJ: Pearson Education, Inc.

Harris, C. , Bates-Jensen, B., Parslow, N., Raizman, R., Singh, M., & Ketchen, R.J. (2010). Bates-Jensen wound assessment tool: pictorial guide validation project. *Journal of Wound, Ostomy & Continence Nursing,37*(3), 253-9. doi: 10.1097/ WON.0b013e3181d73aab

Houser, J. (2011). Evidence-based practice in healthcare. In J. Houser, S. Oman (Eds.). *Evidence-based practice an implementation guide for healthcare organizations,* (p. 7). Sudbury, MA: Jones & Bartlett Learning.

Merck Manual, Professional Edition. *Abrasions.* (2013). Retrieved from http://www.merckmanuals.com/professional/ injuries_poisoning/lacerations/lacerations.html?qt=abrasions&alt=sh#v1110280

Sanford Health. Healthwise. (2010). *Scrapes.* Retrieved from http://www.sanfordhealth.org/HealthInformation/Healthwise/ Topic/srape#hw101236

ALLERGIES

DEFINITION/ETIOLOGY:
The immune system reacts to a foreign substance that is not generally harmful (examples – certain foods, latex, pollen, insect stings/bites, medications or pet dander).

SIGNS AND SYMPTOMS:
Symptoms vary and depend on the persons' specific allergy. Allergy symptoms range from mild to life threatening.

Allergic dermatitis
- Rash (papules/vesicles) at site of contact
- Pruritus
- May have areas of excoriation from scratching
- Thicken dry skin that may ooze

Allergic rhinitis
- Allergic shiners – bluish discoloration and edema below eyes
- Clear nasal discharge
- Sneezing
- Itchy, watery and/or swollen eyes

Atopic dermatitis (type of eczema)
- Thickened, cracked, or scaly patches of skin
- Patches red to brownish-gray in color
- Itchy skin
- Extremely dry skin may ooze

Medication allergy (penicillin, sulfa, anticonvulsants, iodine and insulin preparations are the most common cause of medication allergies)
- Hives
- Rash
- Pruritus
- Difficulty breathing/wheezing
- Anaphylaxis

See *School Nurse Guidelines for:*
- Anaphylaxis
- Food Allergies
- Poison ivy/oak
- Rashes
- Sting allergy

ALLERGIES *(continued from previous page)*

MANAGEMENT/TREATMENT:

General treatment
1. Avoidance of allergen
2. Medications (as prescribed) to reduce symptoms
3. Immunotherapy (allergy shots)
4. Emergency epinephrine

Allergic dermatitis
1. Corticosteroids creams/ointments – to ease itching
2. Corticosteroid (oral) – reduces inflammation, immune response and itching
3. Antihistamines – to relieve severe itching
4. Antibiotics – if lesions are infected from scratching

Allergic rhinitis
1. Antihistamines - relieves sneezing, runny nose, itching, and watery eyes
2. Nasal corticosteroid sprays – start working quickly but may take several weeks to obtain the full effect of the medication
3. Decongestants – reduce symptoms of nasal congestion
4. Leukotriene inhibitor (i.e. Singulair®) to relieve seasonal allergy symptoms
5. Immunotherapy

Atopic dermatitis
1. **Oral corticosteroids – may be prescribed short-term to treat severe cases.**
2. Corticosteroid creams or ointments to ease scaling of skin and itching.
3. Antihistamines to relieve severe itching.
4. Antibiotics to treat bacterial skin infections from scratching.
5. Immunomodulators – reduces atopic dermatitis flare-ups. These medications are approved for children over the age of two. The FDA recommends that these medications be used only when other treatment options have failed.

Medication allergy
1. **Discontinue medication that caused allergic response immediately.**
2. Antihistamines to relieve mild symptoms of rash/hives/itching.
3. Bronchodilators to relieve wheezing.
4. Corticosteroids - reduce inflammation associated with allergic reaction.
5. Epinephrine for severe allergic reaction.

FOLLOW-UP:
- Refer to specialist if symptoms do not respond to treatment.
- Educate as to the importance of avoiding known allergens.
- For severe allergies – provide information regarding the importance of wearing a Medical Alert necklace/bracelet.

ALLERGIES *(continued from previous page)*

- Identify coexisting medical conditions such as asthma – commonly associated with allergic rhinitis and atopic dermatitis.

POTENTIAL COMPLICATIONS:
General
- Skin infections from frequent scratching
- Another allergy
- Anaphylaxis (severe allergic reaction)
- Death

Allergic rhinitis
- Sinusitis
- Otitis Media

NOTES:
An individualized Healthcare Plan AND an Individualized Emergency Plan should be prepared for every child with a serious known food, substance or insect allergy potential. Appropriate school staff (including bus personnel and cafeteria and playground personnel) should receive in-service preparation for dealing with a general allergic reaction and with child specific needs. Staff training in the use of injected epinephrine should be conducted according to state and district laws and policies.

Many states have adopted legislation that allows schools provide undesignated epinephrine auto injectors.

Allergy Resources for School Personnel

American Academy of Allergy and Asthma and Immunology (AAAAI)
1-800-822-ASMA
www.aaaai.org
Professional and patient education resources on the website

Food Allergy and Anaphylaxis Network (FAAN)
4744 Holly Ave.
Fairfax, VA 22030-5647
1-800-929-4040
www.foodallergy.org
www.fankids.org
School guidelines (including school bus and field trips) and teaching materials.

ALLERGIES *(continued from previous page)*

Asthma and Allergy Foundation of America
1233 20th St NW, Ste 402
Washington, DC 20036
800-7-ASTHMA
www.aafa.org
Resources and free student Asthma Action Cards

American Latex Allergy Association
www.latexallergyresources.org

References

Food Allergy and Anaphylaxis Network. (2013). *Types of allergic reactions/Managing food allergies.* Retrieved from
   www.foodallergy.org

Mayo Clinic. (2013). *Allergies.* Retrieved from http:www.mayoclinic.com/health/allergies/DSO01118

Hogate, S., Giel, J., Selekman, J. (2013). Allergy. In J. Selekman (Ed.), *School nursing: A comprehensive text* (2nd ed.) (pp. 784-816).
   Philadelphia, PA: F.A. Davis.

LATEX ALLERGY

DEFINITION/ETIOLOGY (*see also Allergies and Anaphylaxis*):
Latex allergy is a reaction to certain proteins found in natural rubber latex, a product manufactured from a milky fluid that comes from the rubber tree. The more frequently exposed a person is to latex either by direct contact or inhalation (e.g., staff administering daily care requiring use of gloves, persons with spina bifida who use latex catheters), the more likely they are to develop sensitivity. A latex allergy may cause allergic reactions ranging from sneezing or a runny nose to anaphylaxis, a potentially life-threatening condition.

Type IV-Delayed (due to chemicals used in processing latex):
- Itchy, red, mildly swollen skin rash on sites which touched latex
- Typically appearing 24-48 hours after contact
- Blisters appear in severe cases

Type I-Immediate (due to proteins which are part of the natural latex):
- Involves parts of the body that did not touch latex
- Hives on any part of the body
- "Hay fever-like" nasal stuffiness, sneezing, runny nose, itchy nose, eyes or roof of the mouth
- Wheezing, coughing and shortness of breath - *an emergency*
- Anaphylaxis - a life threatening blockage of the airway and shock

MANAGEMENT AND TREATMENT:
1. *Delayed reactions*: short-term, over-the-counter or prescribed steroid topical cream or ointment usually relieve rash.
2. *Hives or "hay fever"-like signs*: over-the-counter antihistamines or decongestants provide relief; health care provider may prescribe cromolyn or corticosteroid nasal spray.
3. *Wheezing, coughing or shortness of breath*: anti-inflammatory and bronchodilator medications for reactive airway.
4. *Anaphylaxis*: epinephrine (e.g., Epi-Pen, Auvi-Q) injected as quickly as possible, followed by immediate transport to a hospital emergency department.

FOLLOW UP:
- Educate persons to avoid contact and exposure to items containing latex (gloves, hair brushes, bandages, balloons, rubber bands, erasers, etc.) A list of common health care and daily items containing latex and alternative products is available through the Latex Allergy Support Group at http://www.lasg.org.uk/information/.
- Persons with a latex allergy may need to avoid certain foods: avocado, banana, kiwi, water chestnut, tomato, "pitted" fruits, and nuts grown in the ground.

LATEX ALLERGY *(continued from previous page)*

- Develop an Individual Healthcare Plan for a student with a latex allergy that includes specific actions to prevent exposure, staff training, and the emergency action plan.
- Schools should provide latex free gloves for staff that use them in their daily job performance.

Resources
NASN's Anaphylaxis Planning Algorithm at http://nasn.org/ToolsResources/ FoodAllergyandAnaphylaxis/AnaphylaxisPlanningAlgorithm

References
American Latex Allergy Association. (n.d.) *About latex allergy.* Retrieved from
    http://www.latexallergyresources.org/about-latex-allergy

Mayo Clinic. (2011). *Latex allergy.* Retrieved from http://www.mayoclinic.com/health/latexallergy/DS00621

Selekman, J., Bochenek, J., & Lukens, M. (2013).Children with chronic conditions. In J. Selekman (2nd Ed.), *School nursing: A comprehensive text (2nd ed.)* (pp. 792, 1031). Philadelphia, PA: F.A. Davis

ANAPHYLAXIS

IMPORTANT: Your district should have a written procedural guideline in place for anaphylaxis. This guideline should be posted in the health room.
- *Students with a known allergic reaction should have an individualized health plan (see sample below) in place and all staff (including bus drivers) must be aware of the emergency plan and how to initiate it.*
- *Determine how epinephrine will be available to the student at all times (on person, in classroom(s)/cafeteria, when on bus or school sponsored event).*
- *Point to consider: Some schools have obtained Standing Orders/or a physician directed nursing protocol for epinephrine from a school physician/physician and non-patient specific stock epinephrine in the health room.*

DEFINITION/ETIOLOGY:
Anaphylaxis is a severe, potentially life-threatening allergic reaction. It may occur in adults or children not previously known to be allergic or hypersensitive. The reaction ranges from mild, self-limited symptoms to rapid death. Symptoms of a reaction can occur within seconds to minutes after exposure.

CAUSES:
Extreme sensitivity to one or more of the following:
- Insect sting, usually bee, wasp or fire ants
- Medication or immunizations, usually by injection
- Food such as peanuts, tree nuts, shellfish, cow's milk or egg (most common triggers in children adolescents and young adults)
- Industrial or office chemicals or their vapors
- Latex rubber

SIGNS AND SYMPTOMS:
Most allergic reactions are not severe enough to cause anaphylaxis. Anaphylaxis has a sudden onset. The severity of the reaction depends on how sensitive, amount ingested and route of exposure. <u>Symptoms that begin within 15 minutes after exposure to trigger agent usually result in the more severe type of anaphylactic reaction.</u>

CAUTION: The severity of the symptoms can change quickly.

ANAPHYLAXIS *(continued from previous page)*

SYMPTOMS OF ANAPHYLAXIS INCLUDE:

Mouth	Itching, swelling of lips and or tongue, tingling (burning) sensation in mouth or around lips or drooling
Throat	Swelling of the tongue and throat, difficulty swallowing, itching, tightness/ closure, hoarseness, changes in quality of voice*
Skin	Itching, hives, redness, swelling
Gut	Abdominal pain/cramping, nausea/vomiting, diarrhea
Lungs	*Respiratory difficulty, shortness of breath, cough, shallow respirations, wheezing, stridor
Heart	Weak pulse, heart palpitations, drop in blood pressure, dizziness, light-headedness, loss of consciousness

Only a few symptoms may be present. **All of the above symptoms can potentially lead to a life-threatening situation. Provide prompt medical attention.**

*Respiratory difficulty and changes in quality of voice are symptoms of laryngeal edema and may signal closure of the airway. Laryngospasm (closure of the vocal cords blocking air intake) can occur as part of anaphylaxis or by itself without any of the above symptoms. **Call 911 immediately.**

MANAGEMENT/TREATMENT:

Follow student's individual emergency care plan. Administer medication as ordered. Plan should include medical orders and staff responsibilities for emergency care.

1. **Immediate injection of adrenalin 1:1000 subcutaneously**
   Age: 3-5 years-----0.15 cc
   Age: 6-8 years-----0.25cc
   Age: 9-18 years---0.3cc
2. **Immediate call to 911** and transport to nearest medical facility despite initial improvement after first epinephrine injection, biphasic reactions often occur. The following information should be sent with the EMS:
   * Allergen to which patient is reacting, if known.
   * Signs and symptoms of distress.
   * Emergency measures instituted.
   * Patient response to emergency measures.
   * Time of all activities, including giving adrenalin.
3. If reaction is known to follow an insect sting, see "Sting Allergies".

16

ANAPHYLAXIS *(continued from previous page)*

4. **If student is still at school in 15-20 minutes, repeat dose of epinephrine <u>according to physician orders.</u>**
5. Monitor vital signs including blood pressure continuously.
6. Place person on their back or other comfortable position with their legs elevated. Do not allow person to sit up.
7. Cover with blankets, if necessary, to keep warm; do not allow blankets to interfere with handling or observation.
8. Refer all cases to physician.

FOLLOW-UP:
- Review the student's individualized emergency plan to make sure there are no changes required based on this incident. If this is the first known incident of an allergic reaction, ensure that an individualized emergency plan (see sample below) is developed and make sure all staff (including bus drivers) are aware of the emergency plan and how to initiate it.
- Provide health education with family, student, and school staff regarding further exposure to sensitizing agent.
- Emphasize wearing Medic Alert tag or bracelets (<u>www.medicalert.org</u>).
- Ask about desensitization procedure by physician.
- Have parent/guardian replace epinephrine if expired or used.
- Record as "Medical Alert" on student's record.

POTENTIAL COMPLICATIONS:
- Cardiac arrest
- Respiratory arrest
- Shock
- Coma
- Death

NOTES:
- Every minute counts with anaphylaxis. Delay in treatment is associated with fatalities.
- Prevention – avoid known allergens.
- Eighty to ninety percent of anaphylactic reactions include skin signs and when they are absent, anaphylaxis is harder to recognize.
- Symptoms of an anaphylactic reaction may vary in multiple episodes in the same person.
- Medications, age-related factors, and co-existent diseases, may contribute to severe or fatal anaphylaxis.
- Co-factors such as infections, exercise, emotional stress, and premenstrual status may possible amplify anaphylaxis.

ANAPHYLAXIS *(continued from previous page)*

- An emergency care plan must be in place and mock drills practiced regularly.
- Do not store injectable epinephrine devices in a frequently opened drawer as repeated motion may cause premature release and injury when handled.
- Do not store injectable epinephrine in car glove box/bus or where it can become overheated.
- Consider sending epinephrine home during school breaks depending on temperature of building when school is not in session.
- Epinephrine that is cloudy or discolored should not be used.
- Do not store in refrigerator. Normal **room temperature** is best. Dispose of used auto-injector according to OSHA guidelines.

Resources

NASN's Anaphylaxis **Planning Algorithm** at http://nasn.org/ToolsResources/FoodAllergyandAnaphylaxis/AnaphylaxisPlanningAlgorithm
(Tools to train school nurses and staff).

World Allergy Organization guidelines for Assessment and Management of Anaphylaxis at http://www.ncbi.nlm.nih.gov/pmc/articles/PMC3500036/ . (Charts include Clinical Criteria for Diagnosing Anaphylaxis, Patient Risk Factors for Severe or Fatal Anaphylaxis and Co-Factors that Amplify Anaphylaxis, Anaphylaxis Mechanisms and Triggers, Clinical Criteria for the Diagnosis of Anaphylaxis, and Symptoms and Signs of Anaphylaxis).

References

Mayo Clinic. (2013). *Anaphylaxis*. Retrieved from http://www.mayoclinic.com/health/anaphylaxis/DS00009

Selekman, J. & Gray, C. (2013). Allergy. In J. Selekman (Ed.), *School nursing: A comprehensive text (2nd ed.)* (pp. 787-790). Philadelphia, PA: F.A. Davis.

Simons, F., Ardussol, L., Bilo, B., Gamal, Y., Ledford, D., Ring, J., Sanchez-Borges, M., Senna, G., Sheikn, A., Thong, B., & World Health Organization. (2011). World allergy organization guidelines for the assessment and management of anaphylaxis. *The World Allergy Organization Journal, 4*(2), pp.13-37. Retrieved from   http://www.ncbi.nlm.nih.gov/pmc/articles/PMC3500036/

American Academy of
Allergy Asthma & Immunology
www.aaaai.org

Anaphylaxis Emergency Action Plan

Patient Name: _____ Age: _____

Allergies: _____

Asthma ☐ Yes *(high risk for severe reaction)*   ☐ No

Additional health problems besides anaphylaxis: _____

_____

Concurrent medications: _____

_____

Symptoms of Anaphylaxis

MOUTH	itching, swelling of lips and/or tongue
THROAT*	itching, tightness/closure, hoarseness
SKIN	itching, hives, redness, swelling
GUT	vomiting, diarrhea, cramps
LUNG*	shortness of breath, cough, wheeze
HEART*	weak pulse, dizziness, passing out

Only a few symptoms may be present. Severity of symptoms can change quickly.
*Some symptoms can be life-threatening. ACT FAST!

Emergency Action Steps - DO NOT HESITATE TO GIVE EPINEPHRINE!

1. Inject epinephrine in thigh using (check one): ☐ Adrenaclick (0.15 mg)   ☐ Adrenaclick (0.3 mg)

☐ Auvi-Q (0.15 mg)   ☐ Auvi-Q (0.3 mg)

☐ EpiPen Jr (0.15 mg)   ☐ EpiPen (0.3 mg)

Epinephrine Injection, USP Auto-injector- authorized generic
☐ (0.15 mg)   ☐ (0.3 mg)

☐ Other (0.15 mg)   ☐ Other (0.3 mg)

Specify others: _____

IMPORTANT: ASTHMA INHALERS AND/OR ANTIHISTAMINES CAN'T BE DEPENDED ON IN ANAPHYLAXIS.

2. Call 911 or rescue squad (before calling contact)

3. Emergency contact #1: home_____ work_____ cell_____

Emergency contact #2: home_____ work_____ cell_____

Emergency contact #3: home_____ work_____ cell_____

Comments: _____

_____

_____

_____

Doctor's Signature/Date/Phone Number

_____

Parent's Signature (for individuals under age 18 yrs)/Date

19

 **FOOD ALLERGY & ANAPHYLAXIS EMERGENCY CARE PLAN**

Name: _____ D.O.B.: _____

Allergy to: _____

Weight: _____ lbs.   **Asthma:** [ ] Yes (higher risk for a severe reaction) [ ] No

PLACE STUDENT'S PICTURE HERE

For a suspected or active food allergy reaction:

FOR **ANY** OF THE FOLLOWING
SEVERE SYMPTOMS

[ ] If checked, give epinephrine immediately if the allergen was definitely eaten, even if there are no symptoms.

LUNG	**HEART**	**THROAT**	**MOUTH**
Short of breath, wheezing, repetitive cough	Pale, blue, faint, weak pulse, dizzy	Tight, hoarse, trouble breathing/ swallowing	Significant swelling of the tongue and/or lips

SKIN	**GUT**	**OTHER**	**OR A COMBINATION**
Many hives over body, widespread redness	Repetitive vomiting or severe diarrhea	Feeling something bad is about to happen, anxiety, confusion	of mild or severe symptoms from different body areas.

NOTE: Do not depend on antihistamines or inhalers (bronchodilators) to treat a severe reaction. **Use Epinephrine.**

1. **INJECT EPINEPHRINE IMMEDIATELY.**
2. **Call 911.** Request ambulance with epinephrine.
- Consider giving additional medications (following or with the epinephrine):
  » Antihistamine
  » Inhaler (bronchodilator) if asthma
- Lay the student flat and raise legs. If breathing is difficult or they are vomiting, let them sit up or lie on their side.
- If symptoms do not improve, or symptoms return, more doses of epinephrine can be given about 5 minutes or more after the last dose.
- Alert emergency contacts.
- Transport student to ER even if symptoms resolve. Student should remain in ER for 4+ hours because symptoms may return.

NOTE: WHEN IN DOUBT, GIVE EPINEPHRINE.
MILD SYMPTOMS

[ ] If checked, give epinephrine immediately for ANY symptoms if the allergen was likely eaten.

NOSE	**MOUTH**
Itchy/runny nose, sneezing	Itchy mouth

SKIN	**GUT**
A few hives, mild itch	Mild nausea/discomfort

1. **GIVE ANTIHISTAMINES, IF ORDERED BY PHYSICIAN**
2. Stay with student; alert emergency contacts.
3. Watch student closely for changes. If symptoms worsen, **GIVE EPINEPHRINE.**

MEDICATIONS/DOSES

Epinephrine Brand: _____

Epinephrine Dose: [ ] 0.15 mg IM   [ ] 0.3 mg IM

Antihistamine Brand or Generic: _____

Antihistamine Dose: _____

Other (e.g., inhaler-bronchodilator if asthmatic): _____

_____

PARENT/GUARDIAN AUTHORIZATION SIGNATURE   DATE   PHYSICIAN/HCP AUTHORIZATION SIGNATURE   DATE

ASTHMA AND ASTHMA EMERGENCIES

DEFINITION/ETIOLOGY:
Asthma is a chronic inflammatory disease of the airways. It is best understood as the clinical result of two linked processes, airway inflammation and bronchial hyper-reactivity. While bronchial hyper-reactivity is often genetically determined, it may be induced by viral infection. Airway inflammation is often triggered by allergies or viral illness. Environmental exposure to known allergens, or cigarette smoke at home may aggravate symptoms and lead to more persistent and significant airways hyper-reactivity.

HISTORY:
Asthma is the most common "medical" cause of chronic school absenteeism and may present in a number of distinct fashions:
- Episodes of wheezing and shortness of breath related to exposure to an allergen, such as cats, dust, outdoor pollens or mold
- Prolonged and often refractory cough and wheeze with shortness of breath related to acute respiratory viral illness
- Shortness of breath, cough or wheeze triggered by exercise or cold-air that takes more than just a minute or two from which to recover

SIGNS AND SYMPTOMS:
Asthma symptoms vary from person to person. Symptoms range from minor wheezing to life-threatening asthma attacks. In most children without active symptoms, physical examination is totally normal.

Early signs and symptoms of asthma may include:
- Nighttime cough
- Chronic fatigue
- Bags under eyes
- Irritability

Persistent cough or shortness of breath may be the only signs of active asthma. Wheezing is often but not always heard. Reduced peak flows from baseline helps separate asthma from other conditions such as bronchitis or poor physical conditioning. A greater than 20% improvement in peak flow rates after albuterol administration is seen in asthma too.

ASTHMA AND ASTHMA EMERGENCIES *(continued from previous page)*

Common signs and symptoms of asthma:
- Shortness of breath
- Tightness (or pain) in chest
- Wheezing
- Coughing
- Difficulty sleeping due to coughing, wheezing and/or shortness of breath.

Children with a *severe asthma attack* often evidence observable signs:
- Sitting upright, leaning forward, using neck muscles to assist inspiration; nasal flaring may be present
- Abnormal breath sounds (decreased/wheezing)
- Prolonged expiration, sometimes with pursed lips
- High pitched cough; irregular high pitched wheeze
- Poor air movement; rapid shallow breathing
- Tachycardia (pulse>120)
- Speaking in very short sentences
- Blue lips or fingernails
- Inability to record a peak flow

> **The presence of signs or symptoms suggestive of a severe asthma attack in a child should be considered a medical emergency and immediate treatment commenced.**

MANAGEMENT/TREATMENT:

General guidelines for dealing with an asthma attack include:
1. Implement child's Asthma Action Plan.
2. Administer inhaled or nebulized bronchodilator (usually albuterol) as per Action Plan.
3. Allow the child to assume a comfortable posture in a quiet setting.
4. Measure peak flow, if possible, to document severity and response to therapy.
5. Record pulse and respiratory rate.
6. Monitor – do not leave student alone.
7. Notify parent/guardian.

> **A child who does not completely and quickly respond to bronchodilator therapy and with normalization of peak flows should not return to class.**

Treat acute symptoms of asthma with as-needed rescue short-acting bronchodilators. Albuterol sulfate *(Proventil, Ventolin, Xopenex)* is the most commonly prescribed metered dose inhaled rescue bronchodilator. It may also be given in tablet, extended release tablet, syrup, or nebulized with the means of an air compressor driven hand-held nebulizer.

ASTHMA AND ASTHMA EMERGENCIES *(continued from previous page)*

Rules of Two®¹ serve as an easy asthma assessment tool to indicate when further medical therapy is needed, and are derived from the content of the NHLBI* *Guidelines for the Diagnosis and Management of Asthma*. Answering "yes" to one of the *Rules of Two®* suggests that anti-inflammatory therapy using an inhaled corticosteroid (such as Flovent Diskus, Flonase, AeroBid, QVAR or Pulmicort) should be added to as-needed bronchodilators. This is especially true in evaluating the asthmatic child who is taking only rescue medication for control.

Rules of Two® ask:
- ✓ Do you need a quick-relief inhaler (rescue) bronchodilator for asthma symptoms more than two times/week?
- ✓ Do you awaken with asthma symptoms at night more than two times/month?
- ✓ Do you refill a canister of rescue bronchodilator more than two times/year?

In low doses, inhaled corticosteroids have been shown to reduce mortality, hospitalizations, emergency asthma flares, exercise and allergen triggering, night-time awakenings from asthma and total cost of care.

If anti-inflammatory therapy is already being utilized, then additional therapy with either a long acting bronchodilator *(Serevent, Foradil, Perforomist)* or leukotriene modifier *(Accolate, Singulair, Zyflo)* may be appropriate. Occasionally theophyllines may be added as long-acting bronchodilators. A combination medication containing both a long-acting beta agonist and a corticosteroid *(Advair, Symbicort, Dulera)* may be another option for better asthma control.

Management should also include avoiding asthma triggers. Specific inquiry into asthma triggers is important and should include symptoms related to exposure to pets, dust, foods, medication (such as aspirin or ibuprofen) or cigarette smoke. Studies have shown that reducing exposure to specific allergens or irritants (such as cigarette smoke) improves asthma symptoms and reduces the amount of medication necessary for good control.

FOLLOW-UP:
- Monitor effectiveness of pharmacological therapy.
- Monitor student inhaler technique. Provide reinforcement as needed.
- Educate student/staff on asthma basics and how to manage an asthma emergency.
- Educate student/staff on how to properly care for inhaler:
    - Clean inhaler weekly – remove canister from jacket and wash jacket with soap and water.
    - Follow HFA priming instructions

---

1   *Rules of Two®* is a registered service mark of Baylor Health Care System, Dallas, Texas.

ASTHMA AND ASTHMA EMERGENCIES *(continued from previous page)*

Prime HFA bronchodilator inhalers per pharmaceutical directions

HFA Bronchodilator	Priming Instructions
ProAir	3 sprays (1st use; after 2 weeks non-use)
Proventil	4 sprays (1st use; after 2 weeks non-use)
Ventolin	4 sprays (1st use; after 2 weeks non-use) [Prime – 1 spray if MDI dropped and 1 spray after washing]
Xopenex	4 sprays (1st use; after 3 days non-use)

ASTHMA EMERGENCIES:
An acute asthma attack is a medical emergency that should be treated promptly and effectively.

IMMEDIATE DANGER SIGNS:
- Struggling to breath – may be hunched over
- Abnormal breath sounds – absent/decreased/wheezing
- Retractions – intercostals, substernal, suprasternal
- Nasal flaring
- Using accessory muscles
- Bluish discoloration (cyanosis) around lips or nailbeds
- Tachycardia
- Tachypnea
- Difficulty walking
- Difficulty carrying on a conversation
- Little relief from bronchodilator – not responding to medication
- *Severely restless*
- *Decreased level of consciousness*
- Symptoms worsening

MANAGEMENT/TREATMENT:
1. Seek immediate emergency care – *CALL 911 IMMEDIATELY.*
2. *Transport to nearest hospital for emergency care.*
3. *Notify Parent/guardian.*

ASTHMA AND ASTHMA EMERGENCIES *(continued from previous page)*

UNTIL EMS ARRIVES:
- Continue to follow physician's orders
- Allow the child to assume a comfortable posture in a quiet setting
- Monitor vital signs
- Keep student calm
- Provide reassurance
- Do not leave student alone

Potential complications of a severe asthma attack include:
- Respiratory failure
- Death

NOTE:
This information is not meant to be substituted for the professional advice /guidance of a physician.

POTENTIAL COMPLICATIONS:
- Complications can range from secondary infections to more serious respiratory arrest.
- Permanent narrowing of the bronchial tubes.
- Unresponsiveness to medications.
- Side effects from long-term use of some asthma medications.
- Severe asthma attack resulting in increased emergency room visits and hospitalizations.

NOTES:
Every child identified with asthma should have a written **Asthma Action Plan** approved by the child's health care provider and available in the school nurse's office.

The goal of asthma management is <u>prevention</u>:
1. Education regarding avoiding known allergies or irritants and the need to use medications as directed is important.
2. Yearly influenza vaccine may be recommended.
3. In some circumstances, children may be allowed to carry short-acting rescue inhaled bronchodilators on their person for use before exercise or with asthma symptoms. This decision should be the joint agreement between the school nurse, parent and child's physician and should be supported by school policy and/or state regulations.
4. Educate student/staff on the importance of avoiding extreme weather conditions. Student may need to stay indoors when:
    - ✓ It is extremely windy
    - ✓ Pollen count is high
    - ✓ Outdoor temperature is <32^0 F (including wind chill factor). Encourage student to cover mouth and nose with a scarf or mask during cold weather!
    - ✓ Outdoor temperature is > 90^0F (including heat index)

ASTHMA AND ASTHMA EMERGENCIES *(continued from previous page)*

5. The school nurse may consider offering a school based asthma education program such as the American Lung Association's "Open Airways For Schools" program to students with asthma. The Open Airways program consist of six 40 minute lessons covering topics such as:
    - Asthma basics
    - Recognizing asthma symptoms
    - Identifying and avoiding asthma triggers
    - Learning how to manage an asthma episode
    - Learning how to manage asthma while at school

Note on inhalers: Albuterol inhalers should have a dose counter. You cannot get an accurate estimate of how much active ingredient is in a canister by floating it in water (and you risk damaging the valve). Counters also help indicate if a person is overusing the inhaler and needs a different controller medication plan.

Resources:
American Academy of Allergy, Asthma, and Immunology
414–272–6071
www.aaaai.org

American Academy of Pediatrics
847–434–4000
www.aap.org

American Lung Association
800–LUNG–USA (800–586–4872)
http://www.lungusa.org/

Asthma and Allergy Foundation of America
800–7–ASTHMA (800–727–8462)
http://aafa.org

Baylor Health Care System
800-422-9567
http://www.baylorhealth.com/PhysiciansLocations/Dallas/SpecialtiesServices/Asthma/Pages/default.aspx

Centers for Disease Control and Prevention
 800–CDC–INFO (800–232–4636)
www.cdc.gov/asthma

ASTHMA AND ASTHMA EMERGENCIES *(continued from previous page)*

Environmental Protection Agency/ Asthma Community Network
www.asthmacommunitynetwork.org
800–490–9198
www.epa.gov/asthma/publications.html (to order EPA publications)

National Association of School Nurses

240–821–1130

www.nasn.org

National Heart, Lung, and Blood Institute

National Institutes of Health, P.O. Box 30105

Bethesda, MD, 20891

Phone: 301–592–8573

http://www.nhlbi.nih.gov/health/health-topics/topics/asthma/

References

Allergy and Asthma Network. (2009). *Mastering hfa inhalers.* Retrieved from
http://www.aanma.org/2009/03/mastering-hfa-inhalers-%E2%80%93-step-by-step-instructions/

American Lung Association. (2013). *About OAS.* Retrieved from
http://www.lung.org/lung-disease/asthma/in-schools/open-airways/about-oas.html

Asthma and Allergy Network. (2013). *Inhaler know-how.* Retrieved from http://www.aanma.org/?s=asthma

Baylor Health Care System. (2013). *Asthma toolbox.* Retrieved from
http://www.baylorhealth.com/PhysiciansLocations/Dallas/SpecialtiesServices/Asthma/Pages/AsthmaToolbox.aspx

Centers for Disease Control and Prevention (CDC). (2013). *Asthma and schools.* Retrieved from
http://www.cdc.gov/healthyyouth/asthma/

Ficca, M. & Moore, C. (2013). Asthma. In J. Selekman (Ed.), *School nursing: A comprehensive text* (2nd ed.) (pp.677-704).
Philadelphia, PA: F. A. Davis.

Mayo Clinic. (2011). *Asthma attack.* Retrieved from
http://www.mayoclinic.com/health/asthma-attack/DS01068/DSECTION=symptoms

MedlinePlus. U.S. National Library of Medicine. (2013). *Signs of an asthma attack.* Retrieved from
www.nlm.nih.gov/medlineplus/asthma.html

Merck Manual Online. (2013). *Asthma.* Retrieved from http://www.merckmanuals.com/professional/pulmonary_disorders/
asthma_and_related_disorders/asthma.html?qt=asthma&alt=sh

National Heart, Lung and Blood Institute. (2012). *What is asthma?* Retrieved from
http://www.nhlbi.nih.gov/health/dci/Diseases/Asthma/Asthma_WhatIs.html

Thompson, J. (2013). *New HFA reliever inhalers for asthma – things you should know.* Retrieved from
http://www.healthcentral.com/allergy/c/3989/19952/hfa-asthmathings

ATTENTION DEFICIT HYPERACTIVITY DISORDER

DEFINITION/ETIOLOGY:

The American Psychiatric Association defines attention deficit hyperactivity disorder (ADHD) as "characterized by a pattern of behavior, present in multiple settings (e.g., school and home), that can result in performance issues in social, educational, or work settings." ADHD is a neurobehavioral disorder that is characterized by inattention, hyperactivity and/or impulsive behaviors that may include behaviors like failure to pay close attention to details, difficulty organizing tasks, and activities, excessive talking, fidgeting, or an inability to remain seated in appropriate situations. The patterns of behavior need to be observed in more than one setting. Children with ADHD differ in their symptoms, causes, prognosis, and responses to treatment. DASome children are thought to have attention deficit without hyperactivity. These students may perform poorly in school despite normal intellect because they cannot sit still, attend, or complete a task. They are often rejected by their peers. Boys are affected more than girls. Symptoms appear by age 3 years but often the condition is not medically diagnosed until school age. ADHD should be considered a chronic illness.

SIGNS/SYMPTOMS:

DIAGNOSTIC CRITERIA:

The DSM- V (2013) sets diagnostic criteria for ADHD. Children must have at least six symptoms from either (or both) the inattention group of criteria and the hyperactivity and impulsivity criteria, while older adolescents and adults (over age 17 years) must present with five. Using DSM-5, several of the individual's ADHD symptoms must be present prior to age 12 years.

The DSM-V lists the following symptoms of inattention . The symptoms must have persisted for at least six months to a degree that is maladaptive and inconsistent with developmental level.

Inattention
- Often fails to give close attention to details or makes careless mistakes in schoolwork, work, or other activities
- Often has difficulty sustaining attention in tasks or play activities
- Often does not seem to listen when spoken to directly
- Often does not follow through on instructions and fails to finish schoolwork or chores (not due to oppositional behavior or failure to understand instructions)
- Often has difficulty organizing tasks and activities
- Often avoids, dislikes, or is reluctant to engage in tasks that require sustained mental effort (such as schoolwork or homework)
- Often loses things necessary for tasks or activities (e.g., toys, school assignments, pencils, books, or tools)
- Is often easily distracted by extraneous stimuli
- Is often forgetful in daily activities

ATTENTION DEFICIT HYPERACTIVITY DISORDER *(continued from previous page)*

The following symptoms of hyperactivity-impulsivity are listed by the DSMV and must have persisted for at least 6 months to a degree that is maladaptive and inconsistent with developmental level.

Hyperactivity
- Often fidgets with hands or feet or squirms in seat
- Often leaves seat in classroom or in other situations in which remaining seated is expected
- Often runs about or climbs excessively in situations in which it is inappropriate (adolescents or adults may only feel restless)
- Often has difficulty playing or engaging in leisure activities quietly
- Is often "on the go" or often acts as if "driven by a motor"
- Often talks excessively

Impulsivity
- Often blurts out answers
- Often has difficulty waiting for a turn
- Often interrupts or intrudes on others

   ✓ Some hyperactive-impulsive or inattentive symptoms that caused impairment were present before age 12 years.

   ✓ Some impairment from the symptoms is present in two or more structured settings (e.g., at school and at home).

   ✓ There must be clear evidence of clinically significant impairment in social, academic, OR occupational functioning.

DIAGNOSTIC PROCEDURES
1. Observations may be conducted:
   - At home, in several locations and circumstances (e.g. meal time, outdoor play, performance of homework and household chores)
   - At doctor's office
   - At school - classroom, cafeteria, and playground
   - At church, restaurants and family gatherings
2. Rating scales: many available
3. Behaviors must cause functional impairment
4. Diagnosis of exclusion
5. Provide all data to physician upon referral

ATTENTION DEFICIT HYPERACTIVITY DISORDER *(continued from previous page)*

MANAGEMENT/TREATMENT:

While there is no cure for ADHD, it can be successfully managed. Treatment management may include medication and educational and behavioral interventions.

- **Educational:** modification of lesson plans, teacher instruction, special class placement. Many strategies are available in educational manuals, such as decreasing environmental stimuli, providing structure, and assisting with organization.
- **Psychological/behavioral:** counseling, (group, individual and family); behavior modification.
- **Medication:** Stimulants are commonly used to treat AHDH. Dosage is not based on body weight, rather dosages are calculated on achieving desired effect with minimal side effects.

Types of Medication
Methylphenidate (Ritalin)
Methylphenidate (sustained release or once daily forms)
Concerta ER (extended release)
Metadate CD
Metadate ER (extended release)
Methylin
Ritalin SR (sustained release)
Daytrana transdermal patch
DextroAmphetamines
Dexedrine
Dexedrine spansules
DextroStat
Adderall (mixture)
Methamphetamine (Desoxyn)
Dexmethylphenidate (Focalin)
Lisdexamfetamine dimesylate (Vyvanse)
Atomoxetine (Strattera) which works on norepinephrine
Pemoline (Cylert)

High blood pressure medication for ADD / ADHD — Certain blood pressure medications can be used to treat ADD / ADHD. Options include clonidine (Catapres) and guanfacine (Tenex). They are especially beneficial for those with tics or Tourette's Syndrome. While these medications can be effective for hyperactivity, impulsivity, and aggression, they are less helpful when it comes to attention problems.

ATTENTION DEFICIT HYPERACTIVITY DISORDER *(continued from previous page)*

FOLLOW-UP:
Stimulants (Ritalin, etc.) can cause loss of appetite: control by taking medication with or after meal. Monitor growth: height and weight three times each school year (e.g. September, January, May).

POTENTIAL COMPLICATIONS:
Monitor for adverse effects of medications. The following are the most common adverse effects. For a complete list, see Physician's Desk Reference® or other drug resource.
- Risk of liver toxicity
- Abdominal pain
- Jitteriness, nervousness, anxiety, irritability
- Sleeplessness if taken after 4-5 P.M.
- New onset tic

NOTES:
Families require support and education regarding the diagnosis and management of this condition.

MEDICATION REMINDER
Dose for each child must be individualized by physician.
- All have side effects and must be monitored closely, especially early in therapy.
- Do not insist that child be put on medication.
- If child is prescribed medication, try to obtain child's assent. All psychoactive medications work better if they are taken willingly by child with parental cooperation.
- It may be necessary to continue medication into adolescence and adult years.
- Children and teens should not take medication without supervision.

ASSOCIATED DISORDERS (Co-morbid conditions)
While ADHD does not cause psychological problems, children with ADHD are more likely to have co-morbid conditions. The most common associated disorders seen with ADHD include: oppositional defiant disorder, conduct disorder and learning disabilities.

CONDUCT DISORDER
A repetitive and persistent pattern of behavior in which the basic rights of others or major age-appropriate societal norms or rules are violated, as manifested by the presence of 3 or more of the following criteria in the past 12 months, with at least one criterion present in the past 6 months.

31

ATTENTION DEFICIT HYPERACTIVITY DISORDER *(continued from previous page)*

Aggression to people and animals
- Often bullies, threatens, or intimidates others
- Often initiates physical fights
- Has used a weapon that can cause serious physical harm to others (e.g., bat, brick, broken bottle, knife, gun)
- Has been physically cruel to people
- Has been physically cruel to animals
- Has stolen while confronting a victim (e.g. mugging, purse snatching, extortion, armed robbery)
- Has forced someone into sexual activity

Destruction of property
- Has deliberately engaged in fire setting with the intention of causing serious damage
- Has deliberately destroyed others' property (other than by fire setting)

Deceitfulness or theft
- Has broken into someone else's house, building, or car
- Often lies to obtain goods or favors or to avoid obligations (i.e. "cons" others)
- Has stolen items of nontrivial value without confronting a victim (e.g., shoplifting, theft without breaking and entering, forgery)

Serious violations of rules
- Often stays out at night despite parental prohibitions, beginning before age 13
- Has run away from home overnight at least twice while living in parental or parental surrogate home (or once without returning for a lengthy period).
- Is often truant from school, beginning before age 13.
- The disturbance in behavior causes clinically significant impairment in social, academic, or occupational functioning.

OPPOSITIONAL DEFIANT DISORDER (ODD)
A pattern of negativistic, hostile, and defiant behavior lasting at least 6 months, during which four (or more) of the following are present:
- Often loses temper
- Often argues with adults
- Often actively defies or refuses to comply with adults' requests or rules
- Often deliberately annoys people
- Often blames others for his or her mistakes or misbehavior
- Is often touchy or easily annoyed by others
- Is often angry and resentful
- Is often spiteful or vindictive

Note: Consider a criterion met only if the behavior occurs more frequently than is typically observed in individuals of comparable age and development level.

ATTENTION DEFICIT HYPERACTIVITY DISORDER *(continued from previous page)*

The disturbance in behavior causes clinically significant impairment in social, academic, or occupational functioning. ODD may start during preschool years. Conduct disorder usually appears in older children (Adapted from: Diagnostic and Statistical Manual of Mental Disorders-V, 2013, Published by Amer. Psych. Assn.)

LEARNING DISABILITES
Learning disabilities are common in children with ADHD. Children with both ADHD and learning disabilities may need extra academic support in the classroom or even special education services.

References

American Psychiatric Association. (2013). *Diagnostic and Statistical Manual of Mental Disorders (5th ed.*). Alexandria, VA: Author.

American Psychiatric Association. (2013). *Attention deficit hyperactivity disorder. Retrieved from* http://www.dsm5.org/Documents/ADHD%20Fact%20Sheet.pdf

Mayo Clinic. (2013). *Attention-deficit/hyperactivity disorder (ADHD) in children*. Retrieved from http://www.mayoclinic.com/helth/adhd/DS00275

National Institutes of Health. (2012). *Attention deficit hyperactivity disorder.* Retrieved from http://www.nimh.nih.gov/health/publications/attention-deficit-hyperactivity-disorder/index.shtml

Selekman, J. & Foley, M. (2013). Attention deficit/ hyperactivity disorder and learning disabilities. In J. Selekman (Ed.), *School nursing: A comprehensive text (2nd ed.)*(pp. 840-871). Philadelphia, PA: F.A. Davis.

Shelton, K.C. & O'Boyle-Jordan, B. (2008). Cognitive-perceptual problems: Attention- deficit/hyperactivity disorder, blindness, deafness, and autism. In C. Burns, M. Brady, A. Dunn, N.B. Starr, C. Blosser (Eds.) *Pediatric primary care (4th ed.*) (pp. 325-336). St. Louis, MO: Saunders Elsevier. http://pediatrics.aappublications.org/content/early/2011/10/14/peds.2011-2654.full.pdf+html

AUTISM SPECTRUM DISORDER

DEFINITION/ETIOLOGY:

Autism Spectrum Disorder (ASD) falls under a group of complex neurodevelopmental disorders. According to the Diagnostic and Statistical Manual of Mental Disorders (DSM) – fifth edition (published by the American Psychiatric Association), **Asperger's Syndrome, Pervasive Developmental Disorder – Not Otherwise Specified and Childhood Disintegrative Disorder are no longer separate autistic diagnosis. All of these subcategories of autism are now incorporated into a single category; the (ASD) diagnosis.** This single ASD diagnostic category has created a sliding scale of severity depending on the child's symptoms.

The exact etiology of autism is unknown. Given the varied severity and symptoms of autism, the etiology is most likely multifactorial. Potential causes include:
- Children with medical conditions such as congenital rubella syndrome, phenylketonuria, tuberous sclerosis, Tourette syndrome, epilepsy or fragile X syndrome have a higher risk of being diagnosed with ASD
- Genetic predisposition – based on sibling research studies, there is also a genetic tendency; families that have one child diagnosed with ASD have a higher occurrence of autism in subsequent children
- Brain structure abnormalities – some children diagnosed with ASD have enlarged ventricles, abnormalities of the cerebellar vermis and of the brain stem nuclei
- Gender – boys are approximately 4 times more likely to be diagnosed with autism
- Environmental – while suspected, there is no proof of an environmental connection to ASD

SIGNS AND SYMPTOMS:

Autism symptoms typically appear within the first three years of life. Symptoms vary from person to person. Diagnostic evaluation involves a multidisciplinary approach. Potential team members include trained physicians (developmental pediatrician/neurologist) and psychiatrist/psychologist who administer specific autistic behavioral testing/evaluations. Diagnosis criteria is based on social communication/interaction and restricted/repetitive behaviors. These symptoms must interfere with functional abilities.

Social communication/interaction symptoms (deficits must be met in each category)
- Impaired social interaction / emotional interaction
  - Difficulty reciprocating social and emotion interactions with others
  - Difficulty making friends
  - Does not display physical affection
  - May reject physical affection
  - Absence of social play

AUTISM SPECTRUM DISORDER *(continued from previous page)*

- Difficulty with nonverbal communication
    - o Tend to avoid eye contact (poor eye contact)
    - o Inability to understand facial expressions, gestures and tone of voice
- Unable to maintain relationships
    - o Lack empathy for others
    - o Difficulty playing with others

Restrictive/repetitive movements (2 of the 4 symptoms must be met)

- Repetitive speech (ECHOLALIA) / motor movements (rocking back and forth, hand flapping)
- Strict adherence to routines/rituals – resistant to change
- Highly restricted interest – these interests are often obsessive and may be limited to specific topics/activities (lining up cars, etc.)
- Hypo/hyper reactive to sensory input
- Self-abusive behaviors (head banging)

MANAGEMENT/TREATMENT:

There is no cure for autism. Early detection and interventions improves quality of life and overall outcomes. Interventions must be based on student need. Interventions may include:

- Speech therapy
- Physical therapy
- Occupational therapy
- Behavioral therapy – social work services
- Special education services
- Pharmacological therapy – antipsychotic medication for aggressive and harmful behaviors, ADHD medications to help treat impulsive and hyperactive behaviors, antidepressant for anxiety, etc.

FOLLOW-UP:

Evaluate effectiveness of interventions. Monitor for potential medication side effects. Some medications can interact, causing dangerous side effects. Report suspected side effects to parent/physician.

POTENTIAL COMPLICATIONS:

Comorbidities may include:

- ADHD
- Pica
- Seizure disorder – more than 20 % of individuals with autism develop seizure disorder by adulthood
- Sleep disorders
- Gastrointestinal issues

AUTISM SPECTRUM DISORDER *(continued from previous page)*

NOTES:
- Controversy remains on whether a link exists between autism and certain childhood vaccines; specifically the measles, mumps and rubella vaccine (MMR). Educate parent/guardian that no reliable study has shown a link between autism and the MMR vaccine and the potential complications of contracting a vaccine preventable disease such as pertussis.
- Some parents/guardians seek alternative therapy in the treatment of autism including chelation therapy. Chelation therapy is thought to remove mercury and heavy metals from the body and is considered dangerous; there have been deaths associated with chelation therapy as an alternative therapy for autism. As needed, educate parents/guardians on the dangers of chelation therapy.
- Dietary interventions – parents/guardians may choose vitamin supplements, gluten-free and a casein-free diet in the treatment of ASD; more research is needed regarding how effective dietary interventions are in addressing ASD. Refer parents/guardians with questions related to dietary interventions to a registered dietician with an expertise in ASD.

RESOURCES
Autism Society of America
http://www.autism-society.org/
1(800) 328-8476

Autism Speaks
http://www.autismspeaks.org/what-autism/symptoms

Centers for Disease Control and Prevention (CDC)
http://www.cdc.gov/ncbddd/autism/facts.html
1(800) 232-4636

National Institute of Neurological Disorders and Stroke
http://www.ninds.nih.gov/disorders/autism/detail_autism.htm

AUTISM SPECTRUM DISORDER *(continued from previous page)*

References

Autism Speaks. (2013). *DSM-5 will be released this weekend.* Retrieved from
http://www.autismspeaks.org/news/news-item/dsm-5-will-be-released-weekend

Centers for Disease Control and Prevention (CDC). (2012). *Autism spectrum disorders.* Retrieved from
http://www.cdc.gov/ncbddd/autism/facts.html

Hyman, S. (2013). New DSM-5 includes changes to autism criteria. *AAP News.* Retrieved from
http://aapnews.aappublications.org/content/early/2013/06/04/aapnews.20130604-1

Mayo Clinic. (2012). *Autism.* Retrieved from http://www.mayoclinic.com/health/autism/DS00348

Merck Manual. (2013). *Autism spectrum disorder.* Retrieved from
http://www.merckmanuals.com/professional/pediatrics/learning_and_developmental_disorders/
autism_spectrum_disorders_asd.html?qt=autism&alt=sh

National Institute of Neurological Disorders and Stroke. (2013). *Autism fact sheets.* Retrieved from
http://www.ninds.nih.gov/disorders/autism/detail_autism.htm

Selekman, J. Diefenbeck, C., & Guthrie, S. (2013). Mental health concerns. In J. Selekman (Ed.),
School nursing: A comprehensive text (2nd ed.) (pp. 927-969). Philadelphia, PA: F. A. Davis.

BACK AND NECK INJURY

DEFINITION/ETIOLOGY:
The etiology of back and neck injury is multifactorial. Severe injuries may occur from a traumatic blow to the back or neck that fractures, dislocates, or compresses a vertebrae. Most injuries are sprains and strains. Back and neck injuries may result from motor vehicle accidents and playground injuries. Youth are at increased risk of injury because they often participate in risky behaviors and physical activities/sports. Severe injuries may occur to athletes (football, soccer, gymnastics, etc.) trampoline jumpers, horseback riders, divers who hit bottom, etc. Neck injuries can occur when the neck is forcefully flexed, and the chin strikes the chest.

SIGNS AND SYMPTOMS:
Symptoms depend on the location of the injury. Symptoms can affect the neck, arms, legs, back and shoulders. Symptoms may include:
- Pain made worse by pressure or movement
- Pain may radiate into arm or leg
- Nerve involvement: weakness, tingling, numbness, or inability to move arm or leg

Signs of a serious injury include:
- **Extreme pain in neck or back**
- **Abnormal positioning of neck or back**
- **Loss of sensation**
- **Loss of bowel and bladder function**
- **Difficulty walking**
- **Difficulty breathing**

When damage to the spinal cord is suspected, DO NOT MOVE STUDENT until assessment is done.

MANAGEMENT AND TREATMENT:
Treatment depends on the extent of the injury.

1. Do not move, bend, or rotate neck of student.

2. *Assess airway, breathing, and circulation – if airway is compromised, and CPR is necessary, use jaw thrust maneuver instead of head tilt. Call 911 immediately.*

3. Perform comprehensive neurological assessment. If you suspect a serious injury, immobilize student until assessment is completed.

4. Assess student's ability to move extremities slowly, and only a small amount. Test response to stimuli such as a finger touch or pin prick. Determine strength by checking hand grasp.

BACK AND NECK INJURY *(continued from previous page)*

5. If severe neck or back injury is suspected or if pain, sensory impairment, or weakness persists, have student remain lying down and **call emergency ambulance for additional evaluation.**

6. If sensation is intact, pain is minimal to absent, and student is able to move all extremities normally, allow student to slowly sit up and then walk.

7. If all neurological signs are normal and student is able to move all extremities freely, ice may be applied to relieve pain.

8. Notify parent/guardian.

9. Refer to physician/healthcare provider for further follow-up and treatment if necessary.

10. Complete injury report.

FOLLOW UP:
*   Student with minor injuries who remains at school should be observed several times during school day.
*   Notify PE teacher of injury and potential accommodations.

NOTES:
BACK PACKS AND BACK PAIN

The amount of weight carried by children in their backpacks is an important issue that deserves serious consideration. Loading of the spine is a risk factor for low back pain not only in adults but also in children; the load that children most commonly carry is their school backpack. **A backpack limit of 10-15% of ideal body weight for students is recommended** (obese children already carry an additional built-in burden which should not be used in calculating 15% of body weight). The backpack should have two wide (at least 2") shoulder straps and a waist or chest strap to distribute the load. Although back pain in children is likely to be multifactorial, heavy backpacks are probably an important contributing cause. Some schools have policies on the use of backpacks and rolling cases.

While increasing numbers of children are developing back pain, it is difficult to assign the cause of this increase to heavy backpack use alone. Students may also have back or neck pain due to postural lordosis, spondylolysis, and/or Scheuermann's kyphosis.

BACK AND NECK INJURY *(continued from previous page)*

References

American Academy of Pediatrics. (2013). *Backpack safety.* Healthychildren.org. Retrieved from
http://www.healthychildren.org/English/safety-prevention/at-play/pages/Backpack-Safety.aspx?nfstatus=401&nftok
en=00000000-0000-0000-0000-000000000000&nfstatusdescription=ERROR%3a+No+local+token

American College of Emergency Physicians. (n.d.). *What to do in a medical emergency: Neck or back injury.* Retrieved from
http://www.emergencycareforyou.org/EmergencyManual/WhatToDoInMedicalEmergency/Default.aspx?id=258&
terms=spinal+injuries

Centers for Disease Control and Prevention (CDC). (2012). *Musculoskeletal disorders.*   Retrieved from
http://www.cdc.gov/niosh/programs/msd/

Cosby, M., Miller, N. & Youngman, K. (2013). Acute measures for emergent problems. In J. Selekman (Ed.), *School nursing:
A comprehensive text* (2nd ed.) (pp.516-577). Philadelphia, PA: F. A. Davis.

Mayo Clinic. (2012). *Spinal injuries: First aid.* Retrieved from http://www.mayoclinic.com/health/first-aid-spinal-injury/FA00010

MedlinePlus. U.S. National Library of Health. (2013). *Back injuries.* Retrieved from
http://www.nlm.nih.gov/medlineplus/backinjuries.html

Merck Manual. (2013). *Evaluation of neck and back pain.* Retrieved from http://www.merckmanuals.com/professional/
musculoskeletal_and_connective_tissue_disorders/neck_and_back_pain/evaluationof_neck_and_back_pain.html?
qt=back%20%20and%20neck%20injuries&alt=sh

BED BUGS

DEFINITION/ETIOLOGY:

Bed bugs (*Cimex lectularius*) are small, reddish brown, wingless, flat, parasitic insects that bite humans and animals while they sleep. They can go without feeding for up to six months. They are not known to transmit or spread disease and should not be considered a medical or public health hazard.

Bedbugs were eradicated at one time in most developed countries because of the use of DDT, a pesticide that is no longer used and is banned because of its toxicity. The discontinuation of DDT use and the increase of international travel are thought to have led to bedbugs becoming a problem again.

Bed bug infestations usually occur around or near the areas where people sleep, e.g. beds, bed frames, mattress seams, box springs, behind wallpaper, or any other clutter or objects around a bed. The insects can travel anywhere from 8 to 100 feet but are found to live usually within 8 feet of where people sleep. Bedbugs hide in luggage and clothing, crawl and hitchhike so they can be transported easily. They may be brought to school in book bags and clothing.

SIGNS AND SYMPTOMS:
- Itchy bites, sometimes in a row
- Bites usually found on face, arms, legs, neck
- Bites may have a red dot in the middle of a raised bump
- Bite marks may take as long as 14 days to develop
- Some people have no reaction to bedbug bites
- Some people may experience an allergic reaction that results in severe itching, blisters or hives
- Difficult to distinguish bed bug bites from other insect bites

MANAGEMENT/TREATMENT:
- **<u>No exclusion is necessary</u>**
- Avoid scratching
- Relief for itching may include:
  - antiseptic creams or lotions
  - prescribed steroid creams
  - antihistamines (such as Benadryl®)

POTENTIAL COMPLICATIONS:
- Scratching may lead to secondary infection
- Boils
- Cellulitis
- Allergic symptoms (e.g. swelling/pain at the bite site)
- Anaphylaxis (on rare occasions)

BED BUGS *(continued from previous page)*

FOLLOW UP:

Family may need to contact their landlord or contact a professional exterminator to eliminate any home infestation. Exterminators may use a combination of pesticides and nonchemical treatments. Nonchemical treatments may include:

- **Vacuuming**
- **Washing clothes in hot water.** Washing clothes and other items in water at least 120 F (49 C) can kill bedbugs.
- **Using clothes dryer.** Placing wet or dry items in a clothes dryer set at medium to high heat for 20 minutes will kill bedbugs and their eggs.

For School Buildings

- Limit items that travel back and forth between home and school.
- Limit clutter.
- Clean cubbies/ lockers routinely (seasonally).
- Vacuum rugs frequently. Dispose of vacuum cleaner bags/filters in tightly sealed plastic bag.
- Avoid fabric-covered furniture, pillows in schools.
- Provide space between coat hooks and backpacks.
- Keep "Lost and Found" clothing, backpacks, etc. in closeable plastic storage bins.
- Involve facilities maintenance and pest management staff to address any bed bug infestation in schools.

NOTES:

The school nurse can be extremely helpful in helping families and staff from overreacting to this nuisance condition. Education is very important, reminding people that bed bugs do not discriminate, and infestations is not a reflection of cleanliness. Bed bugs do not infest the person; they infest the living area and require extermination.

Having a plan/guideline that includes how the school will physically address prevention and elimination of bed bugs and how families will be notified is helpful.

Resources:

Environmental Protection Agency (www.epa.gov/bedbugs)
IdentifyUs (https://identify.us.com/idmybug/bed-bugs/)

References

American Academy of Pediatrics. (2013). *Bedbugs.* In S. Aronson, & T. Shope (Eds.), *Managing infectious diseases in child care and schools (2nd ed.)* (pp. 69-70). Elk Grove Village, IL: American Academy of Pediatrics.

Center for Disease Control. (2013). *Bed bugs FAQs.* Retrieved from www.cdc.gov/parasites/bedbugs/faqs.html

Mayo Clinic. (2012). *Bed bugs.* Retrieved from http://www.mayoclinic.com/health/bedbugs/DS00663

BIPOLAR DISORDER

DEFINITION/ETIOLOGY:
Bipolar disorder (previously called manic depressive disorder) is a mental disorder characterized by extreme changes in energy and affect, mood swings, periods of unusual highs (mania) and lows (depression). The exact etiology is unknown. However, genetics and environment have been linked to bipolar disorder. Bipolar disorder is a life-long illness but in most cases, can be controlled with medications and psychological counseling.

SIGNS AND SYMPTOMS:
Symptoms vary from person to person. Symptoms may include:
Manic stage
- Euphoria
- Flight of ideas
- Feelings of grandiose
- Agitated/irritated
- Aggressive behaviors
- Inflated self-esteem
- Risky behaviors
- Substance/alcohol abuse
- May talk fast
- Decreased need for sleep

Depressive stage:
- Withdrawn
- Sadness/feelings of hopelessness
- Irritability
- Anxiety
- Fatigue
- Difficulty concentrating
- Chronic pain with unknown cause
- May have suicidal thoughts

Children and adolescents may demonstrate symptoms of intense rage, aggressive and impulsive behaviors. These symptoms can be misdiagnosed as Obsessive Compulsive Disorder and/or ADHD.

BIPOLAR DISORDER (*continued from previous page*)

MANAGEMENT/TREATMENT:
1. Primary treatment includes daily medication and psychotherapy.
2. If indicated, administer medication per doctor's orders.
3. Potential medication treatment includes:

Drug	Examples of medications	Comments
Lithium	Lithium- prevents extreme highs and lows, stabilizes mood; may need to take lithium for several weeks before feeling better; physician will order regular blood test to monitor lithium levels	• Monitor for side effects – dry mouth, gastrointestinal issues; **beware of lithium toxicity** – gastrointestinal issues, dizziness, weakness, slurred speech, seizures, nystagmus, coma; follow up with physician immediately if lithium toxicity is suspected • Risk of lithium toxicity increases with dehydration; maintain hydration
Antipsychotics	Used to treat acute mania. Examples include risperidone, olanzapine, ziprasidone , chlorpromazine, aripiprazole, paliperidone, quetiapine)	Side effects may include weight gain, sedation and neurological symptoms
Anticonvulsants	Used to stabilize mood. Examples include carbamazepine, divalproex and lamotrigine	Potential side effects – weight gain, dizziness, drowsiness

FOLLOW UP:
- Be aware that some adolescents are nonadherent to drug regimens (often due to side effects such as weight gain)
- Educate parent/guardian/student that bipolar disorder is a lifelong illness that requires lifelong treatment
- Monitor for medication side effects

POTENTIAL COMPLICATIONS:
- Poor school attendance/performance
- Difficulty maintaining relationships
- Suicide

BIPOLAR DISORDER (*continued from previous page*)

References

American Psychiatric Association. (2012). *Bipolar disease.* Retrieved from http://www.psychiatry.org/bipolar-disorder

Ball, J., Binder, R., & Cowen, K. (Eds.). (2012). Alterations in mental health and cognition. *Principles of Pediatric Nursing: Caring for Children (5th ed.)* (p. 923-924). Upper Saddle River, NJ: Pearson Education, Inc.

Mayo Clinic. (2012). *Bipolar disorder*. Retrieved from http://www.mayoclinic.com/health/bipolar-disorder/DS00356

Merck Manual. (2012). *Bipolar disorders in children and adolescents.* Retrieved from http://www.merckmanuals.com/professional/pediatrics/mental_disorders_in_children_and_adolescents/ bipolar_disorder_in_children_and_adolescents.html?qt=bipolar disorder&alt=sh

Selekman, J. Diefenbeck, C., & Guthrie, S. (2013). Mental health concerns. In J. Selekman (Ed.), *School nursing: A comprehensive text* (2nd ed.) (pp. 927-969). Philadelphia, PA: F. A. Davis.

BITES: Animal and Human (if skin is broken)

DEFINITION/ETIOLOGY:
Soft tissue injuries resulting from animal or human bites and include a puncture wound or crushing injury combined with lacerations. Commonly, such injuries are to the head, face, and neck.

SIGNS AND SYMPTOMS:
- Pain and bleeding
- Puncture wounds and/or lacerations usually jagged; pieces of tissue may be torn away in severe bites

MANAGEMENT/TREATMENT:
1. Wash and irrigate with copious amounts of soap and water.
2. Apply loose dressing.
3. Topical antibiotics may be applied if approved.
4. Refer all but most minor bites (skin not broken) to physician.
5. Record date of last tetanus.

FOLLOW-UP:
Prevention of Infection
- Dog bites likely to be open, jagged lacerations that can be thoroughly irrigated, have a low infection rate, and usually require no prophylactic antibiotics.
- Cat bites are usually deep puncture wounds and have a high infection rate. They often require prophylactic antibiotics.
- **Human bites *that break the skin* have the greatest potential for infection. Also, consider transmission of Hepatitis B to both parties** (consult current AAP Redbook for guidance or follow school district policy).

Prevention of Tetanus
Verify immunization status with student's family physician. If not possible, follow these general guidelines:
- If no previous active immunization with tetanus toxoid, encourage tetanus immune globulin and begin series of tetanus toxoid.
- If active immunization is 10 years ago or longer: Booster of tetanus toxoid (adult Td).
- If active immunization within the past five years: Mild bite—no booster. Severe bite— booster adult Td.
- Severe, neglected, old (over 24 hours) or dirty bites—Adult Td, unless person has had one in the previous 12 months.

BITES: Animal and Human *(continued from previous page)*

POTENTIAL COMPLICATIONS:

Animal bites
- Early cellulitis - *Pasteurella multocida*
- Secondary infection – *Staphyloccoccus aureus*
- Rabies

Human Bites
- Cellulitis
- Infection

NOTES:
- Follow procedure for notifying animal control of animal bites.
- While it is theoretically possible for any mammal to develop rabies, rodents have not been implicated in transmitting the disease; therefore, a child bitten by a squirrel, rat, mouse, gerbil, hamster, or rabbit is not considered to be in danger, but a physician should be consulted.
- Common carriers of rabies are dogs, cats, foxes, skunks, and raccoons. Bats carry rabies but only bite if handled. Children who touch a dead or sick bat are at small risk, but a doctor and public health department should be notified (airborne infection from bat guano is only a theoretical possibility).
- Unprovoked bites (especially from a dog) raise greater suspicion than if animal is provoked or teased. The biting animal must be confined and observed 10 days—notify the health department or police. If the animal cannot be apprehended, then rabies shots may need to be given.
- Isolate all students from area where bite occurred (if on school property) until animal control/police arrive.
- Bites on fingers and face are more dangerous.

References

American Academy of Pediatrics. (2013). Bites (human and animal). In S.S. Aronson & T.R. Shope (Eds.*), Managing infectious diseases in child care and schools, a quick reference guide (3rd ed.)* (pp. 71-72). Elk Grove Village, IL: Author.

American Academy of Pediatrics. (2009). Summaries of infectious disease – parvovirus B19. In L. K. Pickering, C. J. Baker, D. W. Kimberlin, & S. S. Long, (Eds.), *Red Book: 2009 report of the committee on infectious diseases*, (*28th ed.*) (pp. 187-191). Elk Grove Village, IL.: Author.

Barrett, J., & Revis, D.R. (2012). Human bites. *Medscape Reference*. Retrieved from http://emedicine.medscape.com/article/768978-overview

Brehm, C. (2008). Common injuries. In C. Burns, M. Brady, A. Dunn, N.B. Starr, C. Blosser (Eds.), *Pediatric primary care (4th ed.)* (pp. 1097-1098). St. Louis, MO: Saunders Elsevier.

Garth, A. P., Harris, N. S., & Spanierman, C.S. (2012). Animal bites in emergency medicine . *Medscape Reference*. Retrieved from http://emedicine.medscape.com/article/768875-overview

MayoClinic. (2011). *Rabies, prevention*. Retrieved from http://www.mayoclinic.com/health/rabies/DS00484/DSECTION=prevention

Medline Plus, U.S. National Library of Medicine. (2013). *Rabies*. Retrieved from http://www.nlm.nih.gov/medlineplus/ rabies.html#cat11

BLISTERS

DEFINITION/ETIOLOGY:
A blister is a round or oval bubble of fluid under the skin that may or may not be painful or itchy depending on the cause. The cause is varied:

- Irritation (friction/shoes; repetitive activity/rowing, shoveling)
- Burns from intense heat (sunburn, hot liquids or appliances, etc.) or cold (frostbite)
- Contact dermatitis (poison ivy, oak and sumac, detergents, chemicals)
- Allergies (medication)
- Infection (impetigo, eczema, ringworm, herpes, varicella [chicken pox])

SIGNS AND SYMPTOMS:
- Blisters from irritation and burns are red and often painful, particularly if the blister is on a weight bearing part of the body (foot) or in an area that is frequently used (hand).
- Contact dermatitis and allergic skin responses have redness and are itchy.
- The blisters present with some infections are called vesicles. Depending on the source of the infection, these vesicles can be red, itchy, and/or painful.

MANAGEMENT/TREATMENT:
- Treatment is largely symptomatic.
- Skin covering the blister is best left intact. If the blister is broken, skin integrity is compromised leaving an entry for bacteria. Cover the broken blister with a sterile dressing and attempt to avoid activity that requires further friction or pressure on the affected area.
- Monitor for signs of infection.

POTENTIAL COMPLICATIONS:
Infection after blister skins over or blister ruptures. Signs of infection include increasing redness, edema, area warm to touch, area becomes increasingly more painful, or purulent drainage is present.

FOLLOW UP:
Monitor for signs of infection and refer to primary healthcare provider if redness increases, edema present, area warm to touch, area becomes increasingly more painful, or purulent drainage is present.

BLISTERS *(continued from previous page)*

NOTES:
Prevention
- Proper fitting shoes, socks, clothing, and equipment for walking, running and participation in athletic/sports activities.

- If an area of redness appears, stop the activity.

- Observe sun-safety cautions and use sunscreen.

- Dress appropriately for winter weather and know the signs of frostbite.

- Be able to identify poison ivy, oak, and sumac.

- Read instructions accompanying tools, equipment, and appliances. Pay particular attention to safety.

References
Medline Plus, US National Library of Medicine. (2011). *Vesicles.* Retrieved from
http://www.nlm.nih.gov/medlineplus/ency/article/003939.htm

The Merck Manual, Professional Edition. Sunburn. (2012). Retrieved from http://www.merckmanuals.com/professional/dermatologic_disorders/reactions_to_sunlight/sunburn.html?qt=sunburn&alt=sh

Web MD. (2011). *Blisters - Topic overview.* Retrieved from
http://www.webmd.com/skin-problems-and-treatments/tc/blisters-topic-overview

BOILS

DEFINITION/ETIOLOGY:
A furuncle (boil) is a skin infection, consisting of a walled off, puss filled mass that is most commonly staph (*S. aureus*), involving the entire hair follicle and the adjacent subcutaneous tissue. They occur most commonly on sites of friction and swelling such as under the belt, groin, armpit, buttocks, and thighs. Some people are afflicted with many, with little success at prevention. Boils can be a small bump to an abscess filled with pus. They will sometimes drain on their own, but are usually require incision and drainage.

SIGNS AND SYMPTOMS:
- Pain, swelling, and redness
- May be about the size of a marble (1-2 cm) or larger
- May be firm or fluctuant
- Redness progresses to yellowish center of pus

MANAGEMENT/TREATMENT:
- Usually requires incision and drainage for healing.
- Warm, moist dressings several times a day.
- Antibiotic ointment is not generally considered effective but may help eradicate a carrier state. Mupirocin (i.e. Bactroban) is helpful in eradicating nasal carriage of staphylococcus.
- Systemic anti-staphylococcal antibiotics may be required.
- Draining lesions must be cleaned frequently to prevent spread of infection.
- To prevent recurrence, the role of good hygiene should be stressed to student and family.
- Washing with an antibacterial soap may be helpful in the event of frequent episodes.

FOLLOW-UP:
- Refer to physician if abscess does not continue to heal/improve daily.
- Gram stain, culture, and sensitivity may be needed to guide appropriate antibiotic therapy.
- Confer with parents/guardians about other family members with skin infections (impetigo, etc.).
- Discuss and monitor preventive measures if student participates in any contact sport, or sports that use mats (gymnastics, wrestling, martial arts).

POTENTIAL COMPLICATIONS:
- Watch for cellulitis or lymphangitis.
- *Students with continuous or repeated impetigo may harbor Staphylococcus aureus in nose.* Mupirocin (Bactroban) is helpful in eradicating nasal carriage of staphylococcus.
- Methicillin-Resistant Staph Aureus (MRSA)

BOILS *(continued from previous page)*

- Outbreaks of community-associated Methicillin-Resistant Staph Aureus (CA-MRSA)
- MRSA infections have occurred among athletes, inmates at correctional facilities, and is often acquired in a hospital setting. It can be spread in the general community as well. The infection is usually spread from person to person by direct contact with a draining lesion or by contact with an asymptomatic carrier of *S. aureus*. Transmission can occur indirectly through contact with contaminated items (shared towels and athletic gear) or environmental surfaces.
- Bacteremia and secondary dissemination can occur and is a greater risk for those who are immunocompromised or have other chronic health conditions such as diabetes.

NOTES:
The child and their parents/guardians should be advised of the following:
- Try to keep hands off boil.
- Wash hands thoroughly after touching a boil.
- Do not reuse or share towels. Linens in contact with boils should be washed in very hot water.
- Dressings should be discarded in a sealed plastic bag.
- Once boil has formed, antibacterial soap is not effective.

References

American Academy of Pediatrics. (2009). Summaries of infectious disease – staphylococcal infections. In Pickering, L.K., Baker, C.J., Kimberlin, D.W., Long, S.S.(Eds.), *Red Book: 2009 Report of the committee on infectious diseases,*(28th ed.), (pp. 601). American Academy of Pediatrics: Elk Grove Village, IL.

Center for Disease Control. (2010). *Methicillin-resistant staphylococcus aureus (MRSA) in schools*. Retrieved from http://www.cdc.gov/ncidod/dhqp/ar_MRSA_AthletesFAQ.htm

Habif, T. , Campbell, J.L., Chapman, M.S., Dinulos, J.G.H., & Zug, K.A. (2011). *Skin diseases diagnosis and treatment (3rd ed.)*. Philadelphia, PA : Elsevier Saunders

Mayo Clinic. (2010). *Boils and carbuncles, (p.174)*. Retrieved from http://www.mayoclinic.com/health/boils-and-arbuncles/DS00466/DSECTION=prevention

Medline Plus. U.S. National Library of Medicine. (2012). *Boils*. Retrieved from http://www.nlm.nih.gov/medlineplus/ency/article/001474.htm

BURNS

DEFINITION/ETIOLOGY: Lesions caused by extreme heat or other cauterizing agents

Superficial burns or first-degree
Superficial – only affects the top layer of skin (epidermis).
Partial-thickness burns or second-degree
Involves the epidermis and extends into the dermis.
Full thickness burns or third-degree
Full thickness of skin is destroyed and involves the epidermis, dermis, and fat layer. Usually destroys the sweat glands, hair follicles, and nerve endings as well.
Fourth degree burns
Full thickness through all layers of skin into the muscle and bone.

SIGNS AND SYMPTOMS:
1. **Superficial burns**
   - Begins with pain and redness as in minimal sunburn – no blisters.
   - Later, slight to no peeling of skin.
2. **Partial-thickness burns**
   - Begins with pain, redness, and blisters as in moderate to severe sunburn.
   - Later, skin peels in large pieces, scarring only if secondary infection ensues.
3. **Full thickness burns**
   - Begins with little or no pain (nerves are gone), with red, black, or white discoloration.
   - Some unbroken blisters may be present.
   - Third degree burns always scar and often need skin graft.

MANAGEMENT/TREATMENT:
1. **General**
   a. Rapidly immerse burn in cold water. This not only helps stop the pain but it also stops destruction of tissue. There is a correlation between how fast the area is cooled and how fast it heals.
   b. Wash gently but thoroughly with antiseptic soap, pat dry with sterile pad.
   c. Avoid Vaseline®, butter, antibiotic or other greasy ointments.
   d. Avoid tight, air-excluding bandages.
   e. Check date of latest tetanus booster.
   f. Complete injury report.
2. **Superficial burns**
   a. Cool compress or submerge in cold water (not ice).
   b. No further treatment necessary.

BURNS *(continued from previous page)*

3. **Partial-thickness burns**
   a. Cool compress.
   b. Wash gently with antiseptic soap and dry.
   c. DO NOT break blister.
   d. Apply non-sticking dressing that does not exclude air.
   e. Notify parent.
4. **Full thickness burns**
   a. Cover with clean or sterile dressing or sheet.
   b. Evacuate to emergency room or doctor's office.
5. **Chemical burn**
   a. Flush with copious amounts of cool water for 15 minutes.
6. **Chemical or electrical burns: refer in all cases for further medical treatment.**

FOLLOW-UP:
- Change dressing daily (if this is not done at home) until danger of infection has passed.
- Observe for secondary infection.
- Teach student and parent/guardian to clean the affected area gently twice a day with soap and water and keep the area clean.
- Teach student and parent/guardian signs and symptoms of infection and the need to see the physician if they occur.
- Refer to physician for any developing signs of infection or if no improvement after FIRST day of treatment.
- Observe for scarring, especially on flexor areas of arms, legs, and neck.
- Children with facial scarring need emotional support on return to school. Prepare classmates/peers.

POTENTIAL COMPLICATIONS:
- Minor burns are typically superficial and do not cause complications.
- Moderate to severe burns can cause serious complications due to tissue damage and extensive fluid loss. Complications include: dehydration, infection, shock, muscle and tissue damage, chemical imbalances, etc.

NOTES:
- Facial burns: refer to physician in all cases.
- Send date of last tetanus booster with all physician referrals.
- Be alert to possible child abuse, self-tattoo, or deliberate injury.
- Record shape/size of burns as well as document history of event.
- Do not use ice on burns as it can cause further damage

Teach children safety rules such as **stop, drop, and roll** if their clothing catches on fire so they can help extinguish the flame and prevent getting burned more extensively.

BURNS *(continued from previous page)*

References

Bowden, V., & Greenberb, C.(Eds.). (2010) The child with altered skin integrity. *In Bowden, V. Greenberb, C. (Eds.), Children and their families: The continuum of care (*2nd ed.) (p.p. 1348-1349). Philadelphia PA: Lippincott Williams and Wilkins.

Mayo Clinic (2012). *Burns: First aid.* Retrieved from   http://www.mayoclinic.com/health/first-aid-burns/FA00022

CHILDHOOD CANCER

Childhood cancer is the leading cause of death from disease in children. On a positive note, it is still a rare disease, and has a survival rate of 80% (defined as surviving 5 years after diagnosis). Because children are growing, childhood cancer is unlike cancer seen in adults. Adult cancers tend to be slow in growth, but childhood cancers grow quickly, and a child may become ill in a short period of time. Childhood cancers predominate in the areas of the body that exhibit rapid growth such as the blood, lymphatic system, central nervous system, and bones.

DEFINITION/ETIOLOGY:
Cancer is defined as cell growth out of control. The rapid growth results in immature, abnormal cells that invade surrounding tissue. The etiology of childhood cancer varies from adult cancers. Adult cancers tend to be epithelial in nature, while childhood cancers often stem from nonepithelial or embryonal cells.

Numerous types of cancers are seen in children. Following is a brief overview of the most common cancers seen in children.

Leukemia	Leukemia is the most commonly diagnosed childhood cancer. Leukemia is characterized by an abnormal amount of white blood cells (WBC) in the body. It is considered a cancer of the bone marrow and blood. As the WBC's proliferate, the cells they produce are immature. The increasing production of WBC's affects normal production of red blood cells and platelets. Abnormal WBC's are called blast cells. The common types of leukemia in children are acute lymphoblastic leukemia (ALL) and acute myeloid leukemia (AML). Typical symptoms include lethargy, bruising and other abnormal bleeding, bone and joint pain, weakness and weight loss.
Brain tumor	Second most common cancer in children. The overall prognosis is dependent on the size, type, and location of the tumor. Neurological symptoms such as headache, blurred vision, dizziness, change in gait or fine motor skills, nausea, and vomiting are often seen. School staff may note a change in school performance and/or concentration. Typically, occurring tumors include astrocytoma, glioma, medulloblastoma, and ependymoma.
Neuroblastoma	Tumors that form along the sympathetic nervous system chain. They are often found above the kidneys in the adrenal glands, but can start anywhere.
Bone tumors	Tend to occur in older children and in the teenage years. **Osteosarcoma-** usually affects the large bones of the arms and legs. **Ewing's sarcoma-** can occur anywhere but most likely found in spine, ribs or pelvis.

CHILDHOOD CANCER *(continued from previous page)*

Lymphoma	These malignant diseases affect the lymph system and tissues. The two main types of lymphoma are Hodgkin lymphoma (also known as Hodgkin disease) and Non-Hodgkin lymphoma.
Retinoblastoma	Originates in the retina of the eye. Dependent on the size of the tumor, it may be necessary to remove the entire eye. This tumor is often discovered during well child exams, and is rarely seen in children over the age of six.
Wilm's tumor	Also known as nephroblastoma. Wilm's tumor is the most common kidney cancer. Symptoms include swelling or lump in the abdomen. Other symptoms such as poor appetite, fever, pain, or nausea may be present. **Nursing alert: DO NOT** palpate the abdomen if this tumor is suspected.

SIGNS AND SYMPTOMS (General):
- Keep in mind that symptoms may have a relatively fast onset, secondary to the rapidly growing cells in children
- Pain
- Loss of appetite
- Weight loss
- Anemia
- Increased susceptibility to infection
- Bruising
- Prolonged bleeding
- Neurological disturbances: change in behavior, change in gait, headache, dizziness, blurred or double vision

MANAGEMENT/TREATMENT:
1. Treatment is based on the type of cancer and may include surgery, radiation, and/or chemotherapy.
2. In some cases, a bone marrow transplant may be indicated for treatment.
3. In addition to treating the cancer, the effects of the tumor on the body (i.e. pain) and any side effects from treatment must be managed.
4. Be aware that 80% of patients use some type of complementary treatment in addition to conventional care.
5. Cancer therapy is complex and is usually managed by a pediatric oncologist.
6. In most cases, the oncology team develops an individualized treatment plan for the child that may be followed for several years.
7. Side effects from treatment include increased susceptibility to infection, bleeding/ bruising, hair loss, loss of appetite, nausea, vomiting.

CHILDHOOD CANCER *(continued from previous page)*

FOLLOW-UP:

1. Potential for infection
   a. Monitor for signs and symptoms of infection
   b. Notify parent/guardian if temperature > 99.9
   c. Notify parent/guardian of any exposure to communicable diseases
   d. Educate student, staff and class on handwashing techniques
   e. Provide health promotion information

2. Bleeding
   a. Educate staff regarding potential for abnormal bleeding and situations to report to the school nurse
   b. Monitor for petichiae, nosebleeds, bleeding gums or prolonged bleeding
   c. Contact parent/guardian for nosebleeds lasting longer than 10 minutes

3. Pain
   a. Contact parent/guardian with any new complaints of pain or severe pain
   b. Partner with oncology team for chronic pain management
   c. Administer analgesics only if ordered specifically for the student, even if standing orders available.

4. Gastro-intestinal side effects (nausea, vomiting, constipation, diarrhea)
   a. Educate staff on potential GI side effects and importance of notifying school nurse
   b. Maintain adequate hydration
   c. Accommodate for frequent, small meals throughout the day if necessary
   d. Provide opportunities for rest as needed
   e. Notify parent/guardian if vomiting persists

5. Alteration in coping
   a. Assess for stress and coping abilities
   b. Provide resource information to families
   c. Hair loss, surgical scars, and effects of long-term corticosteroids can contribute to altered body image. Monitor for body image disturbances through observation, discussion, and collaboration with parents and school staff.
   d. Art can be a therapeutic form of expression and stress management for the child.
   e. Provide support to siblings and make appropriate referrals as needed

POTENTIAL COMPLICATIONS:

It is important for the school nurse to be aware of late effects of treatment in survivors of childhood cancers. Potential adverse outcomes include decreased growth and development, developmental delays, cognitive disorders, heart or lung disease, infertility and development of secondary cancers.

CHILDHOOD CANCER *(continued from previous page)*

Interventions for the school nurse:
1. Monitor growth
2. Monitor development and refer student if regression is noted
3. Provide psycho-social support and referrals as need
4. Educate staff on potential complications
5. Plan for school re-entry

SCHOOL RE-ENTRY:
It is often recommended that the student remain in school part-time to maintain a sense of normalcy and to continue with established peer relationships. Homebound or hospital-based instruction should be instituted when the student is unable to attend school. Prior to the student returning to school:
- Schedule a meeting with parent/ guardian, school staff such as school nurse, counselor, teacher, school psychologist, principal, health care provider
- Establish guidelines for care while child is at school, along with a plan for any potential emergencies
- Create an Individualized School Healthcare Plan
- Update parent/guardian emergency contact numbers
- With parent/guardian permission, consider a presentation to the class prior to student returning to school. Often a provider from the child's cancer treatment team is willing to assist with transitioning the student back to school.
- Continue to monitor student after the child returns to school, re-evaluate and revise plan as needed.

IMPLICATIONS FOR LEARNING:
- Treatment and follow-up appointments will affect attendance
- Side effects from cancer and treatment impacts learning and performance
- Learning problems may emerge years after treatment is completed
- Common problems seen after treatment:
  - Attention disorders
  - Cognitive deficits
  - Difficulty remembering and processing information
  - Difficulty "keeping up"
  - Difficulty with reading
  - Difficulty with handwriting
  - Difficulty with new material
  - Lower grades than previous to treatment
  - Behavioral disorders
  - Trouble reading social cues

CHILDHOOD CANCER *(continued from previous page)*

It may be necessary to institute and Individual Education Plan (IEP) or 504C Plan to provide the necessary academic accommodations and supports.

NOTE: There may be cases when not all treatment options have been successful. The shift in care will become palliative. Often these students wish to continue to attend school. Accommodations can be made to make the child comfortable and have optimal quality of life while at school.

See **Do Not Attempt Resuscitation (DNAR)** for further information, if needed.

Resources

American Cancer Society- Website contains an abundance of information and resources. http://www.cancer.org/treatment/childrenandcancer/whenyourchildhascancer/children-diagnosed-with-cancer-returning-to-school

Candlelighters Childhood Cancer Foundation- Provides information on cognitive effects in survivors along with advocacy information. www.candlelighters.org

National Cancer Institute Fact Sheet- http://www.cancer.gov/cancertopics/factsheet/NCI/children-adolescents

Welcoming the Child with Cancer Back to School- An excellent downloadable guide for educators. Includes medical information, tips for transitioning back to school, peer support guidelines, and discusses grief and loss. Available at:

http://www.lrhsd.org/cms/lib05/NJ01000316/Centricity/Domain/89/Welcoming%20the%20Child%20with%20Cancer%20Back%20to%20School.pdf

Young people with cancer: A guide for parents-http://www.cancer.gov/cancertopics/coping/youngpeople

References

American Cancer Society. (2013). *Children diagnosed with cancer: Returning to school.* Retrieved from http://www.cancer.org/treatment/childrenandcancer/whenyourchildhascancer/children-diagnosed-with-cancer-returning-to-school

American Cancer Society. (2012). *Cancer in children.* Retrieved from http://www.cancer.org/cancer/cancerinchildren/detailedguide/index

Ball, J., Binder, R., & Cowen, K. (Eds.). (2012). The child with cancer. *Principles of Pediatric Nursing: Caring for Children (5th ed.)* (pp. 706-751). Upper Saddle River, NJ: Pearson Education, Inc.

Selekman, J., Bochenek, J., & Lukens, M. (2013). Alterations in cellular health: The student with cancer. In J. Selekman (Ed.), *School nursing: A comprehensive text (2nd ed.)* (pp. 724-732). Philadelphia, PA: F.A. Davis.

Spencer, J. (2006). The role of cognitive remediation in childhood cancer survivors experiencing neurocognitive late effects. *Journal of Pediatric Oncology Nursing, 23*(6), 321-325. doi: 10.1177/10434542206293270

The Children's Hospital of Philadelphia. (2009, October). *Welcoming the child with cancer back to school: An educator's guide.* Retrieved from http://www.lrhsd.org/cms/lib05/NJ01000316/Centricity/Domain/89/Welcoming the Child with Cancer Back to School.pdf

CHEST PAIN

DEFINITION/ETIOLOGY:
Pediatric chest pain can be classified as cardiac or non-cardiac. Non-cardiac is the most prevalent cause of chest pain in school-aged children and adolescents. Chest pain can originate from any structure in the chest - lungs, ribs, chest wall, diaphragm, joints between sternum and ribs, and heart. It can be caused from injury, infection, respiratory conditions, referred pain from the abdomen, or irritation and can be from stress or anxiety.

Chest pain from the heart is rare (unless child is known to have heart defect or disease). While the pain may be a symptom of serious disease, most chest pain is benign or self-limiting.

SIGNS AND SYMPTOMS:
Signs and symptoms will vary widely with cause and the person's age and personality. For many people, the heart is the most identifiable organ in the chest so they describe discomfort by saying their "heart hurts". It is important to remember this may be a figure of speech and not to over react. The determination of the cause of pain is a diagnostic decision and the term "heart pain" should be assessed similarly to other types of pain, focusing on associated signs and symptoms and severity and conveying that information to a diagnostician.

MANAGEMENT/TREATMENT:
1. Conduct an assessment
   - It is important to take a careful history; make close observation as person describes symptoms. Determine if history of recent injury, presence of underlying health condition (asthma, heart defect or cardiovascular history, recent illness, sickle cell disease, history of genetic disorder).
   - Determine onset of symptoms (acute, gradual, growing worse).
   - Length of time with symptoms?
   - Any association with activity (including at rest, only after activity, on inspiration, after coughing, etc.)?
   - What makes it better?
   - What makes it worse?
   - Determine type of pain - constant, intermittent, sharp, dull, radiating, etc.?
   - Are there associated respiratory symptoms?
   - Assess skin condition (indicative of oxygen exchange).
   - Assess psychological demeanor (calm, anxious, dramatic), history of increased stress.
   - History of huffing, smoking or other drug use.
   - Perform a general physical assessment including vital signs and note any irregularities.

CHEST PAIN *(continued from previous page)*

2. The person who has pain of acute onset that:
    a. interferes with breathing and /or sleep,
    b. is precipitated by exercise, or
    c. is associated with alteration of vital signs and dizziness, palpitations, syncope, or fever should be evaluated by their primary physician/healthcare provider.
    Symptomatic individuals should not be allowed to drive alone.
3. EMS should be contacted if an individual is more seriously compromised, particularly with symptoms of cyanosis, difficulty breathing, and decreased level of consciousness. Activate EMS if open chest wound or signs and symptoms of pneumothorax (rapid/ shallow respiration, painful respiration, cyanosis, and hypotension).

COMMON ILLNESSES THAT CAUSE CHEST PAIN

Costochondritis
A condition where there is inflammation in the cartilage between the sternum and ribs. It may be caused by a viral illness or by frequent coughing. The pain will occur with inhalation. The majority of people will have tenderness over the costochondral joint (depression on side of sternum where rib joins sternum). May be treated with OTC anti-inflammatories.

Musculoskeletal Injury/Pain
The most common cause of pediatric chest pain. Children frequently strain chest wall muscles while wrestling, carrying heavy books, or exercising. Direct trauma to the chest may result in a mild contusion of the chest wall or, with more significant force, a rib fracture, hemothorax, or pneumothorax. In most cases, there is a straightforward history of trauma and the diagnosis is clear.

Respiratory Conditions
Children who have severe, persistent cough, asthma, bronchitis, pleurisy or pneumonia may complain of chest pain due to overuse of chest wall muscles. Some children may complain of chest pain with exercise due to exercise-induced asthma. Pulmonary embolism should be considered in adolescent girls taking oral contraceptives.

Psychogenic Disturbances
Stress or anxiety can precipitate chest pain in both boys and girls. Often the stress that results in somatic complaints is not readily apparent and not all of these children present with hyperventilation or an anxious appearance. However, if the child has had a recent major stressful event, such as separation from friends, divorce in the family, or school failure that correlates temporally with the onset of the chest pain, it is reasonable to conclude that the symptoms are related to the event.

CHEST PAIN *(continued from previous page)*

Gastrointestinal Disorders

Conditions such as reflux esophagitis often cause chest pain in young children and adolescents. The pain is described classically as burning, substernal in location, and worsened by reclining or eating spicy foods. Be aware that students with eating disorders such as purging may have pain secondary to esophageal trauma related to the purging.

Miscellaneous Causes

Some young children will complain of chest pain following ingestion of a coin or other foreign body that lodges in the esophagus. Generally, the child or parent/guardian gives a clear history of recent foreign body ingestion.

Some instances of chest pain are related to an underlying disease. A careful history and physical exam will often sort these out. For instance, sickle cell disease may lead to vaso-occlusive crises or acute chest syndrome. Marfan syndrome may result in chest pain and fatal dissection of an abdominal aortic aneurysm. Collagen vascular disorders may lead to pleural effusions. Shingles may result in severe chest pain that precedes or occurs simultaneously with the classic rash.

References

American Heart Association. (2012). *Commonly asked questions about children and heart disease*. Retrieved from http://www.heart.org/HEARTORG/Conditions/More/CardiovascularConditionsofChildhood/ Commonly-Asked-Questions-About-Children-and-Heart-Disease_UCM_311917_Article.jsp

Ball, J., Binder, R., & Cowen, K. (Eds.). (2012). Alterations in respiratory function. *Principles of Pediatric Nursing: Caring for Children (5th ed.)* (pp. 594-595). Upper Saddle River, NJ: Pearson Education, Inc.

Illinois Emergency Medical Services for Children, (2010). *Guidelines for the nurse in the school setting*. Retrieved from website: http://www.luhs.org/depts/emsc/Schl_Man.pdf

John, R. & Chewey, L.(2013). Common complaints. In J. Selekman (Ed.), *School nursing: A comprehensive text* (pp. 608-610). Philadelphia, PA: F.A. Davis.

Martchenke, J. & Blosser, C. (2008). Cardiovascular disorders. In C. Burns, M. Brady, A. Dunn, N.B. Starr, C. Blosser (Eds.). *Pediatric primary care*, 4th ed. (pp. 753-754). St. Louis, MO: Saunders Elsevier.

Veeram Reddy, S. R., & Singh, H. (2010). Chest pain in children and adolescents. *Pediatrics in Review, 31*(1), p.p. e1-e9.doi: 10.1542/pir.31-1-e1

CHICKENPOX (Varicella)

DEFINITION/ETIOLOGY:
Chickenpox (varicella) is an acute, highly contagious, generalized viral disease that is caused by the zoster virus (human [alpha] herpes virus 3). Transmission occurs through contact with respiratory droplets/secretions and direct contact. It is vaccine preventable.

SIGNS AND SYMPTOMS:
- Usually a history of exposure.
- Sudden onset of slight fever, mild constitutional symptoms and a characteristic skin eruption beginning on scalp, face, or trunk.
- Multiple lesions (usually beginning on face and trunk) which constitute a vesicle on an erythematous base (dewdrop on a rose petal).
- Contagious 1-2 days before the rash appears and until all blisters have formed scabs.
- See also chart on *Rashes.*

MANAGEMENT/TREATMENT:
1. Treatment is supportive with management of itching with antihistamines or oatmeal baths; acetaminophen for fever; and anti-staphylococcal penicillin or cephalosporins for bacterial superinfections.
2. Exclusion from school until all lesions are scabbed over and dry (5-7 days; longer for immunocompromised persons to assure all blisters are crusted). Incubation period averages 14-16 days for new exposures, but may range 10-21 days.
3. Immunosuppressed individuals are particularly at risk and may develop life threatening disease (students with leukemia or HIV). Alert parents of students with immunity problems that their child may have been exposed to chickenpox at school.
4. Also, alert school staff members who may be immunocompromised of the outbreak of chickenpox.
5. Advise parent/guardian:
   DO NOT give aspirin or products containing salicylates due to the link with Reye's Syndrome.
   Oatmeal baths in lukewarm water may be comforting to the itching rash.
   Trim fingernails to reduce secondary infections from scratching.

POTENTIAL COMPLICATIONS:
Complications are uncommon, but may include dehydration from vomiting or diarrhea.
Secondary infections may occur from scratching the blister.
Complications that are more serious include pneumonia and encephalitis.

CHICKENPOX (Varicella) *(continued from previous page)*

NOTES:

> Varicella tends to be more severe in adolescents and adults.
>
> Remind all parents that a vaccine is available and recommended; some states require chickenpox vaccination for school entry.
>
> Adults may get "shingles" after exposure to varicella.
>
> 95% of adults have had chickenpox (even if they do not remember it).

References

American Academy of Pediatrics. (2013). Chickenpox (varicella-zoster infections). In S. Aronson, & T. Shope (Eds.), *Managing infectious diseases in child care and schools (2nd ed.)* (pp. 77-78). Elk Grove Village, IL: American Academy of Pediatrics.

American Academy of Pediatrics. (2009). Summaries of infectious disease – varicella-zoster infections. In L.K. Pickering, C.J. Baker, D.W. Kimberlin, & S.S. Long (Eds.), *Red Book: 2009 report of the committee on infectious diseases (28th ed.)* (pp. 714-726). American Academy of Pediatrics: Elk Grove Village, IL.

Ball, J., Binder, R., & Cowen, K. (Eds.). (2012). Immunizations and communicable diseases. *Principles of Pediatric Nursing: Caring for Children (5th ed.)* (p. 410). Upper Saddle River, NJ: Pearson Education, Inc.

Centers for Disease Control and Prevention . (2013). *Chickenpox information for parents.* Retrieved from http://www.cdc.gov/vaccines/vpd-vac/varicella/downloads/PL-dis-chickenpox-bw-office.pdf

Centers for Disease Control and Prevention, W. Atkinson, S. Wolfe, J. Hamborsky, L. McIntyre (Eds.) (2012). *Epidemiology and prevention of vaccine-preventable diseases (12th ed.)* (p.301). Washington DC: Public Health Foundation.

Centers for Disease Control and Prevention. (2011). *Chickenpox.* Retrieved from http://www.cdc.gov/vaccines/pubs/pinkbook/varicella.html

Mayo Clinic. (2013). *Chickenpox.* Retrieved from http://www.mayoclinic.com/health/chickenpox/DS00053

Medline Plus, U.S. National Library of Medicine. (2013). *Chickenpox.* Retrieved from http://www.nlm.nih.gov/medlineplus/chickenpox.html

Medline Plus, U.S. National Library of Medicine. (2013). *Reye syndrome.* Retrieved from http://www.nlm.nih.gov/medlineplus/reyesyndrome.html

National Institute of Neurological Disorders and Stroke, NIH (2009). *NINDS Reye's Syndrome information page.* Retrieved from http://www.ninds.nih.gov/disorders/reyes_syndrome/reyes_syndrome.htm

National Reye's Syndrome Foundation. (n.d.). *Reye's syndrome.* Retrieved from http://www.reyessyndrome.org/

Selekman, J., & Coates, J. (2013). Disease prevention. In J. Selekman (Ed.), *School nursing: A comprehensive text (2nd ed.)* (pp. 505-506). Philadelphia, PA: F.A. Davis.

CHILD MALTREATMENT

DEFINITION/ETIOLOGY:
Child maltreatment, a component of family violence, is defined as physical, emotional, or sexual abuse and includes physical or emotional neglect. Child maltreatment is an act of commission or omission. Commission is a deliberate or intentional act in which there is harm, potential harm or the threat of harm but harm to the child is unintentional. Omission, an act of negligence is failure to protect or meet the child's basic physical, emotional, medical, safety, or educational needs.

Note: **School Nurses are designated by law as mandatory reporters of suspected child maltreatment.**

Risk Factors for Child Maltreatment

Child	• Children under the age of 1 year (50% of fatalities) • Children under the age of 3 years (75% of fatalities) • Males (60% are abused) • Caucasians (45% are abused) • Special needs children (sometimes place extra burdens on parents/guardians)
Adult	• Most common abuser is the parent/guardian • Women under 40 years of age are the highest abusers • Abused as a child • Young parents/guardians, low education, numerous children, poverty, and/or a single parent • Lack of parenting skills, understanding children's needs and child development • Additional transient adult caregivers in the home, substance abuse, individual or family history of mental health and/or physical health issues • Belief that discipline that is considered child maltreatment is appropriate • Limited social network, lack of family support and/or self esteem • An unwanted pregnancy or the child does meet their expectations
Family	Dysfunctional families that may include violence between spouses
Community	Transient neighborhoods with violence, high poverty and unemployment rates

SIGNS/SYMPTOMS:
All forms of abuse
- Behavior and personality changes
- Changes in relationship with peers, family members and school personnel
- Changes in school attendance and performance
- Apprehensive of certain situations and people

CHILD MALTREATMENT *(continued from previous page)*

Physical Abuse
- Bruises, cuts, burns, fractures healing at different stages
- Marks from a belt, rope or chain located on the face, arms, back, legs and buttocks
- An increase in chronic health condition symptoms may be related from withholding medication
- Wincing indicating pain with movement
- Parts of a handprint on the body
- Behaviors inconsistent with developmental age

Emotional Abuse
- Low self-esteem, low self-image, cries, feelings of shame or guilt
- Trust issues, avoids eye contact, withdrawn
- Social, emotional or academic delay
- Inappropriate behavior (aggressive, destructive, cruel, engages in improper sexual activities)
- Attempts suicide
- Lack of attachment to the parent
- Older children may experiment with substance abuse

Sexually Abuse
- Genital area may exhibit signs of trauma (redness, bruises, bleeding, swelling)
- Sexually transmitted infection, urinary tract infection, difficulty sitting or walking
- Somatic complaints (headache, stomachaches, etc.), bedwetting, night terrors
- Feelings of hostility, guilt, anger, shame, eating disorders

MANAGEMENT/TREATMENT:
- Physical exam and comprehensive history
- Removal of child from the abusive situation if necessary
- Mental health therapy from a trained professional
- Art therapy
- Group or family treatment
- Treatment pursuant to type of abuse may include a physical exams, x-rays, MRI, CT, urine cultures

FOLLOW UP:
- Establish trusting relationship with parent/guardian
- Prevent further injury
- Emphasize the importance of counseling and follow up care
- Support the victims of child maltreatment
- Homecare teaching (family treatment and parenting classes)

CHILD MALTREATMENT *(continued from previous page)*

- Educate staff regarding signs and symptoms of child maltreatment
- Identify students with indicators of maltreatment
- Provide safety education to children
- Provide community resources to victims and families
- Collaborate with community to raise awareness to reduce incidence
- Expected school nurse outcomes include developing nurturing environment for the child, normal growth and development, positive sense of self-esteem, stress relief for parents and absence of episodes of abuse

NOTES:
- Each state provides its own definitions of child abuse and neglect based on minimum standards set by federal law.
- Be aware of the school, district, and state process for reporting child abuse.
- When obtaining information about the injury document the child's and parent's response verbatim.
- Abuse or neglect can influence the health and mental status throughout life.

RESOURCES
Child Welfare Information Gateway, Developing and Sustaining Prevention Programs at
https://www.childwelfare.gov/preventing/developing/index.cfm

References
Ball, J., Binder, R., & Cowen, K. (Eds.). (2012). Assessment and management of social and environmental influences. *Principles of Pediatric Nursing: Caring for Children (5th ed.)* (pp. 461-462). Upper Saddle River, NJ: Pearson Education, Inc.

Centers for Disease Control. (2012). *Child maltreatment-definition.* Retrieved from
http://www.cdc.gov/violenceprevention/childmaltreatment/definitions.html

Children's Bureau. (2012). *Child maltreatment-data tables.* Retrieved from
http://www.acf.hhs.gov/programs/cb/resource/child-maltreatment-2010-data-tables

Selekman, J., Pelt, P., Garnier, S., & Baker, D. (2013). *Youth violence.* In J. Selekman (Ed.), *School nursing: A comprehensive text* (2nd ed.) (pp. 1103-1110). Philadelphia, PA: F.A. Davis.

CONCUSSION/HEAD INJURY

DEFINITION/ETIOLOGY:

Concussion
A concussion is a type of traumatic brain injury (TBI) that affects children, adolescents and young adults. Children and teens take longer to recover than adults. It is caused by a blow, bump or jolt to the head. The impact generally causes the brain to move back and forth in the head. The CDC estimates that approximately 1.6-3.8 million sports/recreation related concussions happen each year and many occur without loss of conciousness. All concussions are serious and recognition and proper response when they first occur can help aid recovery and prevent further injury. Subsequent or repeated concussions can have lifelong complications or even death. Students who experience a concussion may exhibit cognitive and emotional issues that can impact the learning process and requires a collaborative approach in which the school nurse plays a vital role in supporting the student and and educating the school team on potential implications in the school setting.

Other head injuries include:
- **Trauma to scalp:** laceration, bruise, abrasion
- **Trauma to bony skull:** fracture
- **Trauma to brain:** contusion, laceration, hematoma

SIGNS/SYMPTOMS:
1. **Concussion**
   a. **Physical**
      - Headache
      - Nausea or vomiting
      - Dizziness
      - Fatigue, feeling "foggy"
      - Blurry or double vision
      - Sensitivity to light
      - Vomiting
      - Unequal size of pupils
      - Unusually rapid or slow pulse rate
   b. **Cognitive**
      - Difficulty concentrating
      - Difficulty remembering
      - Feeling slowed down
      - Difficulty thinking clearly

CONCUSSION/HEAD INJURY *(continued from previous page)*

    c. **Emotional**
- Irritable
- Sad
- Nervous

2. **Scalp injury:**
- Abrasion
- Laceration: more bleeding than similar cut on other parts of the body because the skin over the scalp has a larger blood supply.
- Bruise: causes mildly painful swelling (synonyms: pump-knot, goose-egg). Edges may feel depressed, but it is not to be mistaken for the depressed skull fracture described below.
- In all these conditions, there is no disturbance of consciousness unless there is accompanying injury to the brain.

3. **Skull fracture:**
- Non-displaced linear fracture: no symptoms except pain unless the base (bottom) of the skull is fractured (X-ray required for diagnosis) .
- Basal skull fracture: usually associated with severe injury which almost always produces disturbance of consciousness or leakage of blood or spinal fluid from the mouth, nose, or ear.
- Depressed skull fracture: due to a fragment or larger piece of bone pressing down on the brain as a result of trauma. Usually it cannot be felt by palpation and requires an X-ray for diagnosis.

MANAGEMENT/TREATMENT:

Concussion:
- Any student expected of having a concussion or head injury should be removed from play immediately and sent for medical evaluation.
- Students and parents/guardians should be educated on the signs and syptoms of a concussion and be instructed on the importance of not hiding their injury.
- Students should return to their normal activities gradually. Only when student's symptoms have reduced significantly, in consultaion with their doctor, should they gradually return to activities.
- Students should get plenty of rest and avoid high risk, high intensity activities until symptoms resolve.
- When returning to school students may need accomodations such as a shortened school day, less testing, rest periods during the day, restrictions on physical education and /or recess or moderations to the work load.
- Prior to returning to sports students should take part in a "return to play" protocol that gradually allows the student to increase activities while monitoring for symptoms.

CONCUSSION/HEAD INJURY *(continued from previous page)*

Scalp injury:
- Abrasion: wash with plain soap. Apply pressure with 4x4 gauze or other clean cloth until bleeding stops. Dressing is usually not necessary.
- Laceration: same as abrasion but apply pressure longer to make sure bleeding stops (see *Laceration Guideline*).
- Bruise: apply cold pack to relieve pain. DO NOT apply pressure. Prognosis excellent if no sign of brain injury.

Skull fracture:
- If skull fracture suspected, refer to healthcare provider.
- Linear: Limitation of activity as directed by physician/ healthcare provider .
- Basal: refer to medical facility.
- Depressed: if fragment is significantly depressed to encroach on brain, surgery may be required to elevate bony segment.

POTENTIAL COMPLICATIONS (SERIOUS):
- Epidural / subdural hematoma
- Intracranial hemorrhage
- Cervical spinal injury
- Skull fracture
- Cerebrospinal fluid leak

Notes
- Students with chronic conditions such as migraines may take longer to recover from a concussion. Students with depression and/or anxiety may also have trouble dealing with the complications of a concussion.
- Neurocognitive testing to access concentration, memory and processing speed may be done to help assess the impact of the concussion.
- Children and adolescents should avoid computer use, texting and video games while symptoms persist.
- After a concussion a collaborative approach to the student's needs in school is needed. Guidance counselors, teachers, nurses and support staff must be educated on the complications of concussions and the impact on learning.

References
Center for Disease Control. (2011). *Heads up: Brain injuries in your practice.* Retrieved from http://www.cdc.gov/concussion/HeadsUp/physicians_tool_kit.html

Mayo Clinic. (2011). *Concussion.* Retrieved from http://www.mayoclinic.com/health/concussion/DS00320

CONJUNCTIVITIS (Pink Eye)

DEFINITION/ETIOLOGY:
Inflammation and/or infection of the conjunctiva (mucous membrane lining the eye), caused by allergens, irritants (e.g., foreign object, dust, smoke), bacterial (staphylococcal, streptococcal, haemophilus) or viral (usually adenovirus, but also herpes simplex) infections.

SIGNS AND SYMPTOMS:
- Redness of sclera
- Discharge: purulent or watery
- Itchiness: student rubs eye(s)
- Eyelids may be red and/or swollen
- Crusts in inner corner of eyes, especially on waking from sleep

Physical Findings That Help Differentiate Cause:

Allergic	<ul><li>Occurs in response to agent causing allergic reaction.</li><li>Discharge remains watery; bilateral</li><li>No contagious period.</li><li>May occur with the common cold</li></ul>
Bacterial	<ul><li>The common meaning of "pink eye": purulent drainage (thick, yellow to green-yellow) and more crusting during sleep.</li><li>Often beginning unilaterally and progressing to bilateral. Is spread to other by hand, contaminated eye mascara, etc</li><li>This is contagious but less easily transmitted to others than viral.</li><li>Contagious period ends when medication is started and symptoms are no longer present.</li><li>May occur with the common cold</li></ul>
Viral	<ul><li>Usually less severe, watery discharge but may be thick and white to pale yellow.</li><li>Lasts 3-5 days.</li><li>Most often bilateral.</li><li>Highly contagious but does not require antibiotics.</li><li>May occur with the common cold.</li><li>Contagious period continues while symptoms are present.</li></ul>
Chemical	<ul><li>Usually appears shortly after contact with irritating substance.</li><li>No contagious period.</li></ul>

CONJUNCTIVITIS (Pink Eye) *(continued from previous page)*

MANAGEMENT/TREATMENT (with specific care based on likely cause or medical diagnosis):
1. Exclusion from school: The registered nurse may not exclude those whose conjunctivitis is mild or associated with a cold or allergy. School policy should direct other personnel to exclude ALL cases for medical evaluation. Health care provider may prescribe antibiotic drops or ointment. Students return to school when treatment has begun.
2. Discourage home treatment with cold ointment or steroid drops.
3. Over-the-counter drops may be used for comfort of mild allergic or viral conjunctivitis. Health care provider may order topical anti-inflammatory drops for significant allergic conjunctivitis.
4. Cool compress for temporary relief.
5. Check visual acuity; it should be normal or unchanged from the student's usual acuity.
6. Check fingers and nose for impetigo.
7. Review handwashing and other measures to prevent spread of infection.
8. Refer any case with subconjunctival hemorrhage.

FOLLOW UP:
Educate about handwashing and keeping fingers/hands away from eyes. Instruct the student to not share face washcloths and eye makeup. Discard unused eye makeup.

POTENTIAL COMPLICATIONS:
Conjunctivitis can be accompanied by an inflammation of the cornea which can affect vision.

NOTES:
The chart that follows presents indicators of iritis (uveitis or inflammation of iris) and keratitis (inflamed cornea).

DIFFERENTIAL DIAGNOSIS OF THREE EYE DISORDERS

PARAMETER	ACUTE CONJUNCTIVITIS	ACUTE IRITIS	KERATITIS
Pain	Mild discomfort	Moderate pain, with photophobia	Moderate to severe with photophobia
Vision	Normal	Slightly to moderately blurred	Blurred
Discharge	Often mucopurulent	Clear	Clear, scanty
Cornea	Clear	Clear	May appear normal
Pupil	Normal	Small and irregular	Normal or small
Response to Light	Normal	Poor	Fair
Injection	Conjunctival only	Conjunctival and circumcorneal	Minimal to Moderate
Blepharospasm	Minimal to None	Moderate	Severe

CONJUNCTIVITIS (Pink Eye) *(continued from previous page)*

References

American Academy of Pediatrics. (2013). Pinkeye (conjunctivitis). In S. Aronson, & T. Shope (Eds.), *Managing infectious diseases in child care and schools (2nd ed.)* (p. 133-134). Elk Grove Village, IL: American Academy of Pediatrics.

American Academy of Pediatrics. (2009). Recommendations for care of children in special circumstances – infections spread by direct contact. . In Pickering, L.K., Baker, C.J., Kimberlin, D.W., & Long, S.S. (Eds.), *Red Book: 2009 Report of the Committee on Infectious Diseases* (28th ed.) (p. 144). American Academy of Pediatrics: Elk Grove Village, IL.

Blosser, C. (2008). Eye disorders. In C. Burns, M. Brady, A. Dunn, N.B. Starr,& C. Blosser (Eds.), *Pediatric primary care (4th ed.)* (pp. 689-694). St. Louis, MO: Saunders Elsevier.

John, R. & Chewey. L. (2013). Common complaints. In J. Selekman (Ed.), *School nursing: A comprehensive text* (2nd ed.) (pp. 587-590). Philadelphia, PA: F.A. Davis.

Mayo Clinic. (2012). *Pink eye (conjunctivitis).* Retrieved from http://www.mayoclinic.com/health/pink-eye/DS00258

American Optometric Association (AOA). (2013). *Conjunctivitis.* Retrieved from http://www.aoa.org/patients-and-public/eye-and-vision-problems/glossary-of-eye-and-vision-conditions/conjunctivitis

CONTACT LENS PROBLEMS

OVERVIEW
Contact lenses are used as a substitute for glasses in most situations. They may also be used to treat certain eye diseases or for cosmetic purposes to change eye color. Children between the ages of 6-9 are prescribed contact lenses for medical reasons only.

LENS TYPES include soft lenses, rigid gas permeable lenses, extended wear lenses, disposable lenses, and specialty lenses. Decorative lenses sold are illegally sold in beauty salons, novelty stores and online. These lenses are non-fitted lenses and cover a larger part of the eye, putting the wearer at a higher risk for a severe complication. Decorative lenses, if desired should be prescribed by an eye care professional.

Most problems encountered from wearing contact lenses are from inexperienced wearers, improper wear or care, or delay in follow-up with the eye healthcare provider. These problems range from a lens being out of position, eye irritations such as dryness, a foreign body on or under lens, to more serious complications such as pink eye, corneal abrasion , infection, corneal ulcer, and permanent vision loss.

SIGNS/SYMPTOMS:
As a new contact lens wearer, it is not uncommon to have:
- Tearing upon insertion
- Scratchy feeling or like there is something in the eye
- Mild light sensitivity
- Slight headache especially if stronger prescription
- Distorted vision that may be caused from:
    - Lens that is not centered
    - Soft lens inside out
    - Wearing disposable lenses beyond the suggested time
    - Not wearing lenses for several days (cornea may lose adaptation)
    - Dirty lens

SIGNS AND SYMTPOMS OF AN EYE IRRITATION, INFECTION, OR SERIOUS COMPLICATION INCLUDE:
- Persistent pain
- Burning and tearing
- Redness that will not clear
- Hazy vision that continues an hour or more after lens removal
- Continued sensitivity to light
- Swelling of eye

CONTACT LENS PROBLEMS *(continued from previous page)*

MANAGEMENT/TREATMENT:

Seek care from eye healthcare professional if symptoms of an eye irritation or infection (above) occur.

Removing Displaced Lenses
- Blink several times to make sure lens is in the eye. Blinking may center the lens.
- Wash hands before touching the eye or lens.
- Use your finger to feel the lens through the eyelid.
- Look in the opposite direction of the lens (downward, upward, to the right or left) to visualize the lens.
- When the lens is visualized, use your finger to move the lens back on the cornea.
- Massaging the lens through eyelid may help move it back in place.
- If you are unable to remove the lens, seek care from an eye doctor.

FOLLOW UP: (Teaching Tips)
- Wash your hands before touching your eye or handling lenses.
- Don't wear lenses longer than prescribed.
- Don't sleep in your lenses unless specifically fitted for that purpose.
- Don't use saliva as a cleaning agent. The risk of bacterial contamination is great.
- Don't use homemade solutions that are not sterile, not distilled or tap water for any part of the cleaning regimen.
- Use only solutions recommended by fitter – some are not compatible with other lenses and/or may be allergenic to wearer.
- Experts consider the "rub and rinse" method to be the superior cleaning method.
- Don't get cosmetics, sprays, etc. on lenses.
- Finish with makeup before handling lenses.
- Don't reuse the solution in your lens case. Throw away and use a new case every three months.
- Don't rinse lenses in hot water or store in a hot or unusually cold place; lens may warp.
- Used lenses stored for 30 days should not be worn without re-disinfecting.
- Frequent blinking is essential for all contacts to maintain moisture and a constant supply of oxygen to the corneas.
- Wearing non-prescription decorative lenses or circle lenses purchased online or in novelty shops can result in permanent eye damage.
- Smokers have a higher incidence of problems wearing contact lenses than non-smokers.

CONTACT LENS PROBLEMS *(continued from previous page)*

References

American Academy of Ophthalmology, Eye Smart. (2013). Contact *lenses for vision correction.* Retrieved from
http://www.geteyesmart.org/eyesmart/glasses-contacts-lasik/contact-lens.cfm

American Academy of Ophthalmology, Eye Smart. (2013). *Removing a displaced content lens.* Retrieved from
http://www.geteyesmart.org/eyesmart/ask/questions/stuck-contact-lens.cfm

Medline Plus. U.S. National Library of Medicine. (2013). *Corneal ulcers and treatment.* Retrieved from http://www.nlm.nih.gov/
medlineplus/ency/article/001032.htm#visualContent

United States Food and Drug and Administration, Medical Devices. (2011). *Contact lenses.* Retrieved from http://www.fda.gov/
MedicalDevices/ProductsandMedicalProcedures/HomeHealthandConsumer/ConsumerProducts/ContactLenses/
default.htm

CYSTIC FIBROSIS

DEFINITION/ETIOLOGY:
Cystic fibrosis is an autosomal recessive genetic disease caused by a mutation of the **Cystic Fibrosis Transmembrane Regulator** (CFTR) gene, altering the salt balance in body secretions. Cystic fibrosis affects mainly the exocrine glands, resulting in a thick, sticky mucous that compromises the organs, primarily the lungs and pancreas. The exocrine glands produce sweat, saliva, pancreatic digestive juice and respiratory tract mucous.

SIGNS AND SYMPTOMS:
Vary with the severity of the disease.
- Salty taste to the skin – increased amount of sodium and chloride in sweat
- Weight loss despite voracious appetite
- Frequent, foul-smelling, greasy stools
- Stools may be gray or clay colored
- Flatulence
- Abdominal pain
- Delayed growth
- Thick sputum
- Productive coughing
- Wheezing
- Frequent respiratory infections

MANAGEMENT/TREATMENT:
There is no cure for cystic fibrosis. Treatment is aimed at alleviating symptoms, primarily to keep the lungs as clear as possible.

1. Chest physical therapy to loosen thick mucus secretions
    a. Postural drainage
    b. Chest percussion
    c. Positive expiratory pressure therapy
    d. Mechanical devices such as Flutter/Vest devices
2. Medications
    a. Pancreatic enzymes to aid in digestion with each meal/snack
    b. Aerosolize drugs (e.g. Pulmozyme®) thins mucus making it easier to cough up
    c. Bronchodilators to open airways
    d. Vitamin supplements (secretions prevent body from absorbing fat soluble vitamins A, D, E and K)
    e. Antibiotics to treat respiratory infections, may need longer duration of treatment than normal

CYSTIC FIBROSIS *(continued from previous page)*

3. Maintain adequate nutrition
    a. High calorie/diet high in protein and fat
    b. May need nutritional supplements
    c. May need supplemental feedings per nasogastric tube, or Total Parenteral Nutrition (TPN)
    d. For long term nutritional support, a gastrostomy or jejunostomy tube may be placed
4. Physical activity as tolerated
    a. Allow student to set their own pace, accommodate for rest periods as needed.
    b. Encourage adequate hydration (especially during hot weather or after exercise – increased salt in sweat – may need supplemental salt).
    c. Physical activity loosens lung secretions.
    d. Improves overall physical condition of heart and lungs.
5. Psychosocial assessment
    a. May feel different from peers
    b. Need for special diet, medications, respiratory management
    c. Potential for bullying from others

FOLLOW-UP:
*   Develop individualized school healthcare plan identifying signs of airway distress and appropriate responses.
*   Assist student with administration of pancreatic enzymes.
*   Act as a liaison with CF care centers to coordinate care for school.
*   Monitor nutritional status – measure height/weight a minimum of 2 times per year.
*   Educate staff regarding chronic cough.
    o   Not contagious
    o   Should not suppress cough – clears secretions
    o   Allow student to keep water bottle on desk
    o   Allow bathroom privileges as needed for digestive problems
    o   Preferential seating near door so student may leave classroom as needed for heavy coughing
    o   Tissues/plastic bag at desk for productive cough

POTENTIAL COMPLICATIONS:
*   Asthma can result from chronic inflammation of the bronchial tubes
*   Chronic respiratory infections
    o   Pneumonia
    o   Bronchitis
    o   Chronic sinusitis

CYSTIC FIBROSIS *(continued from previous page)*

- Liver damage due to blocked bile duct
- Cystic fibrosis-related diabetes (CFRD)– features similar to Type 1 and Type 2 diabetes but considered a separate condition
- Depressed growth rate
- Osteoporosis and/or osteopenia secondary to compromised absorption of calcium and vitamin D
- Infertility – 98% in males
- Death – typically as a result of lung complications

NOTES:

Children with cystic fibrosis are more likely to suffer complications from an illness. Educate regarding the importance of healthy lifestyle behaviors:
- Appropriate handwashing
- Immunizations – pneumococcal and influenza
- Avoiding cigarette smoke
- Healthy eating habits
- Avoid sitting within 6 feet of another student with CF secondary to cross infection

Resources

Cystic Fibrosis Foundation http://www.cff.org/AboutCF/

Cystic Fibrosis Foundation, specific for school: http://www.cff.org/LivingWithCF/AtSchool/

National Lung Heart and Blood Institute

http://www.nhlbi.nih.gov/health/health-topics/topics/cf/

References

Ball, J., Binder, R., & Cowen, K. (Eds.). (2012). Alterations in respiratory function. *Principles of Pediatric Nursing: Caring for Children (5th ed.)* (p.p. 551-599). Upper Saddle River, NJ: Pearson Education, Inc.

Brady, M. (2008). Respiratory disorders. In C. Burns, M. Brady, A. Dunn, N.B. Starr, & C. Blosser (Eds.), *Pediatric primary care* (4th ed.) (pp. 790-791). St. Louis, MO: Saunders Elsevier.

Cystic Fibrosis Foundation. (n.d.). *About cystic fibrosis.* Retrieved from http://www.cff.org/AboutCF/

Cystic Fibrosis Foundation. (2012). *Living with CF at school.* Retrieved from http://www.cff.org/LivingWithCF/AtSchool/

Mayo Clinic. (2012). *Cystic fibrosis.* Retrieved from http://www.mayoclinic.com/health/cystic-fibrosis/DS00287

National Lung, Heart Blood Institute. (2011).What is *cystic fibrosis?* Retrieved from http://www.nhlbi.nih.gov/health/health-topics/topics/cf/

Selekman, J., Bochenek, J., & Lukens, M. (2013). Cystic fibrosis. In J. Selekman (Ed.), *School nursing: A comprehensive text (2nd ed.)* (pp. 721-724). Philadelphia, PA: F.A. Davis.

CYTOMEGALOVIRUS (CMV)

DEFINITION/ETIOLOGY:
Cytomegalovirus (CMV) is one of a group of highly host-specific herpes viruses (herpes 1 & 2, Epstein Barr and varicella/shingles). The virus cycles between stages of an active infection and dormancy and an infected person can "shed" the virus at any time. Depending upon the age and the immune status of the host, CMV can cause a variety of clinical syndromes, collectively known as cytomegalic inclusion disease, although the majority of infections are very mild or subclinical. CMV can be transmitted through body fluids including urine, blood, saliva, secretions (e.g. breast milk, tears, semen, and vaginal fluids), and during the birthing process.

CLINICAL MANIFESTATIONS:
Congential CMV *(Fetus/Newborn)*: may cause intrauterine death or severely affect newborn (microcephaly, hearing loss, vision impairment, chronic liver disease, developmental disabilities, pneumonia, seizures etc.). Symptoms may develop months after birth.

Acquired CMV *(Infant/Toddler)*: milder infections, may be asymptomatic with excretion of virus in the urine.

Older Children/Adults: CMV is present in the environment; about 40% of adults have antibodies against the organism; blood transfusions and organ transplants can convey infection; immunosuppressed and pregnant individuals are at particular risk.

SIGNS AND SYMPTOMS :
- Generally none except in the severely affected newborn; those who survive will usually be served in Special Education due to cognitive impairment and other developmental disabilities.
- An infectious mononucleosis-like syndrome can occur in older children and young adults (fever, sore throat, fatigue, jaundice, and swollen glands).
- Diagnosis is made by rising antibody titer in blood, or isolation of virus from the urine.

MANAGEMENT AND TREATMENT:
1. Acute disease is rarely diagnosed in school-age children.
2. Special education and other school personnel who handle diapers should always use "standard precautions".
3. Quarantine is unnecessary but pregnant teachers should not change diapers of known CMV shedders.
4. No vaccine is available.
5. Specific treatment with I.V. antiviral drugs is generally reserved for individuals who are immunosuppressed.
6. CMV has a predilection for the retina.

80

CYTOMEGALOVIRUS (CMV) *(continued from previous page)*

FOLLOW UP:
- Some children will have serial urine cultures to determine when they stop shedding.
- Educate staff that **pregnant women and immunosuppressed individuals are the only ones at significant risk.**

POTENTIAL COMPLICATIONS:
Most babies born with CMV never develop symptoms or disabilities. However, when babies do have symptoms, some resolve while others can be permanent. Examples of potential complications of CMV include:

Temporary Symptoms	Permanent Symptoms or Disabilities
• Liver problems • Spleen problems • Jaundice (yellow skin and eyes) • Purple skin splotches • Lung problems • Small size at birth • Seizures • Pneumonia	• Hearing loss • Vision loss • Mental disability • Small head (microcephaly) • Lack of coordination • Seizures • Death

PREVENTION:
- Standard Precautions
- Handwashing
- Avoid contact with infectious body fluids
- Avoid contact with tears and saliva of infected child?
- Avoid sharing food, eating utensils and drinking from the same glass
- Do not put a child's pacifier in your mouth
- Do not use someone else's toothbrush
- Do not touch inside of mouth, nose or eye after contact with body fluids of an infection person

NOTES:
- After neonatal infection, virus may be excreted for 5-6 years (children 7 and older rarely pose a threat); CMV is excreted (urine, saliva) by a large number of children in day care centers, which may represent a community reservoir.
- If the mother has a primary CMV infection during pregnancy, the risk of transmitting the disease is high. However, if CMV is reactivated during pregnancy the risk of transmission to the fetus is low.

CYTOMEGALOVIRUS (CMV) *(continued from previous page)*

- If congenital CMV is suspected it is important to test the infant within 3 weeks otherwise it is considered acquired CMV.
- If CMV is found in breast milk, breast feeding is not discouraged as usually no signs, symptoms or disease occur.
- Approximately 50 percent to 80 percent of women have the virus by the age of 40.
- Once CMV is in the body it remains present for life. If healthy, CMV is often dormant and goes undiagnosed.
- CMV does not reactivate unless individual is immunosuppressed.
- No cure is available for CMV but antiviral medication is available to slow down the infection for those at risk.

Resource

Centers for Disease Control and Prevention. (2011). Guide to Infection Prevention for Outpatient Settings: Minimum Expectations for Safe Care. http://www.cdc.gov/HAI/settings/outpatient/outpatient-care-gl-standard-precautions.html

References

American Academy of Pediatrics. (2013). Cytomegalovirus. In S. Aronson, & T. Shope (Eds.), *Managing infectious diseases in child care and schools (2nd ed.)* (p.81). Elk Grove Village, IL: American Academy of Pediatrics.

Centers for Disease Control. (2010). *Cytomegalovirus (CMV) and congenital CMV infection*. Retrieved from http://www.cdc.gov/cmv/overview.html

Gaylord, N. & Yetman, R. (2008). Perinatal conditions. In C. Burns, M. Brady, A. Dunn, N.B. Starr, & C. Blosser (Eds.), *Pediatric primary care*, (4th ed.), (pp. 1070-1071). St. Louis, MO: Saunders Elsevier.

Mayo Clinic. (2011). *Cytomegaloviris (CMV) infection.* Retrieved from http://www.mayoclinic.com/health/cmv/DS00938

National Institute of Neurological Disorders and Stroke. (2011). *NINDS neurological consequences of cytomegalovirus infection information page.* Retrieved from http://www.ninds.nih.gov/disorders/cytomegalic/cytomegalic.htm

DENTAL EMERGENCIES

DEFINITION/ETIOLOGY:

Nearly one half of children have a dental injury to a tooth during their childhood. Tooth and mouth injuries are generally not considered life threatening, but may require immediate dental and/or medical attention. Common causes of dental injuries are related to sport activities, falls, with or without something in the mouth, fights, and automobile accidents. Frequently, injury to a tooth or the oral cavity can be prevented or lessened by use of appropriate equipment or a mouth guard. Prevention education is critical as injuries to permanent teeth can have a lasting impact on a person's self-esteem and confidence.

SIGNS AND SYMPTOMS:
A healthcare provider should be contacted for the following:
- Avulsed tooth (knocked out due to trauma)
- Fractured, chipped or missing tooth (may have been swallowed)
- Luxated/dislocated tooth
- Fractured jaw (pain with opening and closing jaw)
- Infections and/or inflammation
- Sensitivity to pressure or hot/cold
- Bleeding that can't be stopped after 10 minutes
- Problems breathing or swallowing
- A large cut inside the mouth
- An object stuck in any part of the mouth (throat, tongue, cheek)

MANAGEMENT/TREATMENT:

AVULSED TOOTH*
If a knocked out tooth is handled correctly, there is a good possibility the dentist will be able to put the tooth placed back into the socket if the child is seen within 30 minutes. Approximately 85% of avulsed teeth placed in the socket within 5 minutes survive.
1. Don't change the tooth's protective coating by trying to clean it. At most, gently rinse off debris with warm water. **Do not touch the root of the tooth.**
2. If possible, gently place the tooth back into its socket securing it with gauze or aluminum foil around the tooth. If unsuccessful place the tooth in student's mouth between cheek and gum (providing the student is old enough). This natural environment is most protective to the tooth; use milk in the case of students < 7 years.
3. If student is too young, wrap tooth in gauze and immerse in cold milk for transportation.
4. Commercial containers to carry tooth to the dentist are available, but expensive. These containers are convenient but have no proven advantage, are of no proven advantage, but are convenient.
5. Call parent and the dentist to arrange an immediate visit.

*Maxillary central incisor is most frequently avulsed.

DENTAL EMERGENCIES *(continued from previous page)*

6. Do not attempt to insert a primary tooth back in the socket. The tooth should be taken to the dentist so that he or she can be sure the tooth was lost in its entirety and the root not broken.

FRACTURED TOOTH
1. Rinse the mouth with warm water.
2. Call parent.
3. Save fragment/ large chip.
4. Call dentist and describe extent of chip.
5. Cover jagged edge of tooth with gauze.
6. Apply cold compress or a washcloth with ice to the cheek to reduce pain and swelling.

LUXATED/DISLOCATED TOOTH
1. Reposition tooth gently.
2. Call parent and dentist for emergency visit.
3. Put gauze around tooth and have student hold it there during transportation to dentist.
4. For permanent tooth, **time is of the essence**.

FRACTURED JAW
1. Immobilize jaw placing a scarf, tie or towel under the chin. Tie the ends on top of the head.
2. Apply ice to reduce swelling.
3. Call parent and dentist.

PUNCTURE WOUNDS
1. Do not remove the embedded object in any part of the mouth.
2. Seek immediate medical care.
3. This injury may require referral to surgeon.

FOLLOW-UP:
Monitor for:
- Persistent pain.
- Sensitivity to hot and cold.
- Discoloration of tooth.
- Possible tetanus booster if less than 12 years old.
- Persistent bleeding - prolonged or recurrent, after dental injury or extraction of tooth:
  1. Place a sterile gauze pad on the extraction site and have the student gently bite on it for 30 minutes.
  2. Replace soaked gauze pads as necessary.
  3. Consult a dentist if bleeding persists over 1 hour; sooner if bleeding appears excessive. If bleeding is spontaneous without trauma, refer to doctor.

DENTAL EMERGENCIES *(continued from previous page)*

POTENTIAL COMPLICATIONS:
- Dental pulp fracture
- Displaced tooth
- Embedded tooth fragments
- Discoloration of tooth
- Loss of tooth
- Possible root canal, crown in the future
- Wounds may heal with a scar that may affect swallowing and speech

OTHER DENTAL CONCERNS:

Toothache
- Rinse mouth with warm water.
- Floss teeth to remove food particles that may be trapped between teeth.
- All toothaches should be referred to a dentist; severity will dictate the time frame.

Protruding braces wire
- Protruding wire from a brace can be gently bent out of the way to relieve discomfort by using a tongue depressor or pencil eraser. If the wire cannot be bent easily, place small piece of gauze or cotton over the end to prevent irritation to cheek or gum. Do not try to remove any wire embedded in the cheeks, gum, or tongue. (Local orthodontists often donate care kits.)
- Obtain orthodontic care same day.

Red, swollen or sore gums
- Have student rinse mouth thoroughly with a warm salt water solution (1/4 tsp. table salt to 4 oz. glass of water).
- Instruct student to repeat rinses every two hours, and after eating or tooth brushing, and before bedtime.
- If no improvement in 1-2 days, refer to doctor or dentist.
- Check for abscesses below the tooth line.

NOTES:
The Role of the School Nurse
When a facial or dental injury occurs at school, the school nurse, rather than a dentist, may be the first one contacted. Taking a quick, complete, injury specific history is essential.

DENTAL EMERGENCIES *(continued from previous page)*

If the child has no life-threatening symptoms, briefly obtain any additional history that would influence advice, such as past medical history, whether the child has any special healthcare needs, and/or significant social information. Next, it becomes important to determine if the injury is primarily dental or medical. The head, neck, and oral cavity have a tremendous vascular supply; therefore, blood may obscure a significant injury or it may make a mild injury appear much worse that it is. If it is clear the injury is primarily dental, help the caregiver to access a child's dentist immediately.

Other considerations include:
1. Education on prevention of dental injuries
    a. Types and use of mouth guards
    b. Do not put anything but food in the mouth
    c. Sit while eating
    d. Do not chew hard candy, ice, etc.
2. Special hygiene and diet instructions

COMMONLY ASKED DENTAL QUESTIONS:
1. **What should school nurses know about tooth development?**
   Most importantly, the permanent teeth form very close to the apices (roots) of the primary teeth. Any injury to a primary tooth has the potential to damage the permanent tooth below. Primary tooth injuries range in damage from as minor as a small spot on the crown of the tooth to as severe as aborting further development of the permanent tooth bud. Consequently, all primary tooth injuries need evaluation by a dentist. School nurses should also be aware of other things that can affect tooth development such as excessive fluoride, tetracyclines, congenital defects, metabolic diseases and high fever. These can have deleterious effects on the quality of dental hard tissues, especially the enamel.

2. **What are the current indications for orthodontics?**
   Pediatric dentists and orthodontists are adept at recognizing young patients who could benefit from early orthodontic intervention. This involves the diagnosis of growth problems in the jaws, malalignment of tooth problems related to habits such as thumb sucking, as well as discrepancies in the size of the teeth related to jaw size. Appliances may be used to redirect jaw growth, eliminate habits, change the size and shape of the dental arches, etc. Although early intervention may not eliminate the need for full orthodontic treatment when all permanent teeth have erupted, it may minimize the extent and duration of treatment. Additionally, it may make the options of treatment the orthodontist can offer to the patient greater and reduce any need for extraction of permanent teeth in order to straighten the teeth.

DENTAL EMERGENCIES *(continued from previous page)*

3. **What about students with disabilities?**
   They seem to have special problems because of the systemic problem or because of the secondary effects on diet, medications or the because of difficulty in maintaining good oral hygiene. Referral to a pediatric dentist or another dentist who has had advanced training in working with patients with special needs is extremely important. Dentists with special training can help the parent/guardian customize toothbrushes for easier self-care, e.g. placing a toothbrush through a small rubber ball to give the student something larger to grip. If the student is unable to brush his or her teeth, the dentist can assist the caregiver with alternate strategies. These include special positioning and customized tooth brushing techniques, even behavior modification. These students may also need professional dental care more often than the routine 6-month checkups.

References

American Academy of Pediatric Dentistry. (2013). *Fast facts.* Retrieved from http://www.aapd.org/news/fast_facts/

American Dental Association. (2013). *Dental emergencies.* Retrieved from http://www.ada.org/370.aspx

Baginska, J., Wilczynska-Borawska, M. (2012). First aid algorithms in dental avulsion. *Journal of School Nursing 28 (2),* pp.90-94.

McTigue, D. J. & Thompson, A. (2013). *Patient information: Mouth and dental injuries in children.* UptoDate. com. Retrieved from http://www.uptodate.com/contents/mouth-and-dental-injuries-in-children-beyond-the-basics?view=print

Milgrom, P., Tut, O., Chi, D., Draye, M.A., & Acker, M. (2008). Dental and oral disorders. In C. Burns, M. Brady, A. Dunn, N.B. Starr, C. Blosser, (Eds.), *Pediatric primary care* (4th ed.) (pp. 863-864). St. Louis, MO: Saunders Elsevier.

Mosby's Medical Dictionary (8th ed.). (2009). Elsevier. Retrieved from http://medical-dictionary.thefreedictionary.com/dental+emergency

DEPRESSION

DEFINITION/ETIOLOGY:
Depression is an affective illness or mood disorder characterized by dysphoric moods (emotions such as sadness, irritability, mood swings, and hopelessness) and affect (sad facies) and self-devaluation (e.g., feeling worthless). Clinical depression is characterized by a combination of specific symptoms that persist *more than three weeks* and *cause functional problems* at home, school or in social relationships. Depression is a leading cause of school failure, especially in students with learning difficulties, and suicidal ideation.

CAUSES:
Primary or familial-genetic depression. About a third of depressed children have a biological parent who is affectively ill. Research suggests that the right parietotemporal cortex of the brain plays a role in depression. In depressed states, there is a relatively low level of the neurotransmitters serotonin and norepinephrine.

Secondary or symptomatic depression is a response to problems such as early childhood traumas, chronic health conditions, learned patterns of helpless thinking, learning disabilities, peer pressure, significant losses or having a family member commit suicide.

SIGNS AND SYMPTOMS:
Children and adolescents express depression differently. Children are more likely to have:
- somatic complaints
- separation anxiety
- insomnia at night and fears

Adolescents exhibit both emotional and behavioral symptoms:
Emotional:
- Crying spells for no apparent reason
- Irritability
- Difficulty focusing or concentrating – decline in school performance
- Fatigue
- Feelings of helplessness, worthlessness, isolation
- Feeling sad or down
- Tremendous sensitivity to failure or rejection
- Loss of interest and pleasure in developmentally appropriate activities
- Socially withdrawn from friends and family
- Recurrent suicidal ideations

Behavioral:
- Appetite changes associated with weight gain or weight loss
- Agitation, disruptive behavior

DEPRESSION *(continued from previous page)*

- Decrease in school performance
- Insomnia or hypersomnia
- Somatic complaints – headaches, stomachaches, etc.
- Disheveled appearance
- Self mutilation (cutting, burning, excessive piercing/tattooing)

MANAGEMENT/TREATMENT:

1. **If immediate danger is suspected, student must not be left alone while 911 or local emergency crisis number is called.**

2. **Therapy:**
Young children may benefit the most from play therapy. Comprehensive treatment including both individual (cognitive behavioral therapy/interpersonal psychotherapy) and family therapy has been shown to be effective in treating depression in older children and adolescents. The focus is not on emotions, but on behaviors that influence feelings, e.g., "feels sad but act positive to help you feel better."

3. **Medication:**
Treatment may also include the use of antidepressant medication. The choice of drug is related to age, weight, family history of illness and response to medication, and the nature of depression or its related conditions, e.g., bipolar disorder. For children and young adolescents, the drugs of choice are first generation antidepressants (tricyclic antidepressants) which can increase appetite, or imipramine or desipramine for overweight youth. Third generation antidepressants (Prozac or Zoloft) are used if the child or young adolescent does not respond.

    Third generation antidepressants are the drugs of choice for older adolescents. The specific medication depends on the presence of manic moods. For some, a third generation antidepressant is taken in the morning and tricyclic is taken at bedtime.

    Antidepressants may increase the risk that a child/teen may have suicidal ideations. Children/teens who take antidepressants should be watched closely. Educate staff and parents/guardians regarding the warning signs of suicide (talking, writing, or drawing about death, giving belongings away, withdrawing from family and friends, etc.).

4. **School-home Communication**
A team approach with consistent messages from adults at home and school that reassure the child/youth and do not allow him/her to drop routines and social interactions.

DEPRESSION *(continued from previous page)*

FOLLOW UP:
- Consider depression as a significant factor in students with learning failures or discipline infractions, e.g., fights, especially among males.
- Anticipate depression as a response to chronic illness and significant losses or stress.
- Educate staff and students (health education) to recognize that children of any age can experience and exhibit signs of depression.

POTENTIAL COMPLICATIONS:
- Alcohol/Substance Abuse
- Anxiety
- Family/relationship conflicts
- Involvement with the court system
- School problems
- Social isolation
- Self mutilation
- Suicide

NOTES:
The school nurse may suspect depression with:
- Teacher referrals for inattention, falling asleep in class (due to inadequate sleep at night)
- Frequent student visits for tiredness, headache, stomach ache, panic attack, and muscle aches
- Vague vision problems
- Referrals for school avoidance (school "phobia") or declining school performance
- Informal observation of weight change, disheveled appearance, irritability with friends, dropping out of extracurricular activities

The school nurse is the key school professional to:
- Report responses to medication and communicate any concerns for missed or excessive doses with the parent.
- Inform teachers of anticipated side effects, particularly to prevent misinterpreting student behavior as "under the influence of drugs ".
- Develop a care plan, in partnership with the school-home team, to respond constructively to somatic complaints (without minimizing significant illnesses or injuries) and reinforce positive behaviors, e.g., good attendance, engaging in school activities.
- Educate the student about the need for consistent medication use and to not take anyone else's medication.

DEPRESSION *(continued from previous page)*

Other:
- Screening in 12-18 year olds for major depression is recommended by the U.S. Prevention Task Force if support systems are in place for diagnosis, therapy and follow up.
- Some diseases such as hypothyroidism or anemia can cause symptoms that look like depression. The physician may order diagnostic tests to rule out these physical conditions.

References

Bobo, N., Kimel, L., & Bleza, S. (2013). Mental health screening. In J. Selekman (Ed.), *School nursing: A comprehensive text (2nd ed.),* (p. 466). Philadelphia, PA: F.A. Davis.

Gottesman, M.M. & Houck, G. (2008). Coping and stress tolerance: Mental health problems. In C. Burns, M. Brady, A. Dunn, N.B. Starr, & C. Blosser (Eds.), *Pediatric primary care (4th ed.),* (pp. 427-431). St. Louis, MO: Saunders Elsevier.

Mayo Clinic. (2012). *Teen depression.* Retrieved from http://www.mayoclinic.com/health/teen-depression/DS01188

National Institute of Mental Health. (2011). *Depression.* Retrieved from http://www.nimh.nih.gov/health/publications/depression/complete-index.shtml

United States Preventive Task Force. (2013). *Major depressive disorder in children and adolescents.* Retrieved from http://www.uspreventiveservicestaskforce.org/uspstf/uspschdepr.htm

DEVELOPMENTAL DISABILITIES

DEFINITION/ETIOLOGY:

Developmental disabilities (DD) are a diverse group of physical, cognitive, psychological, sensory and speech impairments that are identified prenatally up 18 years of age and are likely to continue throughout life. They result in considerable limitations in three or more of the following areas: comprehension and language skills (receptive and expressive language), learning, self-direction, self- care, mobility, and the ability to function independently without coordinated services (capacity for independent living and economic self-sufficiency). Developmental Disabilities may have a severe adverse effect on educational outcomes.

Type	Description/Characteristics
Autism Spectrum Disorders	Significantly affects verbal and nonverbal communication and social interaction.
ADHD	There are 3 main symptoms, the inability to focus, hyperactivity and impulsivity. May be managed with medication and /or a behavior plan.
Cerebral Palsy	The inability to control muscle responses and/or a weakness of the muscle. AFO's (braces) and splints help support the feet and legs for walking and for use of hands.
Intellectual Development Disabilities (IDD)	Considered a condition, but actually a symptom of numerous different conditions. Average IDD is sub average intelligence (I.Q.>55-70 range) with deficits in adaptive behavior and manifested during a developmental period. Common IDD's are Fragile X syndrome, Fetal Alcohol syndrome, Down syndrome Angelman syndrome, Prader Willie syndrome and toxoplasmosis. IDD's can be diagnosed during pregnancy through blood tests (amniocentesis or chorionic villus). After birth, intelligence quotient (I.Q.) test determine diagnosis in addition to observing behavior and assessing adaptive skills. Children with intellectual disabilities may become functional adults; they are able to learn, but do so slowly, and with difficulty.
Learning Disabilities	Specific types of learning problems, dyscalcula (math), dysgrahia (writing) and dyslexia (reading).
Hearing	Unable to process communication through hearing with or without implication, may be permanent or fluctuate.
Vision Impairment	Depends on what part of the eye is affected, the eye condition, and how much correction is possible through glasses, contacts, surgery or medicine. Senses of smell, touch, taste, and hearing are heightened.
Vision and Hearing Impaired	Causes severe developmental, communication and educational needs which may require a specific program to accommodate blind and deaf students.

DEVELOPMENTAL DISABILITIES *(continued from previous page)*

Developmental Disabilities may be caused by:
- Traumatic Brain Injury and other child maltreatment manifestations (shaken baby syndrome or head trauma)
- Prenatal or after birth nutrition or growth problems
- Prenatal or after birth infections
- Chromosome abnormalities
- Poor maternal diet, lack of prenatal care, substance abuse or OTC drugs
- Prematurity
- Environmental toxins (lead poisoning, infections)

SIGNS/SYMPTOMS:
- Vary depending on condition
- Delay in developmental milestones (walking, talking, etc.)
- Difficulty speaking or delayed speech, can't remember things
- Unable to follow or understand rules of social behavior
- Difficulty solving problems or understanding outcomes of action
- IDD's that show up sooner may indicate a more severe disability

MANAGEMENT/TREATMENT:
- No cure is available
- Treatment specific to disability
- Accessing educational related services resources; physical therapy, occupational therapy, therapeutic speech therapy or nursing services
- Early intervention for children birth -3 years of age
- Development of an Individualized Family Service Plan (IFSP)
- Special education services 3-21 of age (some states extend services)
- Development of an Individualized Educational Plan (IEP)
- Transitional planning for school to community
- Communication devices and computer technology
- Special equipment depending on condition (standers, bikes, braces, wheelchairs, adaptive seating, eating utensils, sensory stimulation etc.)

FOLLOW UP:
- Investigate instructional and classroom accommodations
- Provide interventions based on need of the student and evaluate the impact of the outcomes
- Hearing and vision screening (minimize sensory deficits)
- Dental care (prevent periodontal disease)
- Immunizations (deficiencies in immune system)
- Use multi-sensory approach
- Promote good nutrition

DEVELOPMENTAL DISABILITIES *(continued from previous page)*

- Alert parents/guardians of signs of illness (ear and upper respiratory infections)
- Assist with transition planning from school to the community (IEP planning for transitioning must begin before the age of 16)

NOTES:

- The average I.Q. is 100, IDD can range from mild 55-70 , moderate 40-54, severe 25-39, and profound <25

Laws:

- The Individuals with Disabilities Education Improvement Act (IDEIA) directs how educational services (available through the state, school district and public agencies) are provided to infants, toddlers, children and youth with disabilities http://idea.ed.gov/
- Section 504 of the Rehabilitation Act of 1973 prohibits educational discrimination on the basis of disability and provides students who do not qualify for IDEIA with disabilities services http://www.hhs.gov/ocr/civilrights/resources/factsheets/504.pdf
- The American Disabilities Act (ADA) provides equality for people with disabilities (education, employment, transportation, access to buildings, etc.) http://www.ada.gov/

RESOURCES:

Administration of Community Living, Administration of Intellectual Developmental Disabilities at http://www.acl.gov/Programs/AIDD/Index.aspx

National Dissemination Center for Children with Disabilities at http://nichcy.org/

Partnering with Your Child's School: A Guide for Parents at http://www.hscfoundation.org/aboutus/publications/partnering_with_schools_english_guide.pdf

References

Ball, J., Binder, R., & Cowen, K. (Eds.). (2012). Alterations in mental health and cognition. *Principles of Pediatric Nursing: Caring for Children (5th Ed.)* (pp. 931-939). Upper Saddle River, NJ: Pearson Education, Inc.

Blom, M., Crawford, L., Whitehead, S. (2013).intellectual disabilities. In J. Selekman (Ed.), School *nursing: A comprehensive text (2nd ed.)* (pp. 899-923). Philadelphia: F.A. Davis.

Centers for Disease Control. (2013). *Developmental disabilities.* Retrieved from http://www.cdc.gov/ncbddd/developmentaldisabilities/index.html

MedlinePlus. U.S. National Library of Medicine. (2012). *Developmental disabilities.* Retrieved from http://www.nlm.nih.gov/medlineplus/developmentaldisabilities.html

National Dissemination Center for Children with Disabilities. (n.d.). *Disabilities.* Retrieved from http://nichcy.org/disability

Selekman, J., Bobhenek, J. & Lukens, M. (2013).Children with chronic conditions. In J. Selekman (Ed.), School *nursing: A comprehensive text (2nd ed.)* (p. 702). Philadelphia, PA: F.A. Davis.

DIABETES EMERGENCIES (See Diabetes Type I)

DEFINITION/ETIOLOGY:
A diabetic emergency is a life-threatening condition. Diabetic emergencies occur when there is a severe imbalance between insulin and blood glucose in the body. There are two types of diabetic emergencies: hypoglycemia and hyperglycemia.

HYPOGLYCEMIA

Hypoglycemia is low blood sugar and is considered a medical emergency. Causes are:
- Too much insulin
- Not enough food or student eats more than insulin dose calculation
- Delayed snack or missed meal
- Too much exercise without snack before
- Some prescribed or over-the-counter medication

SIGNS AND SYMPTOMS: HYPOGLYCEMIA
- Vary from person to person
- Symptoms develop rapidly without warning
- Children may not always demonstrate outward symptoms
- Young children especially may not recognize symptoms of hypoglycemia

Mild	Moderate	Severe
○ Blurred vision ○ Difficulty concentrating 　Headache, hungry ○ Irritable ○ Nausea and/or vomiting ○ Shaky, stomach ache, ○ Sweaty and/or pale ○ Fruity breath	○ Disoriented ○ Confusion ○ Poor coordination ○ Restlessness ○ Mood changes (aggression, crying, bizarre behavior)	○ Inability to swallow ○ Seizures ○ Unconscious ○ Permanent brain damage can result if reaction is prolonged.

MANAGEMENT/TREATMENT: HYPOGLYCEMIA
Hypoglycemia low blood sugar (<70 mg/dL or > 70 mg/dL with symptoms)
- Follow student's Emergency Care Plan (ECP)
- If possible, check blood sugar and follow ECP, immediately give 15 gm fast-acting carbohydrate such as one of the following:
    - 3 or 4 glucose tablets
    - 4 oz. fruit juice
    - 6 oz. soft drink (non-dietetic)
    - 1-2 Tablespoons of honey
    - 1 tube glucose gel

DIABETES EMERGENCIES *(continued from previous page)*

- Follow with protein snack plus if it is more than a one hour until meal time
- Recheck blood glucose level 10 – 15 minutes after treatment
- If blood glucose level is still below target range, repeat treatment, contact parent/ guardian

Severe hypoglycemic reaction:
- If student becomes unconscious, has a seizure or is unable to swallow, administer glucagon IM or SQ per licensed healthcare provider's order
- Call 911 if glucagon is administered
- Position student on side as vomiting is a side effect of glucagon

HYPERGLYCEMIA

Hyperglycemia is high blood sugar and is not considered a medical emergency. Untreated hyperglycemia can become ketoacidosis, which is a medical emergency.

Causes are:
- Late or missed insulin
- Illness, infection, stress, hormonal response (e.g., menses)
- Expired insulin
- Problem with insulin pump
- Excess food intake (for amount of insulin or binge eating)
- Insufficient exercise

SIGNS AND SYMPTOMS: HYPERGLYCEMIA
- Usually develops slowly

Mild	Moderate (mild symptoms plus)	Severe
o Increased thirst	o Inability to concentrate	o Nausea and/or vomit
o Increased urination	o Abdominal cramps	o Abdominal cramps
o Stomach ache	o Nausea	o Lethargic
o Blurred vision	o Dry Mouth	o Respiratory problems
o Fatigue	o Light headed	o Weakness
o Hunger, headache		o Confused
o Pale		o Moderate to Large ketones

DIABETES EMERGENCIES *(continued from previous page)*

MANAGEMENT/TREATMENT: HYPERGLYCEMIA (Blood sugar > 300)
- Follow student's ECP
- Check urine for ketones and report findings
- Encourage water and moderate exercise if ketones are negative
- Repeat ketone testing in 1-2 hours or next void
- Supplemental insulin may be ordered by licensed health care provider

ROLE OF THE SCHOOL NURSE:
- Develop and implement an Individualized Healthcare Plan (IHP) and an Emergency Plan (ECP) from student's Diabetes Medical Management Plan which includes:
  - Specific detailed procedures and responsibilities performed by school staff
  - Glucagon administration and storage
  - Specific Possible 504
  - Disaster Plan
- Provide diabetes training (Level I, II or III based on need know) to teachers, cafeteria manager, bus driver and sports coaches
- Manage and monitor trained staff
- Distribution of the ECP to appropriate classrooms and staff
- Students with insulin pumps require the nurse and staff (as appropriate) to be oriented to the specific unit

FOLLOW UP:
- Monitor student for continued sign or symptoms of hypoglycemia or hyperglycemia
- Report incidence to parents/guardians as required by ECP
- Inventory supplies used to treat hypoglycemia or hyperglycemia

PREVENTION:
- Obtain from history and review signs and symptoms of hypoglycemia and hyperglycemia experienced with individual student (if known)
- Consistent routine (meal times, carbohydrate intake and physical activity)
- Notify parents/guardians in advance of schedule changes and special events
- Provide a snack if physical activity occurs just before lunch period or in the late afternoon
- Keep a fast-acting carbohydrate accessible during exercise
- Keep emergency glucose/sugar in key places, especially in large schools (PE, nurse's office, locker, main office)

DIABETES EMERGENCIES *(continued from previous page)*

NOTES:
- Check state laws, nursing practice act and school district policy to determine what can be diabetes care can be delegated to Unlicensed School Personnel
- Glucagon usually works within 15 minutes
- Student should wear Medic Alert identification

ADDITIONAL RESOURCES:
- American Diabetes Association. Provides staff training tools and sample diabetes management and Section 504 plans. www.diabetes.org
- National Association of School Nurses. Helping Administer to the Needs of Students with Diabetes in School (HANDS) is a continuing education resource. http://www.nasn.org/ContinuingEducation/LiveContinuingEducationPrograms/HANDS
- National Diabetes Education Program. Diabetes Resources for Schools and Youth http://www.ndep.nih.gov/hcp-businesses-and-schools/Schools.aspx

References

American Diabetes Association. (n.d.). *Diabetes basics.* Retrieved from http://www.diabetes.org/diabetes-basics/

American Diabetes Association. (n.d.). *Ketoacidosis.* Retrieved from http://www.diabetes.org/living-with-diabetes/complications/ketoacidosis-dka.html

Butler, S., Kaup, T., Swanson, M., & Hoffmann, S. (2013). Diabetes management in the school setting. In J. Selekman (Ed.), *School nursing: A comprehensive text* (2nd ed.) (pp. 888-892). Philadelphia, PA: F.A. Davis

Mayo Clinic. (2012). *Diabetic coma.* Retrieved from http://www.mayoclinic.com/print/diabeticcoma/DS00656/METHOD=print&DSECTION=all

National Association of School Nurses. (2008). *Helping administer to the needs of students with diabetes in school (HANDS).* Retrieved from http://www.nasn.org/ContinuingEducation/LiveContinuingEducationPrograms/HANDS

National Association of School Nurses. (2010). Managing *diabetes at school: Tools for the school nurse.* Silver Spring, MD: Author.

National Diabetes Education Program. (2012). *Helping the student with diabetes succeed: A guide for school personnel.* Retrieved from http://ndep.nih.gov/publications/PublicationDetail.aspx?PubId=97#main

DIABETES - TYPE 1

DEFINITION/ETIOLOGY:

Type 1 Diabetes, previously called juvenile or insulin-dependent diabetes, is an autoimmune disease in which there is destruction of the beta cells (insulin producing cells) of the pancreas and leads to absolute insulin deficiency. Insulin is a hormone that is necessary to convert food into energy for normal body functioning. Without insulin, food is converted into high glucose levels in the blood stream, depriving the brain and muscles of glucose needed to function. The accumulation of glucose within the blood stream damages tissues and blood vessels, leading to nephropathy/kidney disease, retinopathy/eye disease, neuropathy/nervous system, gastroparesis (slowing of the digestive system), heart disease, risk of stroke, poor wound healing and amputations.

Often diagnosed in childhood, there is an increase in diagnosis of Type 1 Diabetes in young adults. Currently, about 215,000 people younger than 20 years have diabetes (type 1 or type 2), about 0.26 percent of all people in this age group. There are no current estimates of undiagnosed diabetes available (NDEP, 2010). Three quarters of all the cases of Type 1 Diabetes are diagnosed at ages <18 years (ADA, 2013).

Type 1 diabetes was thought to be of sudden onset, but research suggests that the autoimmune process progresses over time and presents rather suddenly with hyperglycemia when the declining number of beta-cells can no longer compensate. It is usually diagnosed during childhood and requires insulin administration, by multiple daily injections with syringe/vial or pen/needle or continuous insulin infusion via an insulin pump.

Normal fasting blood glucose is 70-120 mg/dl. Normal postprandial blood glucose is <200 mg/dl. Due to frequent changing needs during times of rapid growth and development, a child may have higher glucose goals. *High blood sugar levels in the blood can lead to Diabetic Ketoacidosis (DKA), breaking down of fat and muscle, resulting in production of ketone (acid) bodies, dehydration, cerebral edema, and potentially death (DKA). Low blood sugar levels in the blood can lead to loss of consciousness, brain damage, and potentially death.*

COMORBID CONDITIONS:
Hypothyroidism
Celiac Disease

DIABETES - TYPE 1 *(continued from previous page)*

SIGNS AND SYMPTOMS:

Hyperglycemia:
- Increased thirst
- Increased urination
- Increased hunger
- Unexplained weight loss
- Fatigue
- Slow healing wounds
- Vision changes

Hypoglycemia*:
- Shakiness
- Dizziness
- Pale skin
- Weakness
- Confusion
- Behavior change/irritability/emotional
- Loss of consciousness
- Seizure

*Some children do not demonstrate any outward symptoms of hypoglycemia or may have hypoglycemic unawareness (inability to recognize symptoms of low blood glucose).

MANAGEMENT/TREATMENT:

1. Monitor blood glucose levels with glucometer (may also have a continuous glucose monitoring system- CGM) per physician orders. Often testing is before snack, lunch, gym/sports and as needed for symptoms of hypoglycemia and hyperglycemia.

2. Insulin- delivery systems vary among children and dosages vary with each administration. Basal/Bolus regimen most mimics the normal pancreatic function. Dosing may be based on a sliding scale, carb to insulin ratio and sensitivity factors.

3. Exercise is important in maintaining stable blood glucose levels. Exercise is a risk factor for hypoglycemia that can occur during the activity, right after the activity and up to 48 hours after an activity. Exercise is not recommended when blood glucose is elevated and/or urine ketones are present due to increased risk of DKA; follow physician orders.

DIABETES - TYPE 1 *(continued from previous page)*

4. Healthy well balanced diet is recommended for all children. Insulin dosing is often related to total carbohydrate count of each meal. Be aware of nutrition changes that may affect the carbohydrate count to avoid overdosing of insulin (many schools are decreasing carbohydrates to improve nutrition).

5. Treatment of hypoglycemia follows "The Rule of 15"- 15 gms of carbohydrate and recheck in 15 minutes for mild hypoglycemia. Moderate episodes of hypoglycemia may require the use of glucose gel if alert, but unable to follow directions. Emergency glucagon administration for episodes of severe hypoglycemia and the child is unconscious or has a seizure. (See Diabetes Emergencies Guidelines).

6. Treatment of hyperglycemia per the child's emergency plan. Encourage drinking water. Urine or blood ketone testing as ordered by physician during episodes of hyperglycemia and illness. (See Diabetes Emergencies Guidelines).

General Management

Diabetes requires an individualized care and lifestyle plan balancing daily dietary intake, physical activity, insulin, and self-monitored blood glucose. Children can learn to use glucometers and be able to interpret results, self-administer insulin, determine insulin dosage, and ultimately self-manage Type 1 Diabetes. Age and developmental stage are factors in identifying tasks children can safely manage.

A lab test called Hemoglobin A1c (HbA1c) measures the past 3-4 months' fasting and post-meal (postprandial) blood glucose levels to indicate the effectiveness of blood glucose control. While a non-diabetic A1c ranges from 4-6%, the goal for persons with diabetes is ≤ 6.5 to 7% with minimal episodes of severe hypoglycemia. These goals vary by age and glucose demand for growth and development. According to the National Diabetes Education Program, children <6 years of age should be ≤ 8.5, but ≥7.5 %; ages 6-12 years should be <8%; and ages 13-19 years should be < 7.7% (NDEP, 2008). Hypoglycemia is a major factor in determining goals for glucose control.

A team approach including students, families, healthcare providers, and school staff (food services, physical education, counseling staff, teachers, bus drivers and administration) led by the school nurse, can assist with risk reduction as well as disease management. The school nurse is the coordinator of care in school, but all staff that have responsibility for the student should have basic training to understand Type 1 diabetes and the needs of these students. Diabetes management training for school personnel is recommended to follow three levels of training. Level One training should be provided as basic information to all personnel. Level Two training is more in depth for those who have direct contact with the child during the school

DIABETES - TYPE 1 *(continued from previous page)*

day. Level Three training is in-depth training for the use of volunteers or unlicensed personnel who will assist with diabetes management, for those states that allow the registered nurse to delegate tasks (see your state Nurse Practice Act) (NASN, 2010).

Physician orders provide the basis of the Diabetes Medical Management Plan (DMMP). From the DMMP, the school nurse develops an individual health plan (IHP) to guide management throughout the school day. An emergency care plan (ECP) is developed to help guide the management during episodes of hypo/hyperglycemia. These documents are necessary attachments to 504 and IEP accommodation plans recommended for all children with Type 1 Diabetes. The school healthcare plan should be adapted to the student's developmental level. As appropriate, the plan includes immediate access to diabetes supplies and permission to self-manage tasks in the classroom or least restrictive setting. The plan also addresses emergency evacuation/school lock-down instructions.

FOLLOW-UP:
- Routine blood glucose monitoring
- Monitor height, weight, and blood pressure
- Dietary goals – reinforce need for healthy eating habits
- Review carbohydrate counting
- Encourage routine exercise

POTENTIAL COMPLICATIONS:
Short term
- Hypoglycemia
- Hyperglycemia
- Diabetic ketoacidosis (DKA)

Long term
- Cognitive deficits related to frequent hypoglycemia or severe episodes of hypoglycemia
- Cardiovascular disease
- Kidney disease
- Neuropathy
- Vision loss
- Susceptible to skin infections

DIABETES - TYPE 1 *(continued from previous page)*

NOTES:

Type 1 diabetes cannot be prevented. Fluctuations in blood glucose are frequent in children and adolescents due to many controllable and uncontrollable factors. Nutrition, exercise, insulin dosing are controllable factors. Illness, stress, hormones, and developmental factors are uncontrollable. Every child is unique in how their body responds to different insulin doses, foods, activities and this changes over time. Many factors must be considered when setting goals and planning for the care of the child with Type 1 Diabetes.

References

American Diabetes Association. (2013a). *Standards of medical care in diabetes—2013, 36* (Supplement 1), S40-44. doi: 10.2337/dc13-S011. Retrieved from http://care.diabetesjournals.org/content/36/Supplement_1/S11.full

American Diabetes Association. (2013b). *Diabetes care in the school and day care setting, 36* (Supplement 1), S75-S79. doi: 10.2337/dc13-S075. Retrieved from http://care.diabetesjournals.org/content/36/Supplement_1/S75.full

Bobo, N. & Silverstein, J. (2010). Designing diabetes management training for school personnel using a three-level approach; *NASN School Nurse, 25,* 216-218.

Burchett, M. Hanna, C. & Steiner, R. (2008). Endocrine and metabolic disorders. In C. Burns, M. Brady, A. Dunn, NB Starr, C. Blosser (Eds.), *Pediatric primary care, 4th ed.* (pp. 595-601). St. Louis, MO: Saunders Elsevier.

Butler, S., Kaup, T., Swanson, M.A., & Hoffman. S.(2013). *Diabetes management in the school setting. In J. Selekman (Ed.), School nursing a comprehensive text* (2nd ed.) (pp. 872-895). Philadelphia, PA: F. A. Davis.

National Association of School Nurses. (2008). *Helping administer to the needs of students with diabetes in school (HANDS).* Silver Spring, MD: Author.

National Association of School Nurses. (2010). Managing *diabetes at school: Tools for the school nurse.* Silver Spring, MD: Author.

National Association of School Nurses. (2012). Diabetes *management in the school setting: Position statement. Retrieved from https://www.nasn.org/PolicyAdvocacy/PositionPapersandReports/NASNPositionStatementsFullView/tabid/462/ArticleId/22/Diabetes-Management-in-the-School-Setting-Adopted-January-2012*

National Diabetes Education Program. (2012). *Helping the student with diabetes succeed: A guide for school personnel. Retrieved from http://www.ndep.nih.gov/publications/PublicationDetail.aspx?PubId=97&redirect=true#main*

DIABETES - TYPE 2

DEFINITION/ETIOLOGY:

Type 2 Diabetes, formerly called adult-onset or non-insulin dependent diabetes, was once an adulthood disease. With the rising incidence of obesity, there is also a rise in Type 2 diabetes in our youth, particularly those 10 years of age and older. Currently, 20-25% of new cases of diabetes in youth are children with Type 2 Diabetes. Statistics are limited due to the lack of diagnosis and proper screening. With an increased focus on this growing pediatric issue, guidelines and recommendations have been developed for screening and treatment, leading to diagnoses that are more accurate.

Type 2 diabetes is defined by impaired secretion of the hormone insulin from the beta cells of the pancreas, insulin-resistance, or a combination of both processes. This "results from a progressive insulin secretory defect on the background of insulin resistance" (ADA, 2013a). This is unlike Type 1 diabetes where there is an absolute insulin deficiency. Insulin is a hormone that is necessary to convert food into energy for normal body functioning. Without enough insulin, food is converted into high glucose levels in the blood stream, depriving the brain and muscles of glucose. The accumulation of glucose within the blood stream damages tissues and blood vessels, leading to nephropathy/kidney disease, retinopathy/eye disease, neuropathy/nervous system, gastroparesis (slowing of the digestive system), heart disease, risk of stroke, poor wound healing and amputations.

Type 2 Diabetes results from a physiological resistance to rising levels of insulin in the presence of being significantly overweight and physically inactive. The addition of high blood pressure and abnormal blood lipids, especially low HDLs and high triglycerides, to diabetes forms a triad called metabolic syndrome that poses a risk for cardiovascular disease associated with diabetes. Obesity is a common precursor. While there is a genetic predisposition for type 2 diabetes, it requires an "environment" to develop -usually being overweight (especially with a body type that stores excess fat around the waist more than the hips) due to high calorie diet and too little activity. Detected early, type 2 can be treated by changes in diet and daily activity but may require oral medication and, at times, insulin injections.

COMORBID CONDITIONS:
- Polycystic Ovarian Syndrome (PCOS)
- Hypertension
- Dyslipidemia
- Fatty liver

DIABETES - TYPE 2 *(continued from previous page)*

RISK FACTORS:
- Obesity- BMI 85th-94th and >95th percentile for age and gender
- Family history of Type 2 Diabetes
- Ethnicity - Hispanic, Non-Hispanic white, African American, Asian/Pacific Islander
- Sedentary lifestyle
- Low socioeconomic status
- Small-for-gestational age birth-weight
- Maternal history of gestational diabetes during pregnancy during the child's gestation

Type 2 diabetes risk factor identification is an important aspect of prevention and control.

SIGNS AND SYMPTOMS:
Hyperglycemia:
- Increased thirst
- Increased urination
- Increased hunger
- Unexplained weight loss/no weight change
- Vaginal yeast infections
- Fatigue
- Slow healing wounds
- Vision changes
- Acanthosis Nigricans (later sign of insulin resistance) - dark, velvety textured skin primarily noted in the axillary, inner elbow, posterior neck and groin areas that signify insulin resistance that may or may not be present with Type 2 Diabetes

Hypoglycemia:
- Shakiness
- Dizziness
- Pale skin
- Weakness
- Confusion
- Behavior change/irritability/emotional
- Loss of consciousness**
- Seizure**

*Some children do not demonstrate any outward symptoms of hypoglycemia or may have hypoglycemic unawareness (inability to recognize symptoms of low blood glucose).
**Severe hypoglycemia is not as common with Type 2 Diabetes, but should be considered when on insulin management.

DIABETES - TYPE 2 *(continued from previous page)*

MANAGEMENT/TREATMENT:

May present in DKA (Diabetic Ketoacidosis) or HHNK (Hyperglycemic Hyperosmolar Nonketotic) state, both life threatening. **(See Diabetes Emergencies Guidelines).**

1. Monitor blood glucose levels with glucometer if ordered (may also have a continuous glucose monitoring system- CGM) per physician orders. Testing recommendations are for those who are taking insulin or oral medications with a risk of hypoglycemia, who may be initiating or changing treatment regimens or have concurrent illnesses.

2. Metformin (only oral medication approved for children with Type 2 Diabetes), may be ordered. Metformin is recommended as a first-line therapy, unless initial diagnosis included DKA or HHNK. If there is significant hyperglycemia, insulin may be initiated to reverse glucose toxicity. Insulin delivery systems and dosages vary. There is potential to discontinue insulin, begin oral therapy and progress to management with diet, and exercise only (unlike Type 1 Diabetes where insulin is the only option for treatment).

3. Exercise to improve blood glucose control because of decreased insulin resistance. Additionally, weight maintenance or weight loss may minimize complications of diabetes. Activity recommendations are for 60 minutes of exercise daily.

4. A healthy, well balanced diet is recommended for all children. If child or youth is being treated with insulin, dosing is often related to total carbohydrate count of each meal. Be aware of nutrition changes that may affect the carbohydrate count to avoid overdosing of insulin (many schools are decreasing carbohydrates to improve nutrition).

5. Treatment of hypoglycemia follows "The Rule of 15"- 15 gms of carbohydrate and recheck in 15 minutes for mild hypoglycemia. Moderate episodes of hypoglycemia may require the use of glucose gel if alert, but unable to follow directions. Emergency glucagon administration for episodes of severe hypoglycemia and the child is unconscious or has a seizure. (See Diabetes Emergencies Guidelines). ** While glucagon may not be prescribed for the child with Type 2 Diabetes, it should be considered if the child is treated with insulin.

6. Treatment of hyperglycemia per the child's emergency plan. Encourage drinking water. Urine or blood ketone testing as ordered by physician during episodes of hyperglycemia and illness. (See Diabetes Emergencies Guidelines). **Often ketone testing is NOT ordered for children with Type 2 Diabetes due to decreased risk for DKA.

DIABETES - TYPE 2 *(continued from previous page)*

General Management

Diabetes requires an individualized care and lifestyle plan balancing daily dietary intake, physical activity, medication (if ordered) and self-monitored blood glucose. Children can learn to use glucometers and, in time, to self-administer insulin as ordered. A lab test called hemoglobin A1c or simply "A1c" measures the past 3-4 months' fasting and post meal blood glucose levels to indicate the effectiveness of blood glucose control. While a non-diabetic A1c ranges from 4-6%, the goal for the child with Type 2 Diabetes is <7% (Copeland et.al, 2013).

A team approach including students, families, healthcare providers, and school staff (food services, physical education, counseling staff, teachers, bus drivers and administration) led by the school nurse, can assist with risk reduction as well as disease management. The school nurse is the coordinator of care in school, but all staff that have responsibility for the student should have basic training to understand Type 2 diabetes and the needs of these students. Diabetes management training for school personnel is recommended to follow three levels of training. Level One training should be provided as basic information to all personnel. Level Two training is more in depth for those who have direct contact with the child during the school day. Level Three training is in-depth training for the use of volunteers or unlicensed personnel who will assist with diabetes management, for those states that allow the registered nurse to delegate tasks (see your state Nurse Practice Act) (NASN, 2010).

Physician orders provide the basis of the Diabetes Medical Management Plan (DMMP). From the DMMP, the school nurse develops an individual health plan (IHP) to guide management throughout the school day. An emergency care plan (ECP) is developed to help guide the management during episodes of hypo/hyperglycemia. These documents are necessary attachments to 504 and IEP accommodation plans recommended for all children with Type 2 Diabetes. The school healthcare plan should be adapted to the student's developmental level. As appropriate, the plan includes immediate access to diabetes supplies and permission to self-manage tasks in the classroom or least restrictive setting. The plan also addresses emergency evacuation/school lock-down instructions.

FOLLOW-UP:
- Routine blood glucose monitoring, if ordered
- Monitor height, weight, and blood pressure
- Dietary goals – reinforce need for healthy eating habits
- Review carbohydrate counting/plate method for healthy nutrition
- Encourage routine exercise - at least 60 minutes of moderate to vigorous activity daily

DIABETES - TYPE 2 *(continued from previous page)*

POTENTIAL COMPLICATIONS:
Short term
- Hypoglycemia
- Hyperglycemia

Long term
- Cognitive deficits related to frequent hypoglycemia or severe episodes of hypoglycemia
- Cardiovascular disease
- Kidney disease
- Neuropathy
- Vision loss
- Susceptible to skin infections

References

American Diabetes Association. (2013a). *Standards of medical care in diabetes—2013, 36* (Supplement 1), S40-44. doi: 10.2337/dc13-S011. Retrieved from http://care.diabetesjournals.org/content/36/Supplement_1/S11.full

American Diabetes Association. (2013b). *Diabetes care in the school and day care setting, 36* (Supplement 1), S75-S79. doi: 10.2337/dc13-S075. Retrieved from http://care.diabetesjournals.org/content/36/Supplement_1/S75.full

Copeland, K.C., Silverstein, J., Moore, K.R., Prazar, G.E., Raymer, T., Shiffman, R.N.,..., & Flinn, S. K. (2013). Management of newly diagnosed type 2 diabetes mellitus (T2DM) in children and adolescents. *Pediatrics, 131*,364-382. *doi: 10.1542/peds.2012-3494*

Flint, A. & Aslanian, S. (2011). Treatment of Type 2 diabetes in youth. *Diabetes Care 2011,34*(Supplement 2), S177-S183. doi: 10.2337/dc11-s215

National Association of School Nurses. (2008). *Helping administer to the needs of students with diabetes in school (HANDS).* Silver Spring, MD: Author.

National Association of School Nurses. (2010). Managing *diabetes at school: Tools for the school nurse.* Silver Spring, MD: Author.

National Diabetes Education Program. (2012). *Helping the student with diabetes succeed: A guide for school personnel.* Retrieved from http://www.ndep.nih.gov/publications/PublicationDetail.aspx?PubId=97&redirect=true#main

Today Study Group. (2010). Design of a family-based lifestyle intervention for youth with type 2 diabetes: the TODAY study. *International Journal of Obesity 2010, 34*(2), 217-26. doi: 10.1038/ijo.2009.195

DIARRHEA

DEFINITION/ETIOLOGY:
Diarrhea is an increase in the number of stools (3 or more per day) and a loosening/softening in consistency in relation to the patient's normal stooling pattern. Severe diarrheal stools are watery, may be green and/or contain mucous or blood. Diarrhea can be acute or chronic. Acute diarrhea typically occurs with parasites and bacterial and viral infections. Diarrhea is considered chronic if it lasts longer than two weeks. There are many causes of diarrhea. The most common causes of diarrhea are viruses, bacteria, parasites, and medications.

Below is a partial list of common causes leading to diarrhea.
Infections
- Acute gastroenteritis (viral) – norovirus, viral hepatitis, rotavirus
- Bacterial diarrhea – salmonella, shigella, E. Coli
- Protozoan (Giardia, amebiasis)

Diseases of the colon
- Celiac disease
- Crohn's disease
- Ulcerative colitis

Psychogenic diarrhea
- Fear/anxiety
- Encopresis

Other
- Cystic fibrosis
- Parasites (round worms, tapeworms)
- Gastrointestinal
- Food allergy / Food intolerance / Lactose intolerance
- Antibiotic diarrhea
- Laxatives
- Dietetic candy with sorbitol
- Constipation with fecal retention

SIGNS AND SYMPTOMS:
- Patients with bacterial enteritis often have a rapid onset of diarrhea without vomiting and > four diarrhea stools per day with blood or mucous
- Viral gastroenteritis – vomiting and frequent watery diarrhea stools
- May have signs of dehydration (decreased urine output, thickening of saliva, thirst, etc.)
- Vital signs—may have increased pulse and lower blood pressure if dehydrated

DIARRHEA *(continued from previous page)*

- Fever is often present, but usually not high
- Abdominal pain, abdominal cramps, or bloating

MANAGEMENT AND TREATMENT:
1. Treatment is dependent on etiology. Treat underlying cause.
2. Monitor for signs and symptoms of dehydration (tachycardia, hypotension, lethargy).
3. If signs of dehydration are present, refer immediately.
4. If well hydrated but acutely ill, notify parent/guardian.
5. If all symptoms are mild, observe in clinic and offer clear liquids or oral rehydrating solution (e.g., Gatorade®). Notify parent/guardian.
6. Although many cases of diarrhea are not caused by an infectious disease, public health guidelines may call for the exclusion of the child from school or child care if the feces are not able to be contained in a diaper or in a toilet.
7. Very young children who attend school or significantly developmentally delayed children of any age, or children whose physical disabilities include lack of bowel control, are the children who may need to be excluded for diarrhea, even if the cause is known to be non-infectious.
8. **Diarrhea from suspected or known food borne-illnesses is reportable to the health department, in most states.**

FOLLOW UP:
- Obtain diagnosis and assess the risk to fellow students
- Examine child on re-entry to school (temperature and hydration status)
- Give medication as prescribed
- Report any relapse

POTENTIAL COMPLICATIONS:
Dehydration is a complication of intense diarrhea due to the loss of excess fluids and electrolytes. Dehydration limits the body's ability to carry out normal functions due to the lack of water/fluid intake. **Serious consequences can result if lost fluids are not replenished. Note:** Immunocompromised individuals are increased risk of dehydration

NOTES:
Prevention
- Proper handwashing prevents the spread of viral diarrhea
- Guard against contaminated food
- Watch what you eat and drink if traveling to developing countries
- Educate parent/guardian(s) on vaccine preventable diarrhea (rotavirus)

DIARRHEA *(continued from previous page)*

References

Centers for Disease Control and Prevention (CDC). (2011).*Viral gastroenteritis*. Retrieved from
   http://www.cdc.gov/ncidod/dvrd/revb/gastro/faq.htm

John, R., & Chewey, L. (2013). Common complaints. In J. Selekman (Ed.), *School nursing: A comprehensive text* (2nd ed.)
   (pp.578-640). Philadelphia, PA: F. A. Davis.

Mayo Clinic. (2013). *Diarrhea*. Retrieved from http://www.mayoclinic.com/health/diarrhea/DS00292/
   DSECTION=lifestyle-and-home-remedies.

Merck Manual. (2012). *Diarrhea in children*. Retrieved from http://www.merckmanuals.com/professional/pediatrics/
   approach_to_the_care_of_normal_infants_and_children/diarrhea_in_children.html?qt=diarrhea&alt=sh

National Digestive Diseases Information Clearinghouse (NDDIC). (2012). *Diarrhea*. Retrieved from
   http://digestive.niddk.nih.gov/ddiseases/pubs/diarrhea/

WebMD. (2012). *The basics of diarrhea*. Retrieved from
   http://www.webmd.com/digestive-disorders/digestive-diseases-diarrhea?page=2

DIPHTHERIA

DEFINITION/ETIOLOGY:
Diphtheria is an acute, highly contagious, potentially life-threatening infection caused by *Corynebacterium diphtheriae* that can either invade the pharyngeal site or present as a cutaneous infection. In the respiratory system the bacteria produces a toxin. It is transmitted from person-to-person through respiratory droplets (coughing or sneezing). Persons can also become infected by coming in contact fomites, an object (telephone, keyboard, doorknobs, toys, and dish) that has been contaminated by an infected person. Contact with infected skin lesions can also spread the infection. Humans are the only known reservoir for *C. diphtheria*. Today, diphtheria is rare in the United States and other developed countries due to widespread vaccination programs.

SIGNS AND SYMPTOMS:
Pharyngeal/Respiratory Diphtheria
- Weakness
- Sore throat
- Fever and chills
- Swollen glands (neck)
- Difficulty swallowing
- Loss of appetite
- Within 2-3 days, a thick coating (pseudomembrane) can build up in the throat or nose
- The toxin may be absorbed into the heart, kidneys, and nerves
- Diagnosis is determined by symptoms
- Definitive diagnosis is made by laboratory results of throat or lesion swabs confirming the presence of toxin in the body

MANAGEMENT/TREATMENT:
- Hospitalization
- Diphtheria Antitoxin (DAT) to counteract toxin
- Antibiotics (penicillin or erythromycin) to kill and eliminate bacteria
- Isolation until no longer able to infect others, usually after completing a 48 hour antibiotic regime
- Untreated person who are infected may be contagious for up to 4 weeks. If the person is treated appropriately, the contagious period can be limited to less than 4 days.
- Recovery from diphtheria is not always followed by life-time immunity
- Diphtheria is a reportable disease (local health department)

DIPHTHERIA *(continued from previous page)*

FOLLOW-UP:

POTENTIAL COMPLICATIONS:
- Obstructed airway
- Myocarditis, endocarditis
- Polyneuropathy
- Paralysis
- Pneumonia
- Respiratory failure
- Septic arthritis
- Mortality rate with treatment is 1 in 10
- Mortality rate without treatment is 1 in 2

NOTES:
Cutaneous Diphtheria
- Rare in the U.S. Persons with poor hygiene or living in crowded conditions are those most often seen with diphtheria.
- Cutaneous diphtheria presents as a scaling rash, lesions, of blisters that can occur anywhere on the body. Lesions may be painful and swollen. The infection is treated by thoroughly cleaning the skin with soap and water and with antibiotics.

Prevention
- Vaccine (primary and post-exposure)
- Post exposure antibiotics
- Diphtheria is a vaccine preventable disease (VPD) when diphtheria vaccine is appropriately given to infants and children, to pre-teens and teens, and to adults
- Adults should receive Td vaccine every 10 years
- Childhood vaccination should be routine
- Follow CDC, AAP, and /or State Departments of Health recommendations for immunization schedules

References
Centers for Disease Control and Prevention. (2013). *Diphtheria*. Retrieved from http://www.cdc.gov/diphtheria/index.html

Mayo Clinic. (2013). *Diphtheria*. Retrieved from http://www.mayoclinic.com/diphtheria/DS00495

Medline Plus. U.S. National Library of Medicine. (2013). *Diphtheria*. Retrieved from http://www.nim.nim.gov/medlineplus/diphtheria.html

Merck Manual, Professional Edition. (2013). *Diphtheria*). Retrieved from http://www.merckmanuals.com/professional/ infectious_diseases/gram-positive_bacilli/diphtheria.html?qt=diphtheria&alt=sh

DISASTER PREPAREDNESS

DEFINITIONS/ETIOLOGY:
Disaster preparedness in the school setting is the development and implementation of a comprehensive plan to respond to a disaster/emergency. Disasters can occur due to a natural event (fire, tornado, hurricane, earthquake, tsunami, etc.), a health epidemic (pandemic influenza, etc.), or a manmade event (hazardous material spill, civil dispute, terrorism, etc.). Disasters directly and indirectly impact the health and well-being of students. When creating a disaster plan, school districts should include in their comprehensive plan a means to provide care to all students and staff.

Disaster preparedness plans set the foundation for necessary actions to take place during an emergency. Survivability may depend on knowing what to do in case of an emergency. Every school district should have a written, realistic and adaptable disaster preparedness plan.

National Response Framework:
Events can happen at any time. During a disaster, the traumatic event (situation) outweighs actual available resources. The Federal Emergency Management Agency (FEMA) provides a unified "National Response Framework" to utilize during disaster preparedness planning. Phases of the "National Response Framework" include prevention, preparedness, response, and recovery planning.

Prevention/mitigation
- Identify potential hazards (natural, pandemics, and acts of terrorism).
- Involve community leaders (police departments, local health departments, local hospitals, emergency medical services, fire department, etc.).
- Improve building safety to prevent potential acts of terrorism.

Preparedness
- Prepare for the event before it occurs.
- Collaborate with community leaders to develop comprehensive plans and algorithms that prepares for generic geographical risks (tornados, hurricanes, tsunami, etc.).
- Identify "Incident Commander" – typically the principal; establish a chain of command.
- Identify necessary resources and equipment that may be needed during a disaster.
- When creating a plan, consider loss of utilities (heat/electric), food, and water.
- The plan must provide for the entire school community including children and staff with special health care needs.
  - If the district has ventilator (or other technology) dependent students, then a strategy for a second means of power **must** be included into the plan.

DISASTER PREPAREDNESS *(continued from previous page)*

- It is recommended that food, water, diabetic supplies (glucometer, strips, lancets, insulin, syringe/pen supplies, carbohydrates for hypoglycemia), medical supplies, and medications be stockpiled for 72 hours; check supply expiration dates periodically.

Response
- Implement disaster plan.
- Respond to the emergency.
- Triage – assist injured students and staff.
- Administer first aid.
- Accountability – are all students and staff accounted for?
- Reunify student with parent/guardian(s) according to disaster plan.

Recovery
- Collaborate with community leaders to promote healing. A disaster (whether natural or man-made) is traumatic. Children respond to trauma differently than adults. Following the event, the school (district) must restore a safe and healthy learning environment.
- After the incident, analyze the event, what needs to be improved.

School Nurse responsibilities before a disaster:
- Create a disaster kit to be utilized in the event of an emergency.
  - The kit should contain first aid supplies, emergency medication, bottled water, diabetic supplies, etc.
- Identify who is certified in CPR and First Aid (FA); consider offering additional CPR/FA classes to increase/maintain building certification.
- Identify and plan for special needs students (chronic health conditions, students with autism, and/or cognitively impaired) prior to an emergency.
  - What will their health needs be during a disaster/emergency?

School Nurse responsibilities during a disaster:
- Triage
- First Aid (coordination)
- Direct hands-on care

FOLLOW UP:
- Debriefing of the incident
- Disaster preparedness is a continual improvement process.
  - What went well?
  - What were the limitations of the plan?
  - What needs to be done to improve the process?

DISASTER PREPAREDNESS *(continued from previous page)*

- Children and youth respond to trauma differently than adults; provide support/ counseling to help youth deal with the aftermath of the trauma
  - ○ Recognize signs and symptoms of posttraumatic stress disorder (PTSD)
    - ▪ Intrusive memories – flashbacks, upsetting dreams about the traumatic event (reliving the traumatic event)
    - ▪ Avoidance behaviors – avoids talking/thinking about the event, avoids activities that they once enjoyed, avoids to the point of developing a phobia of person/place that reminds them of the traumatic incident
    - ▪ Increased anxiety – easily startled or frightened, difficulty sleeping, irritability, anger, has trouble concentrating/focusing
    - ▪ Monitor for somatic symptoms. Somatic symptoms of PTSD may include: sleep

      disturbances, muscle tension, headaches, gastrointestinal disturbances, fatigue, etc.

POTENTIAL COMPLICATIONS:
- PTSD secondary to disaster trauma
- Life-changing (altering) physical injuries
- Death

NOTES:
- Student may feel guilt/shame surrounding the event; provide support as needed.
- In disasters, include children in efforts to help others more affected; helping others assists the child in regaining a sense of normalcy.
- Help the child/youth convey their emotions/feelings through talk, writing, drawing, play, and singing.

References

American Academy of Pediatrics. (2010). *Policy statement—Emergency information forms and emergency preparedness for children with special health care needs.* Retrieved from http://pediatrics.aappublications.org/content/125/4/829.full.pdf+html?sid=7c67bbc1-aed3-4c97-8841-f058a9e1dc58

Doyle, J. (2013). Emergency management, crisis response, and the school nurse's role. In J. Selekman (Ed.), *School nursing: A comprehensive text* (2nd ed.) (pp.1216-1244). Philadelphia: F. A. Davis.

Federal Emergency Management Agency (FEMA). (2013). *National incident management system.* Retrieved from http://www.fema.gov/national-incident-management-system

Foley, M. (2013). Health services management. In J. Selekman (Ed.), *School nursing: A comprehensive text* (2nd ed.) (pp.1190-1215). Philadelphia, PA: F. A. Davis.

DISASTER PREPAREDNESS *(continued from previous page)*

MedlinePlus. U.S. National Library of Medicine. (2013). *Disaster preparation and recovery.* Retrieved from
    http://www.nlm.nih.gov/medlineplus/disasterpreparationandrecovery.html

National Association of School Nurses. (2011). *Emergency preparedness – the role of the school nurse* (Position Statement).
    Retrieved from http://www.nasn.org/Portals/0/positions/2011psemergency.pdf

National Association of State Boards of Education. (2013). *State school healthy policy database.* Retrieved from
    http://www.nasbe.org/healthy_schools/hs/bytopics.php?topicid=3140

O'Meara, S. (2013). *School safety and emergency preparedness.* Retrieved from http://www.nsba.org/SchoolLaw/COSA/
    School-Law-Seminar/School-Safety-and-Emergency-Preparedness.pdf

Strouse, D. (2010). *The role of school nurses in school emergency management planning.* Retrieved from
    http://rems.ed.gov/docs/webinars/Training_SchoolNursesInSEM_101213.pdf

Substance Abuse and Mental Health Services Administration. (2012). *Tips for talking with and helping children and youth cope
    after a disaster or traumatic event.* Retrieved from http://www.samhsa.gov/dtac/docs/KEN01-0093R.pdf

DO NOT ATTEMPT RESUSCITATION (DNAR)

OVERVIEW
An increasing number of students with complex, life-threatening medical issues are attending school. Due to medical advances along with federal laws such as IDEIA, more children with complex chronic conditions are attending school. Chronic conditions include terminal illness, congenital disease and anomalies, and injuries. There are developmental, psychosocial, and emotional benefits for the child to continue to attend school. School attendance maintains a sense of community and normalcy for the student and family.

Parents/guardians and schools are making difficult end of life decisions about steps to be taken in the event that respiratory/cardiac arrest occurs at school. Schools may receive *Do Not Attempt Resuscitation* (DNAR) orders from the physician and/or parents/guardians requesting that life support procedures be withheld in the event respirations and heartbeat have ceased and that the student be allowed to die without emergency intervention. This also may be referred to as *Do Not Resuscitate* (DNR) or *Allow Natural Death* (AND) orders. It is important to note that a DNAR order is not an order to stand by and not intervene in anyway, rather supportive and comfort measures may be integrated into the plan of care. Spiritual and emotional needs also should be addressed in the plan.

POLICIES and GUIDELINES
In the presence of DNAR directives, schools are faced with difficult decisions that are framed by medical, emotional, legal, and ethical issues for the educational setting and that reflect the need of school districts to have local, school-based policies and guidelines. Consideration given to the following may be helpful in reaching sound decisions related to the development of policy, guidelines, and a plan of action.
1. Identification of federal, state, and local laws related to DNAR directives in the educational setting and the care of medically fragile children at school. (General Counsel at the state Department of Education is a good resource to define federal, state, and local laws and the ability of schools to comply with "do not attempt resuscitation" directive in the school district).
2. Local policy development and the development of guidelines that support policy should include both members of the school community (i.e. attorney for the school board of education, school administrator), the school nurse, other members of the school services team, and a member of the medical community (Emergency Medical Services [EMS], and funeral director).

DO NOT ATTEMPT RESUSCITATION (DNAR) *(continued from previous page)*

3. DNAR policy and guideline development teams should:
   * Be able to define and clearly understand what life-supporting measures are being directed to withhold (i.e. cardio-pulmonary resuscitation (CPR), intubation, ventilation, Auto External Defibrillators [AED], or medication).
   * Clearly understand what palliative measures are acceptable (i.e. positioning for comfort and other needed care, oxygen, suctioning, Heimlich maneuver for choking, control of bleeding and pain) (Selekman, Bochenek & Lukens, 2013).
   * That plans are individualized for each student. The following is a non-limiting list of those who should be involved in the development of the plan: the primary care provider, parents/guardians, the school nurse, school administrator, religious advisor, EMS, and the student.
   * Find it imperative that the student has an IHP, including the DNAR order, written by a registered school nurse.

Role of the School Nurse
* Obtain release of information and DNAR order.
* Organize team meeting including school staff, parents/guardians, and palliative care team. Other community members that may be considered: clergy, local EMS, funeral home director, physician.
* Provide student assessment and assessment of staffing needs.
* Develop an Individualized School Health Plan. Components to consider:
  o Disease-directed treatment
  o Symptom control
  o Copy of the DNAR order
  o Specific explanation of what actions may be taken by staff members
  o Comfort measures such as holding the child, providing oxygen, keeping student warm (AAP, 2010)
  o Address spiritual needs
  o Clear instructions on classroom management should child's health status change, i.e. a code that elicits quick staff response, privacy considerations for student
  o Re-evaluation of the plan annually, at minimum
  o Education of identified school staff to include defining staff roles and accommodations for bus transportation

DO NOT ATTEMPT RESUSCITATION (DNAR) *(continued from previous page)*

Resources:
- American Academy of Pediatrics at www.aap.org (See Policy Statement).
- National Association of School Nurses at www.nasn/org (See Position Statement).
- Schwab, N., and Gelfman, M. (2005). Legal Issues In School Health Services. Sunrise River Press, North Branch, MN.
- NASN School Nurse. March 2013. *Do Not Attempt Resuscitation (DNAR) Orders in School Settings*. Excellent article that provides a comprehensive checklist for planning for a DNAR order for a child at school. See reference list for complete information.
- Hospice/Palliative care team caring for the child

References

American Academy of Pediatrics. (2010). Policy statement: Honoring do-not-attempt resuscitation requests in schools. *Pediatrics, 125*, 1073-1077. doi: 10.1542/peds.2010-0452

National Association of School Nurses. (2012). *Do not attempt resuscitation (DNAR): Issue brief.* Retrieved from http://www.nasn.org/PolicyAdvocacy/PositionPapersandReports/NASNIssueBriefsFullView/tabid/445/ArticleId/305/Do-Not-Attempt-Resuscitation-DNAR-2012

Selekman, J., Bochenek, J., & Lukens, M. (2013). Do not resuscitate orders. In J. Selekman (Ed.), *School nursing: A comprehensive text (2nd ed.)* (pp. 713-714). Philadelphia, PA: F.A. Davis.

Weise, K. L. (2010). Do-not-attempt-resuscitation orders in public schools. *American Medical Association Journal of Ethics, 12*(7), 569-572. Retrieved from http://virtualmentor.ama-assn.org/2010/07/pfor1-1007.html

Zacharski, S., Minchella, L., Gomez, S., Grogan, S., Porter, S., & Robarge, D. (2013). Do not attempt resuscitation (DNAR) orders in school settings: Special needs nurses review current research and issues. *NASN School Nurse, 28*(2), 71-75. doi: 10.177/1942602X12472540

EAR PAIN

DEFINITION/ETIOLOGY:
Otalgia or earache/pain can be caused by external or middle ear conditions or by referred pain from other sources. Infections of the ear are one of the most common diseases of childhood. The incidence of middle ear infection increases in winter and spring. Conditions of the ear can be responsible for transient hearing loss in students and therefore can have a great impact in the educational setting.

External ear including external auditory canal
- Infection/ inflammation (otitis externa, cellulitis, furuncle or abscess, perichondritis of the pinna)
- Cerumen (wax) impaction
- Trauma
- Foreign object
- Tumor or growth

Middle ear - Eustachian tube, and Mastoid
- Infection/inflammation (otitis media , middle ear effusion, mastoiditis)
- Trauma
- Tumor or growth
- Allergies

Referred ear pain
- Pharyngeal lesions (peritonsillar abscess, retropharyngeal abscess, nasopharyngeal fibroma)
- Mouth lesions (acute stomatitis or glossitis, dental problem)
- Laryngeal and esophageal sources, e.g., laryngeal ulceration, esophageal foreign body, esophageal reflux (acid reflux)

Other
- Temporomandibular joint (TMJ) dysfunction

SIGNS AND SYMPTOMS:
- **Otitis externa**, or inflammation of the external ear canal, is also called "swimmer's ear." It is commonly seen after frequent exposure to moisture or swimming. *Pseudomonas aeruginosa* is the most common pathogen responsible for otitis externa and *staphylococcus aureus* is also common. The student has pain which may begin gradually or suddenly, and is increased with pressure on the tragus or when the pinna is moved. Otorrhea (discharge coming from the external canal) is common.   Erythema (redness) of the ear canal, itching and irritation, pressure and fullness in the ear may be reported. There may be hearing loss if there is enough swelling to occlude the canal.

EAR PAIN (*continued from previous page*)

- **Otitis Media (OM)** is an acute inflammation of the middle ear. It is the most common cause of ear pain, and may accompany a simple "cold". The tympanic membrane is dull, often bulging, and sometimes erythematous (red). It often resolves spontaneously. Ear pain, fever, inability to sleep, lethargy, diarrhea and vomiting may be present. Sudden hearing loss may occur. Otitis media may also be classified as Acute Otitis Media (AOM) referring to a sudden onset and the presence of a middle ear effusion.

- **Middle Ear Effusion (**MEE) may complicate an upper respiratory infection. A collection of watery fluid fills the middle ear canal and can interfere with hearing. In most cases, the fluid is absorbed spontaneously within 3 months, but if it persists, it can lead to a hearing loss. The child is often asymptomatic and afebrile but may have mild or intermittent ear pain, fullness, or "popping" in the ear, dizziness, or loss of balance.

- **Otitis Media with Effusion (OME)** is an accumulation of serous fluid in the middle ear without signs and symptoms of acute infection. Between 50 and 79% of children may develop OME after a course of antibiotics for AOM. Bubbles or fluid levels may be seen behind the tympanic membrane.

- **Impacted Cerumen** may cause ear pain if the cerumen hardens and touches the tympanic membrane. Although cerumen is a naturally forming lubricant and protector of the ear canal, excessive production may block the ear canal causing hearing loss until removed.

> **Severe ear pain** may be a sign of a ruptured eardrum or foreign body, especially if the onset is sudden.

MANAGEMENT/TREATMENT:

1. The student with severe pain should be evaluated promptly. If a live insect is the cause of pain, inspection by otoscope may be difficult because the light may aggravate an insect and cause additional pain. Notify parents/guardians and advise taking the child to his/her primary care provider.

EAR PAIN *(continued from previous page)*

2. For otitis externa, the parents/guardians should be advised to take the student to the healthcare provider. Clean any drainage gently from pinna of the ear using clean technique/standard precautions and apply a warm dry compress to the affected ear to relieve pain. Topical antibiotic treatment (ear drops) may be prescribed, but only after confirming that the eardrum is intact. In the eardrum has been perforated a nontoxic topical medication will be ordered. Swimming should be discouraged for 7-10 days and moisture in the ear should be avoided for 4-6 weeks. The parent/guardian should be advised to have the child use ear plugs when swimming. Prevent recurrence (which is common) by instilling 2-3 drops of isopropyl alcohol in the ear canals after swimming, showering or during hot humid weather. Otitis externa should resolve in 7 days.

3. For healthy school- aged children with OM, guidelines recommend observation and pain management for 48 to 72 hours as the majority of OM will resolve spontaneously.

4. Removal of cerumen should be done in the office of the health care provider and may be done using a curette or irrigation.

FOLLOW UP:
Screening hearing acuity and comparing the result with a previous screen can be helpful after the student recovers from an acute ear infection. If mild hearing loss is found on screening in the absence of any other signs or discomfort, re-check after about 3 weeks. Most OME will resolve without treatment, but if OME persists for 3 months or at any time there is a language delay, learning problem, or a significant hearing loss is suspected, a medical referral is indicated.

References

Bowden, V. R. & Greenberg, C. S. (2010). The child with altered sensory status. In *Children and their families: The continuum of care (2nd edition) (pp. 1497-1503). Philadelphia PA: Lippincott Williams and Wilkins.*

Medline Plus, U.S. National Library of Medicine. (2013). *Earache.* Retrieved from
http://www.nlm.nih.gov/medlineplus/ency/article/003046.htm

EATING DISORDERS

An eating disorder is marked by severe disturbances in eating behavior, such as extreme reduction of food intake or extreme overeating, along with feelings of significant concern about body weight or shape. Eating disorders have complicated genetic, biological, behavioral, and social causes. According to the National Institute of Mental Health, eating disorders primarily affect females. However, males can also be vulnerable to eating disorders. Two main types are <u>anorexia nervosa</u> and <u>bulimia nervosa</u>. A third category is eating disorders not otherwise specified or EDNOS. These are similar to anorexia or bulimia with slightly different characteristics, such as binge-eating disorder. Eating disorders will often surface during adolescence but can occur at any age. Females are more likely to develop an eating disorder. It affects 10 to 15% of males, and one-third of males affected develop binge-eating disorder. People with eating disorders frequently have other psychiatric disorders including depression, substance abuse, or anxiety. They also can develop serious physical complications such as heart or kidney disorders that can be fatal.

ANOREXIA NERVOSA

DEFINITION/ETIOLOGY:
Anorexia is characterized by induced and sustained weight loss. Speculation on traits that may lead to this disorder are low self-esteem, rigid self-control, fear of maturation, obsession with appearance, and perfectionism.

SIGNS/SYMPTOMS:
The term anorexia is a misnomer since loss of appetite is rare.
- Refusal to maintain body weight at minimal normal weight for age and height, e.g., weight loss leading to body weight at least 15% below that expected; or failure to make expected weight gain during period of growth
- Intense fear of gaining weight or becoming fat, even though underweight
- Disturbance in the way in which one's body weight, size, or shape is experienced, e.g., the person claims to "feel fat" even if emaciated, believes that one area of the body is "too fat" even when obviously underweight
- In females, absence of at least three consecutive menstrual cycles when otherwise expected to occur (primary or secondary amenorrhea). A woman is considered to have amenorrhea if her periods occur only following hormone, e.g. estrogen, administration
- Weight loss accomplished by reduction in total food intake, often with extensive exercising
- Frequently there is self-induced vomiting, use of laxatives, enemas or diuretics (in such cases Bulimia Nervosa may also be present)

EATING DISORDERS *(continued from previous page)*

- Often undiagnosed until weight loss is marked. By the time the person is profoundly underweight, there are other signs, such as hypothermia, bradycardia, hypotension, edema, lanugo (fine hair), and a variety of metabolic changes. In most cases, amenorrhea follows weight loss, but may appear before noticeable weight loss has occurred.

MANAGEMENT/TREATMENT:
1. **Initial diagnosis** is most important.
   a. Often not suspected at home because child is not seen unclothed.
   b. Alert the PE teacher to monitor.
2. Refer for psychiatric evaluation and counseling as appropriate.
3. Effective treatment is long term.
4. Establish liaison with parents/guardians, physician, and therapists – develop multidisciplinary approach in health plan in consultation with healthcare provider and therapist along with school mental health staff.

FOLLOW UP:
- Provide safe haven in clinic where the student can freely discuss problems.
- Monitor for secondary physical effects of under-nutrition.
- Relapse is common.
- **Significant mortality if not treated:** involuntary commitment may be considered if refusal to seek psychiatric care.

COMPLICATIONS:
Under-nutrition can become severe enough to affect secondary endocrine, metabolic, and electrolyte disturbances of bodily functions, including osteoporosis. Prolonged anorexia may lead to alcohol and substance addiction, fertility problems and death due to cardiac arrhythmia, congestive heart failure, or suicide.

BULIMIA NERVOSA

DIAGNOSIS/ETIOLOGY:
No single etiological factor; may be combined neurochemical, developmental, cultural, psychological, family, and environment. Dieting is often precursor to disordered eating. A higher rate of reported sexual abuse in females. In order to qualify for this diagnosis, person must have had a minimum of two binge eating episodes per week for at least three months.

EATING DISORDERS *(continued from previous page)*

SIGNS/SYMPTOMS:
- Recurrent episodes of binge eating
- Rapid consumption of a large amount of food in a discrete period of time, usually done in secrecy
- A feeling of lack of control over eating behavior during the eating binges.
- Self-induced vomiting, use of laxatives or diuretics, strict dieting or fasting
- Vigorous exercise in order to prevent weight gain
- Persistent over concern with body shape and weight
- Chapped, cracked, irritated, or sore fingers from self-induced vomiting
- If person purges by vomiting, may have tooth enamel damage and sore throats
- Frequent trips to bathroom following meal
- Although most people with Bulimia Nervosa are within a normal weight range, some may be slightly underweight and others may be overweight. Extreme thinness (25% below normal weight) may result
- A depressed mood that may be part of a depressive disorder is commonly observed

MANAGEMENT / TREATMENT:
1. Refer for nutritional counseling or psychotherapy as appropriate.
2. Cognitive Behavioral Therapy (CBT) may benefit to help focus on and solve problems related to bulimia. CBT may be individual or group-based and is effective in changing binge-eating /purging behaviors and attitudes towards eating.
3. Develop multidisciplinary approach (described in an individualized health plan).
4. Psychotherapeutic drugs may be prescribed if depression is present.

FOLLOW UP:
- Monitor behavior and compliance to mental health and eating plan.
  Note: *Eating binges may be planned. The food consumed during a binge often has a high caloric content, a sweet taste, and a texture that facilitates rapid eating. The food is usually eaten in secrecy. The food is usually gobbled rapidly with little chewing. Once eating has begun, additional food may be sought to continue the binge. A binge is usually terminated by abdominal discomfort, sleep, social interruption, or induced vomiting. Vomiting decreases the physical pain of abdominal distention allowing either continued eating or termination of the binge and often reduces post-binge anguish. In some cases, vomiting may itself be desired so that the person will binge in order to vomit or will vomit after eating a small amount of food. Although eating binges may be pleasurable, disparaging self-criticism and a depressed mood often follow.*
- Frequent weight fluctuations due to alternating binges and fasts are common. Often persons with bulimia feel that their life is dominated by conflicts about eating.

EATING DISORDERS *(continued from previous page)*

COMPLICATIONS:
- Some people with this disorder are subject to psychoactive substance abuse or dependence, most frequently involving sedatives, amphetamines, cocaine, or alcohol.
- Repeated vomiting can cause inflammation or tears in the lining of the esophagus and erosion of tooth enamel.
- Electrolyte imbalance may lead to cardiac arrhythmia.
- Under-nutrition can become severe enough to affect secondary endocrine, metabolic, and electrolyte disturbances of bodily functions, including osteoporosis.
- Prolonged bulimia may lead to alcohol and substance addiction, fertility problems and death due to cardiac arrhythmia, congestive heart failure, or suicide.

NOTE:
Anorexia and bulimia are two serious life threatening conditions which are curable if identified early, treated by trained therapists, and supplemented by support groups.

References:

American Psychological Association. (2011), *Eating disorders*. Retrieved from http://www.apa.org/helpcenter/eating.aspx

Dunn, A. (2008). Nutrition. In C. Burns, M. Brady, A. Dunn, N.B. Starr, C. Blosser (Eds.), *Pediatric primary care*, 4th ed. (pp. 218-220). St. Louis, MO: Saunders Elsevier.

Selekman, J., Diefenbeck, & Guthrie, S. (2013.). Mental health concerns. In J. Selekman (Ed.), *School nursing: A comprehensive text* (2nd ed.) (pp. 956-959). Philadelphia, PA: F.A. Davis.

National Institute of Mental Health. (2011). *Eating disorders*. Retrieved on July 24, 2013 from http://www.nimh.nih.gov/health/publications/eating-disorders/complete-index.shtml.

ECZEMA (Atopic Dermatitis)

DEFINITION/ETIOLOGY:
Eczema is a form of dermatitis or inflamed skin. Atopic (allergic nature) dermatitis is a common type of eczema characterized by acute or chronic skin eruptions. Eczema affects between 5-20% of children through age 11. Most states require the exclusion of children from school if they have signs or symptoms of communicable diseases. Eczema may be difficult to distinguish from other rashes. An unidentified rash is a classic symptom of some communicable diseases. Therefore, children should be excluded unless the rash is identified as non-communicable.

SIGNS AND SYMPTOMS:
- **Acute:** Skin is intensely itchy, moist, weepy, red, with generalized rash, usually on front of elbows, back of knees, face and neck. Usually seen in children under age two years.
- **Chronic or atopic:** Areas of involvement are wrist, neck, ankles (feet), front of elbows, back of knees, face and neck. Usually dry, scaly, easily irritated. May be red or depigmented. Usually seen in school age children. Crusting may be present. Atopic eczema is chronic and characterized by remissions and exacerbations. Be aware of the Allergy Triad: Allergies-Eczema-Asthma either with the child or with positive family history.
- **"Itch-scratch cycle":** Scratching or rubbing itchy skin causes further irritation and traumatizes sensitive tissue that increases the risk of secondary infection.
- Symptoms range from a small patch to a painful rash affecting large areas of the body

DIFFERENTIAL DIAGNOSES:
- Seborrheic dermatitis (severe dandruff)
- Fungal infections
- Contact dermatitis, e.g., poison ivy
- Irritant dermatitis, e.g., friction from tight clothing

MANAGEMENT/TREATMENT:
1. Mild cases may be treated in school clinic; refer significant cases to physician. Physicians may order allergy testing, topical steroids or phototherapy, etc.
2. Acute: moist, cold compress relieves itching. NO powder or lotion on weepy skin.
3. Chronic: if dry, add moisturizer (e.g. Lubriderm®) or plain calamine for itch.
4. Keep skin hydrated:
   - Keep baths brief. Pat dry.
   - Avoid excessive soap exposure; use mild soap or lipid-free cleanser (e.g. Cetaphil®, Aquaphil®).
   - Seal water into skin after bathing (e.g. Alpha-Keri®, Nivea®, Aquaphor®, Eucerin®).

ECZEMA (Atopic Dermatitis) *(continued from previous page)*

5. Antibiotic ointment for secondary infection.
6. Oral antihistamine to relieve itching; used at bedtime, watch for drowsiness.
7. Use soft cotton clothing and bedding. Avoid wool or rough fabrics. Do not rub skin with washcloth.
8. Control temperature and humidity extremes (high or low); gently pat sweaty skin dry.
9. Treatment is aimed at breaking the "itch-scratch" cycle.

FOLLOW UP:

- Secondary infection is common, especially due to scratching. Resembles impetigo at the edges of eczematous skin; may show as isolated circular crusts with moist or dry pus underneath.
- Observe for cellulitis or lymphangitis.
- Study flare-ups for possible allergies to chemicals, foods, or environmental factors, e.g., dust mites.
- Medical evaluation is necessary for any severe diet restrictions.
- Advise others that eczema is not contagious (unless a secondary infection is present).
- Children are subject to teasing and social distancing which exacerbates stress and low self-esteem.
- Emotions do not cause atopic dermatitis but can trigger the "itch-scratch cycle".
- Anger and frustration can lead to flushing and itchiness.
- Sleep disturbances are common, particularly during flare-ups. If the child is tired or irritable, ask the parent/guardian about night symptoms and management.
- Encourage patience. Some parents/guardians try different products without allowing enough time for anyone to show effectiveness.
- Involve children in their care by asking about their experiences and giving them choices and some control over treatment, such as who applies the topical product, and privacy.

References

Kids Health. (2012). *Eczema*. Retrieved from http://kidshealth.org/parent/infections/skin/eczema_atopic_dermatitis.html

Fennessy, M., Coupland, S., Popay, J., & Naysmith, K. (2000). The epidemiology and experience of atopic eczema during childhood: A discussion paper on the implications of current knowledge for health care, public health policy and research. *The Journal of Epidemiology and Community Health, 54*(8), 581-589. doi:10.1136/jech.54.8.581

Goodhue, C. & Brady, M. (2008). Atopic and phematic disorders. In C. Burns, M. Brady, A. Dunn, N.B. Starr, & C. Blosser (Eds.), *Pediatric primary care (4*th ed.) (pp. 571-575). St. Louis, MO: Saunders Elsevier.

Mayo Clinic. (2011). *Atopic dermatitis (eczema)*. Retrieved from http://www.mayoclinic.com/health/eczema/DS00986

Zheng, T., Yu, J., Oh, M. H., & Zhu, Z. (2011). The atopic march: Progression from atopic dermatitis to allergic rhinitis and asthma. *Allergy Asthma Immunology Research, 3*(2), 67-73. doi: 10.4168/aair.2011.3.2.67

ENCOPRESIS

DEFINITION/ETIOLOGY:

Encopresis is defined as stool incontinence by a child of an age that should be able to control bowel movements, usually over 4 years old. Most cases are due to chronic constipation that results in the large intestine stretching and filling with stool. This is considered functional encopresis and 90% of cases fall into this category. The incontinence occurs as stool leaks around the impaction and it cannot be controlled by the child. The cause for encopresis is unclear but may be due to physiologic and/or psychological factors. Physiologic factors may include inadequate fluid intake, change in diet, lack of exercise, stress, and inappropriate use of laxatives. It may be seen with a change in routine such as the start of a school year, when access to the bathroom is more controlled, or the child is too busy playing to use the bathroom. It also may be secondary to an anal fissure causing painful bowel movement. Nonfunctional encopresis is less common and may be due to congenital anal strictures or bands, or Hirschprung's Disease (congenital megacolon) or other organic anomalies (rare). Psychological factors may include "withholding" stool due to excessively stringent and/or too early toilet training (less common) or other emotional problems. The child may be too young to be toilet trained; children between 3 and 5 often are not yet fully trained. Research supports that children with psychological disorders have a higher incidence of encopresis. Additionally, major life or family adjustment may be a factor as well as possible physical or sexual abuse.

Prevalence: Constipation is seen in 16-37% of school-aged children. Encopresis occurs in 4% of pre-school aged children, and 1-2% of school-aged children. In autistic children, the rate climbs to 10-20%.

SIGNS/SYMPTOMS:
- Fecal impaction with leaking of liquefied stool around impaction (most common)
- Fecal soiling of clothes
- Fecal odor
- Loss of appetite
- Abdominal pain
- Urinary symptoms: urinary tract infections, urine incontinence
- Sometimes anemia and/or under nutrition

EMOTIONAL/BEHAVIORAL FINDINGS:
- Student may be aggressive/disruptive or passive/withdrawn, depending on personality.
- Poor peer acceptance, scape-goating.
- Shame and lack of self-esteem. The rate of attention problems, obsession and compulsion, and oppositional behavior is high among frequently soiling children (Johnson et al., 2006).
- Often behaviors are secondary to the encopresis, and dissipate once the encopresis is resolved.

ENCOPRESIS *(continued from previous page)*

MANAGEMENT/TREATMENT:

1. Differentiate between staining of underpants with small amounts of stool and pants that contain a full-size bowel movement. Children with impaction show lesser amounts of stool.

2. Make change of clothing plus wash-up facilities available. Protect child's problem from other children as much as possible.

3. Disimpaction: Physician may prescribe 2-4 oz. mineral oil retention enema once a day for 24 days, or Fleet enemas may be used (or in combination). Suppositories may also be recommended.

4. Disimpaction is followed by mild laxatives (bulking agents as first choice, then osmotic laxatives such as Miralax®, then stimulants), bowel training, and increased fiber and fluids in diet. The school nurse should work with the parents/guardians, if possible, so that the enemas and laxatives do not "work" during school or school bus times.

5. Bowel training includes a toileting schedule encouraging the child to sit on the toilet for 10-15 minutes after each meal in a private, non-stressful environment.

6. Start school counseling and/or professional mental health counseling for help with associated emotional/behavioral problems.

7. Liaison with healthcare provider/medical facility to ensure that a digital rectal exam has been done (it is surprising how often this is overlooked, especially at mental health clinics).

8. Enlist parent or other person in home to assist with diet, prescribed laxatives, and regular bowel training. The home and school plan for times, rewards or behavioral techniques, appropriate foods, etc. should be jointly developed so that the school staff and family are consistent in their management.

COMPLICATIONS

- Child may experience ridicule or shame.
- Teachers may be disgusted or frustrated.
- Parents/guardians may experience guilt, anger, or frustration.
- Social, interpersonal, and family relations are at grave risk (Dunn, 2008).

FOLLOW UP:

- Maintain liaison with classroom and PE teacher, parents and doctor.
- Maintain toilet schedule at school that matches child's usual BM habits.

ENCOPRESIS *(continued from previous page)*

Resources

University of Virginia School of Medicine has a wealth of information on their website, including an extensive reference list.
http://www.medicine.virginia.edu/clinical/departments/pediatrics/clinical-services/tutorials/constipation/encopresis

Printable informational flyer for parents/guardians: http://www.gikids.org/files/documents/digestive%20topics/english/Constipation%20and%20fecal%20soiling.pdf

Books for children:
Clouds and Clocks: A Story for Children Who Soil, by Matthew Galvin
Everyone Poops, by T. Gomi

Websites for Children:

Are Your Bowels Moving? http://kidshealth.org/kid/stay_healthy/body/bowel.html
The Real Deal on the Digestive System http://kidshealth.org/kid/htbw/digestive_system.html

References

Boyse, K. (2008). *Encopresis (constipation and soiling)*. University of Michigan Health System. Retrieved from
http://www.med.umich.edu/yourchild/topics/encopre.htm

Dunn, A. (2008). Elimination patterns. In C. Burns, M. Brady, A. Dunn, N.B. Starr, C. Blosser(Eds.), *Pediatric primary care* (4th ed.) (pp. 257-261). St. Louis, MO: Saunders Elsevier.

Garman, K., & Ficca, M. (2012). Managing encopresis in the elementary school setting: The school nurse's role. *The Journal of School Nursing, 28*(3), 175-180. doi: 10.177/1059840511429685

Joinson, C., Heron, J., Butler, U., von Gontard, A., The Avon Longitudinal Study of Parents and Children Study Team. (2006). Psychological differences between children with and without soiling problems. *Pediatrics,117*(5),1575-1584. *doi: 10.1542/peds.2005-1773*

Rappaport, L., & Dunn, K. (2010). *Encopresis*. Boston Children's Hospital. Retrieved from
http://www.childrenshospital.org/az/Site835/mainpageS835P0.html

University of Virginia, School of Medicine. (2011). *About encopresis*. Retrieved from
http://www.medicine.virginia.edu/clinical/departments/pediatrics/clinical-services/tutorials/constipation/encopresis

ENURESIS

DEFINITION/ETIOLOGY:
Enuresis (involuntary urination) is repeated, spontaneous urinary voiding in clothes or in bed after the age when toilet training should be complete (usually age 5 years or under). Enuresis is typically diagnosed after the age of five. It does not usually indicate a physical or emotional problem. It is twice as common in boys. Enuresis usually takes the form of bed wetting.

CAUSES:
- Idiopathic hereditary type (primary nocturnal enuresis) is the most common cause of enuresis (if both parents had a history of enuresis, the rate of nocturnal enuresis found in children is approximately 80%
- Some children have unusually deep sleep patterns
- Child is too young to be toilet trained; children 3-5 need a bathroom in or near classroom
- Meatal stenosis in boys
- Boys with excessively long foreskin with poor hygiene
- Chronic urinary tract infection
- Small bladder capacity, irritable bladder, poor sphincter control, or other organic conditions
- Various emotional/psychological problems, including sexual abuse

SIGNS AND SYMPTOMS:
- Urine-stained and wet clothes
- Odor
- Urgency to void
- Bed wetting
- Emotional/behavioral problems, but not as pervasive or common as in children with encopresis
- Symptoms of chronic infection: poor nutritional status plus anemia, itching, foul odor, low-grade fever, stained underpants from constant dribbling, redness and/or impetigo in genital area
- Small caliber of urinary stream in boys with meatal stenosis
- Infection under an excessively long foreskin

MANAGEMENT/TREATMENT:
1. Bed wetting
   - Children may outgrow bed wetting without any intervention
   - Behavior modification with rewards may help
   - Bladder control training
   - Limiting fluids at bedtime alone does not appear to be effective
   - Alarm devices which wake child when the bed is wet – most effective long-term strategy

ENURESIS *(continued from previous page)*

- Healthcare provider may prescribe medication – drugs can decrease bed wetting; results are often not sustained after treatment is stopped
    - ✓ Oral desmopressin (DDAVP) along with limiting fluids reduces urine production in children with normal bladder capacity. (Side effect – DDAVP increases the potential for seizures)
    - ✓ Imipramine (Tofranil) may help increase bladder capacity **(rarely used).** (Caution – Tofranil overdose could be fatal; generally only prescribed when all other treatment modalities have failed)

2. At school:
    - Protect privacy of child's problem from other children.
    - Eliminate shame, guilt, or punishment.
    - Make toilet, washing, and change of clothing facilities available
    - Keep extra clothing at school.
    - Help child make pre-need trips to bathroom.
    - Liaison with parent/guardian(s) and healthcare provider as necessary. The healthcare provider may request a diary to understand the pattern of daytime urination and bowel movements, diet, etc.
    - Educate the child that, during sleep, his/her brain may not "hear" his/her full bladder's signal to help him/her understand the condition and how medication or other interventions (alarm) may help.

FOLLOW-UP:
- If prescribed, monitor for side effects of medication.
- Monitor for medical conditions – enuresis may be a symptom of a physical condition (diabetes mellitus, diabetes insipidus, sickle cell anemia, urethral obstruction, etc.).
- If indicated, refer to healthcare provider for further diagnostic workup.
- **RED FLAG** – enuresis could be a sign of sexual abuse; monitor; if indicated, report to child protective services per school and state guidelines.

POSSIBLE COMPLICATIONS:
- Contributes to poor self-esteem
- Disrupts family interactions
- May disrupt peer/social interactions

NOTES:
- Children with significant ADHD more likely to also be enuretic (at night).

ENURESIS *(continued from previous page)*

References

John, R. & Chewey, L. (2013). Common complaints. In J. Selekman (Ed.), *School nursing: A comprehensive text* (2nd ed.) (pp. 578-640). Philadelphia, PA: F. A. Davis.

Mayo Clinic. (2011). *Bed-wetting.* Retrieved from http://www.mayoclinic.com/health/bed-wetting/DS00611

Merck Manual. (2013). *Urinary incontinence in children.* Retrieved from http://www.merckmanuals.com/professional/ pediatrics/incontinence_in_children/urinary_incontinence_in_children.html?qt=enuresis&alt=sh

ENVIRONMENTAL HEALTH

DEFINITION/ETIOLOGY:

Environmental health is a division of public health that addresses how physical, chemical and biological factors affect a person's health. Examples of environmental exposures that a child might encounter in the school setting include: poor indoor air quality, chemical exposure (secondary to pest management, cleaning products, etc.), injuries/death due to building code violations, playground injuries, air pollutants (such as exhaust fumes), heating and cooling ventilation, etc.

Environment-related diseases affect a child's current and future health and potentially the child's academic success.

Children are more vulnerable to environmental exposures and usually suffer more harm from exposure to these toxic substances than adults due to physiological, metabolic and behavioral differences.

Environmental toxin exposure has been linked to the following:
- Asthma (allergens/pesticides/pollutants/poor indoor air quality/ventilation, etc.)
- Lead poisoning—cognitive deficits, aggressive behaviors, learning disabilities, hearing problems, headaches, ADHD symptoms
- Birth defects secondary to mother's exposure to environmental toxicants (mercury, PCBs, pesticides)
- Childhood cancer (pesticides)

MANAGEMENT:
Create a healthier environment:
1. Implement and enforce "no idling" of bus and car engines while waiting to pick up children.
2. Maintain school grounds (cut grass) after school hours.
3. Clean school buildings with "green cleaners".
4. Inspect air and water quality routinely.
    a. Change furnace filters every 3 months.
5. Maintain adequate lighting and ventilation in classrooms/buildings.
6. Minimize the use of fragrances (perfumes/air fresheners).
7. Reduce indoor allergens.
    a. Minimally, vacuum classroom carpets weekly with vacuum cleaner equipped with high-efficiency particulate air (HEPA) filter.
    b. Steam clean carpets every 8 weeks.
8. Avoid classroom pets.

ENVIRONMENTAL HEALTH *(continued from previous page)*

9. Inspect and maintain playground structures to promote safety and minimize injuries.
10. Consider using organic lawn products.
11. Pest prevention – improve school sanitary conditions to avoid insect infestation.
12. Minimize the use of chemical pesticides.
    a. Pesticide application – as a last resort use least toxic pesticide.
    b. Many states require school districts to notify parents/guardians prior to pesticide application.
    c. Post signs notifying parents/guardians of upcoming pesticide application.
    d. Students/staff should not be allowed into the building within 2 hours of pest extermination; follow product health warnings.

FOLLOW-UP:
Role of the school nurse:
- Be alert to maintenance (building and playground) concerns that could be contributing to environmental health issues; notify appropriate staff regarding potential issues.
- Track and identify building trends in health problems that may be linked to environmental toxins.
- Participate in school committees that advocate for reducing exposures to environmental contaminants.
- Advocate for moderation in the use of fragrances; may need to intervene if odors become too strong.

POTENTIAL COMPLICATIONS:
- Lead poisoning: cognitive impairment
- Asthma/allergies: respiratory distress/death
- Cancer/death

Notes:
Children living in poverty are especially vulnerable to environmental toxic exposures. Pollutants, such as lead (paint chips, lead dust, etc.), molds, pollution (commerce, diesel exhaust, etc.) are more prevalent in lower socioeconomic communities. They may lack the resources and finances needed to reduce their child's exposure to the toxins. The school nurse may need to act as a liaison between the school, community, and healthcare provider to meet the health needs of the most vulnerable.

ENVIRONMENTAL HEALTH *(continued from previous page)*

References

Children's Environmental Health Network. (2012). *Educational brief on children's environmental health.* Retrieved from http://www.cehn.org/files/EducationalBriefonChildrensEnvironmentalHealth1112.pdf

Environmental Protection Agency. (2010). *How does indoor air quality impact student health and academic performance.* Retrieved from http://www.epa.gov/iaq/schools/pdf/student_performance_findings.pdf

Institute of Medicine. (2011). *Climate change, the indoor environment, and health.* Retrieved from http://www.iom.edu/Reports/2011/Climate-Change-the-Indoor-Environment-and-Health.aspx

National Association of School Nurses [NASN]. (2012). *Environmental health concerns in the school setting.* Retrieved from http://www.nasn.org/Portals/0/briefs/2012briefenvironmental.pdf

Owens, K. (2009). *Pesticides and you.* Retrieved from http://www.beyondpesticides.org/schools/publications/Schooling2010.pdf

Proctor, S. (2013). Standards of practice. In J. Selekman (Ed.), *School nursing: A comprehensive text* (2nd ed.) (pp. 48-78). Philadelphia, PA: F. A. Davis.

U.S. Environmental Protection Agency. (2012). *Diesel school buses.* Retrieved from http://cfpub.epa.gov/schools/top_sub.cfm?t_id=37&s_id=38

EYE TRAUMA

DEFINITION/ETIOLOGY:
Eye injuries in children commonly result from sport injuries or projectiles. Baseball is the leading cause of sports-related injuries. Facial injuries often accompany eye trauma.

Chemical burns to the eye are ophthalmologic emergencies and must be referred for immediate emergency care.

Corneal abrasion may result from a direct contact injury, contact lens, or a foreign body with or without penetration.

Foreign Body injuries to the eye may present as either non-penetrating or penetrating. Penetrating injuries are ophthalmologic emergencies and must be referred for immediate emergency care.

SIGNS AND SYMPTOMS:

ASSESSMENT
- Obtain history and nature of physical injury or chemical exposure.
- Assess visual acuity first by using Snellen Chart or "E" test (preschool children). Each eye should be checked individually. The only exception is an acute chemical exposure/injury that requires immediate irrigation (flush with water).
- If student is unable to open eye, do not force.
- Check for visible contusion/lacerations on lids or eye ball.
- Check for blood in anterior chamber (between iris and cornea), called "hyphema".
- Check extra-ocular movements.
- Check for double vision (diplopia).
- Check for unequal or irregular pupils.

MANAGEMENT/TREATMENT:
Emergency referral to primary care provider:
- All cases with chemical burn after irrigation with copious amount of water or saline.
- Impaired vision in any way.
- Painful eye or feels like a foreign object.
- Contusion or laceration on eyelid or eyeball.
- Red eye persists for more than one hour (suggests corneal abrasion or foreign object).

EYE TRAUMA *(continued from previous page)*

Eye trauma without above symptoms:

- Small abrasion or laceration of skin around the eye- without other symptoms- can be washed and left uncovered.
- Red spot limited to the sclera (white of the eye) is related to coughing or vomiting (subconjunctival hemorrhage will resolve spontaneously).
- Cold pack may be useful for minor trauma if primary care provider referral is not necessary.
- Avoid using any eye drops or ointments. Ophthalmic corticosteroids are contraindicated, as they tend to promote growth of fungi and reactivate herpes simplex virus.

Chemical Burn

Ophthalmic burns to the cornea and conjunctiva are an **ophthalmic emergency** and treatment should begin immediately. The eye will be painful, sensitive to light (photophobic) and exhibit excessive tearing (lacrimation).

1. Determine chemical if possible. Alkali burns are generally worse than acid burns. Send available chemical (name of chemical and ph) information with student to emergency treatment center.
2. *Immediately,* flush/irrigate eye with copious amounts of water or saline solution while both eyelids are held open. If only one eye has been exposed to the chemical, attempt to irrigate the eye with the person lying on his/her side. If possible, pour water from the inner corner flowing toward the outer corner.
3. Notify parent/guardian.
4. Refer for emergency medical treatment. Eye should be examined by an ophthalmologist as soon as possible, no longer than 24 hours after exposure.
5. Cool compress to the surrounding area may provide comfort.

Corneal Abrasion

The eye will be painful, sensitive to light (photophobic) and exhibit excessive tearing (lacrimation).

1. Remove contact lens, if present.
2. Examine the eye for the presence of a foreign body. The absence of a *visible* foreign body does not negate the presence of or irritation from a foreign body.
3. Notify parent/guardian.
4. Refer to ophthalmologist for evaluation and necessary treatment.
5. To minimize eye movement, patch <u>both</u> eyes with 4x4 gauze pads prior to travel to primary care provider or ophthalmologist.

EYE TRAUMA *(continued from previous page)*

Foreign Body (non-penetrating)
The eye will be painful, sensitive to light (photophobic), exhibit excessive tearing (lacrimation), and have the sensation of a foreign body presence in the eye.
1. Remove contact lens, if present.
2. Examine the eye for the presence of a foreign body. It may be necessary to invert the upper lid to see the presence of a foreign body.
3. If foreign body (speck of dirt, sand, eyelash, etc.) is obvious, try to remove it with moistened cotton tipped applicator, flushing the lid. Have the student blink several times while the eye is immersed in water (as if opening eyes while swimming under water), or by "sweeping" the upper lid over the lower lid. Pull the upper lid out and down over the lower lid. As the upper lid moves back into position, the lower lid and tears may remove the foreign object.
4. If these attempts and maneuvers fail, notify parents/guardians and refer to the primary care provider.
5. To minimize eye movement, patch <u>both</u> eyes with 4x4 gauze pads prior to travel to primary care provider or ophthalmologist.

Foreign Body (penetrating)
The patient will experience intense pain, sensitivity to light (photophobic) and exhibit excessive tearing (lacrimation). You may be able to visualize the penetrating object. **Penetrating injuries are ophthalmologic emergencies**. Make no attempt to remove the object or flush the eye.
- Cover the injured eye with an eye shield or small paper cup. Anchor in place. Patch other eye to minimize eye movement.
- Notify parent/guardian.
- Refer to emergency medical center or ophthalmologist for *immediate* care.

FOLLOW UP:
- If student returned to class, re-examine eye later that day and on the following day. Continue to monitor for pain and infection.
- For eye trauma without emergency symptoms, re-check visual acuity the 3-4 days after treatment and refer to primary care provider if there is difference from prior screening.
- Implement primary care provider's instructions for care after initial evaluation and treatment.
- Primary care provider may recommend not wearing contact lens for a few days following eye trauma requiring emergency care. This may have implications for reading and classroom work.

EYE TRAUMA (*continued from previous page*)

NOTES:
Prevention
Stress the importance of wearing protective eyewear when participating in contact and ball sports, working with metal and glass projects, hammering metal on metal, and handling chemicals.

References
American Academy of Ophthalmology. (2013). *Clinical statement: Protective eyewear for young athletes.* Retrieved from
http://one.aao.org/CE/PracticeGuidelines/ClinicalStatements_Content.aspx?cid=1fda605b-97b9-47e3-90d1-11b7a9607797

Blosser, C. (2008). Eye disorders. In C. Burns, M. Brady, A. Dunn, N.B. Starr, & C. Blosser (Eds.), *Pediatric primary care, (4th ed.)* (pp. 698-702). St. Louis, MO: Saunders Elsevier.

Merck Manual, Professional Edition. (2012). *Corneal abrasions & foreign bodies. (2012).* Retrieved from
http://www.merckmanuals.com/professional/injuries_poisoning/eye_trauma/
corneal_abrasions_and_foreign_bodies.html?qt=corneal%20abrasions&alt=sh

Merck Manual, Professional Edition. *(2012). Ocular burns.* Retrieved from
http://www.merckmanuals.com/professional/injuries_poisoning/eye_trauma/ocular_burns.html

FAINTING (Syncope)

DEFINITION/ETIOLOGY:

Syncope is a brief, partial or complete loss of consciousness due to diminished oxygen supply to the brain. It may be caused by low blood sugar, standing in place for a long time, headache, seizure, drugs, depression or panic attack or may be as a result of more serious situation such as head injury or an underlying condition such as heart disease/complications.

In children and adolescents most episodes of syncope are benign and most commonly result from vaso-vagal episodes. These are commonly precipitated by trigger events such as unpleasant sights or smells, anxiety, anticipated pain or fear.

Orthostatic hypotension is also a common cause of syncope. This occurs when the child stands and there is a transient increase in the heart rate and inadequate cerebral perfusion resulting in low blood pressure. Dehydration may also be a contributing cause.

Although rare, syncope may be due to cardiac disease such as dysrhythmias or valvular disease. Syncope due to cardiac disease may present on exertion and with generalized weakness and pallor. If an arrhythmia occurs the child often presents with a brief loss of consciousness, palpitations and no warning.

SIGNS/SYMPTOMS:
- Loss of consciousness may be preceded by pale, cool, wet skin, lightheadedness, nausea, frequent yawn, and/or restless feeling.
- Loss of consciousness.
- As person begins to lose consciousness, they may have a brief eye roll and/or body twitching.
- Fainting related to hyperventilation is often accompanied by numbness around the mouth and fingers.
- How fainting may be different from a seizure:
  - Fainters usually know when it is going to happen.
  - Seizures occur with no warning except occasional aura.
  - Seizure twitching is more severe and lasts longer.
  - Post seizure sleep is longer and deeper.
  - Fainters usually remember what happened after they wake up.

MANAGEMENT/TREATMENT:
1. If observe person about to faint, instruct them to lie down to prevent falling.
2. Help ease person to floor or reclining position.
3. Place person on back with no pillow and elevate feet 8 to 12 inches to encourage blood flow to head.

FAINTING (Syncope) *(continued from previous page)*

4. Roll person to side if they vomit.
5. As person awakens, do not allow them to stand immediately (be prepared to have person resume reclining position if dizzy).
6. If person does not awaken within 1-2 minutes, <u>seek immediate medical attention</u>. Prepare for possibility of CPR.
7. If fainting is as a result of head injury<u>, seek immediate medical care</u>.
8. If person is known to have diabetes, proceed with diabetes emergency action plan.
9. Refer to the physician to rule out serious cause of syncope.

FOLLOW UP:
- Determine history of fainting and if applicable, results of past medical evaluation for fainting.
- If prior evaluation determined no cause or need for medical intervention, educate frequent fainters about safety; when experiencing warning symptoms, sit down in a chair, position head between knees close to floor. If they are embarrassed to do this in public, they can pretend to remove something from their shoe. Educate students with postural hypotension about getting up slowly.

NOTE:
Inhaling ammonia or amyl nitrite is **not** recommended.

References
American College of Emergency Physicians Foundation. (n.d.) *Fainting*. Retrieved from
   http://www.emergencycareforyou.org/EmergencyManual/WhatToDoInMedicalEmergency/Default.aspx?id=240

Mayo Clinic. (2013). *Vasovagal syncope*. Retrieved from
   http://www.mayoclinic.com/health/vasovagal-syncope/DS00806/DSECTION=symptoms

FEVER

DEFINITION/ETIOLOGY:
Fever is a physiological response to inflammation or an infection which probably helps the body's defense mechanism. Fever is one of the body's responses to illness or injury, but it can also be a result from heat exposure. Fever is not always cause for alarm, but sometimes it is a sign of a serious problem.

Fever can improve the immune response at lower temperatures and impair some microorganisms and viruses. However, fever can be uncomfortable, dehydrate, and stress the cardio-respiratory system. An oral temperature of over 100.4 degrees Fahrenheit is considered a fever.

SIGNS/SYMPTOMS:
- May feel cold or shiver with an elevated temperature.
- May have signs and symptoms of infectious disease such as cough, diarrhea, vomiting, general weakness and muscle ache.
- Skin may feel sensitive to touch; described as "prickly".
- Eyes may appear glassy.
- Face may be flushed.
- Skin will be warm to touch.
- Dehydration with extended increased temperature.
- There is generally an increase of 10 pulse beats for every degree of fever and respirations increase 4 breaths per minute per degree.

MANAGEMENT/TREATMENT:
1. Assess vital signs.
2. Ensure accurate temperature reading; wait several minutes to take temperature if student has been out in cold or if has just consumed hot or cold liquid.
3. Provide comfort measures; cool compress on the forehead.
4. Remove extra outer clothing (but not to point to create shivering which will increase temperature).
5. Give fluids to drink.
6. Assess for signs of infectious disease and use social distancing.
7. Follow school exclusion policies for elevated temperature.
8. Fever that causes enough discomfort to need medication probably indicates that the student should not be in school.
9. Follow school policy regarding over-the-counter (OTC) medications. Since a low grade fever may be beneficial, withhold acetaminophen unless physician/nurse practitioner orders.

FEVER *(continued from previous page)*

10. Recheck the student's temperature 30-60 minutes after giving medication and note if medication was effective.

NOTES:
- Children with fever, headache, neck stiffness and petechiae or purpura may have significant illness and should be evaluated by a healthcare provider.
- Children with fever that are lethargic, unusually drowsy, altered level of consciousness, or extremely pale or cyanotic should be evaluated by a healthcare provider.
- Never give aspirin to a child or teen under 19 during episodes of fever-causing illnesses as aspirin has been linked to the life-threatening disorder Reye's syndrome.
- Some children are prone to seizures from a high fever.
- Children should be fever free for 24 hours before returning to school.

References

Blosser, C.G., Brady, M. & Muller, W. (2008). Infectious diseases and immunizations. In C. Burns, M. Brady, A. Dunn, N.B. Starr, C. Blosser (Eds.), *Pediatric primary care* (4th ed.) (pp. 539-542). St. Louis, MO: Saunders Elsevier.

John, R. & Chewey, L. (2013). Common complaints. In J. Selekman (Ed.), *School nursing: A comprehensive text (2nd ed.)* (pp. 580-582). Philadelphia, PA: F. A. Davis.

Mayo Clinic. (2011). *Fever.* Retrieved from http://www.mayoclinic.com/health/fever/DS00077

Subbarao, I., Lyznicki, J., & James, J.(Eds.). (2009). *AMA Handbook of First Aid and Emergency Care.* New York: Random House.

The Merck Manuals: The Merck Manual for Healthcare Professionals. (2012). *Fever.* Retrieved from http://www.merckmanuals.com/professional/infectious_diseases/biology_of_infectious_disease/fever.html

FIFTH DISEASE (Erythema Infectiosum)

DEFINITION/ETIOLOGY:
"Fifth Disease" is named that because it was identified after rubeola, rubella, scarlet fever, and roseola. It is caused by Human Parvovirus (*parvovirus B19*)—related to, but not the same as dog parvovirus. It is a common viral infection and occurs in preschool and school aged children. Transmission or spread is by droplets from respiratory secretions or secondarily by hands before the rash appears. About 50% of adults have had the disease as children and thus are immune. The incubation period is 4-14 days but can be as long as 21 days. Rash symptoms occur 1-3 weeks after infection.

SIGNS AND SYMPTOMS:
- About a week after exposure, the patient may develop a low grade fever, headache, cold symptoms and or muscle aches which may last 5-7 days, after which the child recovers with no other symptoms.
- About 1-3 weeks after the fever goes away, a distinctive rash may appear. The rash has a slapped cheek appearance and a faint, lacy rash on the trunk, arms and legs may develop about 1 day later.
- Adults, especially women, may have joint pain and swelling at this stage. The rash fades in 1-2 weeks but may recur for several weeks brought on by exposure to sunlight, heat, exercise, or stress.
- Often there is neither fever nor rash with this disease (sub-clinical form).

MANAGEMENT AND TREATMENT:
1. The most contagious period is just before onset of fever, gradually declining during the next week and low to absent by the time the rash appears. An outbreak of this disease often occurs in late winter and spring. Therefore Fifth Disease may be suspected in the pre-rash, infective stage, if it has occurred in other family members. Transmission of Fifth Disease is enhanced by household contact. A susceptible parent/guardian has a 50% chance of catching the disease from their child. In contrast, during an extensive school outbreak, about 20% of susceptible teachers may develop the infection.
2. Children with the rash of Fifth Disease do not need to be isolated because they are *no longer contagious by the time the rash appears.*
3. Pregnant women who become infected in the *first 4-5 months are at a risk of spontaneous abortion.*
4. Available data suggest that a susceptible woman exposed to her own infected child during the first 20 weeks of pregnancy runs an increased risk (about 1-2%) of having a spontaneous abortion.
5. If the exposure is at school or another job site, the risk is lower because of less intimate contact.

FIFTH DISEASE (Erythema Infectiosum) *(continued from previous page)*

6. Hand washing and proper tissue disposal should be scrupulously practiced.
7. Encourage pregnant family members and staff that expect to have contact with children in school to consult with their health professional about their risk for infection. A blood test to determine if they are already immune may help to alleviate their concern.
8. No treatment is usually required.

POTENTIAL COMPLICATIONS:

- Children with unusual long-term blood disease such as sickle cell anemia, immunodeficiency, etc. need special consideration.
- *Exposed pregnant women need advice from their doctor or an infectious disease specialist.*
- Testing for susceptibility may be available.
- Teachers and day care workers are at increased risk of exposure, but a routine policy of exclusion of pregnant women from these work places is not recommended.

References

American Academy of Pediatrics. (2009). Summaries of infectious disease – parvovirus B19. In L. K. Pickering, C. J. Baker, D. W. Kimberlin, & S. S. Long (Eds.), *Red Book: 2009 report of the committee on infectious diseases,*(28th ed.) (pp. 491-493). American Academy of Pediatrics: Elk Grove Village, IL.

American Academy of Pediatrics. (2013). Fifth disease (human parvovirus B19). In S. Aronson, & T. Shope (Eds.), *Managing infectious diseases in child care and schools (2nd ed.)* (pp. 93-94). Elk Grove Village, IL: American Academy of Pediatrics.

Medline Plus. U.S. National Library of Medicine. (2013a). *Fifth disease.* Retrieved from http://www.nlm.nih.gov/medlineplus/ency/article/000977.htm

Medline Plus. U.S National Library of Medicine. (2013b). *Fifth disease.* Retrieved from http://www.nlm.nih.gov/medlineplus/fifthdisease.html#cat59

National Center for Immunization and Respiratory Disease, CDC. (2012).*Parvovirus B19 (fifth disease) fact sheet.* Retrieved from http://www.cdc.gov/ncidod/dvrd/revb/respiratory/parvo_b19.htm

FOOD ALLERGY (Also see Allergies and Anaphylaxis)

DEFINITION/ETIOLOGY:

A food allergy is an exaggerated immune system response to any food (most commonly milk, eggs, peanuts, tree nuts, soy, wheat, fish, and shellfish, or some other specific food). Food intolerance is an adverse reaction to certain foods but which does not involve the immune system. In a true food allergy, the immune system reacts to exposure to a certain food. An allergic antibody called Immunoglobulin E (IgE), found in people with allergies, causes this. Food allergies may develop at any time, even after eating the food repeatedly in the past without having problems. Symptoms may occur after that allergic individual consumes or is exposed to even a small amount of the food.

SIGNS AND SYMPTOMS:
- Hives on any part of the body
- Rash
- Vomiting, diarrhea and abdominal cramping
- Wheezing, coughing and shortness of breath - an emergency
- Anaphylaxis - a life threatening blockage of the airway and in severe cases can cause shock

Anaphylaxis signs & symptoms can include:
- Uneasiness and agitation
- Facial flushing
- Rapid pulse, palpitations, thready or unobtainable pulse
- Generalized itching/tingling/rash
- Swelling of face, lips, tongue, and/or eyelids
- Blue or gray color around the lips or nail beds
- Dizziness
- Throbbing in the ears
- Difficulty breathing, coughing and/or wheezing
- Nausea, vomiting
- Fall in blood pressure
- Fainting, unresponsiveness

Not ALL signs and symptoms need be present in anaphylaxis.

Please note: Symptoms of anaphylaxis may appear within 1 to 15 minutes and progress rapidly. In some cases, the severe reaction may be delayed. Although most serious reactions occur within the first hour of contact with the allergen, anaphylaxis has been known to occur up to several hours later. Severe allergic reactions may be a precursor to anaphylaxis.

FOOD ALLERGY (*continued from previous page*)

MANAGEMENT/TREATMENT:

Most allergic reactions are not severe enough to cause anaphylaxis. Intervention may not be necessary unless the student develops one of the following. <u>Follow local school policy and procedures.</u>

1. Rash: over-the-counter or prescribed steroid topical cream or ointment usually relieve rash.
2. Hives: over-the-counter antihistamines or decongestants provide relief; possibly prescription Cromolyn or corticosteroid nasal spray.
3. Vomiting, diarrhea: offer small sips of water, avoid dehydration.
4. Wheezing, coughing or shortness of breath: anti-inflammatory and bronchodilator medications for reactive airway.
5. Anaphylaxis: adrenalin (epinephrine) medication injected as quickly as possible, followed by **immediate call to 911** and transport to a hospital emergency department. (Despite initial improvement after first injectable epinephrine (adrenalin), symptoms often recur).
6. A copy of the child/youth's record should be sent with the emergency medical services (EMS) and should include:
   - Allergen to which child/youth is reacting, if known
   - Signs and symptoms of distress
   - Emergency measures instituted
   - Child/youth's response to emergency measures
   - Time of all activities, including giving injectable epinephrine (adrenalin)
   - Signature of nurse and phone number
7. **If student is still at school in 15-20 minutes, repeat dose of injectable epinephrine (adrenalin).** (Plans need to be made in advance with parents/guardians for 2 doses of injectable epinephrine (adrenalin) to be in place if school does not stock injectable epinephrine (adrenalin).)
8. Monitor blood pressure. Elevate legs if blood pressure is low.
9. Cover with blankets if necessary to keep warm; don't allow blankets to interfere with handling or observation.
10. Notify parents/guardians and physician.

FOLLOW UP:

- Avoid contact and exposure to foods which trigger allergic reactions.
- Develop an **Individual Healthcare Plan** with input from the physician and family that includes specific actions to prevent exposure, staff training, and the emergency action plan with individualized orders.
- Assess the student's classroom and school for possible environmental triggers that may cause allergic reactions.
- Environmental controls to avoid the symptoms that cause allergic reactions.
- Suggest to parent/guardian that child wear a Medic Alert bracelet or tag.

FOOD ALLERGY (*continued from previous page*)

- If injectable epinephrine (adrenalin) is ordered, suggest student keep the product/device at hand at all times and replace if expired or used.

NOTES:
Controlling Food Allergies

Food allergy reactions and life-threatening anaphylaxis may occur at school or during school-sponsored activities. The risk of accidental exposure to trigger foods can be reduced in the school setting if schools communicate with students, parents, and physicians to minimize risks and provide a safe educational environment for food-allergic students. Schools need to ensure that:

1. Staff (i.e., teachers, cafeteria personnel, lunch and bus monitors) and parent/guardian are educated about food allergies and preventive measures, e.g., checking food and container labels;
2. Individual healthcare plans are developed for students known to have a food allergy; and
3. There is immediate access to emergency medications, including epinephrine, and local emergency medical services.

Resources

The Food Allergy Research & Education (FARE) has an extensive website with tools and resources for schools including sample action plans at: http://www.foodallergy.org

FARE's School Food Allergy Program (SFAP) is a comprehensive multimedia educational resource that includes the Safe@School® training presentation component. The program can assist schools in developing a food allergy management policy. Call: 800/929-4040 or email store@foodallergy.org.

References

American Academy of Allergy, Asthma & Immunology. (2101). *Anaphylaxis in schools and other child-care settings: Position Statement.* Retrieved from http://www.aaaai.org/Aaaai/media/MediaLibrary/PDF%20Documents/ Practice%20and%20Parameters/AAP-managing-food-allergy-in-schools-2010.pdf

Dunn, A. (2008). Nutrition. In C. Burns, M. Brady, A. Dunn, N.B. Starr, C. Blosser (Eds.), *Pediatric primary* care (4th ed.) (pp. 224-228). St. Louis, MO: Saunders Elsevier.

Food Allergy Research & Education (FARE) (n.d.). *Food allergy action plan.* (2013). Retrieved from http://www.foodallergy.org/faap

Food Allergy Research & Education (FARE). (2013).*Managing students with food allergy during a shelter in place emergency.* Retrieved from http://www.foodallergy.org/managing-food-allergies/at-school/shelter-in-place

Hogate, S., Giel, J. & Selekman, J. (2013). Allergy. In J. Selekman (Ed.), *School nursing: A comprehensive text* (2nd ed.) (pp. 784-838). Philadelphia, PA: F.A. Davis.

National Association of School Nurses. (2012*). Allergy/anaphylaxis management in the school setting: Position statement.* Retrieved from http://www.nasn.org/PolicyAdvocacy/PositionPapersandReports/NASNPositionStatementsFullView/ tabid/462/ArticleId/9/Allergy-Anaphylaxis-Management-in-the-School-Setting-Revised-June-2012

FOODBORNE ILLNESS

DEFINITION/ETIOLOGY:
Foodborne Illness (food poisoning) is an illness that results from consuming or handling contaminated food or beverages. Foodborne illnesses are associated with the lack of adequate knowledge regarding food preparation, storage, hygiene and increasing amounts, and types of imported foods.

NOTIFICATION
It is important to have established criteria with the local or state health department about when and how they are to be involved if a foodborne illness is known or suspected. Many such illnesses are reportable not only to the local or state department of health but also to the Centers for Disease Control. It is important to involve the health department almost immediately because of the actions they can take to identify whether or not the illness is indeed foodborne and to prevent further spread of the outbreak.

CAUSE
Foodborne illness arises from the ingestion of food that is contaminated with bacteria, viruses, parasites, or chemicals both natural and manufactured. An outbreak is generally defined by the Centers for Disease Control and Prevention (CDC) as "an incident in which two or more persons experience a similar illness after ingesting a common food, which epidemiologic analysis implicates as the source of the illness".

Outbreaks have been associated with consumption of cold foods, including salads, sandwiches and bakery products. Liquid items (e.g., salad dressings or cake icing) that allow a virus to mix evenly have also been implicated in outbreaks. Food can be contaminated at its source (e.g., oysters harvested from contaminated waters have been associated with widespread outbreaks). Rough, wet, uncooked foods and contaminated produce are at highest risk of transmission of norovirus. Most foodborne outbreaks of norovirus illness arise from direct contamination of food by a food handler immediately before the food is eaten.

Top Five Pathogens Causing Foodborne Illness	Top Five Pathogens Causing Hospitalization	Top Five Pathogens Causing Death
Norovirus	Salmonella nontyphoidal	Salmonella, non typhoidal
Salmonella	Norovirus	Toxoplasma gondii
Clostridium perfringens	Campylobacter	Listeria monocytogenes
Campylobacter	Toxoplasma gondii	Norovirus
Staphylococcus	E.coli	Campylobacter

(CDC 2011)

FOODBORNE ILLNESS *(continued from previous page)*

SIGNS AND SYMPTOMS:
- History of exposure to suspect food
- Frequent vomiting
- Often abdominal pain
- Hyperactive bowel sounds
- Diarrhea may be present after the onset of vomiting
- Little or no fever
- Chills
- Dehydration
- Depend on the type and amount of the source
- Last for a few hours to several days
- Range from mild to severe and death

MANAGEMENT AND TREATMENT:
1. Report cluster of cases to health department; they will usually:
    a. Investigate food source (possible cultures)
    b. Interview individuals (possible stool cultures)
    c. Inspect food preparation area and handlers
2. Refer individuals to physician/healthcare provider or emergency room (some students may require hospitalization; others merely antibiotics for treatment)
3. Replace fluids and electrolytes

FOLLOW UP:
- Obtain results of any cultures taken and determine from treating physician/healthcare provider if any student returning to school might pose a threat to others (e.g., carrier state of Salmonella)
- Monitor student's state of hydration, temperature and general status
- Report relapses and new cases to health department
- Additional information for student/family education can be found at CDC (www.cdc.gov), National Food Safety Program (www.foodsafety.gov) which hosts National Food Safety Education Month (September) and the Food and Drug Administration (http://www.fightbac.org/)

POTENTIAL COMPLICATIONS:
- Dehydration
- Hemolytic uremic syndrome (rare - affects children under 10 years old)
- Thrombotic purpura

FOODBORNE ILLNESS *(continued from previous page)*

NOTES:
- Children are at greatest risk for diarrhea and dehydration when exposed to foodborne illness.
- The food handler is the most common source of food contamination (this includes volunteers who conduct food events at school).

PREVENTION:
- Hand washing by food handlers is the single most effective means of minimizing foodborne illness transmission.
- Follow recommended or required techniques for food storage, preparation, and holding (hot or cold, covered, etc.).
- Sanitize food preparation and serving areas and of items used to prepare and serve food.
- Most food if properly cooked/heated is rendered harmless (temperature depends on the type of food).
- Avoid cross contamination by separating foods.
- Refrigerate food promptly.
- Uncooked foods such as salads require the greatest care with preparation because *E. coli*, norovirus and hepatitis A can be transmitted.
- Sometimes food suppliers are the source of contamination (eggs, poultry, ground meat, instant mashed potatoes).

Resources

Diagnosis and Management of Foodborne Illnesses – A Primer for Physicians and Other Healthcare Provider at http://www.cdc.gov/mmwr/preview/mmwrhtml/rr5304a1.htm

References

Ball, J., Binder, R., & Cowen, K. (Eds.). (2012). Child and adolescent nutrition. *Principles of Pediatric Nursing: Caring for Children (5th ed.)* (pp. 349, 353). Upper Saddle River, NJ: Pearson Education, Inc.

Centers for Disease Control. (2011). *Food safety*. Retrieved from http://www.cdc.gov/foodsafety/facts.html

Medline Plus, U.S. National Library of Medicine. (2013). *Foodborne illness*. Retrieved from http://www.nlm.nih.gov/medlineplus/foodborneillness.html

National Digestive Diseases Information Clearinghouse. (2012). *Foodborne illness*. Retrieved from http://digestive.niddk.nih.gov/ddiseases/pubs/bacteria/#1

National Institute of Allergy and Infectious Disease. (2012). Foodborne *diseases*. Retrieved from http://www.niaid.nih.gov/topics/foodborne/Pages/Default.aspx

U.S. Department of health and Human services. (2013). *Food poisoning*. Retrieved from http://www.foodsafety.gov/poisoning/index.html

U.S. Food and Drug Administration. (2013). *What you should know about government response to foodborne illness outbreaks*. Retrieved from http://www.fda.gov/Food/RecallsOutbreaksEmergencies/Outbreaks/ucm180323.htm

FOREIGN BODIES: Eye, Ear (including earwax), Nose

DEFINITION/ETIOLOGY:
It is not uncommon for children to present with a foreign body in the eye, ear, or nose. A variety of inanimate objects and vegetable materials can get in the ear and nose. Environmental materials such as dust, dirt, sand, and insects can also get in the eyes, ears, and nose. Children less than three years old are more likely to put objects in their noses, and children under eight years are more likely to put things in their ears.

SIGNS AND SYMPTOMS:
- *Eye:* pain, tearing, irritation, inflammation.
- *Ear:* usually no discomfort. Child reports something in ear.
- *Nose:* Usually no symptoms at first. Child may report having put something in nose. After few days, a unilateral sero-purulent foul-smelling discharge.

MANAGEMENT/TREATMENT:
EYE (see also Eye Trauma)
1. Never remove an intraocular foreign body or if history indicates there was a projectile object involved. Refer immediately to ophthalmologist.
2. Pull down lower lid with tip of index finger. If foreign body can be seen in the sac of the lower lid, remove with a moistened cotton-tipped applicator.
3. If not successful after 1-2 attempts or if foreign body is in any other location, refer to primary care provider.
4. To minimize eye movement, patch <u>both</u> eyes with 4x4 gauze pads prior to travel to primary care provider or ophthalmologist.

Minor irritation from foreign object, e.g., glitter, sand in eye:
1. Fill paper cup to brim with tap water.
2. Have student position irritated eye in water, look into cup, and blink eye, much like opening eyes in swimming pool. *Or*
3. Flush eye at eyewash station or with hand held eyewash bottle.

EAR
1. ***Do not*** *try to remove unless foreign body can be easily seen and grasped with forceps or fingers. Frequently swabs, forceps, and fingers push the object farther into the ear canal.*
2. If the object is an insect, do not attempt to examine with an otoscope as the light may irritate the insect causing it to move and creating discomfort for the student. Take the student into a dark room and shine a flashlight into the ear and the insect may crawl toward the light and out of the ear canal.
3. If policy/protocol permits and with parent/guardian's permission, ear wax may be treated by instilling mineral oil into ear and after 10 minutes turn onto affected side and allow to drain.
4. If these attempts are not successful, refer to primary care provider.

FOREIGN BODIES: Eye, Ear (including earwax), Nose *(continued from previous page)*

NOSE

1. Try having child blow nose forcibly while holding the unaffected nostril shut.
2. ***Do not*** *attempt to remove object unless object can be seen and can be grasped with forceps or fingers.*
3. While removing visible object, press the nose above the object so you cannot push it farther in.
4. Refer to primary care provider if unsuccessful.

FOLLOW UP:

1. *Eye:* Ask teacher to report any further symptoms. Recheck visual acuity 3-4 days after treatment.
2. *Ear:* No follow up if object has been removed.
3. *Nose:* None if object removed. Check for cessation of nasal discharge.

Also see School Nurse Guideline – Eye Trauma.

References

Eyes:

Blosser, C. (2008). Eye disorders. In C. Burns, M. Brady, A. Dunn, N.B. Starr, & C. Blosser (Eds.), *Pediatric primary care(4th* ed.) (pp. 699-700). St. Louis, MO: Saunders Elsevier.

Medline Plus, U.S. National Library of Medicine. (2011). *Eye pain.* Retrieved from http://www.nlm.nih.gov/medlineplus/ency/article/003032.htm

Medline Plus, U.S. National Library of Medicine. (2013*). Eye emergencies.* Retrieved from http://www.nlm.nih.gov/medlineplus/ency/article/000054.htm

Ears:

Mayo Clinic. (2011). *Foreign object in the ear: First aid.* Retrieved from http://www.mayoclinic.com/print/fiRST-aid/HQ00061

Mayo Clinic. (2011). *Earwax blockage.* Retrieved from http://www.mayoclinic.com/health/earwax-blockage/DS00052

Medline Plus, U.S. National Library of Medicine. (2012). *Ear emergencies.* Retrieved from http://www.nlm.nih.gov/medlineplus/ency/article/000052.htm

Merck Manual, Professional Edition. (2013). *External ear obstructions, foreign bodies.* Retrieved from http://www.merckmanuals.com/professional/ear_nose_and_throat_disorders/external_ear_disorders/external_ear_obstructions.html

Nose:

Medline Plus, U.S. National Library of Medicine. (2013). *Foreign body in the nose.* Retrieved from http://www.nlm.nih.gov/medlineplus/ency/article/000037.htm

Merck Manual, Professional Edition. (2012). *Nasal foreign bodies.* Retrieved from http://www.merckmanuals.com/professional/ear_nose_and_throat_disorders/nose_and_paranasal_sinus_disorders/nasal_foreign_bodies.html

FRACTURE (see also Sprains/Strains)

DEFINITIONS/ETIOLOGY:
A fracture is a broken bone most frequently associated with an injury to surrounding tissue caused from direct trauma. Fractures may also be caused from diseases that weaken the bone such as osteogenesis.
- Simple fracture – the bone is lined up and does not need to be set, just immobilized
- Hairline fracture – a fine crack; this may not show immediately on x-ray
- Greenstick fracture – split on one side but not the other
- Displaced fracture – end of bones are not lined up and may actually overlap
- Impacted fracture – two broken ends are jammed together
- Compound fracture – both ends are apart and one or both protrudes through broken skin

SIGNS AND SYMPTOMS:
- Localized pain following trauma
- Asymmetry compared to opposite side, but not always present
- Deformity is associated with severe pain
- Swelling and discoloration are not always present, but the likelihood of a fracture is greater if discoloration appears within 30 minutes
- Suspect "stress" fracture if painful from excess exercise, jogging, gymnastics, ballet training, etc. Produces pain without swelling at site of fracture, especially on movement
- Most frequently missed fractures: ribs, fingers/toes (chipped), elbow, knee, and end of the radius in the forearm

MANAGEMENT/ TREATMENT
1. Do not move the student until an assessment is complete.
2. Do not move the student if a fracture of the leg bones, pelvis or head, neck or spine is suspected unless the student is in grave danger by being left where he is. If a student must be moved under these circumstances, utilize multiple people and devices such as backboards or other large flat items in order to keep the student immobilized.
3. Inspect for deformity, pain, bleeding, protruding bone and edema.
4. Calm student. Watch for signs of shock.
5. Check for pulses near injury; if skin color is white/pale or pulse is absent, gently reposition
   only until circulation improves. If limb resists movement, stop. Immobilize beyond joints above and below ends of suspected fracture, leaving the limb in position. Splint only with a pillow if calling for emergency services. Raise body part above the heart if possible.
6. Cover exposed bone with sterile/clean bandage. DO NOT wash or probe.
7. Apply cold. If using ice, wrap in a towel before applying to the area.

FRACTURE *(continued from previous page)*

8. Summon emergency services and/or parent/guardian, depending on:
   - Severity and need for special transportation
   - Discolored or numb
   - Limb or joint is deformed
   - Bone is piercing the skin
   - Heavy bleeding
9. Monitor pulse(s) and breathing rate, checking for shock, every five minutes until emergency services arrive.
10. Fingers/Toes:
    - If suspect fracture, tape to adjacent finger/toe ("buddy" splint). Refer to be seen within the day, sooner if deformity is present.
    - Jammed finger: buddy tape to adjacent digit. Check onset of discoloration; usually within 12-15 hours if fractured and more than 15 hours if only "jammed."

FOLLOW-UP:
- Splint/cast care as directed.
- Check fingers/toes for adequate circulation and sensation.
- Assist with modifications for classes, writing, keeping cast dry, etc.
- Assess proper crutch use.
- Promote mobility.

POTENTIAL COMPLICATIONS:
- Damage to blood vessels
- Fat embolism
- Nerve damage
- Osteomyelitis

OTHER MUSCULOSKELETAL CONCERNS
- Dislocation – injury to a joint in which the ends of your bones are forced from their normal positions. Can occur in major joints such as the shoulder, hip, knee, elbow and ankle or in the smaller joints (fingers, thumbs and toes).
- Subluxation – partial dislocation
- Sprain – tearing or stretching of ligament (caused by injury)
- Strain- tearing or stretching of muscle or tendon (caused by overuse)

Signs and Symptoms:
- Joint looks visibly deformed or out of place
- Area swollen
- Immovable
- Area intensely painful

FRACTURE *(continued from previous page)*

Complications
- Failure to reduce subluxation/dislocation
- Nerve damage
- Blood vessel damage

Treatment/management – depends on the severity of the injury
- The healthcare provider may try to gently maneuver the dislocated bone back into place (this is called reduction).
- If dislocation is severe – may need local or general anesthesia.
- May need to immobilize joint with a sling or splint.
- May need RICE (rest, ice, compression, elevation).

NOTES:
- Encourage children to wear protective gear such as helmets, elbow pads, kneepads and shin pads while biking, roller blading, and participating in contact sports.
- Repeated fractures can be an indication of other health conditions.
- Child abuse should be considered if there are reoccurring fractures without a medical indication or if the type of fracture is uncommon for a particular age group.
- Compartment Syndrome (mostly in lower limbs) is rare but can occur when there is swelling in a muscle group that has a fibrous covering. The lining does not allow for swelling from the injury and excessive pressure is place on the muscle that decreases blood flow to the muscle and can cause damage. Compartment Syndrome can also be caused from a splint or cast.
- The most common fractures in children are the clavicle, distal forearm, ulna, tibia and femur.

Resources
Medline Plus. (2012). Creating a Sling.
http://www.nlm.nih.gov/medlineplus/ency/presentations/100137_1.htm

References
American Academy of Pediatrics. (2013). Alterations in musculoskeletal function. In S. Aronson, & T. Shope (Eds.), *Managing infectious diseases in child care and schools (2ⁿᵈed.)* (p.p.979-979). Elk Grove Village, IL: American Academy of Pediatrics.

Mayo Clinic. (2012). *Fractures (broken bones): First aid.* Retrieved from
http://www.mayoclinic.com/health/first-aid-fractures/FA00058

The Merck Manual, Professional Edition. (2008). *Overview of fractures.* Retrieved http://www.merckmanuals.com/home/injuries_and_poisoning/fractures/overview_of_fractures.html?qt=fractures&alt=sh

HEADACHE(S)

DEFINITION/ETIOLOGY:
Headaches are common in children and have a wide range of causes with many levels of severity. Headaches are thought to be caused by changes in chemicals, nerves, or blood vessels in the area which send pain messages to the brain and bring on a headache. Children get the same types of headaches as adults and generally headaches are often hereditary. Headaches can be caused by a variety of triggers or certain infections.

Headaches can be considered <u>primary</u>, meaning that they are not due to any underlying condition or <u>secondary or organic</u>, meaning it is secondary to another disease or disorder.

Primary Headaches:
Migraine
Cluster
Tension type

Secondary Headaches:
Tumors
High blood pressure
Head injuries
Other disease processes

Other Important Causes to Consider:
- Fatigue (probe reason if inadequate sleep), skipped breakfast, not wearing vision correction
- Sinusitis
- Central nervous system bleeding
- Increased intracranial pressure (chronic progressive headache)
- Tension
- Exertion

SIGNS AND SYMPTOMS:
Findings with principal causes:
- **Tension-type headache**: the most common type in adolescence: "dull/achy," diffuse, bilateral, radiates to cervical neck, nausea may accompany but rarely vomiting. It is described as a general pain around the head. Precipitating factors include emotional stress and fatigue.

HEADACHE(S) *(continued from previous page)*

- **Vascular headaches**:
  - **Migraine:** "throbbing/pounding," usually unilateral. Generalized headaches are more common than unilateral headaches in children. It is common to experience nausea and vomiting and sensitivity to light which makes it difficult to carry out activities of daily living. About 1/3 of migraine sufferers also experience an "aura" prior to the headache that may be describes as a visual disturbance such as blinking lights or loss of vision. The presence of auras is less common in children than adults. Hunger may precede a childhood migraine. Dizziness, light-headedness, pallor, or purple bags around the eyes may also occur. Headaches last between 4 and 72 hours and are often hereditary.
  - **Cluster:** Often described as "burning/stabbing", often felt most around one eye. These headaches generally start suddenly and are of short duration but may reoccur for several months at a time. They are most common in spring and autumn.
  - **Exertion** (exercise-related): Straining (Valsalva maneuver) triggers severe throbbing, **usually at the base of the head**; felt as a dull ache for 4-6 hours and may recur in later weeks or months upon exertion.
- **Secondary to other conditions**, e.g., sinusitis, dental problem, eye strain. May be associated with other symptoms such as cough, fever or blurred vision.
- **Pathological conditions**:
  - **Traction headaches:** brain tumor, intracranial hemorrhage or disorder of cerebrospinal fluid pressure.
  - **Infection/inflammation:** meningitis, encephalitis and brain abscess. The nature of headache is sudden onset, increasingly severe within days, may be persistently one-sided or localized. Headaches are followed in time by abnormal neurological signs, such as vomiting without nausea, headaches that awaken the person, staggering gait and/or confusion.

ASSESSMENT:
- History: Ask about occurrences, such as surrounding events (injury, stressor such as lack of food or sleep), frequency, duration, cyclic nature, location, and severity of headache (e.g., stops playing, causes school absenteeism). Determine associated symptoms and use of any medications or other care.
- The most important part of the evaluation is to ascertain if this is a benign condition or a pathological condition. If exam is abnormal, especially neurological exam and history (e.g., irritability, mental confusion, fatigue or blurred/altered vision), then there is heightened concern for a more serious pathological condition causing the headache.

HEADACHE(S) *(continued from previous page)*

MANAGEMENT AND TREATMENT:
1. If student has a suspected pathological condition underlying the headache, notify the parent/guardian immediately and refer to the student's healthcare provider.
2. For benign conditions, headache diaries are useful for evaluation. A long-term plan can be suggested by the school nurse, working with the student's healthcare provider.
3. Intervention is based on the cause.

   Non-medication measures
   - Rest in quiet, darkened room
   - Cool or warm cloth on forehead
   - Stress management/relaxation techniques
   - Eliminate precipitating factors
   - Biofeedback, good posture and daily exercise

   Medications
   - **Tension headache**:
     - Non-prescription analgesics.
     - No food or caffeine restrictions unless the food is a confirmed trigger.
   - **Migraine type**:
     - Treat the headache as soon as it starts; do not wait for nausea or other symptoms.
     - Prompt treatment turns off the mediators of inflammation and should be available at school.
     - Over-the-counter analgesics, including acetaminophen, non-steroidal anti-inflammatory drugs (NSAID) such as ibuprofen and naproxen, may not be sufficient.
     - Triptans and serotonin antagonists are commonly prescribed (e.g. sumatriptan nasal spray).
     - School absences or inability to perform at school due to migraine suggests that prophylactic agents are indicated. Prophylactic agents (such as tricyclic antidepressants (amitriptyline), propranolol, and calcium channel blockers) are used when auras present or in severe cases.
   - **Cluster headache**: Children are usually referred to pediatric neurologists.

FOLLOW UP:
- Gauge continuing symptoms with a headache diary.
- Re-evaluation is warranted any time initial impressions do not fit, when symptoms persist or worsen with time, or when new symptoms emerge.
- Monitor complications such as side effects of medications and disruption of activities (e.g. school absences, poor academic performance).

HEADACHE(S) *(continued from previous page)*

- Assist those with migraine or tension headache to follow their medical and non-medical regimens.
- Healthy lifestyle strategies such as adequate sleep, good diet and relaxation techniques can be helpful.

POTENTIAL COMPLICATIONS:

Headaches can be painful and debilitating but are generally not due to dangerous conditions. However, occasionally headaches can be a sign of something more serious including very severe high blood pressure greater than 180/110 mm Hg, stroke, brain tumor, or meningitis.

It is critical to seek emergency medical care if a headache • **gets worse over days or weeks** • **is accompanied by impaired neurological function** • **is accompanied by persistent nausea and vomiting** • **is accompanied by fever or stiff neck** • **is accompanied by seizure, mental disturbance, or loss of consciousness** • **is different than usual headaches, strikes suddenly with great intensity, or** • **wakes you from sleep and is worse when you lay down**

NOTES: (PREVENTION)

Migraine-specific preventive interventions:

- Do not skip meals; a morning snack can help if hunger is a trigger. The role of specific food triggers is controversial, but parents/guardians may want child to avoid one food at a time to see if there is a benefit.
- Stay well hydrated; dehydration is a trigger for some migraines.
- Regular sleep routines and stress management.
- Daily exercise (20-30 minutes).

References

Ball, J., Binder, R., & Cowen, K. (Eds.). (2012). Alterations in neurological function. *Principles of pediatric nursing: Caring for children (5th ed.)* (p.p. 870-8729). Upper Saddle River, NJ: Pearson Education, Inc.

Classic Anthology of Anatomical Charts (7th ed.). (2010). Volume 2: Pathology (p. 6). Philadelphia, PA: Lippincott Williams and Wilkins.

Kids Health from Nemours. (2013). *Headaches.* Retrieved from http://kidshealth.org/parent/general/aches/headache.html.

MediResource Inc. (n.d.). *Headaches.* Retrieved from http://bodyandhealth.canada.com/ channel_condition_info_details.asp?channel_id=42&relation_id=10900&disease_id=67&page_no=2#Treatment

HEAT-RELATED ILLNESS

DEFINITION/ETIOLOGY:
Hyperthermia is a life-threatening increase in body core temperature. Heat-related illness occurs when the body's temperature-regulating mechanisms are over-whelmed. Core body temperature may rise above a safe level. Initially, the loss of salt and potassium from heavy perspiring may lead to **muscle cramps,** referred to as **heat cramps.** If the person is not cooled, this may lead to **heat exhaustion** due to dehydration. The most serious form of heat illness is **heatstroke** which can lead to shock, brain damage, and death.

Hot environments such as outdoors on a hot and humid day or indoors in a hot, poorly ventilated area are the most common causes of heat-related illness. Certain medications can alter the body's response to heat and sun. It is also associated with alcohol, inappropriate use of drugs, prolonged exertion and dehydration.

SIGNS/SYMPTOMS:
HEAT CRAMPS
- Muscle cramps often in the abdomen or legs
- Excess perspiration
- Weakness, lightheadedness

HEAT EXHAUSTION
- Cool, pale and clammy skin
- Heavy sweating
- Weakness or tiredness
- Dizziness or fainting
- Headache
- Nausea/vomiting
- Muscle cramping
- Rapid heart rate

HEAT STROKE
- Hot, red, dry skin
- Absence of sweating
- Rapid and strong pulse
- Extremely high body temperature (may be up to 106 degrees)
- Rapid breathing
- Confusion/lack of coordination
- Unconscious/seizures

HEAT-RELATED ILLNESS *(continued from previous page)*

MANAGEMENT / TREATMENT:
HEAT CRAMPS
1. Move person to cool place and instruct person to rest.
2. Give sips of fluids (4 oz every 15 minutes).
3. Do not give liquids with caffeine.
4. Do not give salt tablets.
5. If person does not improve or if worsens call EMS.

HEAT EXHAUSTION
1. Move person to cool area.
2. Stop activity and instruct person to lie down and elevate feet 8-12 inches.
3. Loosen clothing.
4. Apply cool, wet cloths to neck, armpits, groin.
5. Use fan to cool (evaporation) and/or move to air-conditioned area
6. Sips of fluids (may use sports drink with carbohydrate content under 6 percent).
7. If nausea or vomiting occurs, discontinue fluids.
8. Seek immediate medical attention if symptoms are severe, worsen, or last over an hour.

HEAT STROKE
1. Call 911.
2. Meanwhile, move the victim to a cooler environment.
3. Reduce body temperature with cold bath or sponging, wet sheets, or towels..
4. Remove clothing, use fans, air-conditioners.
5. Be alert for vomiting and prevent aspiration.
6. Monitor consciousness and prepare for CPR.

NOTE:
Untreated heat cramps and exhaustion may lead to Heat Stroke.

HEAT STROKE IS A SEVERE MEDICAL EMERGENCY. SUMMON EMERGENCY MEDICAL ASSISTANCE OR GET THE VICTIM TO A HOSPITAL IMMEDIATELY. DELAY CAN BE FATAL.

HEAT-RELATED ILLNESS *(continued from previous page)*

References

American Red Cross. (2008). *Heat-related illness. Do you know what to do?* Retrieved from http://american.redcross.org/site/PageServer?pagename=ItsHotOutHere

Brehm, C. (2008). Common injuries. In C. Burns, M. Brady, A. Dunn, N.B. Starr, & C. Blosser (Eds.), *Pediatric primary care (4th ed.)* (pp. 1007- 1008). St. Louis, MO: Saunders Elsevier.

Emedicine Health. (2013). *Cooling techniques for hyperthermia.* Retrieved from http://emedicine.medscape.com/article/149546-overview

Mattey, E. (2013). Growth and development: Preschool through adolescence. In J. Selekman (Ed.), *School nursing: A comprehensive text* (2nd ed.)(p. 346). Philadelphia, PA: F.A. Davis.

Medline Plus, U.S. National Library of Medicine. (2013). *Heat emergencies.* Retrieved from http://www.nlm.nih.gov/medlineplus/ency/article/000056.htm

Subbarao, I., Lyznicki, J., & James, J. Editors (2009). *AMA Handbook of First Aid and Emergency Care.* New York, NY: Random House.

HEAT-RELATED ILLNESS *(continued from previous page)*

Apparent Temperature Scale (Heat Index)*

Relative Humidity (%)

Temp °F	30%	40%	50%	60%	70%	80%	90%
86	84.4	86.3	88.3	91.0	95.0	99.4	104.6
88	86.5	88.8	91.4	94.9	99.8	105.6	111.8
90	88.8	91.5	94.9	99.3	105.2	112.3	119.5
92	91.2	94.4	98.9	104.3	111.3	119.5	127.7
94	94.0	97.6	103.3	109.9	118.2	127.1	136.3
96	96.9	101.2	108.1	116.1	125.4	135.1	145.3
98	99.8	105.1	113.2	122.4	132.8	143.4	154.6
100	103.0	109.3	118.6	128.9	140.4	152.0	164.2
102	106.1	113.8	124.3	136.0	148.3	160.9	174.1
104	109.5	118.7	130.4	143.3	156.6	170.2	184.4
106	113.4	124.0	136.9	151.0	165.3	179.9	195.1
108	117.7	129.7	143.8	159.1	174.4	190.0	206.2
110	122.4	135.8	151.1	167.6	183.9	200.5	217.7

HI 90 - 105 = Hot: Heat cramps and heat exhaustion **possible** with prolonged exposure and physical activity.

HI 105-130 = Very Hot: Heat cramps or heat exhaustion **likely**. Heatstroke possible with prolonged exposure and physical activity.

HI 130+ = Extremely Hot: Heatstroke **imminent** with prolonged exposure and physical activity.

Adapted from Texas Department of Health

HEMOPHILIA

DEFINITION/ETIOLOGY:
Hemophilia is a common hereditary blood clotting disorder, primarily affecting males. The severity of hemophilia depends on the amount of clotting factor in the blood (ranging from mild to severe). Clotting factor is a protein in the blood that is needed for normal clotting. Hemophilia is a life-long disease.

TYPES:
- *Hemophilia A*: classic hemophilia (80% of cases), usually severe
- *Hemophilia B*: "Christmas disease"—first diagnosed in child whose last name was Christmas (15% *of cases)*, severity varies
- *Hemophilia C*: usually mild with bleeding problems only after surgery or major injury

SIGNS AND SYMPTOMS:
- External bleed: mild cut, bruises, nose bleeds, abrasions; not a serious problem; bleed longer, not faster
- Internal bleeding may occur anywhere in body. **This is a serious problem**. Symptoms of internal bleeding depend on the location of the bleeding, the amount of bleeding, and structures/functions of the body affected. **If you suspect an internal bleed, seek medical treatment immediately!** Below are examples of internal bleeds:

Location of Bleed	Potential symptom(s)
Kidneys	<ul><li>Blood in urine</li><li>Flank pain</li></ul>
Joint bleed	<ul><li>Can occur without obvious injury</li><li>Feeling of tightness in joint</li><li>Swelling around joint</li><li>Warm to touch</li><li>Pain around joint</li></ul>
Intracranial bleed	<ul><li>Headache</li><li>May have neck pain/stiffness</li><li>Alerted mental function</li><li>Double vision</li><li>Seizures</li></ul>
Intra-abdominal bleeding	<ul><li>Lightheaded</li><li>Short of breath</li><li>Shock</li><li>Decreased blood pressure</li><li>Gastrointestinal bleed – may vomit bright red blood or have black tarry stools, bruising around umbilical area</li></ul>

HEMOPHILIA *(continued from previous page)*

MANAGEMENT AND TREATMENT:
Specific orders should be obtained for all students with a diagnosis of hemophilia. Students must have an Individualized Healthcare Plan and Emergency Plans. They may be eligible for Section 504 or special education services.

Student may be receiving frequent transfusions with special blood products. Open communication between parent/guardian(s) and school staff, including the school nurse, is important in providing safe and effective care in the school setting for students with hemophilia.

School policies and procedures can provide guidance in caring for hemophilia in the school setting. A school nurse may be needed to be available for continuity of care and success in school for students with hemophilia.

1. Apply firm pressure for 10 minutes over skin lacerations or abrasions.
2. Apply ice pack to small bleeds under the skin.
3. Carefully observe student following minor trauma for possible internal bleeding.
4. **If you suspect an internal bleed; seek medical treatment immediately.**
5. Notify parent/guardian after all accidents (even if there is no visible sign of injury).
6. NO ASPIRIN or IBUPROFEN (prolongs bleeding time) nor other medications without doctor's orders.
7. No injections at school unless under a doctor's order because of possible hemorrhage into muscle.
8. Follow physician's orders for PE participation. Contact and hard ball sports are contraindicated.
9. Establish liaison with playground supervisors, PE teacher, parent/guardian(s), and healthcare provider.
10. Educate student about play and sport safety. Restrict activity as little as possible within medical limits.
11. May receive transfusions; increased risk of infection through blood products.
    a. Educate parent/guardian regarding the importance of being up-to-date on Hepatitis A and B vaccination.

FOLLOW UP:
- Provide accommodations for frequent doctors' appointments.
- Observe for early bleeding episodes. Many children do not report early bleeding even if they know it is beginning. Children with hemophilia can learn about the signs and symptoms of internal bleeding and are encouraged to notify an adult when he or she senses bleeding to prevent long-term damage.
- Encourage non-contact sports: golf, swimming.
- Resume activity gradually after external bleeding episode.

HEMOPHILIA *(continued from previous page)*

- Follow healthcare provider's activity orders following an internal bleeding episode.
- Help student feel at ease if returns to school in a wheelchair or with a sling to relieve pressure.
- Educate child/parent/guardian regarding injury prevention when riding bicycle; wear kneepads, elbow pads, helmets, etc.
- If indicated, (with parent permission) provide hemophilia education to classmates.
- Promote good oral hygiene to prevent dental extractions

POTENTIAL COMPLICATIONS:
- Internal bleeding
- Joint damage
- Infections

NOTES:

People with hemophilia can live relatively normal lives with proper treatment. However, prognosis is guarded without adequate treatment.

References

Centers for Disease Control and Prevention. (2011). *Hemophilia*. Retrieved from
http://www.cdc.gov/ncbddd/hemophilia/facts.html

Mayo Clinic. (2011). *Hemophilia*. Retrieved from http://www.mayoclinic.com/health/hemophilia/DS00218

Merck Manual. (2012). *Hemophilia*. Retrieved from http://www.cdc.gov/ncbddd/hemophilia/facts.html

National Heart, Lung, and Blood Institute. (2011). *Signs and symptoms of hemophilia*. Retrieved from
http://www.nhlbi.nih.gov/health/health-topics/topics/hemophilia/signs.html

Selekman, J., Bochenek, J. & Lukens, M. (2013). Children with chronic conditions. In J. Selekman (Ed.), *School nursing: A comprehensive text* (2nd ed.) (pp. 700-783). Philadelphia, PA: F. A. Davis.

HEPATITIS (VIRAL, TYPES A, B, AND C)

DEFINITION/ETIOLOGY:

The term hepatitis describes inflammation of the liver. Hepatitis may be caused by alcohol, drugs, autoimmune diseases, metabolic diseases, and viruses. Acute viral hepatitis is the most common cause of jaundice (conjugated hyperbilirubinemia) in childhood and adolescence. Three types of hepatitis (A, B, C) are reportable illnesses in most states. These viruses affect the liver and produce similar symptoms. The incubation period, the mode of transmission, and results of serologic tests help to distinguish the different types of viral hepatitis.

The five types of viral hepatitis are Hepatitis A (HAV), Hepatitis B (HBV), Hepatitis C (HCV), Hepatitis D (HDV), and Hepatitis E (HEV). In the United States, HAV is the most common cause of acute hepatitis and HCV is the most common cause of chronic hepatitis. The information provided in this guideline will focus on HAV, HBV, and HCV infections in the pediatric population.

CAUSE

Hepatitis: Characteristics of Virus Types			
	Hepatitis A	**Hepatitis B**	**Hepatitis C**
Transmission	fecal-oral route, contaminated water/food	parenteral, blood, blood product, sexual contact, body fluid	parenteral, blood , blood product, sexual contact, drug use
Incubation period	2-6 weeks (average 4 weeks)	1-6 months (average 3 mos.)	2 weeks – 6 months (average 6-7 weeks)
May be a carrier	not long-term	yes	yes
Treatment (acute)	immune globulin within 2 weeks of exposure	Hepatitis B immunoglobulin after exposure	none
Treatment (chronic)	supportive	supportive	Supportive –interferon see below
Vaccine	available (recommended 2 doses for all children 12 months and older)	available (recommended shortly after birth with 2 additional doses)	not available

HEPATITIS (VIRAL, TYPES A, B, AND C) *(continued from previous page)*

SIGNS/SYMPTOMS:
- Fever, malaise, fatigue, headache, joint pain
- Dark urine and lighter-color stools
- Loss of appetite, nausea, vomiting, stomachache
- Jaundice (yellow eyes and skin)
- Most cases in young children are mild

HEPATITIS A (HAV)
- Symptomatic hepatitis A infection occurs in approximately 30% of infected children younger than six years of age; most infected children have no jaundice. Among older children and adults, infection usually is symptomatic and typically lasts several weeks, with jaundice occurring in approximately 70% of cases.
- The highest titer of HAV in stool occurs during one to two weeks before the onset of illness. HAV is transmitted from person-to-person by food and water. The risk of transmission subsequently diminishes by one week after onset of jaundice. However, HAV can be detected in stool for long periods, especially in young children.
- Post-exposure prophylaxis: Immune globulin (IG) is recommended for un-immunized close personal contacts within two weeks after exposure, e.g., member of household, day care center for un-immunized employees and all younger children not yet toilet trained. In a center in which all children are toilet trained, IG is recommend for only the children in the same rooms as the index case. Exposure at **regular school** is _not_ considered a close contact and IG is not recommended except under unusual circumstances.
- Children with hepatitis A should be referred to the healthcare provider and excluded for 1 week after onset of illness.
- Adults with acute HAV infection who work as food handlers or in child care settings should be excluded until one week after onset of the illness, until the IG prophylaxis program has been completed, or as directed by the health department.
- Active immunization (HAV vaccine) is effective for children and adults.

HEPATITIS B (HBV)
- HBV has two phases, acute and chronic. Acute HBV is new and is short-term, occurring shortly after exposure to the virus. Chronic HBV is ongoing and long-term lasting longer than six months. Chronic HBV may not go away completely.
- Young children usually do not have jaundice or other symptoms. Sometimes, HBV affects other parts of the body resulting in arthritis, rash or thrombocytopenia. More than 90% of infants who are infected perinatally will develop chronic infection, whereas 25%-50% of children infected between one and five years of age and 10% of infected older children and adults develop a chronic case.

HEPATITIS (VIRAL, TYPES A, B, AND C) *(continued from previous page)*

- HBV virus is transmitted through blood and body fluids, including exudates, semen, cervical secretions and uncommonly with saliva. Person-to-person contact can occur in any setting involving interpersonal contact over an extended period. HBV virus can survive in the environment for one week, so transmission from shared objects, such as razor blades or toothbrushes also may occur but is uncommon. Among adolescents and adults, those at highest risk include users of injection drugs and those with multiple sexual patters.
- HBV is almost always preventable. Pre-exposure HBV immunization is the universally recommended preventive measure for infants, un-immunized children and adolescents.
- School nurses, athletic trainers, and teachers of students who are severely developmentally delayed and positive for Hepatitis B surface antigens (HBsAg) are candidates for immunization.
- Most children with hepatitis B should be admitted to school without restrictions. If the student has weeping sores, or behaviors that would lead to bleeding exclusion may be necessary.
- Post-exposure prophylaxis: Hepatitis B Immune Globulin (HBIG) is indicated for people at risk of developing HBV due to recent exposure of body fluids of someone infected with HBV. This includes babies of mothers infected with HBV, healthcare workers, emergency first responders, and morticians. HBIG is effective because it provides temporary induced immunity by the transfer of immunoglobulin.

HEPATITIS C (HCV)

- Acute disease tends to be mild and insidious in onset and most infections are asymptomatic. Persistent infection with HCV occurs in 50% to 60% of infected children but without significant liver damage.
- Risk factors are blood transfusions, kidney dialysis, and injected illicit drug use.
- Treatment is with interferon-alfa alone or in combination with ribavirin in chronic hepatitis C in adults. Combination therapy results in higher sustained response rates in 40% of cases but has not received FDA approval for those less than 18 years of age.
- Children with chronic infection should be screened periodically for chronic hepatitis because of potential risk of chronic liver disease.

MANAGEMENT/TREATMENT:

1. Notify the parent/guardian of symptoms of concern and refer to physician.
2. Follow state regulations and school policy on reporting to health department.

HEPATITIS (VIRAL, TYPES A, B, AND C) *(continued from previous page)*

3. Recommendations for immune globulin are only for those with close contact, not general classroom contact. Immune globulin recommendation depends on type of hepatitis and indications. HAV: serologic testing of contacts is not recommended, because testing may delay administration of IG. HBV: serologic test for anti-HBs is recommended in exposed person with previous immunization but unknown response. Work with Public Health authorities.
4. Use good hand washing techniques at all times and instruct children as necessary.

FOLLOW UP:
- Educate campus personnel and students on Universal/ Standard Precautions (see Section III).
- Teach about specific routes of transmission, incubation periods, and signs of infection.
- Athletes should cover existing cuts, abrasions, wounds, or other areas of broken skin with a dressing.
- Inquire about other cases in family and after-school care, group or club.
- Inform about requirements and availability of Hepatitis A and Hepatitis B vaccines.

References

American Academy of Pediatrics. (2009). Recommendations for care of children in special circumstances – infections spread by blood and body fluids. In L.K. Pickering, C.J. Baker, D.W. Kimberlin, & S.S. Long (Eds.), *Red Book: 2009 report of the committee on infectious diseases (28th ed.)* (pp. 146-148). American Academy of Pediatrics: Elk Grove Village, IL.

American Academy of Pediatrics. (2013). Hepatitis A infection; Hepatitis B infection. In S. Aronson, & T. Shope (Eds.), *Managing infectious diseases in child care and schools (2nd ed.)* (pp. 101-104). Elk Grove Village, IL: American Academy of Pediatrics.

Atkinson, W., Wolfe, S,, Hamborsky, J., & McIntyre, L. (eds.). *Epidemiology and prevention of vaccine-preventable diseases* (11th ed.). Washington DC: Public Health Foundation.

Buggs, A. M. (2012). *Hepatitis: Viral.* Retrieved from http://emedicine.medscape.com/article/185463-overview

Centers for Disease Control and Prevention. (2013). *Viral hepatitis.* http://www.cdc.gov/HEPATITIS/

HERPES SIMPLEX - ORAL (cold sore, fever blister)

DEFINITION/ETIOLOGY:
An acute, viral infection with a local primary lesion (cold sore or fever blister occurring on the lips, mouth or face), which is frequently latent and has a tendency to recur. Most persons are initially infected by school age. During the first infection people may shed the virus for at least a week and possibly several weeks after signs and symptoms appear. The virus remains dormant in the body and may recur when triggered by local skin trauma, sun exposure, or systemic changes such as fatigue, menstruation, fever or stress. People with recurrent sores shed the virus for 3-4 days after symptoms appear. Two to five percent of healthy persons with no visible lesions carry herpes simplex virus in their saliva. The virus is often spread by people with no signs or symptoms, often adults and is spread by direct contact through kissing or contact with open sores.

Etiology: *Herpes simplex virus* (HSV), type 1 is the usual cause of mouth sores and herpes simplex virus, type 2 is the usual causative for most genital herpes lesions. At times, type 1 may cause infection in the genital area and type 2 can cause infection in the mouth.

SIGNS AND SYMPTOMS:
- Painful superficial, fluid filled blisters on an erythematous base, usually on the mouth, lips, and face, and are slow to crust over.
- May have an itchy or tingling sensation before blister appears.
- May have tender lymph nodes.
- During an episode the typical duration is 7-10 days.
- Contagious until the lesion is completely crusted over.

MANAGEMENT/TREATMENT:
1. No exclusion from school.
2. Use good hand-washing techniques at all times.
3. There is no cure for herpes simplex.
4. Glyoxide, campho-phenique, and aloe vera relieve burning and itching briefly.
5. Blisters should be kept clean to prevent bacterial infection.
6. Lesions are contagious (spread by skin to skin contact), so hands should be washed after touching lesions.
7. Refrain from kissing when blisters are present.
8. Refer to healthcare provider if severe, frequently recurring or long lasting.
9. Some physicians prescribe oral acyclovir for early use in frequently recurring or severe cases.
10. A child with type 2 lesions should be evaluated for possible sexual abuse.

HERPES SIMPLEX - ORAL (Cold sore, fever blister) *(continued from previous page)*

FOLLOW UP:
Sunscreen on lips reduces risk of recurrence.

POTENTIAL COMPLICATIONS:
- Avoid cross-contamination. Keep hands away from eyes. Herpes simplex infections of the eye can cause scarring of the cornea which can potentially lead to blindness.
- Can cause meningitis or encephalitis if the herpes simplex virus spreads to the brain.

NOTES:
The herpes simplex virus can be life-threatening to a person with a compromised immune system.

SPECIAL INFORMATION on HERPES SIMPLEX, type 2
1. Genital herpes simplex (type 2) does not require exclusion from school.
2. Oral acyclovir is prescribed to suppress painful lesions.
3. Educate staff and pregnant students about dangers to fetus if herpes simplex is acquired during pregnancy.
4. Newborn baby may acquire the infection during vaginal delivery if mother has active type 2 lesions.

Reference
American Academy of Pediatrics. (2013). Herpes simplex virus. In S. Aronson, & T. Shope (Eds.), *Managing infectious diseases in child care and schools (2nd ed.)* (pp. 105-106). Elk Grove Village, IL: American Academy of Pediatrics.

American Academy of Pediatrics. (2009). Summaries of infectious disease – herpes simplex. In L.K. Pickering, C.J. Baker, D.W. Kimberlin, & S.S. Long (Eds.), *Red Book: 2009 report of the committee on infectious diseases (28th ed.)* (pp. 363-373). Elk Grove Village, IL: American Academy of Pediatrics.

Aronson S., & Shope T. (2009). Managing infectious diseases in child care and schools (p.87-88). Elk Grove Village, IL: American Academy of Pediatrics.

Smith, S. (2013). *Herpes labialis.* Retrieved from http://www.nlm.nih.gov/medlineplus/ency/article/000606.htm

HIV

DEFINITION/ETIOLOGY:

The human immunodeficiency virus (HIV) interferes with the body's ability to fight the organisms that cause disease. HIV is a sexually transmitted infection and can spread by contact with infected blood, or from mother to child during pregnancy, childbirth or breastfeeding. HIV affects specific cells in the immune system called T cells or CD4 cells. CD4 cells are a specific type of white blood cell that helps the body to fight disease. HIV weakens the immune system and can destroy so many of the CD4 cells in the body over time and the body cannot fight off infections and disease. When the CD4 count falls below 200, HIV infection leads to a chronic, potentially life threatening condition known as Acquired Immunodeficiency Syndrome (AIDS). Although there are medications available that can slow the progression of the disease, currently there is no safe and effective cure for HIV/AIDS. However, with proper medical care and treatment with antiretroviral therapy (ART), HIV can be controlled.

CAUSES OF HIV:

Scientists identified a specific type of chimpanzees and monkeys in West Africa as the original source of HIV infection in humans. The scientists believe simian immunodeficiency virus (SIV) was most likely transmitted to humans via contact with an infected monkey's blood during butchering or cooking allowing the virus to cross into humans and become HIV.

HIV is one of several bloodborne pathogens. Only certain body fluids from an HIV-infected person that come in contact with mucus membranes, damaged tissue, or injected directly into the bloodstream can transmit HIV. These fluids include:
- Blood
- Semen
- Vaginal secretions
- Rectal secretions
- Breast milk

Note: HIV is not spread by casual contact.

SYMPTOMS:

The symptoms of HIV and AIDS may vary depending on the phase of the infection. The phases of infection include primary infection, clinical latent infection, early symptomatic HIV infection, and progression to AIDS. Table 1 provides a summary of symptoms noted in each phase of HIV infection.

HIV *(continued from previous page)*

Table 1 - Symptoms of HIV Infection

Primary Infection	Clinical Latent Infection	Early Symptomatic HIV Infection	Progression to AIDS
Flu-like illness develops within one to two months after the virus enters the body. **Symptoms:** • Fever • Muscle soreness • Rash • Headache • Sore throat • Mouth or genital ulcers • Swollen lymph glands in the neck • Joint pain • Night sweats • Diarrhea	Typically lasts 8 to 10 years. **Symptoms**: • Persistent swelling of lymph nodes	Virus continues to multiply and destroys the cells of the immune systems. **Symptoms:** • Mild infections • Chronic symptoms • Fever • Fatigue • Swollen lymph nodes • Diarrhea • Weight loss • Cough • Shortness of breath	The disease progresses to AIDS in about 10 years if no treatment for HIV is received. **Symptoms:** • Susceptible to opportunistic infections • Profuse night sweats • Fever >100°F • Chronic diarrhea • Persistent lesions on the tongue or in the mouth • Headaches • Persistent fatigue • Blurred and distorted vision • Weight loss • Skin rashes or bumps
Note: The viral load of HIV in the blood stream is high during the primary infection phase and HIV infection spreads more efficiently during this phase.	**Note**: HIV remains in the body as free virus and in the infected white blood cells		

HIV *(continued from previous page)*

POTENTIAL RISKS and COMPLICATIONS:
- Infections - Tuberculosis, Salmonellosis, Cytomegalovirus, Candidiasis, Cryptococcal meningitis, Toxoplasmosis, Cryptosporidiosis
- Cancers - Kaposi's sarcoma, Lymphomas
- Other complications - Wasting syndrome, Neurological, Kidney disease

MANAGEMENT IN THE SCHOOL SETTING:

Standard/Universal Precautions
The implementation of standard/universal precautions is advised for all school personnel to promote infection control and prevent the spread of bloodborne pathogens such as HIV/AIDS. Standard/universal precautions include the use of gloves and other protective equipment when there is a risk of exposure to human blood and body fluids known to transmit HIV. Annual training for standard/universal precautions should be provided to all school staff at the beginning of the school year. The training should include the mode of transmission for HIV and proper use of personal protective equipment.

Confidentiality
All health records, including notes and other documents referencing a student's HIV status, should be kept in a secure location. Access to confidential student records is only shared with school officials with a legitimate need to know the information. Parents/guardians and students are not required to disclose a student's HIV infection status in order for the student to enroll in and attend school. However, if the parents/guardians or student choose to disclose the HIV status to school staff, the confidentiality of this information should be emphasized.

School Attendance and School Placement
Students with HIV infections have the same right to attend school and receive educational services as any other student. The student's HIV status should not the deciding factor in determining educational services and participation in school sponsored activities. Thus, decisions regarding school attendance, school placement, or special health care needs should be considered on a case-by-case basis including maintaining respect for the rights to privacy of the student and family.

HIV *(continued from previous page)*

References

Centers for Disease Control and Prevention. (2013). *HIV basics*. Retrieved from http://www.cdc.gov/hiv/basics/index.html

Centers for Disease Control and Prevention. (2013). HIV transmission. Retrieved from http://www.cdc.gov/hiv/basics/transmission.html

Mayo Clinic. (2012). *HIV/AIDS*. Retrieved from http://www.mayoclinic.com/health/hiv-aids/DS00005

National Institute of Allergy and Infectious Diseases. (2009). *HIV/AIDS*. Retrieved from http://www.niaid.nih.gov/topics/HIVAIDS/Understanding/Pages/symptoms.aspx.

United States Department of Labor, Occupational Safety and Health Administration. (2013). *Universal precautions*. Retrieved from https://www.osha.gov/SLTC/etools/hospital/hazards/univprec/univ.html

HIVES (URTICARIA)

DEFINITION/ETIOLOGY:
Urticaria is the medical name for hives and is defined as an allergic reaction or hypersensitivity with characteristic skin appearance. Hives appear as localized, pale, itchy, pink wheals (swellings) that may cause the skin to itch, burn, or sting. They may occur singularly or in groups on any part of the skin and are very common. At least 10 to 20 percent of the population will experience at least one episode of hives in their lifetime.

CAUSES:
Chronic hives (urticaria) are triggered by an inflammation in the skin due to mast cells releasing histamines and other chemicals into the blood stream. This causes small blood vessels to leak. Triggers for hives can be difficult to pinpoint and the underlying cause may be difficult to identify. Allergy or reaction to the following may trigger or cause hives:
- Foods
- Medications
- Emotional factors
- Inhalants (e.g., pollens, dust)
- Contact substances (e.g., dust, plants)
- Physical factors (e.g., sun, cold)
- Bacterial, viral or fungal infections

SIGNS/SYMPTOMS:
Hives can last from 30 minutes to 36 hours and as hives disappear, new hives may develop. Some people may experience angioedema with hives which manifests as swelling of the skin around the eyes, lips, hands, feed, genitalia, and inside the throat. Other physical findings with hives include:

- Round, reddish-pink wheals on skin surface varying in size from 1/2 cm to 2-3 cm
- May run together causing irregular, larger wheal
- Tend to be clear in center with surrounding redness
- Not tender or painful, but itchy
- Seem to be intensified with heat
- Characteristically short-lived, but reappear often in other parts of body
- May be accompanied by swelling of lips, eyes, fingers, genitalia
- Never contagious
- **LARYNGEAL EDEMA (hoarseness and difficulty breathing) IS THE MOST SERIOUS COMPLICATION.** It requires immediate establishment of an airway and a call to 911.

HIVES (URTICARIA) *(continued from previous page)*

MANAGEMENT/TREATMENT:
1. Cool moist compresses to help control itching.
2. Avoid implicated foods or other suspect allergens.
3. Antihistamines if accidentally re-exposed.
4. Notify parents/guardians of occurrence of hives especially if the child is not known to have allergies. If there are any known or suspected contributing causes of the hives, communicate that information to the parents/guardians also.
5. A child with hives that persist should be monitored carefully for signs and symptoms of a progressive and serious allergic reaction (potentially anaphylaxis).

FOLLOW UP:
Precautions helpful in avoiding hives or angioedema include:
- avoiding known triggers
- avoiding medications that trigger hives
- keeping a diary or journal of activities to help the healthcare provider identify new triggers.

References

American Academy of Dermatology. (2013). *Hives*. Retrieved from
http://www.aad.org/dermatology-a-to-z/diseases-and-treatments/e---h/hives

American College of Osteopathic Dermatology. (2013). *Uticaria (hives)*. Retrieved from
http://www.aocd.org/skin/dermatologic_diseases/urticaria.html

Mayo Clinic. (2011). *Chronic hives*. Retrieved from http://www.mayoclinic.com/health/chronic-hives/DS00980

Vernon, P., Brady, M. & Starr, N.B. (2008). Dermatologic diseases. In C. Burns, M. Brady, A. Dunn, N.B. Starr, C. Blosser (Eds.), *Pediatric primary care* (4th ed.) (pp. 982-983). St. Louis, MO: Saunders Elsevier.

HPV

DEFINITION/ETIOLOGY:

The Human papillomavirus (HPV) is the most common sexually transmitted infection in the United States. HPVs are small, double-stranded DNA viruses that infect the epithelium. There are more than 100 types of HPV existing and the HPV infection can cause warts on different parts of the body. For example, HPV can cause plantar warts on the feet and other varieties of HPV infection commonly cause warts that occur on the hands or face. While there are more than 40 different strains of HPV that specifically infect the mucosal epithelium affecting the genital area, most of the HPV infections do not lead to cancer. However, some types of genital HPV can cause cancer of the cervix. HPV vaccines can help protect against strains of genital HPV which are most likely to cause genital warts or cervical cancer.

CAUSES OF HPV:

HPV is primarily transferred by skin-to-skin contact. The infection occurs when the virus may enter the body through:

- A cut in the skin
- An abrasion
- A small tear in the outer layer of your skin

Note: Genital HPV infections are transmitted through sexual intercourse, anal sex, and other skin-to-skin contact in the genital area. HPV infection is very rarely transmitted from mother to infant during delivery. However, if exposure occurs during delivery, it may cause HPV infection in the baby's genitals and upper respiratory system.

SIGNS AND SYMPTOMS:

Most often, the immune system defeats HPV infection before warts are created. However, when warts do appear as a result of HPV infection, the appearance may vary depending on the type of HPV involved. Below are descriptions of the various types of warts resulting from HPV infection.

- Genital warts are flat lesions, small cauliflower-like bumps, or tiny stem-like protrusions.
    - In women, genital warts appear on the vulva and may occur on the cervix or in the vagina.
    - In men, genital warts appear on the penis and scrotum or around the anus.
    - Genital warts rarely cause discomfort or pain.
    - Common warts are rough, raise bumps occurring on hands, fingers, and around fingernails. These warts may be painful and susceptible to bleeding/injury.
- Plantar warts are hard and grainy growths commonly appear on heels or balls of feet and may cause discomfort.

HPV *(continued from previous page)*

- Flat warts are flat topped in appearance, are slightly raised lesions, and may appear darker that regular skin color on face, neck, hands, wrists, elbows, or knees. Flat warts usually affect children, adolescents, and young adults.
- Cervical cancer can be caused by two specific types of genital HPV; do not cause warts and no signs or symptoms in the early stages of cervical cancer.
  - Annual Pap tests are important to detect precancerous changes in the cervix.
- Recurrent respiratory papillomatosis (RRP) are very rare. Warts grow on the throat. They may occur in children (juvenile onset) or in adults (adult onset). Growths can block the airway causing hoarse voice and difficulty breathing.

POTENTIAL RISKS and COMPLICATIONS:
Risk factors for HPV infection include:
- Number of sexual partners
- Age – Common warts occur most often in children and adolescents. Genital warts occur most often in adolescents and young adults.
- Weakened immune system may lead to a greater risk of HPV infections. (Note: immune systems may be weakened by HIV/AIDS or by drugs that may suppress the immune system).
- Damaged skin
- Personal contact

Complications of HPV may include:
- Oral and upper respiratory lesions
- Cancer, e.g. cancers of the genitals, anus, mouth, and upper respiratory tract

MANAGEMENT AND PREVENTION EFFORTS:
HPV can be managed and prevented in several ways:
1. Currently two HPV vaccines are used in the United States. They are available and recommended for boys and girls ages 11 to 12 years old. The vaccines are given in three shots over a six-month period.
   - Gardasil®, a quadrivalent vaccine was "first licensed vaccine developed to prevent cervical cancer and other diseases in females caused by genital HPV infection"[1] and approved in 2006 by the Food and Drug Administration (FDA)
   - Cervarix® a bivalent vaccine was approved in 2009 for the prevention of HPV.

---

1 Bellia-Weiss, T., Parsons, M., Sebach, A.M., and Rockelli, L.A. *Promoting HPV Prevention in the School Setting.* NASN School Nurse, 2013 March; 28(2):86-93.

HPV *(continued from previous page)*

2. Protection for sexually active individuals: condoms may lower the risk of HPV infection and HPV related diseases.
3. Limiting the number of sex partners can lower chances of getting HPV.

INTERVENTIONS: The Role of the School Nurse

The school nurse can assist in the management and prevention of HPV infection among children and adolescents in the following ways:

- Conduct health promotion education sessions in the school setting to increase awareness among youth and parents/guardians about HPV prevention and available vaccines.
- Coordinate with school-based health centers (when available in the school setting) to increase awareness about prevention education and immunizations available for HPV. (Note: School-based health centers provide an ideal setting for prevention education for sexually transmitted infections such as HPV.)

References

Atkinson, W., Wolfe, S., Hamborsky, J., & McIntyre, L. (Eds.) (2012). *Epidemiology and prevention of vaccine-preventable diseases* (12th ed.). Washington DC: Public Health Foundation/ Centers for Disease Control and Prevention. Retrieved from http://www.cdc.gov/vaccines/pubs/pinkbook/table-of-contents.html

Bellia-Weiss, T., Parsons, M., Sebach, A.M., & Rockelli, L.A. (2013). Promoting HPV prevention in the school setting. *NASN School Nurse, 28*(2), 86-93. doi: 10.1177/1942602X12463249

Centers for Disease Control and Prevention (CDC). (2012). *Human papillomavirus.* Retrieved from http://www.cdc.gov/vaccines/pubs/pinkbook/hpv.html

Centers for Disease Control and Prevention (CDC). (2013). *Human papillomavirus (HPV).* Retrieved from http://www.cdc.gov/hpv/

Mayo Clinic. (2013). *HPV Infection*. Retrieved from http://www.mayoclinic.com/health/hpv-infection/DS00906

HOMELESSNESS

DEFINITION/ETIOLOGY:
Federal law defines homeless children and youth as those who lack a fixed, regular, and adequate nighttime residence. According to the National Center on Family Homelessness, approximately one in 45 children experience homelessness in America each year. 1.6 million American children are homeless each year. Homeless families comprise roughly 1/3 of the total homeless population.

The McKinney Homeless Assistance Act (1987) was created in response to findings that half of the homeless children were not regularly attending school. The McKinney Act ensures homeless children receive free transportation to and from school. The Act further requires schools to register homeless children even if they lack normally required documents, such as immunization records or proof of residence.

Homeless children live in shelters, cars, homes of parents/guardians' friends or relatives or strangers, shared single-family quarters, motels on a weekly pay basis, tents and under bridges. Attendance suffers with length-of-stay rules in shelters, short stays in relatives' homes, and parent/guardian's relocation to seek work. They may have no storage for possessions such as donated clothing, no place to study or do homework, and irregular sleep and eating times.

CAUSES OF HOMELESSNESS (FOR FAMILIES):
- Lack of affordable housing
- Poverty
- Unemployment

POTENTIAL RISKS and COMPLICATIONS:
- Chronic health conditions (asthma, chronic otitis media, anemia, etc.)
- Behavioral problems
- Developmental delay
- Early initiation of substance abuse
- Social isolation
- Mental health problems (anxiety, depression, and withdrawal)
- Tuberculosis

MANAGEMENT:
States and communities are expected to remove barriers to enrollment, attendance, and success of these children, including preschool age children. Potential barriers include:

HOMELESSNESS *(continued from previous page)*

1. **Barriers to enrollment** - Lack of birth certificate, guardianship papers, previous school record transfer, lack of residence address for school assignment, and immunization records.
2. **Barriers to attendance** - Transportation, family mobility, poor health (e.g., untreated asthma), inadequate food, no clean clothing, no school supplies.
3. **Barriers to success** - Difficulty getting evaluation for special education or gifted programs, transportation and materials for extra-curricular events, counseling services and/or after-school care.

INTERVENTIONS: SCHOOL NURSE ROLE
1. **Enrollment**
   a. Follow laws with respect to admitting homeless children and secure up-to-date immunizations and records as quickly as possible.

2. **Attendance (School Nurse Concerns)**
   a. Assess for undiagnosed or untreated problems; e.g., poor growth, chronic infections, reactive airway disease, wounds, physical and mental health conditions.
   b. Coordinate with public health and community clinics for complete treatment including immediate access to immunizations.

3. **TB test follow up**
   a. Secure tuberculosis testing promptly (in accord with state or local requirements) as homeless children and youth are at greater risk of exposure.
   b. Assure that positive TB skin tests are adequately evaluated, and if medication is needed, assist the parent to assure medication completion.

4. **Provide support**
   a. Coordinate with shelters and social services for clothing (possibly facilitating shower and change at school), school meals, school supplies and after-school homework centers, adjusted assignments or tutoring to assure completion of schoolwork.
   b. A backpack or packet with class pictures, preserved samples of quality work, and stamped post cards to stay in touch with classmates helps to meet mental health needs of children who change schools.

HOMELESSNESS *(continued from previous page)*

References

Brady, M. & Dunn, A. (2008). Role relationships. In C. Burns, M. Brady, A. Dunn, N.B. Starr, C. Blosser (Eds.), *Pediatric primary care* (4th ed.) (pp. 377-378). St. Louis, MO: Saunders Elsevier.

Cory, A. & Jovanovic, J. A. (2013). The student's family. In J. Selekman (Ed.), *School nursing: A comprehensive text (2nd ed.)* (pp. 383-406). Philadelphia, PA: F.A. Davis.

National Coalition for the Homeless. (2012). *Homeless families with children.* Retrieved from http://www.nationalhomeless.org/factsheets/families.html

McKinney-Vento Homeless Education Assistance Improvements Act of 2001 (U.S.C. 42). Retrieved from http://www.ed.gov/policy/elsec/leg/esea02/pg116.html

Substance Abuse and Mental Health Services Administration. (2013). *Homelessness resource center.* Retrieved from http://homeless.samhsa.gov/

National Coalition for the Homeless. (2012). *Homeless families with children.* Retrieved from http://www.nationalhomeless.org/factsheets/families.html

The National Center for Family Homelessness. American Institutes for Research. (2010). *Children.* Retrieved from http://www.familyhomelessness.org/children.php?p=ts

HYPOTHERMIA

DEFINITION/ETIOLOGY:
Hypothermia is a medical emergency and can occur when the body loses heat faster than it can produce heat. This causes a dangerously low body temperature. The normal body temperature is 98.6°F (37°C) and hypothermia occurs as the body temperature decreases below 95°F (35°C). Once the body temperature decreases, the heart, nervous system, and other vital organ cannot function properly. If hypothermia is left untreated, complete failure of the heart and respiratory system can occur and lead to death.

CAUSES OF HYPOTHERMIA
- Exposure to cold weather conditions
- Accidental exposure to or immersion in a cold body of water
- Staying out in the cold too long
- Being cold and wet
- Wearing inappropriate clothing for cold weather conditions
- Inadequate heating in the home or air conditioning too cold

Note: The body may lose heat through various mechanisms including
- Radiated heat: heat loss is due to heat radiated from unprotected body surfaces.
- Direct contact: Heat is conducted away from the body when in direct contact with something very cold, e.g. cold water, cold ground.
- Wind: removes body heat at the surface of the skin.

SIGNS AND SYMPTOMS:
The human body automatically responses to cold weather by shivering in an attempt to create heat and warm up. Constant shivering is major sign of hypothermia. Hypothermia may range from moderate to severe. The signs and symptoms include:
- Shivering
- Lack of coordination, clumsiness, stumbling
- Slurred speech, mumbling
- Confusion, difficulty thinking
- Poor decision making
- Low energy or drowsiness
- Lack of concern, apathy
- Progressive loss of consciousness
- Weak pulse
- Slow and shallow breathing

HYPOTHERMIA *(continued from previous page)*

MANAGEMENT/TREATMENT:
- Call 911 – monitor breathing and provide cardiopulmonary resuscitation (CPR) immediately if breathing stops or seems slow and shallow.
- Move the person out of the cold or protect from wind/cold weather and insulate from the cold area.
- Remove wet clothing and replace with warm, dry covering.
- Do not apply direct heat; use warm compresses and apply to the center of the body, e.g. head, neck, chest, and groin. Heat applied to the extremities (i.e. arms and legs) can force a cold block toward the central organs (i.e. heart, lungs, and brain) and can result in a decrease in the core body temperature, which can be fatal.
- Avoid massaging frostbitten skin as rubbing can cause severe damage to the tissues.

Note: Emergency medical care for hypothermia will be guided by the severity of hypothermia. Various interventions can be used to increase the body temperature back to normal including blood rewarming, warm intravenous fluids, airway rewarming, and cavity lavage.

POTENTIAL RISKS and COMPLICATIONS:
An increased risk of hypothermia may occur with various factors:
- Age can be a risk factor for hypothermia
    - Older age: The body's ability to regulate temperature may decrease with age. Decreased ability to communicate and mobility are contributing factors for the elderly.
    - Younger age: Children can lose heat faster than adults due to the larger head to body ratio in children. Inappropriate dressing in the colder weather may increase the risk of hypothermia in children.
- Mental illness: May interfere with judgment and can affect appropriate dressing for the weather.
- Alcohol and drug use: Alcohol may make the body feel warm inside resulting in rapid heat loss from the skin surface. Additionally, the use of alcohol and drugs may affect judgment regarding weather conditions.
- Medical conditions: Certain medical conditions can affect the body's ability to regulate heat, i.e. underactive thyroid gland, poor nutrition, stroke, severe arthritis, chronic conditions affecting sensation, and conditions that limit the normal circulation/blood flow.
- Medications: Certain medications can alter the body's ability to regulate temperature.

HYPOTHERMIA *(continued from previous page)*

Complications of hypothermia may lead to the following:
- Frostbite – freezing of body tissues
- Gangrene – decay and death of tissue due to interrupted blood flow
- Chilblains – damage to the nerves and small blood vessels in the hands or feet due to prolonged exposure to cold temperatures.
- Trench foot – damage to nerves and small blood vessels because of prolonged immersion in cold water.

FOLLOW-UP AND PREVENTION EFFORTS:
School nurses can play a valuable role in educating children and families about outdoor activities during the cold weather to prevent hypothermia. Prevention for keeping children warm in cold weather includes the following:
- Cover up with appropriate clothing for cold weather, e.g. hats, mittens, to prevent body heat from escaping.
- Avoid overexertion to prevent sweating and quick loss of body heat.
- Encourage children to wear layers of clothing – loose fitting and lightweight.
- Encourage children to stay as dry as possible and to change wet clothing as soon as possible.
- Limit amount of time spent outside during cold weather.
- Educate youth and adolescents about risky behaviors and the importance to abstain from alcohol and drug use, especially during periods of prolonged cold weather exposure.

References
Centers for Disease Control and Prevention. (2012). *Emergency preparedness and response, winter weather: Hypothermia.* Retrieved from http://emergency.cdc.gov/disasters/winter/staysafe/hypothermia.asp

Mayo Clinic. (2013). *Hypothermia.* Retrieved from http://www.mayoclinic.com/health/hypothermia/DS00333

U.S. National Library of Medicine, National Institutes of Health. (2013). *Hypothermia.* Retrieved from http://www.nlm.nih.gov/medlineplus/hypothermia.html.

ILLNESS FALSIFICATION (Factitious Disorder)

DEFINITION/ETIOLOGY:

Illness falsification is considered a factitious disorder.

1. **Factitious disorders** are conditions in which a person acts as if he or she has an illness by deliberately producing, feigning, or exaggerating symptoms. People with factitious disorders seek painful or risky tests and operations in order to obtain attention. While the cause of factitious disorders is unknown, some theories believe there is both a biological and psychological cause. Numerous people with Factitious Disorder also experience mental health disorders especially personality disorders.

2. **Pediatric Condition Falsification (PCF)** (formerly referred to as Munchausen by Proxy) is a form of child abuse in which a parent/guardian/caregiver (most often the mother) deliberately produces false physical or psychological symptoms in a child under their care causing the victim to be regarded as ill or impaired by others. The child is presented for medical treatment and the parent or caregiver fails to acknowledge the deception. PCF often involves physical abuse, neglect, and emotional abuse. **A child who is subjected to this behavior is a victim of child abuse by PCF.**

Factitious disorders must be distinguished from **malingering** (faking illness to avoid other responsibilities). In malingering, the individual also produces the symptoms intentionally, but has a *goal that is recognizable* when the circumstances are known. For example, the falsification of symptoms to avoid a math test would be called malingering.

Medical conditions fabricated by children may go undetected or be diagnosed as somatization (see Note). Further study of children who falsify symptoms may in some cases help identify earlier experiences of PCF abuse (parent/guardian involvement) or covert parental coaching of illness falsification, and provide more effective interventions. Better understanding and identification of these children is likely to help prevent the development of more chronic adult factitious disorders.

NOTES:

Somatization refers to the occurrence of physical complaints for which medical evaluation reveals no physical pathology, or when pathology is present, the complaints are grossly in excess of what would be expected from the physical findings. Pain and somatic symptoms are problematic when, regardless of cause, they become a dominant force in the child's life and impair functioning. Somatic complaints often have associated psychiatric symptoms, particularly anxiety or depression, although the cause of the condition remains unclear.

ILLNESS FALSIFICATION (Factitious Disorder) *(continued from previous page)*

SIGNS AND SYMPTOMS:
Factitious Disorder
- Child may present with an inconsistent medical history
- Child may seek treatment from the school nurse/health office personnel frequently
- May present with reports of symptoms that are not observable
- May demonstrate an extensive knowledge of medical terminology and descriptions of illness
- Presence of bruises or infection
- Evidence of self-bruising or ingestion of substances to cause illness
- Presence of symptoms only when the child is alone or not being observed
- Willingness or eagerness to have medical tests, operations, or other procedures
- Reluctance by the child to have the school nurse speak with their parent/guardian (s) or healthcare providers
- Seeking treatment from multiple doctor's, clinic, hospitals, etc.
- New symptoms after obtaining negative results

Pediatric Condition Falsification
- Seizures, fever, diarrhea, apnea, nervous system dysfunction, signs of bleeding (urine and stool) and rashes
- Most common in children under 1 and up to age 6 years old
- A parent or caregiver fabricates symptoms of illness in a child
- The child is presented for medical assessment and care, usually persistently, often resulting in multiple medical procedures and hospitalizations
- The perpetrator denies the etiology of the child's illness
- Symptoms of illness abate upon separation of the child from the perpetrator
- Improvement of symptoms occurs when child is hospitalized but return on discharge

Possible exceptions: when the child has suffered permanent damage as a result of the abuse; child is actively colluding with the parent/guardian; child has developed a psychiatric disorder.

MANAGEMENT/TREATMENT:
1. Be alert to the possibility of Pediatric Condition Falsification and Factitious Disorder.
2. If there are concerns regarding illness fabrication or discrepancies between the parent/guardian's reports of health problems in the child and the school nurse's observations of the child's health:
   - Review the child's past medical history.
   - Consult with the child's physician/healthcare provider to review the child's diagnosis and health status. Discuss implications for school attendance and participation in school activities. Inform the provider of observations of the child in the school setting.

ILLNESS FALSIFICATION (Factitious Disorder) *(continued from previous page)*

- Maintain a trusting relationship with the perpetrator.
- Document child/parent/guardian interactions.
3. Information about the child's attendance, school health records, parental reports of medical/health problems, educational testing, and staff observations of health and behavioral issues are relevant and may be requested by the physician or legal authorities.
4. Be prepared to provide information should the family be referred to Child Protective Services. Follow district policy.
5. Factitious disorders are usually treated with psychotherapy and/or family therapy. Behavior modification is the first goal.
6. Medication may be used to treat related disorders such as depression or anxiety.

POTENTIAL COMPLICATIONS:

Factitious Disorder including PCF

- Absences from school which affect academic success
- Side effects of use of drugs or medical tests used to explore cause of reported physical or psychological symptoms
- Fear
- Pain and suffering
- Loss of normal attachment to parent/caregiver (especially with PCF)
- Loss of normal developmental experiences (i.e., kept out of school [PCF] or staying home from school in cases of Factitious Disorder)
- Loss of normal social experiences
- Death

References

American Psychiatric Association. (2013). *Highlights of changes from DSM-IV-TR- DSM-5.* Retrieved from http://www.psychiatry.org/practice/dsm/dsm-frequently-asked-questions

Ball, J., Binder, R., & Cowen, K. (Eds.). (2012). Assessment and management of social and environmental influences. *Principles of Pediatric Nursing: Caring for Children (5th ed.)* (pp. 461-462). Upper Saddle River, NJ: Pearson Education, Inc.

The Cleveland Clinic Foundation. (2013). *An overview of factitious disorders.* Retrieved from http://my.clevelandclinic.org/disorders/factitious_disorders/hic_an_overview_of_factitious_disorders.aspx

IMPETIGO

DEFINITION/ETIOLOGY:

Impetigo is a highly contagious skin infection characterized by eruptions caused by either *Streptococcal* or *Staphylococcal* bacteria. Minor skin injuries, insect bites, and dermatitis may be the portal for the infectious agent. The eruptions may proceed through vesicular, pustular, and encrusted stages. It usually appears as red bumps that form on the face (particularly around the nose and mouth) or extremities. The red bumps fill with pus, break open, and form a honey-colored crust. The lesions are usually itchy, but not painful. Symptoms usually begin 1-3 days after exposure for *Streptococcus*; usually 4-10 days for *Staphylococcus*. Infection is spread by direct contact with secretions from lesions.

SIGNS AND SYMPTOMS:

- Begins as a red sore, pimple or fluid-filled blister, most often found on face but may be anywhere on body.
- Blisters that rupture easily, leave a red, raw looking base.
- Itchy blisters, filled with honey-colored fluid that may be oozing and crusting over.
- May have swollen lymph nodes near the infection (lymphadenopathy).

MANAGEMENT/TREATMENT:

1. An untreated person can spread the bacteria for as long as drainage occurs from lesions. Infected individuals do not transmit the infection 24 hours after antibiotic treatment is underway.
2. Parents/guardians should keep contagious children home until 24 hours after starting topical or oral antibiotic therapy. Contacts of cases do not need to be excluded.
3. Hygienic measures: Wash the skin several times a day with an antibiotic soap to gently remove crusts and drainage.
4. Antibiotic therapy: Mild cases may be treated with prescribed topical antibiotic ointment or antibacterial cream. Before applying the topical medication, scabs need to be gently removed so that the medication can penetrate the lesion. More severe cases may require oral antibiotics.
5. Draining lesions should be covered with a dressing.

FOLLOW UP:

- Encourage diligence in skin cleansing.
- Monitor completion of antibiotic course even though lesions are healed.
- Have family observe close contacts and family members for lesions. Watch for additional cases.

IMPETIGO *(continued from previous page)*

POTENTIAL COMPLICATIONS:
- Post streptococcal glomerulonephritis (PSGN) (rare)
- Spread of the infection to other parts of the body
- Cellulitis (see Skin Infection)
- Methicillin-resistant *Staphylococcus aureus* (see MRSA)

NOTES:
Prevention
- Infected person should:
  - Use a clean towel and wash cloth each time.
  - Not share towels, clothing, razors, and other personal care products with others.
  - Wash hands thoroughly after touching skin lesions.
- Caregiver should wear gloves when washing lesions and applying antibiotic medication. Wash hands thoroughly afterwards.

References

American Academy of Pediatrics. (2013). Impetigo. In S. Aronson, & T. Shope (Eds.), *Managing infectious diseases in child care and schools (2nd ed.)* (p. 109). Elk Grove Village, IL: American Academy of Pediatrics.

American Academy of Pediatrics. (2009). Recommendations for care of children in special circumstances –recommendations for inclusion or exclusion. In L.K. Pickering, C.J. Baker, D.W. Kimberlin, & S.S. Long (Eds.), *Red Book: 2009 report of the committee on infectious diseases (28th ed.)* (p. 129). American Academy of Pediatrics: Elk Grove Village, IL.

Ball, J., Binder, R., & Cowen, K. (Eds.). (2012). Alterations in skin integrity. *Principles of Pediatric Nursing: Caring for Children (5th ed.)* (p. 1038-1039). Upper Saddle River, NJ: Pearson Education, Inc.

Centers for Disease Control and Prevention. (2008). *Group A streptococcal (GAS) disease.* Retrieved from http://www.cdc.gov/ncidod/dbmd/diseaseinfo/groupastreptococcal_g.htm

Mayo Clinic (2013). *Impetigo.* Retrieved from http://www.mayoclinic.com/health/impetigo/DS00464

Medline Plus, U.S. National Library of Medicine (2012). *Impetigo.* Retrieved from *http://www.nlm.nih.gov/medlineplus/impetigo.html*

Merck Manual, Professional Edition. *Impetigo and ecthyma.* (2013). Retrieved from *http://www.merckmanuals.com/professional/dermatologic_disorders/bacterial_skin_infections/impetigo_and_ecthyma.html?qt=impetigo&alt=sh*

National Institute of Allergy and Infectious Diseases (2009). *Impetigo.* Retrieved from *http://www.niaid.nih.gov/topics/impetigo/Pages/Default.aspx*

Vernon, P., Brady, M. & Starr, N.B. (2008). Dermatologic diseases. In C. Burns, M. Brady, A. Dunn, N.B. Starr, & C. Blosser (Eds.), *Pediatric primary care (4*th ed.) (pp. 951-952). St. Louis, MO: Saunders Elsevier.

INFLUENZA

DEFINITION/ETIOLOGY:
Influenza is a respiratory virus affecting the nose, throat, and lungs. There are 3 different influenza viruses: A, B and C. Most illnesses are caused by the type A and B influenza antigens. The symptoms are typically more severe with Influenza type A. Influenza type B is typically milder. Type B primarily affects children. The incubation period is 1 –4 days. May be contagious from 1 day before the symptoms start to more than 7 days after the onset of influenza. Symptoms typically last 3 – 5 days.

The virus is spread by airborne respiratory droplets, hand to hand contact or by contact with contaminated objects. Influenza is prevalent in the United States from October to March.

SIGNS AND SYMPTOMS:
- Fever –usually high (100-102 degrees); abrupt onset; fever may last up to 5 days
- Chills
- Headache
- General aches and pains
- Fatigue
- Nasal congestion
- Sneezing
- Sore throat
- Chest discomfort
- Cough (nonproductive)
- Mild pinkeye

MANAGEMENT/TREATMENT:
1. Encourage fluids and bedrest.
2. Physician/healthcare provider may prescribe antiviral medication (Tamiflu or Relenza) to shorten the duration of the symptoms and to reduce the risk of complications.
   - Benefit of taking antiviral medication is greatest if started within 48 hours of onset of illness.
   - If physician prescribes antiviral medication, monitor for side effects such as nausea and vomiting.
3. May administer acetaminophen if ordered to help alleviate flu symptoms (aches, pains, elevated temperature, etc.); follow medication orders.
4. Do not administer aspirin to children under the age of 18. Aspirin can play a role in causing Reye's Syndrome (rare but potentially fatal disease).
5. Instruct parent/guardian to call physician if symptoms worsen.
6. Instruct parent/guardian to keep child home from school until the child is fever free for 24 hours (without the use of antipyretics).
7. Educate parent/guardian(s) on potential complications of influenza.

INFLUENZA *(continued from previous page)*

FOLLOW UP:
- Refer to physician if symptoms reappear after illness has subsided.
- If need be, reiterate to the parent/guardian that the child should be kept home for 24 hours after the fever subsides (without antipyretic medication).

POTENTIAL COMPLICATIONS:
Students with chronic diseases such as asthma, diabetes, heart conditions, etc. may be at increased risk of complications.

Flu complications
- Pneumonia – most serious complication
- Sinus infection
- Ear infection
- Febrile seizure
- Bronchitis

NOTES:
Educate on the importance of:
- Yearly influenza vaccine (contraindicated in individuals with egg allergies)
- Controlling the spread of influenza; avoid crowds during peak influenza season
- Do not share food or drink
- Preventing the spread of influenza
  - Promote good handwashing
  - Cover mouth and nose with tissue when cough and/or sneeze; dispose of tissue properly; wash hands or use an alcohol-based hand sanitizer to remove germs
  - If tissue is not available, cough and/or sneeze into shoulder or elbow

References

American Academy of Pediatrics. (2013). Influenza. In S. Aronson, & T. Shope (Eds.), *Managing infectious diseases in child care and schools (2nd ed.)* (p.p. 111-112). Elk Grove Village, IL: American Academy of Pediatrics.

Ball, J., Binder, R., & Cowen, K. (Eds.). (2012). Immunization of communicable diseases. *Principles of Pediatric Nursing: Caring for Children (5th ed.)* (pp. 412-413). Upper Saddle River, NJ: Pearson Education, Inc.

Mayo Clinic. (2013). *Influenza (flu).* Retrieved from http://www.mayoclinic.com/health/influenza/DS00081

Merck Manual. (2012). *Influenza.* Retrieved from http://www.merckmanuals.com/professional/infectious_diseases/respiratory_viruses/influenza.html?qt=Influenza&alt=sh

Selekman, J., & Coates, J. (2013). Disease prevention. In J. Selekman (Ed.), *School nursing: A comprehensive text* (2nd ed.) (pp.473-515). Philadelphia, PA: F. A. Davis.

LACERATIONS

DEFINITION/ETIOLOGY:
A laceration is a tearing or jagged wound of the soft tissue. Soft tissue tears/cuts (lacerations) are common in children and are often the result of falls, blows, collisions or contact with sharp objects. Lacerations can occur anywhere on the body, but they are more common over bony areas (fingers, hand, knee, foot).

SIGNS AND SYMPTOMS:
- Torn or jagged wound of the soft tissue
- Wound edges may be separated

MANAGEMENT/TREATMENT:
1. Educate student in the proper process to wash, apply pressure and apply bandage to their wound. Encouraging supervised self-care minimizes bloodborne pathogen exposure and encourages student to become more participatory in their own self-care.
2. Treatment for superficial lacerations include:
   - Wear gloves if assisting student to clean and cover
   - Apply firm pressure with sterile or clean dressing until bleeding stops
   - Clean wound and surrounding skin with tap water or normal saline; if necessary to remove debris, irrigate with copious amounts of water

   Note: *Hydrogen peroxide is not appropriate for fresh wounds; it damages tissues and interferes with healing*
   - If unable to remove debris from wound, refer to physician for follow-up treatment
   - If no contraindications – apply topical antibiotic (follow school district policy) and bandage
   - If necessary, dry and apply butterfly dressing or Steri-Strip as directed
3. Treatment for cuts which are contaminated, deeper, longer or wider than above, or located on the face or flexor surface (knee, elbow) include:
   - Apply firm pressure until bleeding stops
   - Cover with sterile dressing.
   - May apply cold pack to prevent swelling
   - Refer to healthcare provider
   - If sutures are needed, they must be placed within 6 hours
4. Review immunization record; check last tetanus date; provide copy to parent/guardian to accompany to physician referral.

FOLLOW UP:
- Change bandage as needed.
- Note signs and symptoms of infection that require a revisit to physician/healthcare provider.
   - Early signs and symptoms of infection include: increased pain, redness around the edge of wound, swelling and tenderness.

LACERATIONS *(continued from previous page)*

- o Late signs and symptoms of infection include: fever, purulent drainage and lymphangitis (infection of the lymph vessel caused by a bacterial infection); look for red streak from infected area to armpit or groin.
- Observe for signs of cellulitis.
- Refer student to physician if exhibits signs of wound or systemic infection.
    - o If there are sutures, watch for swelling which causes tension on sutures and tissues.
    - o Observe sutures for signs of infection; infection appears first as a tiny red circle around each stitch.
- Follow primary care provider orders or local protocol if wound irrigation and dressing change is require/needed during the school day.

POTENTIAL COMPLICATIONS:
- Wound infection
- Lymphangitis
- Cellulitis

NOTES:
Watch for pyogenic granuloma.
- Small raised red benign growth
- Lesion is vascular; bleeds easily
- Pyrogenic granulomas appear following an injury (typically to the hand, arm or face)
- Small pyogenic granulomas often resolve on own; larger lesions may need to be surgically removed

References

John, R., & Chewey, L. (2013). *Common complaints.* In J. Selekman (Ed.), *School nursing: A comprehensive text* (2nd ed.) (pp. 578-640). Philadelphia, PA: F. A. Davis.

Medline Plus. U.S. National Library of Medicine. (2013). *Lymphangitis.* Retrieved from http://www.nlm.nih.gov/medlineplus/ency/article/007296.htm

Medline Plus. U.S. National Library of Medicine. (2013). *Wounds.* Retrieved from http://www.nlm.nih.gov/medlineplus/wounds.html

The Merck Manual, Professional Edition. (2013). *Lacerations.* Retrieved from http://www.merckmanuals.com/professional/injuries_poisoning/lacerations/lacerations.html?qt=lacerations&alt=sh

National Library of Medicine. (2012). *Pyogenic granuloma.* Retrieved from http://www.ncbi.nlm.nih.gov/pubmedhealth/PMH0002435/

WebMD. (2010*). First aid & emergencies.* Retrieved from http://firstaid.webmd.com/tc/cuts-topic-overview

LEAD POISONING (Plumbism)

DEFINITION/ETIOLOGY:
Lead is a natural metal occurring in the environment. Lead poisoning occurs when there is a build-up of lead in the body. People are exposed to lead by eating food or drinking water that is contaminated with lead. Old homes may have lead in the water pipes or may be painted with lead based paints. Children may be exposed to lead by playing in soil that has been contaminated with lead and/or eating lead-based paint chips. Lead poisoning most often occurs in young children under the age of six. Lead poisoning is often considered a chronic disorder.

SIGNS AND SYPMTOMS:
Symptoms are minimal at first. Symptoms are not obvious until blood levels become elevated. If not treated may have irreversible effects. Lead poisoning can affect every organ in the body.

Signs and symptoms of acute lead poisoning
- Irritable/moody
- Anorexia
- Fatigue
- Gastrointestinal symptoms – abdominal pain/vomiting/constipation

Signs and symptoms of chronic lead poisoning
- Cognitive deficits (risk increases with whole blood level $\geq$ 10 µg/dL)
- Seizure disorders
- Aggressive behaviors
- Anemia (lead interferes with hemoglobin formation)
- Peripheral neuropathy
- Muscle and joint pain
- Kidney damage

Blood level $\geq$ 50 µg/dL
- Gastrointestinal symptoms
  - Abdominal cramping (chronic)
  - Constipation
- Hand tremors
- Irritability/changes in mood

MANAGEMENT/TREATMENT:
- Eliminate source of lead exposure
- Children with blood lead levels of 5 µg/dL should be monitored; the child's vitamin and nutritional status should be assessed; children with diets low in fat and high in iron and calcium absorb less lead
- Chelation therapy for children diagnosed with encephalopathy or with blood lead levels greater than 45 µg/dL

LEAD POISONING *(continued from previous page)*

FOLLOW-UP:
- Refer student to support team to evaluate if child is eligible for Special Education or Section 504 accommodations.
- Lead poisoning is preventable. Consider writing a newsletter article educating parent/guardian(s) on lead poisoning prevention and the signs and symptoms of lead poisoning.

POTENTIAL COMPLICATIONS:
- Irreversible organ damage
- Encephalopathy
- Death – high lead levels cause brain damage and kidney failure which ultimately lead to death

NOTES:

Cultural implications. The following products _may_ contain lead:
- Some folk remedies (Greta or Azarcon – Hispanic home remedy)
- Some ethnic health-care products (Litargirio – used as deodorant)
- Imported herbal products/medicinal herbs may contain lead
- Some candies from Mexico
- Toys produced overseas may contain lead

References

Centers for Disease Control and Prevention. (2013). *Lead poisoning*. Retrieved from http://www.cdc.gov/nceh/lead/

Mayo Clinic. (2011). *Lead poisoning*. Retrieved from http://www.mayoclinic.com/health/lead-poisoning/FL00068

Medline Plus. U.S. National Library of Medicine. (2013). *Lead poisoning*. Retrieved from http://www.nlm.nih.gov/medlineplus/leadpoisoning.html

The Merck Manual, Professional Edition. (2013). *Lead poisoning*. Retrieved from http://www.merckmanuals.com/professional/injuries_poisoning/poisoning/lead_poisoning.html?qt=lead%20poisoning&alt=sh

United States Environmental Protection Agency. (2012). *Protect your family from lead in your home*. Retrieved from http://www.cpsc.gov/PageFiles/121956/426.pdf

LESBIAN, GAY, BISEXUAL, AND TRANSGENDER (LGBT) YOUTH

DEFINITION/ETIOLOGY:

Sexual orientation refers to an enduring pattern of emotional, romantic, and sexual attractions to men, women, or both sexes. Additionally, sexual orientation may refer to a person's sense of identity based on attractions, related behaviors, and membership in a community of others who share similar attractions.[1] Sexual orientation is often discussed in relation to the following three categories:

1. Homosexual – having emotional, romantic, or sexual attractions to members of the same sex, i.e. "Gay" refers to men who have emotional and physical attraction to men; and "Lesbian" refers to women who have emotional and physical attraction to women.
2. Heterosexual – having emotional or physical attraction to members of the opposite sex.
3. Bisexual – men or women having emotional or physical attraction to both sexes.

Transgender individuals have a strong sense of incongruence between their birth sex and their self-identified gender. Also, transgender individuals may identify as being heterosexual, homosexual, or bisexual.

Homosexuality is not a psychiatric disorder. Approximately 9 million Americans identify as lesbian, gay, bisexual or transgender (Gates, 2011). Homosexuality, bisexuality, and questioning one's own sexual orientation are no longer considered health conditions/disorders that need or respond to treatment or remediation (NASN, 2012).

The fact that gay and lesbian youth are more likely to attempt suicide or leave school to avoid ill treatment by adults or peers calls for educational leadership to teach that hatred and intolerance is unacceptable.

MANAGEMENT/POLICY:

1. Use gender neutral, non-judgmental language. Avoid the term "sexual preference" as this suggests choice (which current research does not support); sexual orientation is preferred.
2. Ensure confidentiality.
3. Do not endorse unsafe behaviors, e.g., risky sexual activity, alcohol abuse, driving while intoxicated, etc., while accepting the person who views him or herself as gay, lesbian or bisexual.
4. Suggest keeping a private journal to write about stresses and challenges, personal strengths, and possible solutions or ambitions. Journaling helps separate minor from major issues.

---

1 American Psychological Association (2013). Sexual orientation and homosexuality. http://www.apa.org/helpcenter/sexual-orientation.aspx

LESBIAN, GAY, BISEXUAL, & TRANSGENDER (LGBT) YOUTH *(continued from previous page)*

5. Be non-judgmental when asking questions about sexual activity or orientation in order to be effective in encouraging the student to share concerns and behaviors.
6. Reassure youth who are distressed about homosexual experience.
7. Offer to help or refer those who need help telling parents or who are having trouble in school or with peers.
8. Develop a network of community resources for youth and their parents for social and emotional support.

FOLLOW UP:
- Observe for depression and suicidal ideation.
- All adults in schools share the responsibility to help all youth develop into well-adjusted adults and to create a safe school and community environment that respects individual difference.
- Health education about tolerance and acceptance of diversity in the school and about sexual activity and sexually transmitted diseases.

POTENTIAL COMPLICATIONS:
- Lesbians – increased risk of sexually transmitted disease, depression, and substance abuse.[2]
- Homosexuals – increased risk of sexually transmitted disease, depression, and poor body image.[3]
- Other potential complications[4]:
  - Human Immunodeficiency Virus/Acquired Immunodeficiency Syndrome (HIV/AIDS)
  - Human Papilloma Virus (HPV)
  - Stigma
  - Suicide
  - Sexually transmitted diseases (STDs)
  - Substance abuse (club drugs)
  - Body image and disordered eating
  - Homelessness
  - Domestic Violence and victimization

---

2 Mayo Clinic. (2012). Health issues for lesbians. http://www.mayoclinic.com/health/health-issues-for-lesbians/MY00739
3 Mayo Clinic. (2012). Health issues for gay men: Tips to stay healthy. http://mayoclinic.com/health/health-issues-for-gay-men/MY00738
4 Gerlt, T., Blosser, C. & Dunn, A. (2008). Sexuality. In C. Burns, M. Brady, A. Dunn, N.B. Starr, C. Blosser (Eds.). *Pediatric primary care*, 4th ed. (pp. 406-408). St. Louis, MO: Saunders Elsevier.

LESBIAN, GAY, BISEXUAL, & TRANSGENDER (LGBT) YOUTH *(continued from previous page)*

NOTES:

Guidelines for Health Education include

- Do not refer to homosexuality as a medical term by limiting the mention of lesbian and gay issues in health education and HIV prevention curricula.
- Avoid "sexualizing" or defining homosexuality only by sexual activity; heterosexuals do not define themselves by their sex lives.
- In HIV and AIDS prevention education, all students need to recognize risk-taking behaviors; worldwide, heterosexual transmission is significant.
- Reduce "them" versus "us" thinking and behavior. In-service and professional development can help educators reflect on their own biases, deal with their feelings, and recognize actions that covertly reinforce stereotypical ideas about LGBT youth.

Characteristics of successful school programs include

- Keep disclosure in confidence.
- Use inclusive language, e.g., "parent" (not mother, father), "seeing anyone" or "date" (not boy or girlfriend), that conveys acceptance.
- Include LGBT issues in discussing multicultural issues.
- Establish and enforce policies that protect students from harassment, violence and discriminatory jokes or slurs by adults or students.
- Support students whose families include people in the LGBT community.

Resources

American Psychological Association (APA)
http://www.apa.org/

Lesbian, Gay, Bisexual, and Transgender Concerns Office (LGBTCO)
750 First Street N.E.
Washington, DC 20002
http://www.apa.org/pi/lgbt/index.aspx Centers for Disease Control (CDC)

LGBT Youth Resources
http://www.cdc.gov/lgbthealth/youth-resources.htm

National Gay and Lesbian Task Force
1325 Massachusetts Ave NW, Suite 600
Washington, DC 20005
Phone: (202) 393-5177
TTY: (202) 393-2284
Fax: (202 393-2241
http://www.ngltf.org/

LESBIAN, GAY, BISEXUAL, & TRANSGENDER (LGBT) YOUTH *(continued from previous page)*

References

American Psychological Association. (2013). *Sexual orientation and homosexuality*. Retrieved from http://www.apa.org/helpcenter/sexual-orientation.aspx

Centers for Disease Control and Prevention. (2013). *Lesbian, gay, bisexual, and transgender health*. Retrieved from http://www.cdc.gov/lgbthealth/about.htm

Gates, G. L. (2011). *How many people are lesbian, gay, bisexual and transgender?* Williams Institute of the UCLA School of Law.

Gerlt, T., Blosser, C. & Dunn, A. (2008). Sexuality. In C. Burns, M. Brady, A. Dunn, N.B. Starr, C. Blosser (Eds.), *Pediatric primary care* (4th ed.) (pp. 406-408). St. Louis, MO: Saunders Elsevier.

Institute of Medicine. (2011). The health of lesbian, gay, bisexual, and transgender people: Building a foundation for better understanding. Washington, DC: The National Academy of Sciences. Retrieved from http://www.nap.edu/download.php?record_id=13128/health/health-i

Mayo Clinic. (2012). *Health issues for lesbians.* Retrieved from http://www.mayoclinic.com/health/health-issues-for-lesbians/my00739

Mayo Clinic. (2012). *Health issues for gay men: Tips to stay healthy.* Retrieved from http://mayoclinic.com/health/health-issues-for-gay-men/MY00738

National Association of School Nurses [NASN] (2011). *Sexual Orientation and Gender Identity/Expression* (Sexual Minority Students): School Nurse Practice: *Position Paper.* Retrieved from http://www.nasn.org/PolicyAdvocacy/PositionPapersandReports/NASNPositionStatementsFullView/tabid/462/ArticleId/47/Sexual-Orientation-and-Gender-Identity-Expression-Sexual-Minority-Students-School-Nurse-Practice-Rev

Riley-Lawless, K. (2013). Demographics of children and adolescents. In J. Selekman (Ed.), *School nursing: A comprehensive text* (2nd ed.)(pp. 331-332). Philadelphia, PA: F.A. Davis.

LEUKEMIA

DEFINITION/ETIOLOGY:

Leukemia is the most common childhood cancer, defined as cancer of the white blood cells (WBC). There is an increase in the production of abnormal WBCs in leukemia, which replaces normal bone marrow and spills over into the circulating blood. Leukemic cells may infiltrate any organ: liver, spleen, lymph nodes, kidneys, testes, and the central nervous system (brain and spinal cord).

The initial period of drug therapy is usually 2 1/2 - 3 years. After the initial period of drug therapy, the type of medication and length of therapy is individualized.

CAUSES:

The exact cause of leukemia is not fully understood by scientists. Leukemia appears to develop from a combination of genetic and environmental factors.

TYPES:

1. <u>Acute Lymphocytic Leukemia</u> *(ALL)* accounts for approximately 76% of cases. ALL is most common in ages 2-4 years and has the best prognosis during this time period. The survival rate is just under 90%. There are several subtypes of ALL which are identified by bone marrow appearance and other blood tests. Treatment and prognosis depend on age of onset, subtypes of ALL, and other blood factors.
2. <u>Acute Non-lymphocytic Leukemia</u> accounts for approximately 20% of cases. The survival rate is approximately 71%.
3. <u>Acute Myelogenous Leukemia</u> (AML) and other types account for approximately 2-4% of cases. AML is most common is the teenage years.
4. <u>Chronic Myelogenous Leukemia</u> (CML) is rare in children. Survival rates are 60-80%.

SIGNS/SYMPTOMS:

- Onset may be insidious or acute
- Bone and joint pain due to pressure and irritation from infiltration by white blood cells
- Anemia, pallor, fatigue, weakness, lethargy
- Increased susceptibility to fevers and recurrent infections due to low white blood cell count and weakened immune system
- Bleeding under the skin; pinpoint hemorrhages (petechiae) or larger areas; bleeding of nose or gums; blood in stool or urine
- Headache due to infiltration of the brain
- Seizures, balance problems, or abnormal vision
- Vomiting from bleeding in stomach or increased intracranial pressure
- Breathing problems and interference with blood flow to and from the heart
- Enlarged liver, spleen or swollen lymph nodes
- Weight loss

LEUKEMIA *(continued from previous page)*

MANAGEMENT/TREATMENT:
- Drug therapy
- Chemotherapy
- Radiation
- Bone marrow or blood stem transplants (required for aggressive ALL)

Side Effects of Treatment:
- Hair loss from drug therapy
- Weight gain from therapy (prednisone)
- High blood pressure
- Breathing problems and interference with blood flow to and from the heart
- One third to 1/2 of survivors have poor short term memory, short attention span, or other learning difficulties
- Blood stem transplants may affect child's growth
- Emotional and psychological problems (which may affect school work)

FOLLOW UP:
An individual healthcare plan should be developed and may include:
- Homebound instruction for limited periods
- Notify teacher of symptoms of possible illness
- Emphasize that the condition may make the student vulnerable to contagious viral illnesses of others
- Notify cafeteria manager if child needs extra food
- Obtain immunization exemption from doctor if necessary
- Coordinate with physical education (PE) teacher
- Accommodation of physical/emotional needs (possible 504/IEP)
- Educate classmates before student returns to school
- Notify parent/guardian(s) and doctors of unusual symptoms and the occurrence of contagious illnesses, e.g., chickenpox, in the school
- Continuous follow up care is important and essential for the child diagnosed with leukemia

NOTES:
- Special treatment is required for exposure to chicken pox.
- A diagnosis of leukemia may be devastating for the family of a child who is newly diagnosed.
- Siblings are "at risk" for contracting leukemia.
- Children treated for leukemia have an increased risk for developing cancer in adulthood.
- Some school districts and hospitals have a school re-entry program.

LEUKEMIA *(continued from previous page)*

Resources
"Returning to School", Leukemia and Lymphoma Society at <u>http://www.livestrong.org/</u> <u>What-We-Do/Our-Actions/Professional-Tools-Training/For-Educators/Returning-to-School</u>

References

American Cancer Society. (2013). *How is childhood leukemia diagnosed? Signs and symptoms of childhood leukemia.* Retrieved from <u>http://www.cancer.org/cancer/leukemiainchildren/detailedguide/childhood-leukemia-diagnosis</u>

Kids Health. (2012). *Leukemia.* Retrieved from <u>http://kidshealth.org/parent/medical/cancer/cancer_leukemia.html</u>

Mayo Clinic. (2013). *Leukemia.* Retrieved from <u>http://www.mayoclinic.com/health/leukemia/DS00351</u>

Medline Plus. U.S. National Library of Medicine. (2013). *Childhood Leukemia.* Retrieved from <u>http://www.nlm.nih.gov/medlineplus/childhoodleukemia.html</u>

Selekman, J., Bobhenek, J. & Lukens, M. (2013).Children with chronic conditions. In J. Selekman (Ed.), *School nursing: A comprehensive text* (2nd ed.) (p. 728). Philadelphia, PA: F.A. Davis.

LICE (HEAD) - Pediculosis humanus capitis

DEFINITION/ETIOLOGY:
Head lice are parasitic insects that live with a glue-like substance. Nymphs hatch from the eggs in 7-10 days, and grow to adults capable of reproduction (lay eggs) in 9-12 days, with a life span of 30 days. Only eggs deposited by inseminated female lice will hatch close to the human scalp, feed on human blood, and humans are their only host. The female lays about 6 eggs per day (more than 100 in a lifetime), attaching them firmly to the hair shaft near the scalp. Head lice move by crawling; they cannot fly or jump and commonly affect people with good hygiene. They are spread most commonly by head to head contact, for example during play at home or school, slumber parties, sports activities and camp. Although uncommon, it can be spread by contact with clothing such as hats, scarves, combs, brushes or towels. Only lice, not nits, spread the infection.

Head lice are not dangerous and do not transmit disease but they are contagious until killed from a chemical agent. They most commonly occur in children ages 3-11 years old.

SIGNS AND SYMPTOMS:
- Head lice infestations can be asymptomatic, particularly with a first **infestation or when an infestation is light.**
- Itching (pruritus), the most common symptom of head lice infestation, is caused by an allergic reaction to the saliva associated with louse bites. It may take 4-6 weeks for itching to appear the first time a person has head lice.
- The student may report a tickling feeling or a sensation of something moving in the hair.
- Student irritability and sleeplessness may be present.
- Sores on the head may be caused by scratching. These sores and scabs, caused by scratching, can sometimes become infected with bacteria normally found on a person's skin. These may also be associated with swollen lymph nodes.

The assessment of a child who is suspected of having head lice includes:
- In good lighting, use a wood applicator to separate the hair in small sections. Give particular **attention to the scalp behind the ears and at the nape of the neck, areas of optimal temperature for head lice. Dispose of the applicator after each use.**
- The nurse needs to learn to recognize head lice and nits to avoid misidentification of dandruff and other debris as nits or lice.
- New nits will be found close to the scalp and will not easily be removed from the hair shaft as will dandruff, hairspray droplets and other hair products, dirt particles, other insects (fleas, bedbugs, etc.) and scabs. Magnification may be helpful in making this assessment.

LICE (HEAD) - Pediculosis humanus capitis *(continued from previous page)*

MANAGEMENT AND TREATMENT:
Exclusion:
Policies should be based on scientific evidence and best practice. Administrators, school nurses, local private and public health physicians and concerned parent/guardian(s) can cooperate to develop rational and epidemiologically sound school policies. Policy can be further supported through faculty and staff in-service and parent/community educational programs. School nurse practice includes the dual roles of child advocate and collaboration in policy development.

1. The American Academy of Pediatrics, National Association of School Nurses, Centers for Disease Control and Prevention, and Harvard School of Public Health do not recommend a "no-nit" policy.
2. Children with live head lice should be referred to their parent/guardian(s) for treatment. Data does not support school exclusion for nits (NASN, 2011).
3. The discovery of nits or live lice should not cause the student to be sent home from school or isolated while at school.
4. Notify parent/guardian(s) at the end of the day of the suspected infestation and recommended management.
5. Student may be transported home as usual.
6. Screenings of entire classes or school have not been found to be cost effective are not recommended.
7. Parents/guardians should be instructed to check their family at least weekly for the presence of lice.
8. **In cases that involve head lice, as in all school health issues, it is vital that the school nurse prevent stigmatizing and maintain the student's privacy as well as the family's right to confidentiality.**

TREATMENT:
Educate and assist families to enable them to be able to effectively and efficiently treat head lice so that the student can return to school the next day.
1. Only students with live (moving) lice need treatment with an over-the-counter (OTC) or prescription medication (pediculicide). Some medications may require 2 treatments. Some resistance to these products has been reported and may require referral to the health care provider.
2. Parents/caregivers should persistently work to remove nits. All nits should be removed to limit newly hatched nymphs (7-10 days).
3. "Preventive" use of lice shampoo is NOT advised. Some lice survive sub-lethal doses of residual chemicals and mutate over generations to resist low doses of pediculicide.
4. There is no clear evidence to support the use of food-grade oil, salad dressing, tea tree oil, enzymes, hot air blowers, or other 'remedies.'

211

LICE (HEAD) - Pediculosis humanus capitis *(continued from previous page)*

5. Articles such as clothing and bedding should be washed at 130 degrees and dried on the hot setting.
6. Parent/guardian(s) should check and treat all household members who have lice, following the instructions only
7. Students with severe or persistent infestation should be referred to their primary care provider for treatment or to social services to assist with accessing treatment.
8. Supplemental Measures:
    a. Articles such as clothing and bedding should be washed at 130 degrees and dried on the hot setting.
    b. Soak combs and brushes in hot water (at least 130°) for 5-10 minutes.
    c. Vacuum carpet, pillows, and furniture where the infested person sat or lay. The risk of being infested by a louse that has fallen onto a rug or carpet or furniture is very small. Head lice survive less than 1-2 days if they fall off a person and cannot feed; nits cannot hatch and usually die within a week if they do not stay at the warm temperature found close to the human scalp. Spending much time and money on housecleaning activities is not necessary to avoid re-infestation by lice or nits that may have fallen off the head or crawled onto furniture or clothing.

FOLLOW UP:
- Monitor progress toward effective eradication of live lice and nits.
- "Treatment failure" may be due to misdiagnosis or misidentification of nits, non-adherence to directions for treatment, a new exposure after treatment, or inadequate or low residual ovicidal (egg-killing) action of the lice medication used.
- Seek information from reliable, evidence-based, science-based sources.

POTENTIAL COMPLICATIONS:
- Secondary bacterial infections (impetigo)
- Enlarged lymph nodes

NOTES:
Education/Prevention for Faculty/Staff/Students
- Educate parent/guardian(s), students and staff about prevention, recognition, and treatment of head lice before cases or outbreaks occur.
- Inform staff about appropriate follow-up and dispel myths (e.g., lice fly or hop).
- Ask teachers to observe and refer children who scratch or have visible lice/nits.
- Educate teachers and students to avoid "head-to-head" contact, e.g., during telling secrets, team work, team sports, babysitting, sleepovers, etc.
- Encourage teachers to minimize student use of dress-up hats and neck wear if cases have occurred during the year.

LICE (HEAD) - Pediculosis humanus capitis *(continued from previous page)*

- Watch for head contact with fabric items, e.g., daily vacuuming of carpet if students lie on it; keep personal use pillows or blankets for naps stored separately.
- Non-fabric items are low risk. Clean headphones, vinyl bus seat backs, and solid helmets for general hygiene.
- Do not let children pile their winter coats/hats. Although there is no clear evidence of effectiveness, some schools separate coats and back packs on hooks, chair backs. Hats may be tucked into coat sleeves.

Education/Prevention for Parent/Guardian(s) /Students
- Offer clear instructions about effective treatment products and safe actions.
- Utilize multiple instructional strategies that are appropriate for intended audience (parent/guardian(s) /students/staff):
  - Verbal instructions/explanations, and videos.
  - Written head lice information, treatment instructions/directions related to treatment, policy, pamphlets, letters, and newsletters. Use appropriate reading level and languages for intended audience(s) when developing or selecting print materials.
  - Hands-on strategies include demonstration-return demonstration for scalp inspection, head lice and nit identification, and nit combing technique.
- Assess family needs for treatment assistance and follow-through with nit combing and re-treatment if necessary.

References
Andresen, K., & McCarthy, A.M. (2009). A policy change strategy for head lice management. *The Journal of School Nursing*. 25 (6) 407-416. doi:10.1177/1059840509347316

American Academy of Pediatrics. (2009). Summaries of infectious disease – pediculosis capitis, pediculosis corporis. In L.K. Pickering, C.J. Baker, D.W. Kimberlin, & S.S. Long (Eds.), *Red Book: 2009 report of the committee on infectious diseases (28th ed.)* (pp. 495-497). American Academy of Pediatrics: Elk Grove Village, IL.

Center for Disease Control. (2010). *Parasites-lice-head lice*. Retrieved from http://www.cdc.gov/parasites/lice/head/

National Association of School Nurses. (2011). *Pediculosis management in the school setting: Position statement*. Retrieved from http://www.nasn.org/PolicyAdvocacy/PositionPapersandReports/NASNPositionStatementsFullView/tabid/462/ArticleId/40/Pediculosis-Management-in-the-School-Setting-Revised-2011

MENINGITIS

DEFINITION/ETIOLOGY:
Meningitis is an inflammation of leptomeninges, a covering of the brain and spinal cord. Meningitis may be caused by bacteria, viruses or, rarely, fungi. It is important to know whether meningitis is caused by viral or bacterial infection because the severity of illness and treatment differ depending on the cause.

CAUSES
- **Viral** meningitis is generally less severe and clears up without treatment. The most common viruses causing meningitis are enteroviruses (85-95%).
- **Bacterial** meningitis can be quite severe and may result in brain damage, hearing loss, or learning disabilities. The importance of knowing the type of bacteria causing the meningitis is helpful in providing the appropriate antibiotic treatment to prevent some types from spreading and infecting other people.
  - In children 2 months to 12 years of age, this was traditionally the result of infection with *Streptococcus pneumoniae, Haemophilus influenzae* or *Neisseria meningitides*.
  - In those who are 9 years old or older, common causes have traditionally been *Streptococcus pneumoniae* or *Neisseria meningitides*.
  - Recent advances immunizations have led to decrease of disease associated with *Streptococcus pneumoniae* and *Haemophilus influenza*.
  - In children who have ventriculoperitoneal (VP) shunt, meningitis is the result of *Staphylococcus epidermidis* and, less commonly, *Staphylococcus aureus*.
- **Fungal and Mycobacterium** tuberculosis: uncommon, but should be considered in immuno-compromised host.

SIGNS/SYMPTOMS:
- Classic triad for suspicion: fever, headache and stiff neck; but these findings are most common in children >2 years of age.
- Signs of brain dysfunction such as altered mental status or consciousness, seizures.
- Signs of increased of intracranial pressure (ICP): headache, vomiting or papilledema.

MANAGEMENT/TREATMENT:
1. **Meningitis is an emergency condition** and REQUIRES diagnosis and appropriate treatment as soon as possible to prevent serious complications.
2. Suspected cases should be referred to a physician/healthcare provider with concomitant notification of parents/guardians.
3. Closely monitor vital signs and physical findings, especially neurological findings such as level of consciousness.

MENINGITIS *(continued from previous page)*

4. Specific treatment of meningitis depends on confirmed diagnosis:
    o For suspected viral meningitis: supportive care may be done as an outpatient, *except* herpes meningitis (for which antiviral therapy occurs with close supervision in hospital setting).
    o For suspected bacterial meningitis, treatment is initially directed to the most common pathogens based on child's age and setting. All children need to be admitted for close monitoring.
5. Chemoprophylaxis of close contacts are considered, and based on the type of pathogen that was cultured (*Haemophilus influenzae* or *Neisseria meningitides*), age, and other aspects of the situation surrounding exposure. Contact Public Health Department with details.
6. Work closely with health department and school officials to reduce public anxiety.
7. Follow local and/or state public health officials' decisions regarding outbreak control and management.

POSSIBLE COMPLICATIONS:
*   Up to 50% of those with bacterial meningitis sustain sequelae such as hearing loss, seizures, learning disabilities, blindness, ataxia, or hydrocephalus.
*   Poor prognosis is associated with young age, long duration of illness before effective antibiotic therapy, late onset seizure, coma, shock, and immuno-compromised status.
*   Most children with non-herpetic viral meningitis recover completely.

FOLLOW UP:
*   All children with meningitis should have a hearing evaluation before hospital release and follow-up visit.
*   After hospitalization, children need to be transitioned to rehabilitation at home until there is complete recovery.
*   When children return to school: monitor for mental, social, and functional alterations that may be present and provide planning with a multi-disciplinary team, e.g., 504 plan.
*   Monitor side effects of medical therapy (i.e., anticonvulsant drugs).

NOTES:
Following good hygiene practices is effective in reducing the spread of infection causes by viruses. Proper hand hygiene and respiratory etiquette can reduce the spread of viral infections such as viral meningitis. Cleaning contaminated surfaces, avoid sharing items with sick people, and obtaining childhood vaccinations can reduce the chances of becoming infected with a virus or spreading infection to others.

MENINGITIS *(continued from previous page)*

References

American Academy of Pediatrics. (2013). *Menigitis.* In S. Aronson, & T. Shope (Eds.), *Managing infectious diseases in child care and schools (2nd ed.)* (pp. 119-120). Elk Grove Village, IL: American Academy of Pediatrics.

American Academy of Pediatrics. (2009). Summaries of infectious disease. In L.K. Pickering, C. J. Baker, D.W. Kimberlin, & S.S.Long (Eds.), *Red Book: 2009 Report of the Committee on Infectious Diseases (*28th ed.) (pp. 455-463). Elk Grove Village, IL: American Academy of Pediatrics.

Atkinson, W., Wolfe, S., Hamborsky, J., & McIntyre, L. (Eds.) (2012). *Epidemiology and prevention of vaccine-preventable diseases (*12th ed.). Washington DC: Public Health Foundation/ Centers for Disease Control and Prevention. Retrieved from http://www.cdc.gov/vaccines/pubs/pinkbook/table-of-contents.html

Blosser, C.G., Brady, M. & Muller, W. (2008). Infectious diseases and immunizations. In C. Burns, M. Brady, A. Dunn, N.B. Starr, C. Blosser (Eds.). *Pediatric primary care (* 4th ed.) (pp. 532-533). St. Louis, MO: Saunders Elsevier

Centers for Disease Control and Prevention (CDC). (2012). *Meningitis.* Retrieved from http://www.cdc.gov/meningitis/index.html

Selekman, J. & Coates, J. (2013). Disease prevention. In J. Selekman (Ed.), *School nursing: A comprehensive text* (2nd ed.) (pp. 509-510). Philadelphia, PA: F.A. Davis.

MENSTRUAL DISORDERS

DEFINITION AND ETIOLOGY:

Term	Definition
Amenorrhea	Absence of menstruation.
Dysmenorrhea	Defined as "difficult menstrual flow" and can cause painful menstruation (cramps). Primary dysmenorrhea is the result of increased prostaglandin production (in the absence of pelvic pathology). Secondary dysmenorrhea is painful uterine contractions related to an identified cause, e.g. endometriosis, pelvic inflammatory disease. Typically occurs in the first three years after initial menstruation.
Hypermenorrhea	Excessive bleeding in amount and duration, at regular intervals (also called *menorrhagia*).
Intermenstrual	Not excessive bleeding, occurring between otherwise regular menstrual periods.
Menarche	Onset of menses. Average age of onset is 12, but may occur from 8-15 years. Menstrual periods are often irregular during first six months to two years.
Menometrorrhagia	Excessive and prolonged bleeding, frequent and irregular intervals.
Metrorrhagia	Not excessive bleeding, but intervals are irregular.
Mittelschmerz	Intermenstrual pain and/or bleeding, lasting a few hours to 3 days. Pain is usually associated with ovulation.
Oligomenorrhea	Infrequent, irregular episodes of bleeding, usually occurring at intervals greater than 40 days.
Polymenorrhea	Frequent but regular episodes of bleeding, occurring at intervals of 21 days or less.
Dysfunctional Uterine Bleeding	Irregular, painless bleeding that is prolonged and excessive.

SIGNS AND SYMPTOMS:
Dysmenorrhea
- **Primary dysmenorrheal** - pain, usually the first day or two of menses
- Suprapubic pain radiating to the thigh and lower back
- Associated nausea, vomiting, and diarrhea
- Breast tenderness
- Headache, fatigue, sleep disturbances
- Dizziness, nervousness, syncope

MENSTRUAL DISORDERS *(continued from previous page)*

Amenorrhea
Requires evaluation when:
- Menarche delayed beyond age 15
- No secondary sexual characteristics develop by age 14 (breasts, pubic and axillary hair)
- Three years after developing secondary sexual characteristics if menstruation has not begun

Persons at risk:
- Runners, gymnasts, ballet dancers (excessive exercise)
- Girls with too little body fat, e.g. anorexia nervosa, extreme dieters such as vegan vegetarians
- Possible development of osteoporosis due to lack of estrogen (female hormone)

Excessive Uterine Bleeding
- It is helpful to divide cases in to mild, moderate or severe to determine treatment
- Hemoglobin < 8 with tachycardia, pallor would indicate a severe case
- Hemoglobin between 9-11 would indicate moderate hemorrhage
- In mild cases there is no anemia

MANAGEMENT/TREATMENT:
Anovulatory cycles where there is a lack of a progesterone peak, are present in the majority of girls within 24 months of menarche and are responsible for irregular menses. Irregular cycles after 24 months post menarche should be evaluated.

1. **Primary dysmenorrhea**
   - Analgesic medication specifically NSAIDS (non-steroid anti-inflammatories) which reduce prostaglandin level.
   - Educate on proper use of NSAIDS to avoid stomach irritation or overdose.
   - Warm pad to lower abdomen and position of comfort.
   - Encourage physical exercise and balanced diet.
   - Refer severe disorders for medical evaluation.
   - Hormonal contraception can be used to treat dysmenorrhea when NSAIDS are ineffective.
2. **Amenorrhea**
   - Refer for medical evaluation girls who should have begun menstruating or have stopped.
   - Consider the possibility of pregnancy.

MENSTRUAL DISORDERS *(continued from previous page)*

3. Excessive Uterine Bleeding
- For severe cases, hospitalization and transfusion may be necessary.
- Oral hormonal therapy may be used to regulate cycles and decrease bleeding.
- Reassurance, a high iron diet, and the use of a multivitamin with iron should be encouraged.

POTENTIAL COMPLICATIONS:
Refer to primary healthcare provider if:
- Menstruation has not begun by the age of 15.
- Menstruation has not begun within 3 years after breast growth began, or if breasts have not started to grow by age 13.
- Period suddenly stops for more than 90 days.
- Periods become very irregular after having had regular, monthly cycles.
- Periods occurs more often than every 21 days or less often than every 35 days.
- Bleeding for more than 7 days.
- Bleeding is heavier than usual or using more than 1 pad or tampon every 1 to 2 hours.
- Bleeding occurs between periods.
- There is severe pain during period.
- Sudden fever and feel sick after using tampons.

NOTES:
- Educate students to keep diary of menstrual cycles to share with parent/guardian and healthcare provider.
- Encourage students to keep sanitary napkins/tampons at school. An emergency supply of sanitary napkins and tampons should be kept in health room.
- Students may keep medication for discomfort at school following school policy and guidelines for medication at school.
- Be alert to history and signs that suggest pregnancy or secondary dysmenorrhea, e.g., PID (pelvic inflammatory disease).
- Irregular menstrual cycles in a girl within two years of menarche can usually be observed before an extensive work up. Provide reassurance.

References
Carey, A. & Murray, P. (2011). Menstrual disorders: Dysmenorrhea and premenstrual syndrome. In M. Fisher, E. Alderman, R. Kreipe, W. Rosenfeld, W.(Eds.). *Textbook of adolescent health care* (pp. 589-610). Elk Grove Village, IL: American Academy of Pediatrics.

Mayo Clinic. (2011). *Menstrual cramps*. Retrieved from http://www.mayoclinic.com/health/menstrual-cramps/DS00506

Medline Plus, U.S. National Library of Medicine. (2011). *Menorrhagia (heavy menstrual bleeding)*. Retrieved from http://www.mayoclinic.com/health/menorrhagia/DS00394

MONONUCLEOSIS (Glandular Fever, Infectious Mono)

DEFINITION/ETIOLOGY:
An acute viral infection caused by the Epstein-Barr virus (EBV). Incubation period is 4-6 weeks. The virus is present in pharyngeal secretions and is spread by saliva. The virus can be excreted for many months after infection and can even occur intermittently throughout life. It can occur at any age, but is most common in adolescents.

SIGNS AND SYPMTOMS (COMMON):
- Milder and often undiagnosed in young children, more severe in high school and college age
- Fever, malaise, headache, and fatigue
- Sore throat and enlarged, red, exudative tonsils
- Lymph nodes swollen in axilla, groin, above elbow, and especially in neck (post cervical)
- Enlarged spleen
- Maculopapular confluent rash if treated with penicillin
- Fever may last 1-2 weeks; fatigue and malaise may last 4-6 weeks

MANAGEMENT/TREATMENT:
There is no treatment; most patients recover in 4-6 weeks without medication.
1. Refer to physician/healthcare provider; laboratory tests are needed for diagnosis; strep throat may accompany.
2. Symptomatic support for sore throat (gargle) and fever (fluids).
3. Return to school on advice of physician/healthcare provider.
4. May be in school during illness if temperature is below 100° and able to tolerate activity.
5. Rest and contact sports restrictions may be needed for a month or longer.

FOLLOW UP:
- Monitor 1-2 weeks after return to school for full recovery.

POTENTIAL COMPLICATIONS:
- Complications are rare : encephalitis, Guillain-Barré syndrome.
- Danger of ruptured spleen. Protect from contact sports for 1 month or until splenomegaly has resolved.

MONONUCLEOSIS (Glandular Fever, Infectious Mono) *(continued from previous page)*

NOTES:

Health education:

- Transmitted person-to-person via saliva. Virus may remain in saliva several weeks during and after convalescence.
- Avoid kissing on the mouth and sharing food from the same container and/or by sharing things like eating utensils, glasses, toothbrushes and lipstick or lip gloss.
- Use good handwashing techniques at all times.

References

American Academy of Pediatrics. (2013). Mononucleois. In S. Aronson, & T. Shope (Eds.), *Managing infectious diseases in child care and schools. (2nded.)* (p.123). Elk Grove Village, IL: American Academy of Pediatrics.

American Academy of Pediatrics. (2009). Summaries of infectious disease – Epstein-barr virus infections. In L.K. Pickering, C.J. Baker , D.W. Kimberlin, & S.S. Long (Eds.), *Red Book: 2009 Report of the committee on infectious diseases(28th ed.)* (pp. 289-292). American Academy of Pediatrics: Elk Grove Village, IL.

Centers for Disease Control and Prevention (CDC), National Center for Infectious Diseases. (2006). *Epstein-Barr Virus and Infectious Mononucleosi.* Retrieved from CDC website at http://www.cdc.gov/ncidod/diseases/ebv.htm

Mayo Clinic. (2012). *Mononucleosis.* Retrieved from http://www.mayoclinic.com/health/mononucleosis/DS00352

Smith, S., & Vorvick, L. (2013). *Mononucleosis.* Retrieved from http://www.nlm.nih.gov/medlineplus/ency/article/000591.htm

MOSQUITO-BORNE DISEASES

DEFINITION/ETIOLOGY:
A mosquito-borne disease is a transmitted from a mosquito infected from a virus or parasite. Mosquitoes become infected by feeding off of birds, mammals or people who are carriers of diseases. Most people infected with a mosquito-borne disease do not become ill except with Malaria. However, the potential for them to become ill fluctuates from mild, flu like symptoms to severe illness and even death.

Types

Eastern Equine Encephalitis (EEE)	A rare illness in humans and only a few cases are reported in the United States each year. EEE is considered the most serious mosquito-borne disease in the United States. Most cases occur in the Atlantic and Gulf Coast states.
Western equine encephalitis	Most cases of Western equine encephalitis occur in the eastern and central states.
La Crosse encephalitis	Most cases of La Crosse encephalitis occur in the southeastern states, upper mid-Western, and mid-Atlantic states. Children under the age of 16 usually have the most severe cases.
West Nile Virus (WNV)	Most cases of WNV occur in the summer to fall months in North America. Mosquitoes infect people, horses, and mammals with the virus. Although the risk is very low, WNV has been known to spread through organ transplants, blood transfusions, breast-feeding and during pregnancy from mother to baby.
Dengue	Dengue is uncommon in United States, but has been seen in Texas, Florida, and Hawaii. Dengue is vaccine preventable.
Malaria	A small amount of malaria cases exist in the United States. Those infected typically become ill.

SIGNS/SYMPTOMS:
- Range from none to severe
- Depends on the virus or parasite transmitted
- Mild, flu like (fever, body aches, headache, vomiting, nausea)
- Rash
- High fever
- Altered mental status
- Swollen lymph glands
- Convulsions
- Encephalitis
- Meningitis
- Coma, paralysis, death

MOSQUITO-BORNE DISEASES *(continued from previous page)*

MANAGEMENT/TREATMENT:
- No specific treatment
- Based on symptoms
- Pain control
- OTC medications to alleviate flu like symptoms
- Avoid ibuprofen, naproxen sodium which may increase bleeding disorders
- Close medical monitoring is required for severe symptoms

PREVENTION /CONTROL
Educate students, families, staff, and the community on prevention:
- Wear protective clothing (long pants, long sleeves and socks)
- Use insect repellents (containing diethyltoluamide, amount used is determined by number of hours of protection needed)
- Install screens on windows and doors
- Remove standing water around your home (flower pots, buckets, pool cover, bird baths, pet dishes, etc.)
- Avoid shaded and wooded areas
- Limit outdoor exposure between dawn and dusk
- Community-wide mosquito prevention programs

NOTES:
- Report sick or dead bird, or mammal to local health department

References
American Academy of Pediatrics. (2013). Mosquito-borne diseases. In S. Aronson, & T. Shope (Eds.), *Managing infectious diseases in child care and schools (2nded.)* (p. 125). Elk Grove Village, IL: American Academy of Pediatrics.

Centers for Disease Control. (2012). *Division of vector-borne diseases.* Retrieved from http://www.cdc.gov/ncezid/dvbd/index.html

Centers for Disease Control. (2012). *Malaria facts.* Retrieved from http://www.cdc.gov/malaria/about/facts.html

Mayo Clinic. (2012). *West nile virus.* Retrieved from http://www.mayoclinic.com/health/west-nile-virus/DS00438/DSECTION=symptoms

Oakland County Health Department. (2013). *West nile virus what you need to know.* Retrieved from http://www.oakgov.com/health/Documents/Facts%20Sheets/fs_west_nile_virus.pdf

MUMPS

DEFINITION/ETIOLOGY:
Mumps is a systemic disease characterized by swelling of one or more of salivary glands, usually the parotid glands.

Mumps is caused by *Rubulavirus* that infects the respiratory tract. Others causes of parotitis include with *cytomegalovirus, parainfluenza virus types 1 and 3, influenza A virus, coxackieviruses* and *enteroviruses.* The virus is spread by direct contact with respiratory droplets and saliva. The incubation period is generally 16-18 days (range 12-25 days) from time of exposure to onset of symptoms. Mumps virus has been isolated from saliva from between 2 and 7 days before symptom onset until 9 days after onset of symptoms. Interactions of students during sporting or other inter-collegiate events and mass mobilization of students during holidays are opportunities for transmission among students from geographically diverse parts of the country and world. Mumps is a vaccine preventable disease (VPD).

SIGNS AND SYMPTOMS:
- Non-specific prodrome, which includes myalgia, anorexia, malaise, headache, and fever
- Unilateral or bilateral tender swelling of parotid or other salivary glands
- 30%-70% of mumps infections are associated with typical acute parotitis
- Up to 20% of infections are asymptomatic
- Nearly 50% are associated with non-specific or primarily respiratory symptoms, with or without parotitis

MANAGEMENT/TREATMENT:
1. Rapidly identify infected and susceptible persons and report to public health department.
2. There is no specific treatment for mumps. The healthcare provider may recommend that parent/guardian(s) apply ice or heat packs to the neck and the administration of non-aspirin analgesics (e.g. Tylenol®). Do not give aspirin to children with a viral illness because of the risk of Reye's Syndrome.
3. Infected student should be excluded for 5 days from onset of parotid glands swelling.
4. Susceptible children or adolescents born during or after 1957 should have received two doses of mumps immunization (usually as MMR).
5. The routine use of vaccine is not advised for people born before 1957, however immunization is not contraindicated in those people having unknown serologic status.
6. Mumps vaccine has not been effective in preventing of infection after exposure; however, immunization will provide protection to subsequent exposures.
7. Recommend that unimmunized, pregnant females exposed to mumps consult with their healthcare provider.
8. Follow local and/or state public health officials' decisions regarding outbreak control and management.

MUMPS *(continued from previous page)*

Potential Complications:
- Aseptic meningitis
- Orchitis (in older men)
- Nerve deafness

NOTES:

PREVENTION
- Mumps is a vaccine preventable disease.
- Mumps immunization status should be assessed. Mumps vaccine should be given as an MMR for students and staff who have not already had mumps or mumps vaccine.
- The effectiveness of MMR against mumps is approximately 80% after one dose and approximately 90% after two doses.
- Because the vaccine is not 100% effective, some cases can occur in vaccinated persons.
- Students should be kept home until 9 days after the onset of paratoid swelling.

References

American Academy of Pediatrics. (2013). Mumps. In S. Aronson, & T. Shope (Eds.), *Managing infectious diseases in child care and schools (2nd ed.)* (pp. 131-132). Elk Grove Village, IL: American Academy of Pediatrics.

American Academy of Pediatrics. (2009). Summaries of infectious disease – mumps. In L.K. Pickering, C.J. Baker, D.W. Kimberlin, & S.S. Long (Eds.), *Red Book: 2009 report of the committee on infectious diseases (28th ed.)* (pp. 468-472). American Academy of Pediatrics: Elk Grove Village, IL.

Ball, J., Binder, R., & Cowen, K. (Eds.). (2012). Immunizations and communicable diseases. *Principles of Pediatric Nursing: Caring for Children (5th ed.)* (p. 415). Upper Saddle River, NJ: Pearson Education, Inc.

Blosser, C.G., Brady, M. & Muller, W. (2008). Infectious diseases and immunizations. . In C. Burns, M. Brady, A. Dunn, N.B. Starr, & C. Blosser (Eds.), *Pediatric primary care* (4th ed.) (pp. 520-521). St. Louis, MO: Saunders Elsevier.

Centers for Disease Control and Prevention, W. Atkinson, S. Wolfe, J. Hamborsky, L. McIntyre (Eds.) (2012). *Epidemiology and prevention of vaccine-preventable diseases (12th ed.)* (p.301). Washington DC: Public Health Foundation.

Merck Manual, Professional Edition. *Mumps (epidemic parotitis).* (2013). Retrieved from *http://www.merckmanuals.com/ professional/pediatrics/miscellaneous_viral_infections_in_infants_and_children/mumps.html?q=mumps&alt=sh*

Selekman, J., & Coates, J. (2013). Disease prevention. In J. Selekman (Ed.), *School nursing: A comprehensive text (2nd ed.)* (p. 503). Philadelphia, PA: F.A. Davis.

MUSCULAR DYSTROPHY

DEFINITION/ETIOLOGY:

Muscular dystrophy is a group of genetic, degenerative diseases primarily affecting voluntary muscles. Muscles become progressively weaker. In the late stages of muscular dystrophy, fat and connective tissue often replace muscle fibers. Some types of muscular dystrophy affect heart muscles, other involuntary muscles, and organs. The most common types of muscular dystrophy appear to be due to a genetic deficiency of the muscle protein dystrophin. There is no cure for muscular dystrophy. Supportive care, therapy, and medications can prolong functionality and slow the course of the disease.

SIGNS AND SYMPTOMS:

Duchenne Muscular Dystrophy

- Most common and most severe form of muscular dystrophy.
- Occurs mostly in males. Child may experience delay in walking, usually evident by age 3 and obvious by 5-6.
- May exhibit language delays.
- Early symptoms are clumsiness, toe walking, swayback, frequent falling, difficulty with stairs and getting up from floor, weakness in lower leg muscles resulting in difficulty running and jumping, waddling gait, and constipation.
- Always progressive, leading to need for leg braces, wheelchair dependency, contractures, obesity, respiratory complications (may progress to need for oral suctioning, tracheostomy and ventilator) and cardiac symptoms. Some may exhibit curvature of the spine (scoliosis).
- Calf and some other muscles enlarge due to fatty infiltration.
- Intellectual impairment is often present.
- Life expectancy age 20-30s, often from pneumonia, respiratory muscle weakness, or cardiac complications.

Other forms of muscular dystrophy

Becker's muscular dystrophy

- Milder form of muscular dystrophy
- Affects older boys and young men with onset around age 11, but may not occur until mid-20s or later. Most are able to walk through their teens and into adulthood.

Myotonicdystrophy (Steinert's Disease), Facioscapulohumeral muscular dystrophy (Landouzy-Dejerine dystrophy), Emery-Dreifuss muscular dystrophy, Limb-Girdle muscular dystrophy, Congenital muscular dystrophy, Oculopharyngeal muscular dystrophy, are other forms of muscular dystrophy. All vary in age onset, severity, rapidity of progression, associated intellectual impairment, and years of life.

MUSCULAR DYSTROPHY *(continued from previous page)*

MANAGEMENT/TREATMENT:
1. **Medication** - Corticosteroids, immunosuppressive drugs, anticonvulsants, skeletal muscle relaxants and antiarrhythmic drugs may be used improve muscle strength and delay progression for muscle weakness, delay the damage to dying muscle cells and to manage the muscle spasms, rigidity and affected cardiac muscles in certain types of muscular dystrophy.
2. **Physical therapy** keeps joints flexible and delays the progression of contractures.
3. **Assistive devices** such as braces, walkers, canes, and wheel chairs improve mobility and independence. Ventilators assist with oxygenation if muscles used to facilitate respiration become weakened.
4. **Surgery** may be necessary to relieve painful contractures. Curvatures of the spine, significant enough to compromise respiratory function may warrant surgical consideration.
5. Cardiac muscle may become compromised treated with medication or pacemaker.
6. When swallowing affected, family may opt for gastrostomy tube placement for nutrition.
7. As respiratory muscles weaken, respiratory support in the form of Nocturnal Nasal Intermittent Positive Pressure Ventilation (NNIPPV) or a ventilator may be used.
8. Altered cough secondary to neuromuscular weakness may require manual or mechanical cough assist.
9. May require oral suctioning to clear the airway.

FOLLOW-UP:
- Continually monitor for progress toward goals and watchful for signs and symptoms of complications.
- Update the Individualized Healthcare Plan (IHP) as necessary and update appropriate faculty and staff of changes in the care plan.
- Individualized Education Plan (IEP) or 504 plan for special services and accommodations, if needed.

POTENTIAL COMPLICATIONS:
- Obesity
- Contractures and spinal curvature
- Diminished fine motor skills
- Compromised skin integrity
- Urinary tract infections
- Constipation
- Respiratory infections
- Decline in independence with ADL's
- Swallowing difficulties

MUSCULAR DYSTROPHY *(continued from previous page)*

- Cardiac inefficiency
- Emotional/mental health issues secondary to condition itself, medications, or living with a chronic illness
- Sense of helplessness and hopelessness (depression)

Role of the school nurse
- Child and family advocate
- To partner with the physician, parents/guardians and other members of the school health team to develop the Individualized Healthcare Plan (IHP)
- To assemble and lead the school's child care team. The team and their focus may include:
  School physician
    - Coordinate medical management plan with the student's primary care provider, parent/guardian(s), and support services
    - Monitor immunization, influenza, and pneumonia status
  School nurse
    - Case management
    - Health education and health counseling
    - Staff development/in-service
    - Monitor respiratory status, early intervention can decrease severity of respiratory illness and prevent hospitalization
    - Monitor growth
  Physical therapist
    - Assess range of motion and ambulation abilities
    - Develop a plan for both active and passive range of motion, stretching exercises, ambulation, transfer (to chair, toilet, positioning blocks/devices, etc.), and positioning needs
  Occupational therapist
    - Assess activities of daily living skills, large motor skills, and fine motor skills
    - Develop a plan for work surfaces, note taking/adapted technology, dietary assistance (special utensils, lunch tray set-up, food served to meet mastication needs [bite size pieces], may need assistance with feeding or to be fed, feeding tube).
  Speech/language therapist
    - Assess mastication/swallowing abilities and needs and coordinate plan with school food service personnel
    - Assess speaking abilities for students with tracheostomies/ventilators and develop a communication plan

MUSCULAR DYSTROPHY *(continued from previous page)*

<u>School dietitian</u>
- o Coordinate special dietary needs with occupational therapist and speech therapist
- o Coordinate with school physician to develop an appropriate nutritional plan for caloric intake, sodium intake/steroid therapy, vitamins and minerals, and antioxidants

<u>School counselor/social worker</u>
- o Assess mental health status
- o Plan for appropriate student, sibling, friends, and family supports

<u>Director of transportation</u>
- o Coordinate special transportation needs with physical therapist and occupational therapist

<u>Education specialists</u>
- o Develop appropriate educational plans and may include:
  - ✓ Special education
  - ✓ General education
  - ✓ Adapted physical education

NOTE: As the disease progresses the student may be followed by a palliative care team or hospice. Often these students wish to continue to attend school. Accommodations can be made to make the child comfortable and have optimal quality of life while at school.
See **Do Not Attempt Resuscitation (DNAR)** for further information, if needed.

Resources

Education Matters: A Teacher's Guide to Duchenne Muscular Dystrophy. Downloadable from: http://www.parentprojectmd.org/site/DocServer/EdMatters-TeachersGuide.pdf

Learning and Behavior in Duchenne Muscular Dystrophy for Parents and Educators. Downloadable from: http://www.columbia.edu/cu/md/Learning_and_Behavior_Guide.pdf

Muscular Dystrophy Association: Research, information, support at http://mda.org

Parent Project Muscular Dystrophy: 1-800-714-5437

References
Centers for Disease Control. (2012). *Muscular Dystrophy*. Retrieved from http://www.cdc.gov/ncbddd/musculardystrophy/

Kravitz, R. (2009). Airway clearance in duchenne muscular dystrophy. *Pediatrics in Review, 123*(Supplement), S231-S235. doi: 10.1542/peds.2008-2952G

Mayo Clinic. (2012). *Muscular dystrophy*. Retrieved from http://www.mayoclinic.com/health/muscular-dystrophy/DS00200

Selekman, J., Bochenek, J., & Lukens, M. (2013). Muscular dystrophy. In J. Selekman (Ed.), *School nursing: A comprehensive text (2nd ed.)* (pp. 751-755). Philadelphia, PA: F.A. Davis.

NOSEBLEED (Epistaxis)

DEFINITION/ETIOLOGY:
A nosebleed can be caused by trauma, scratching the nose, picking the nose; repeated nose blowing that irritates the mucous membranes and may start with sudden temperature change, dry air, or infection. Students with nosebleeds may also have a foreign body in the nose. Most nosebleeds come from blood vessels in the front of the nose.

SIGNS/SYMPTOMS:
- Blood coming from the nose
- Complaint of tasting blood or swallowing blood

MANAGEMENT / TREATMENT:
1. Instruct person to breathe through their mouth. Reassure the young or anxious child that he can still breathe through the mouth.
2. Have the person sit down and lean forward. This minimizes the amount of blood swallowed that may cause vomiting.
3. Assist the student to firmly pinch his anterior nose (nostrils closed) below the bone continuously for 10 minutes.
4. If bleeding continues, hold nose closed an additional 15 minutes.
5. If bleeding continues for more than 20 minutes, contact the parent/guardian to refer for medical care, e.g., vasoconstricting nose drops.
6. Additionally, a cold compress or ice applied to the bridge of the nose may help.
7. Seek medical help if person is dizzy, light-headed, pale or has a rapid heart rate, or if person taking blood thinners.

FOLLOW UP:
- Restrict excessive physical exertion remainder of that day.
- For the rest of the day, avoid blowing, sniffing, probing/picking the nose and dislodging the clot.
- Inquire about any clotting abnormalities and use of aspirin or anticoagulants.
- Repeated nosebleeds: refer to primary care provider.
- Assess if family history of bleeding disorders.
- Assess if there is possible substance abuse by nasal snorting.
- Assess if history of other types of frequent or excess bleeding, for example with menstruation.
- Assess if history of blood in stool (black or tarry appearance).

NOSEBLEED (Epistaxis) *(continued from previous page)*

POTENTIAL COMPLICTIONS:
- Choking on blood
- Vomiting from swallowed blood
- Anemia with frequent nosebleeds

NOTE: Young children have more nosebleeds because the blood vessels are more fragile. Most nosebleeds that occur in children are not serious and usually stop within a few minutes. High blood pressure does not cause nosebleeds, but it may increase the severity.

References

Mayo Clinic. (2011). *Nosebleeds: First aid.* Retrieved from http://www.mayoclinic.com/health/first-aid-nosebleeds/hq00105

Medline Plus, U.S. National Library of Medicine. (2013). *Nosebleeds.* Retrieved from
http://www.nlm.nih.gov/medlineplus/ency/article/003106.htm

Merck Manual, Professional Edition. *Epistaxis.* (2012). Retrieved from http://www.merckmanuals.com/professional/
ear_nose_and_throat_disorders/approach_to_the_patient_with_nasal_and_pharyngeal_symptoms/
epistaxis.html?qt=nosebleeds&alt=sh

PERTUSSIS (WHOOPING COUGH)

DEFINITION/ETIOLOGY:

Pertussis is a highly contagious bacterial infection caused by *Bordetella pertussis*. Other agents that may cause a similar cough-like illness: *Bordetella parapertussis*, *Mycoplasma pneumoniae*, *Chlamydia trachomatis*, and *Chlamydia pneumonia*. Incubation period for *Bordetella pertussus* is from 6-21 days, usually 7-10 days and is spread from person to person through airborne droplets in close contact (coughing and sneezing). Pertussis is a vaccine preventable disease (VPD).

SIGNS AND SYMPTOMS:
- Pertussis is divided in 3 stages:
  1. The <u>catarrhal stage</u> lasts 1-2 weeks, may not be recognized or non-specific symptoms such as rhinorrhea (runny nose), sneezing, mild cough, slight sore throat, sinus congestion, and low-grade fever. Pertussis is most contagious from catarrhal stage until 2 weeks after onset of cough, without appropriate treatment.
  2. The <u>paroxysmal stage</u> lasts 2-4 weeks or longer, characterized by paroxysmal cough or whooping cough.
  3. The <u>convalescent stage</u> lasts 1-2 weeks, but cough can persist for several months.
- The duration of classic pertussis is 6-10 weeks or longer.
- Vomiting and exhaustion are common following coughing episodes.

MANAGEMENT/TREATMENT:
1. Refer to primary healthcare provider for diagnosis and appropriate treatment.
   a. (The macrolide agents erythromycin, clarithromycin, and azithromycin are preferred for the treatment of pertussis. Trimethoprim-sulfamethoxazole is an acceptable alternative. After the catarrhal stage, antibiotics cannot shorten the duration of the illness, but reduce the amount of time an infected person can transmit the bacteria to others.)

2. Implement state health regulations/ school policy for control measures.
   a. Students and staff with pertussis should be excluded from school and may return 5 days after they begin appropriate therapy.
   b. Those who do not receive antimicrobial therapy should be excluded from school for 21 days after onset of symptoms (coughing).
   c. School-wide or classroom chemoprophylaxis generally has <u>not</u> been recommended because of the delay in recognition of outbreak.
   d. People who have been in contact with an infected person should be monitored closely for respiratory tract symptoms for 21 days after last contact.

3. For household contacts: un-immunized children who are younger than 7 years of age or those who have received fewer than 4 doses of pertussis vaccine should have pertussis immunization according to recommended schedule.

PERTUSSIS (WHOOPING COUGH) *(continued from previous page)*

4. Chemoprophylaxis: A macrolide such as erythromycin for 14 days is recommended for all household contacts. Prompt use of chemoprophylaxis in household contacts can limit secondary transmission.

5. Cough medicine will <u>not</u> likely help and should not be given unless instructed by the primary healthcare provider.

FOLLOW-UP:
Monitor nutritional status. To avoid vomiting after coughing, eat smaller, more frequent meals instead of larger meals.

POTENTIAL COMPLICATIONS:
- Pertussis causes disease in every age group, but has the most significant impact on un-immunized young children.
- Major complications are most common among infants and young children. Complications include bacterial pneumonia, seizure, encephalopathy, and death. Most deaths occur among unvaccinated children or children too young to be vaccinated.
- Other complications may include difficulty sleeping, loss of weight, urinary incontinence, syncope, and rib fracture curing violent coughing.
- Previously immunized adolescents can become susceptible when immunity wanes, but they can receive a booster (Tdap) if they previously received only the tetanus-diphtheria toxoids (Td) booster at age 11-13 years.

References

American Academy of Pediatrics. (2013). Whooping cough (pertussis). In S. Aronson, & T. Shope (Eds.), *Managing infectious diseases in child care and schools (2nd ed.)* (pp. 173-174). Elk Grove Village, IL: American Academy of Pediatrics.

American Academy of Pediatrics. (2009). Summaries of infectious disease – pertussis (whooping cough). In L.K. Pickering, C.J. Baker, D.W. Kimberlin, & S.S. Long (Eds.), *Red Book: 2009 report of the committee on infectious diseases (28th ed.)* (pp. 504-519). American Academy of Pediatrics: Elk Grove Village, IL.

Ball, J., Binder, R., & Cowen, K. (Eds.). (2012). Immunizations and communicable diseases. *Principles of Pediatric Nursing: Caring for Children (5th ed.)* (p. 415-416). Upper Saddle River, NJ: Pearson Education, Inc.

Brady, M. (2008). Respiratory disorders. In C. Burns, M. Brady, A. Dunn, N.B. Starr, & C. Blosser (Eds.), *Pediatric primary care (4th ed.)* (pp. 778- 779). St. Louis, MO: Saunders Elsevier.

Centers for Disease Control and Prevention, Atkinson, W., Wolfe, S., & Hamborsky, J. (Eds.). (2012). *Epidemiology and prevention of vaccine-preventable diseases,12th ed.* Washington DC: Public Health Foundation.

Centers for Disease Control. (2013). *Pertussis outbreak trends.* Retrieved from http://www.cdc.gov/pertussis/outbreaks/trends.html

Centers for Disease Control. (2013). *Recommended immunization schedules for persons aged 0 through 18 years — United States, 2013.* Retrieved from http://www.cdc.gov/vaccines/schedules/downloads/child/0-18yrs-schedule.pdf

Merck Manual, Professional Edition. (2012). *Pertussis.* Retrieved from http://www.merckmanuals.com/professional/infectious_diseases/gram-negative_bacilli/pertussis.html?qt=pertussis&alt=sh

PINWORM INFECTION (Enterobiasis)

DEFINITION/ETIOLOGY:

Pinworms are the most common of all roundworm infections. They are small thread-like roundworms measuring about 1/4 to 1/2 inch in length. The ova of the parasite transfers from the perineal area to fomites, are picked up by a new host, transferred to the mouth, and swallowed. The lifecycle of the pinworm - egg, larva (immature stage), and mature worm takes place inside the colon and requires 3-6 weeks to complete. Eggs can be carried to the mouth by contaminated food, drink, or fingers and are capable of clinging to bedding, clothes, toys, doorknobs, furniture, or faucets for up to two weeks. Pinworms are found more commonly among people living in crowded conditions, day-care facilities, and schools.

SIGNS AND SYMPTOMS:
- More common in children
- Many people have no symptoms at all
- Itching around the anus and vagina
- Intense itching that may interfere with sleep.
- Intermittent abdominal pain and nausea

MANAGEMENT/TREATMENT:
1. Eggs may be collected with a strip of sticky, clear tape and identified by a healthcare provider.
2. Mild infections may not need medication.
3. If medication (Mebendazole, Pyrantel Pamaoate, or Albendazole (Albenza) is indicated, the entire household should be treated.
4. Children that are infected are likely to become re-infected outside the home; therefore, major efforts to eliminate eggs from the home are of little help.
5. Antipruritic creams and ointments may be recommended to relieve anal itching.

FOLLOW UP:
Monitor for sleepiness and weight loss.

POTENTIAL COMPLICATIONS:
- Infection of the female genitalia and reproductive system
- Abdominal pain
- Weight loss

PINWORM INFECTION (Enterobiasis) *(continued from previous page)*

NOTES:
Prevention
- Bathe after waking.
- Wash nightclothes and bedding often.
- Frequent hand washing, especially after using the bathroom or changing diapers, and before eating.
- Change underclothes each day.
- Avoid nail biting.
- Avoid scratching anal area.

References

Centers for Disease Control and Prevention. (2013). *Parasites- enterobaisis (also known as pinworm infection). (2013).* Retrieved from http://www.cdc.gov/parasites/pinworm/treatment.html

Mayo Clinic. *Pinworm infection.* (2012). Retrieved from http://www.mayoclinic.com/health/pinworm/DS00687

Medline Plus. U.S. National Library of Medicine. *Pinworms.* (2013). Retrieved from http://www.nlm.nih.gov/medlineplus/pinworms.html

Merck Manual, Professional Edition. *Pinworm infestation. (2012).* Retrieved from http://www.merckmanuals.com/professional/infectious_diseases/nematodes_roundworms/pinworm_infestation.html?qt=pinworms&alt=sh

National Institute of Allergy & Infectious Diseases, National Institute of Health. (2010). *Pinworm infection.* Retrieved from http://www.niaid.nih.gov/topics/pinworm/Pages/treatment.aspx

PNEUMONIA

DEFINITION/ETIOLOGY:
Pneumonia is an infection of the lungs and may occur in one or both lungs. When pneumonia occurs, the air sac of one or both lungs become inflamed. During the pneumonia infection, the air sacs may fill with fluid or pus, causing cough with phlegm or pus, fever, chills and difficulty breathing. Pneumonia may be caused by bacteria, viruses, and fungi.

Pneumonia can range from mild to life-threatening and is most serious for infants and young children, as well as adults older than 65 years of age. Also, people with underlying health problems or weakened immune systems are at increased risk of pneumonia complications. Antibiotics and antiviral medications are used to treat many common forms of pneumonia.

CAUSES OF PNEUMONIA
Pneumonia may be caused by many small germs. There are five main causes of pneumonia:
- Bacteria
- Viruses
- Mycoplasmas
- Fungi and other infectious agents
- Various chemicals

TYPES OF PNEUMONIA
Pneumonia is classified according to the location where the infection is acquired. Below are four types of pneumonia based on the specific acquired location and the specific organisms associated with the cause.

- Community-acquired pneumonia – most common type and may be caused by the following:
  - Bacteria: Streptococcus pneumoniae
  - Bacteria-like organisms: Mycoplasma pneumoniae produces milder signs and symptoms. The term Walking Pneumonia may result from Mycoplasma pneumoniae.
  - Viruses: Most common cause of pneumonia in children younger than two years of age. Usually mild and can become severe when caused by certain influenza viruses such as sudden acute respiratory syndrome (SARS).

236

PNEUMONIA *(continued from previous page)*

- Hospital-acquired pneumonia –bacterial infection; occurs within 48 hours after being hospitalized for another condition.
  - Bacteria causing this type of pneumonia may be resistant to antibiotics.
  - People who are assisted by a ventilator for breathing are at higher risk for hospital-acquired pneumonia.

- Health care-acquired pneumonia – bacterial infection; general occurs among people when living in a long-term care facility or if treated by an outpatient center/clinic.
  - Bacteria may be resistant to antibiotic treatment.

- Aspiration pneumonia - occurs when food, drink, vomit, or saliva are inhaled into the lungs.
  - May occur if the normal gag reflex is disturbed by brain injury, swallowing problems, or excessive use of drugs and alcohol

SIGNS AND SYMPTOMS OF PNEUMONIA:
- Fever and shaking chills
- Sweating and clammy skin
- Lower than normal temperature in people with weakened immune system or poor health
- Cough with thick, sticky fluid
- Chest pain with deep breathing and coughing
- Shortness of breath
- Wheezing (may be more common in viral pneumonia)
- Muscle aches and muscle fatigue
- Nausea, vomiting, and diarrhea
- Headache

POTENTIAL RISKS AND COMPLICATIONS:
- Chronic health conditions (asthma, chronic otitis media, anemia, etc.)
- Behavioral problems
- Developmental delay
- Early initiation of substance abuse
- Social isolation
- Mental health problems (anxiety, depression, and withdrawal)
- Tuberculosis

PNEUMONIA *(continued from previous page)*

Other risk factors include:
- Chronic diseases such as asthma, chronic obstructive pulmonary disease (COPD), and heart disease.
- Weak, compromised or suppressed immune system.
- Smoking because it damages the body's natural defenses against bacteria and viruses causing pneumonia.
- Using ventilator assistance for breathing while hospitalized.

Complications:
- Bacteremia – bacteria in the bloodstream can cause organ failure.
- Abscess in the lung due to formation of pus in the lung cavity.
- Pleural effusion – fluid accumulation around the lungs; chest tube may be necessary to drain infected fluid.
- Difficulty breathing

MANAGEMENT AND TREATMENT:

General Information
- Hospitalization is recommended for severe cases of pneumonia
- Immunizations provide protection against pneumonia, e.g. Pertussis, Influenza and pneumococcal vaccines
- Adequate nutrition helps to improve the natural immunity of children
- Promote good hygiene practices, e.g. handwashing

Bacterial Pneumonia
- Treated with oral antibiotics
- Proper diet
- Oxygen as needed
- Other medications for chest pain and coughing as needed

Viral Pneumonia
- May be treated with antiviral medication
- Usually improves in one to three weeks

Mycoplasma Pneumonia
- May be weak for extended period of time
- Adequate rest is important for progression toward full recovery

PNEUMONIA *(continued from previous page)*

References

American Lung Association. (2013). *Pneumonia*. Retrieved from http://www.lung.org/lung-disease/pneumonia/

Centers of Disease Control and Prevention (CDC). (2012). *Pneumonia can be prevented – Vaccines can help*. Retrieved from http://www.cdc.gov/Features/Pneumonia/

Mayo Clinic. (2013). *Pneumonia*. Retrieved from http://www.mayoclinic.com/health/pneumonia/DS00135

World Health Organization (WHO). (2013). *Pneumonia factsheet*. Retrieved from http://www.who.int/mediacentre/factsheets/fs331/en/

POISON IVY/OAK (Contact Dermatitis)

DEFINITION/ETIOLOGY:

Poison ivy/oak is a skin reaction (contact dermatitis) due to the allergen, urushiol, which is found in all parts (stem, flowers, berries, and roots) of the poison ivy, oak and sumac (rhus) plant. Poison ivy/oak grows as a low-lying shrub and a short or high trailing vine. Leaves appear in groups of three with white berries and greenish flowers. A rash only occurs in people sensitive to these plants when the skin directly touches the urushiol from the plant, contaminated objects or smoke from burning plants. A reaction is most commonly seen on the hands, forearms, and face.

SIGNS AND SYMPTOMS:

Reaction typically begins 12-48 hours after exposure but can also take as long as a week.
- Red, itchy rash
    - Small papules and vesicles
    - Rash may have a linear appearance were the plant brushes against the skin
- May have large blisters and generalized weeping of skin
- Localized swelling
- Dryness, crusting and gradual shedding of crusts and scabs is a sign of healing which may take 2-3 weeks

MANAGEMENT/TREATMENT:

1. Wash skin and fingernails thoroughly with a degreasing detergent (dishwashing soap) and cool water within 10 minutes of exposure or with a commercial product (e.g., Tecnu® or Zanfel® cleansers) as soon as possible to prevent or decrease a reaction.
2. Continue to rinse the area frequently to prevent wash solutions from drying on the skin and the spread of urushiol.
3. To relieve itching, apply cool packs (every 15-20 minutes, 3-4 times daily), and/or a warm baking soda or colloidal oatmeal bath.
4. Plain calamine lotion may be applied to dry lesions.
5. Topical corticosteroid cream may be used to reduce inflammation.
6. Healthcare provider may prescribe oral steroids for extensive cases.
7. Oral antihistamines are usually not helpful for itch, but hydroxyzine (Atarax®) may be prescribed.
8. Applying a loose dressing may help discourage scratching.
9. Refer to healthcare provider if itching is distracting child from attention to tasks, rash is extensive, or involving eye, face or mucous membranes.

POISON IVY/OAK (Contact Dermatitis) *(continued from previous page)*

FOLLOW UP:
- Observe for infection and treat as needed.
- Wear disposable rubber gloves to:
  - Promptly wash contaminated clothing such shoes, shoelaces, socks, pants, and shirts in detergent and hot water.
  - Clean additional contaminated objects used outdoors such as garden tools and jewelry with hot water and detergent.
- Educate regarding how to identify poison ivy/oak and to avoid re-exposure.
- If on school or public play property, report location for safe removal (without burning).

POTENTIAL COMPLICATIONS:
Scratching the rash with dirty fingernails can cause a secondary infection.

NOTES:
- Do not exclude from school; educate staff on transmission of urushiol.
- Contents of blisters and weepy skin CANNOT cause rash in another individual or even in another location on patient.
- Inhaling smoke from burning poison ivy/oak plants may cause a severe respiratory reaction. A reaction if burning particles land on your skin.
- To prevent a potential exposure, an over the counter barrier cream containing bantoquatam may be used. However, avoidance is the best protection.
- Urushiol can remain active for five (5) years. If contaminated objects are not cleaned, contact with them at a later date may cause a reaction.
- Consider pet fur as possible source of exposure.

References

American Academy of Dermatology. (2013). *Poison ivy, oak, and sumac.* Retrieved from http://www.aad.org/dermatology-a-to-z/diseases- http://www.aad.org/dermatology-a-to-z/diseases-and-treatments/m---p/poison-ivy and-treatments/m---p/poison-ivy

Mayo Clinic. (2012). *Poison ivy rash.* Retrieved from http://www.mayoclinic.com/health/poison-ivy/DS00774

Renzi, L. & Clark Graham, M. (2013). Skin disorders. In J. Selekman (Ed.), *School nursing: A comprehensive text* (p. 693). Philadelphia, PA: F.A. Davis.

National Institute for Occupational Safety & Health, Centers for Disease Control and Prevention. (2010). NIOSH *fast facts: Protecting yourself from poisonous plants* (Publication No. 2010-118). Retrieved from http://www.cdc.gov/niosh/docs/2010-118/

Vernon, P., Brady, M., & Starr, N.B. (2009). Dermatologic diseases. In C. Burns, M. Brady, A. Dunn, N.B. Starr, C. Blosser (Eds.), *Pediatric primary care* (4th ed.) (pp. 974-975). St. Louis, MO: Saunders Elsevier.

PUBERTAL GROWTH AND DEVELOPMENT

DEFINITION/ETIOLOGY:
Puberty refers to the physiologic and anatomic changes associated with reproduction. Puberty causes dramatic changes in almost every body system. The sequences of body changes are visible and predictable. The onset of these changes is influenced by nutritional status, genetics and environmental factors and can vary greatly from person to person. These changes are known as Tanner stages. There are five stages for pubic hair and genital development in males and females.

STAGES OF NORMAL DEVELOPMENT:

A. **Females - Pubic hair development**
   Tanner Stage 1- pre-pubertal, pubic hair is absent
   Tanner Stage 2- fine sparse, straight hair along the vulva
   Tanner Stage 3-darker, coarser, and slightly curly that extends over the mid pubis
   Tanner Stage 4-adult type hair that covers the eternal genitalia but does not extend to the thighs
   Tanner Stage 5-adult type hair that extends to the medial thighs

B. **Females - Breast Development**
   Tanner Stage 1- no palpable breast and a small areola without tissue beyond the chest plane
   Tanner Stage 2- a breast "bud" under the enlarging areola
   Tanner Stage 3- further enlargement of the breast tissue beyond the margins of the areola
   Tanner Stage 4- formation of a secondary mound of the widening and darkening areola above the breast tissue (considered sexual maturity)
   Tanner Stage 5- recession of the areola to the same level of skin overlying breast tissue and and projection of the papilla beyond the areola and breast. (some normal adult women only reach stage 5 in pregnancy)

C. **Males - Pubic Hair Development**
   Tanner Stage 1- pre-pubertal pubic hair is absent
   Tanner Stage 2-fine sparse straight hair at the base of the penis
   Tanner Stage 3-darker, coarser, slightly curly hair over the mid pubis
   Tanner Stage 4- thicker, more curled adult like hair but covers eternal genitalia but not thighs
   Tanner Stage 5-adult like hair that extends to the medial thigh

PUBERTAL GROWTH AND DEVELOPMENT *(continued from previous page)*

NOTES:
- Black boys and girls reach sexual development on an average of one year before their white peers.
- Generally, with pubertal maturation there are also changes in cognition and social development.
- Girls experience a pubertal growth spurt approximately one year after the onset of breast development.
- After menarche (the initiation of menstruation) growth decreases with girls growing no more than 2 inches.
- Boys typically enter puberty later than girls.
- Testicular enlargement is the first clinically significant pubertal event in boys.
- Growth in height for boys can go into young adulthood.
- Bone health is very important for girls entering puberty and has a great effect for later in life bone health.
- Menarche generally takes place 2 years after the onset of pubertal development.
- The age of menarche has steadily decreased over time with the average age now being 12.5 years.
- Approximately one half to one third of boys develop gynecomastia (visible or palpable development of breast tissue in males) during mid- puberty and may last 12 to 18 months.

POTENTIAL COMPLICATIONS:
- The absence of menses after a female has achieved breast development to stage Tanner 4 and completed has growth spurt may be a cause for concern and a referral to a healthcare provider is indicated.
- The onset of vaginal bleeding without and growth spurt or breast development may be a cause for concern and a referral to a healthcare provider is indicated.
- Breast masses may present in about 3.2% of the population and may be caused by a variety of etiologies but malignancy is very rare.
- Breast asymmetry is the most common breast condition in adolescents. It usually improves once development is complete.
- Abrupt testicular pain should be an immediate referral for evaluation of potential testicular torsion.
- Gynecomastia that is unresolved or resembles the breasts of a female in stage 3-5 of development should be evaluated for a potential pathological condition.

PUBERTAL GROWTH AND DEVELOPMENT *(continued from previous page)*

References

Bowden, V. , & Greenberb, C. (2010). *Children and their families: The continuum of care (2nd edition) (p. 103). Philadelphia PA: Lippincott Williams and Wilkins*

Fisher, M. , & Alderman, E., et al. (2011). *Textbook of adolescent health care* (pp. 23-31). Elk Grove Village, IL: American Academy of Pediatrics.

PUNCTURE WOUNDS

DEFINITION/ETIOLOGY:
Small but deep hole produced by penetrating object. Sharp pointed objects such as nails, tacks, pencils, knife and teeth can cause puncture wounds. Most often occurs in hands and feet but can be any body surface area. Object may penetrate the skin and leave a hole or remain partially or completely in wound. Puncture wounds are typically deeper than lacerations or abrasions.

SIGNS/SYMPTOMS:
If small object:
- Small hole at puncture site
- Little to no bleeding
- Potential for retained foreign body
- History of injury

If larger object:
- May be medical emergency
- May cause heavy bleeding and injury to areas beneath puncture site

Puncture wounds to the eye, neck, chest or abdomen are serious. Seek medical treatment. If necessary, call 911.

MANAGEMENT/TREATMENT:
1. Wash around the wound with soap and water.
2. Irrigate the wound with water to remove debris.
3. If debris remains in wound after irrigation with water, do not probe or pull debris from a wound as it may splinter and leave pieces; refer to physician/healthcare provider for follow-up care.
4. If embedded object in wound, minimize movement and leave object in place.
5. Do not try to clean a major wound as it may cause heavy bleeding.
6. Do not clean the wound with *Hydrogen peroxide. Hydrogen peroxide is not appropriate for fresh wounds; it damages tissues and interferes with healing.*
7. Apply antibiotic ointment and bandage per school district policy. Do not seal the hole with non-porous bandage.
8. Determine cause of puncture, e.g., nail, glass, wood, human or animal bite, etc.
9. If student was bitten by an animal, contact animal control.
10. Determine date of last tetanus booster.
11. Seek emergency medical services if wound is deep, bleeding heavily or a large object is embedded in the wound.

PUNCTURE WOUNDS *(continued from previous page)*

FOLLOW-UP:
- Monitor of signs of infection. Signs and symptoms of infection that require a visit to physician/healthcare provider include:
    - Early signs and symptoms of infection include: increased pain, redness around the edge of wound, swelling and tenderness
    - Late signs and symptoms of infection include: fever, purulent drainage and lymphangitis (infection of the lymph vessel caused by a bacterial infection); look for red streak from infected area to armpit or groin

POTENTIAL COMPLICATIONS:
- Puncture wounds are hard to clean resulting in increased risk of infection
- Wounds can often be deep with little bleeding so there is an increased risk of infection because germs are imbedded deeply and not washed out by the flow of blood.
- Tetanus is a danger with puncture wound because tetanus bacteria (*Clostridium tetani*) grow well in a deep wound with little oxygen.
- Puncture wounds obtained by stepping on a nail has increased risk of contracting a pseudomonas infection.
- Wounds resulting from an animal or human bite are at increased risk of becoming infected.

NOTES:
- Pencils are not made of lead but nontoxic graphite. Pencil lead is rarely embedded after puncture but more likely the "tattoo" from the graphite leaving a mark

References
John, R., & Chewey, L. (2013). *Common complaints.* In J. Selekman (Ed.), *School nursing: A comprehensive text* (2nd ed.) (pp.578-640). Philadelphia, PA: F. A. Davis.

Mayo Clinic. (2012*). Puncture wounds: First aid.* Retrieved from http://www.mayoclinic.com/health/first-aid-puncture-wounds/FA00014

MedlinePlus. U.S. National Library of Medicine. (2013). *Cuts and puncture wounds.* Retrieved from http://www.nlm.nih.gov/medlineplus/ency/article/000043.htm

Subbarao, I., Lyznicki, J., & James, J. (2009). *AMA Handbook of First Aid and Emergency Care.* New York, NY: Random House.

WebMD. (2010*). First aid & emergencies.* Retrieved from http://firstaid.webmd.com/tc/cuts-topic-overview

RASHES
Differential Diagnosis of Common Childhood Disease Associated with Rash

	Rubeola (measles)	Rubella (German measles)	Roseola	Scarlet Fever (scarlatina)	Fifth Disease	Varicella (chicken pox)
Etiology	Viral	Viral	Viral, Human Herpes virus 6 & herpes 7	Streptococcus Bacteria	Human Parvovirus B19	Varicella zoster virus
Characteristics of Rash	Generalized dusky red blotchy maculopapular rash begins on day 3-7 and last 4-7 days	Large, light pink or light red flat blotches that often flow into one another Rash usually follows 5-10 days after infection occurs May resemble measles, scarlet fever, or fifth disease Approximately ½ of infections do not have a rash	Small flat pink spots or patches not usually itchy Last 2-3 days	Bright red rash, feels like sandpaper lasts 2-5 days Tongue may appear strawberry-like When rash fades, skin peels from tips of fingers and toes	Red, patchy facial rash ("slapped cheek") Cold-like symptoms may precede rash May be asymptomatic Not contagious before development of rash	Consists of maculopapular rash for a few hours, then fluid filled vesicles for 3-4 days drying and crusting over "New" vesicles can continue to appear for 4-7 Rash is itchy and scratching can produce skin abrasions and lead to secondary infection
Part of body rash first appears on	Behind the ears or on forehead/ face	Face	Chest and back	Neck, face, palms of hands and tips of fingers and toes	Face and cheeks	Face, abdomen and back
Spreads to	Arms, trunk, thighs, legs, and feet Small white spots (Koplik's spots) are inside mouth	Trunk, arms legs and then disappearing in the same order	Abdomen, neck and arms	Chest, back, and rest of body	May spread to rest of body in lace-like pattern	Rest of the body including the mouth, arms, genitals and scalp

RASHES *(continued from previous page)*

	Rubeola (measles)	Rubella (German measles)	Roseola	Scarlet Fever (scarlatina)	Fifth Disease	Varicella (chicken pox)
Progression and time intervals for diagnosis	Usually 8-12 days from exposure to onset of symptoms Average interval between appearance of rash after exposure is 7-14 days; range 7-18 days	Usually 16-18 days; range 14-23 days	Usually 10 days; range 5-15 days	1-3 days, can be up to 5 days	Variable, 4-20 days	Usually 14-16 days from exposure to rash, but may range from 10-21 days
Severity of illness	Usually severe	Usually mild	Mild , but moderate mild to high mild	Mild to moderate	Mild, resolves on its own	Severe in older adolescents and adults
Associated symptoms other than rash	Sudden onset of chills followed by sneezing, runny nose, conjunctivitis, photophobia, fever, dry cough, Koplik's spots, sore throat	Mild illness with low fever, mild rash, usually associated with enlargement of nodes on the back of the neck, headache, stuffy nose, inflamed red eye	Cough, runny nose, sore throat before sudden onset of high fever greater than 103 degrees which may last 3-5 days	Fever and sore throat/tonsillitis with tender, enlarged lymph nodes	Fever, headache, runny nose Joint swelling and pain is more common is adults	Slight to moderate fever and itching
Complications	Otitis media, bronchitis, croup, pneumonia, encephalitis, low platelet count, pregnancy loss	Usually none. Women sometimes have arthritis in knees, fingers and wrist. Complications to an unborn can be severe	Usually none Can cause febrile seizures in children and is a risk for those with weak immune system	Rheumatic fever, carditis, painful joints, otitis media, and pneumonia	Usually none Can cause Pneumonia	Occasional arthritis encephalitis arthritis, recurrent breakthrough infections later on in life (shingle)

248

RASHES *(continued from previous page)*

	Rubeola (measles)	Rubella (German measles)	Roseola	Scarlet Fever (scarlatina)	Fifth Disease	Varicella (chicken pox)
Period of Infectivity	Contagious in nose or throat 4 days before rash to 4 days after appearance of the rash Immuno-compromised children can be contagious for the duration of the illness	Maximal communicability is from 10 days before rash to 1-2 weeks days after onset of rash Children with congenital rubella syndrome may be infectious for up to 1 year. Highly communicable	Unknown	Infectious for 10-21 days if untreated or until 24 hours after start of antibiotic treatment	Most infectious before the onset of rash; not contagious after rash appears	From 1-2 days before rash appears, to when all lesions are completely crusted over Persons who are susceptible to varicella should be considered to be infectious from 10- 21 days after exposure NOTE: Persons with weakened immune systems may be communicable for longer periods
Additional information	Vaccine preventable More likely to contract measles if diet if deficient in Vitamin A Do not use aspirin	Vaccination is the key preventive measure	No specific control or preventive measures indicated	Curable with Penicillin. Control measures: Emphasize respiratory etiquette ("cover your cough") and frequent hand washing	No Vaccine or medicine to available Proper hand hygiene encouraged	Vaccine is key preventive measure Do not use aspirin or ibuprofen to treat symptoms

RASHES *(continued from previous page)*

NOTES:
Infection control measures should be considered in regards to the anticipated contact to prevent the spread of communicable diseases. In general, children may be excluded from school for medical reasons related to communicable diseases or due to program or staffing requirements.

Follow local health department or school policy in regards to exclusion from school. In general, exclusion should be considered based on the following criteria:

- If children are not able to fully participate in the program,
- When the level of care during and illness is not able to be met without jeopardizing the safety of other children, or
- When the risk or spread of disease to other children cannot be avoided with the appropriate environmental or individual management.

References

Indiana Department of Health, Epidemiology Resource Center. (2012) *Communicable disease reference guide for schools: 2012 edition.* Retrieved from http://www.state.in.us/isdh/23291.htm

Mayo Clinic. (2012). *Measles.* Retrieved from http://www.mayoclinic.com/health/measles/DS00331/DSECTION=complications

Mayo Clinic. (2012). *Rubella.* Retrieved from http://www.mayoclinic.com/health/rubella/DS00332/DSECTION

Mayo Clinic. (2012). *Roseola.* Retrieved from http://www.mayoclinic.com/health/roseola/DS00452/DSECTION=complications.

Mayo Clinic. (2011). *Scarlet fever.* Retrieved from http://www.mayoclinic.com/health/scarlet-ever/DS00917/DSECTION=complications.

Medline Plus. U.S. National Library of Medicine. (2013). *Chicken pox.* Retrieved from http://www.nlm.nih.gov/medlineplus/ency/article/001592.htm

Medline Plus. U.S. National Library of Medicine. (2013). *Roseola.* Retrieved from http://www.nlm.nih.gov/medlineplus/ency/article/000968.htm

RINGWORM – TINEA

DEFINITION/ETIOLOGY:
Ringworm is caused by a fungus which can affect the skin, nails and hair.

Tinea corporis:	Ringworm of the body
Tinea capitis:	Ringworm of the scalp
Tinea cruris:	Ringworm of the groin area (also called jock itch)
Tinea pedis:	Ringworm of the feet (also called athlete's foot)
Onychomycosis:	Ringworm of the nails
Tinea faciei:	Ringworm of the face

Ringworm on the skin of a child is considered infectious as long as the fungus stays present in the skin lesion. Ringworm can be spread as long as lesions are present and viable fungus persists on contaminated materials and surfaces. The fungus is considered eradicated when the lesion begins to shrink. The fungi that cause ringworm thrive in warm, moist environments. Pets can be carriers of the fungus. Cats are an especially common carrier.

SIGNS AND SYMPTOMS:
Tinea pedis: Scaly lesions between toes. Itchy, vesiculo-papular (blisters or tiny pimples) or scaly lesions on sides of the feet. Lesions may become infected due to scratching. It is most commonly seen in adolescents, especially adolescent males.

Tinea cruris: Discolored areas (sharply demarcated scaling patches, usually itchy) between upper thighs extending onto groin and buttocks. Also referred to as "jock itch". Frequently involve males and especially obese males. It is rarely seen in females.

Tinea corporis: Small (1-3 cm) red bump or papule on the body or face that spreads outward so that each affected area takes on the appearance of a red, scaly outer ring with a clear central area. The lesions are frequently itchy and can become infected if scratched. There may be single or multiple lesions. Tinea corporis is not uncommon in student wrestlers and more often seen in warm climates.

Tinea capitis: In early stages, asymptomatic, but the scalp or back of the neck may itch. A tender, boggy lesion called a kerion may form which is from a hypersensitivity reaction to the fungus. A Flaky scalp that resembles dandruff may be present. Balding, round, oval or confluent patches on the scalp may be present. Patches may be a small as 1-2 cm up to 10 cm. with hairs broken off in the center of the patch. Lesion will generally appear as an itchy, bald patch of scaly skin. This form of ringworm is most common in children.

Onychomycosis: thick and yellowed nails (rare in children).

RINGWORM – TINEA *(continued from previous page)*

MANAGEMENT/TREATMENT:
1. Keep skin and feet clean and dry.
2. When used as directed, over-the-counter (OTC) anti-fungal medications (creams) can effectively treat mild cases of ringworm. More severe cases or cases that do not respond in 2-4 weeks with OTC medications should be referred to the healthcare provider for additional medication.
3. Topical antifungal medications are not effective for the treatment of tinea capitis. Systemic antifungal medication is required for up to 4-8 weeks and should be used for 2 weeks after resolution.
4. Students with tinea capitis should be instructed not to share combs, hats, hair ribbons, or brushes.
5. Avoid contact sports, such as wrestling, for at least 48 hours after treatment was started.
6. Haircuts, shaving of the head, or wearing a cap for tinea capitus during treatment is unnecessary.
7. Students with tinea cruris, tinea corporis, or tinea pedis should be excluded at the end of the school day and be readmitted once treatment is initiated.
8. Students with tinea pedis should be excluded from swimming pools, and from walking barefoot on locker room and shower floors until treatment has been initiated.
9. Siblings and household contacts should be evaluated.

FOLLOW-UP:
- Refer cases with scalp and nail lesions to primary healthcare provider.
- Refer severe cases (those which do not improve within 2-4 weeks of starting treatment) or for a secondary bacterial infection which may require an antibiotic.
- Inform parent/guardian to check contacts, family members, and pets.
- Work with maintenance personnel, teachers, and coaches to assure proper cleaning of headphones, swimming pool and locker areas, PE mats, wrestling headgear, and other equipment with which skin contact is common.

POTENTIAL COMPLICATIONS:
Secondary bacterial infections

NOTES:
Prevention
- Wash hands thoroughly and often.
- Keep skin dry and clean.
- Shampoo hair regularly, especially after haircuts.
- Do not share clothing, shoes, towels, hairbrushes, combs, headgear, or other personal care items.

RINGWORM – TINEA *(continued from previous page)*

- Avoid walking barefoot in public places.
- Wear waterproof shoes or "flip-flops" in public showers and swimming pool areas.
- Change wet socks.
- Use powder on feet to absorb moisture.
- Check pets for areas of hair loss. Consult a veterinarian. Avoid touching pets with bald spots.
- Keep all clothing and bed clothing clean.
- Stay cool and dry.
- Change clothing that becomes sweaty or wet.
- Make sure safety mats and other surfaces that might be home to infectious bacteria, such as MRSA, ringworm and impetigo, are disinfected often (preferably daily).
- Cleaning and draining the school shower areas should be done frequently.

References

American Academy of Pediatrics. (2009). Summaries of infectious disease – tinea capitis, tinea corporis, tinea cruris, tinea pedis and tinea unguium. In L.K. Pickering, C.J. Baker, D.W. Kimberlin, & S.S. Long (Eds.), *Red Book: 2009 report of the committee on infectious diseases (28th ed.)* (pp. 661-666). Elk Grove Village, IL: American Academy of Pediatrics.

American Academy of Pediatrics. (2013). Ringworm. In S. Aronson, & T. Shope (Eds.), *Managing infectious diseases in child care and schools (2nd ed.)* (p.p. 141-142). Elk Grove Village, IL: American Academy of Pediatrics.

Cole, G.W. (2013). *Jock itch overview.* In E medicine Health. Retrieved from http://www.emedicinehealth.com/jock_itch/article_em.htm

Denehy, J. (2013). Athlete health promotion. In J. Selekman (Ed.), *School nursing: A comprehensive text,* (pp. 565-585). Philadelphia, PA: F.A. Davis.

E medicine Health. (2012). *Slideshow pictures: Ringworm -- causes, types, symptoms and treatment.* Retrieved from http://www.emedicinehealth.com/slideshow_ringworm_pictures/article_em.htm

Harvey. A. *(2013). Ringworm on the body.* In E medicine Health. Retrieved from http://www.emedicinehealth.com/ringworm_on_body/article_em.htm

Mayo Clinic. (2010). *Athlete's foot.* Retrieved from http://www.mayoclinic.com/health/athletes-foot/DS00317

Mayo Clinic. (2010). *Ringworm (body).* Retrieved from http://www.mayoclinic.com/health/ringworm/DS00489

Mayo Clinic. (2011). *Ringworm (scalp) definition.* Retrieved from http://www.mayoclinic.com/health/ringworm/DS00892

Oishi, M. L., & Irizarry, L. (2013). *Ringworm on scalp.* In E medicine Health. Retrieved from http://www.emedicinehealth.com/ringworm_on_scalp/article_em.htm

ROTAVIRUS

DEFINITION/ETIOLOGY:
Rotavirus is the most common cause of gastroenteritis and severe diarrhea among infants and children worldwide. Most children experience rotavirus at least one time by the age of two or three. The incubation period for rotavirus ranges from 1-3 days. The name rotavirus is derived from the Latin word *rota* meaning "wheel." When a rotavirus is viewed under an electron microscope, the virus has a characteristic wheel-like appearance. Rotaviruses are non-enveloped double-shelled viruses and are stable in the environment.

CAUSES:
Rotavirus is present in an infected person's stool several days before symptoms appear and up to 10 days after symptoms subside. The virus spreads very easily through hand to mouth contact. There are many types of rotaviruses and it is possible to be infected more than once.

The primary mode of transmission is fecal-oral, although low titers of the virus have been reported in respiratory tract secretions and other body fluids. Laboratory testing of stool specimens is necessary to diagnose rotavirus infection. Because of the rotavirus stability in the environment, transmission can occur through ingestion of contaminated food and water and contact with contaminated surfaces. In the United States, the disease has a winter seasonal pattern and epidemics generally occur from November through April.

SIGNS/SYMPTOMS:
- Fever
- Three to eight days of watery diarrhea and vomiting
- Abdominal pain
- Pale skin
- Dry lips
- Sunken eyes

The physician/healthcare provider should be called if the child has:
- Severe or bloody diarrhea
- Frequent episodes of vomiting for more than three hours
- Temperature of 102°F or higher
- Seems lethargic, irritable, or in pain
- Has signs or symptoms of dehydration, e.g. dry mouth, crying without tears, little or no urination, unusual sleepiness or unresponsiveness

ROTAVIRUS *(continued from previous page)*

MANAGEMENT/TREATMENT:
There is no specific treatment for rotavirus infection as antibiotics are not effective for viral infections. Rotavirus infections generally resolve in three to eight days. Prevention of dehydration during rotavirus infection is the most important concern.

Drinking plenty of fluids, e.g. clear liquids, while rotavirus infection runs its course will help prevent dehydration. Oral rehydration such as Pedialyte® for infants and a rehydration fluid for children replace lost electrolytes more effectively than water or other liquids. Severe dehydration may require hospitalization for intravenous fluids.

FOLLOW UP:
The Advisory Committee on Immunization Practices (ACIP) recommends routine vaccination of infants in the United States. Two different rotavirus vaccines, RotaTeq® (RV5) and Rotarix® (RV1), are currently licensed for infants in the United States.

Both vaccines are live oral vaccines recommended for infants (6-24 months) to prevent subsequent disease later.

COMPLICATIONS:
Intussusception is an uncommon type of bowel obstruction that occurs when the bowel folds on itself. Intussusception is most common in young children and can occur with viral infections. RotaShield® vaccine was taken off the market in the United States as of October 2, 1999 and is no longer offered for infants because of its association between the vaccine and intussusception.

NOTES:
Prevention
- Proper hand hygiene can reduce the spread of rotavirus infection.
- Surfaces should be cleaned with soap and water.
- Approved vaccinations for rotavirus are offered to infants 6 to 24 months for the prevention of rotavirus infection.

ROTAVIRUS *(continued from previous page)*

References

American Academy of Pediatrics. (2009). Summaries of infectious disease. In L.K. Pickering, C. J. Baker, D.W. Kimberlin, & S.S.Long (Eds.), *Red Book: 2009 Report of the Committee on Infectious Diseases* (28th ed.) (pp. 576-579). Elk Grove Village, IL: American Academy of Pediatrics.

Centers for Disease Control and Prevention. (2013). Rotavirus *(Rotavirus Infection).* Retrieved from http://www.cdc.gov/rotavirus/

Centers for Disease Control and Prevention. (2013). Vaccine safety: Rotavirus. Retrieved from http://www.cdc.gov/vaccinesafety/vaccines/rotavsb.html

Centers for Disease Control and Prevention (CDC). (2011). *Rotavirus vaccine (Rotashield) and Intussusception.* Retrieved from http://www.cdc.gov/vaccines/vpd-vac/rotavirus/vac-rotashield-historical.htm

Centers for Disease Control and Prevention. (2009). Recommendations of the advisory committee on immunization practices (ACIP). *Mortality and Morbidity Weekly Report (MMWR), 58*(RR02), 1-25. Retrieved from http://www.cdc.gov/mmwr/preview/mmwrhtml/rr5802a1.htm

Cortese, M. & Parashar, U. (2009). *Prevention of rotavirus gastroenteritis among infants and children.* Centers for Disease Control and Prevention.

Immunization Action Coalition. (2011). *Vaccine information for the public and health professionals: Vaccine information statement Rotavirus VIS.* Retrieved from http://www.immunize.org/vis/vis_rotavirus.asp

Mayo Clinic. (2013). *Rotavirus.* Retrieved from http://www.mayoclinic.com/health/rotavirus/DS00783

SCABIES

DEFINITION/ETIOLOGY:
Scabies is caused by a tiny, eight-legged burrowing mite called *Sarcoptes scabiei*. It is a highly contagious infection spread through direct, prolonged, skin-to-skin contact and shared clothing or linen. A person infected for the first time may not exhibit symptoms for 2-6 weeks and can transmit scabies to another person during that time. A person previously infected with scabies may exhibit symptoms as early as 1-4 days after exposure.

SIGNS AND SYMPTOMS:
- Typical lesion is a "burrow": a tiny, pale, irregular line that marks the path of the scabies mite.
- Rash: tiny (1-2 mm) erythematous papules, vesicles, pustule and scabs. Sometimes with tiny, linear dark scabs 0.5-1) mm long.
- Location: between fingers webs, flexor surface of wrist and elbow, axillary lady folds, waist, and can also spread to breasts and penis.
- **The face, neck, palms and soles** may be involved in infants and very young children **(a good assessment clue).**
- Itching is intense, especially at night and the appearance of rash.
- Frequently found in other family members.
- Secondary skin infections (pustules) are frequent due to scratching.
- Itching is related to an allergic reaction to mites and may persist a month after successful treatment until top layers of skin are shed.
- Diagnostic hints:
  1) Appearance and distribution of rash and the presence of burrows.
  2) Color suspected burrow and surrounding skin with purple felt marker and wipe off with alcohol. Burrow will be outlined in purple.
  3) Microscopic examination of skin scrapings for mites, eggs or fecal matter.

MANAGEMENT/TREATMENT:
1. Exclude from school for prompt treatment. May return 8 hours/next day after proper treatment.
2. Steroid ointments or lotions are contraindicated.
3. Instruct parent/guardian to wash clothes, towels, and bed linen used by the infected person within the previous 2 days at 130 º F or hotter, and dry in hot dryer.
4. MEDICATIONS:
   - No over the counter (OTC) products have been approved to treat human scabies.
   - Scabacides are available by prescription from the primary healthcare provider. Follow label directions.

SCABIES *(continued from previous page)*

- The usual prescription product is permethrin 5% cream (Elimite®). Crotamiton 10% cream (Eurax®) for scabies nodules is approved only for adults. Lindane 1% lotion is available, but is rarely used due to side effects. Evidence suggests that oral ivermectin may be effective in the treatment of scabies, but there is no FDA approval at this time.
- Scabacide lotions should be applied to the entire body (chin-line to toes.) NEVER ON THE FACE. The lotions should be left on as recommended on the package insert, and then washed off thoroughly with soap and water.
- Anti-scabetic lotions/creams should not be used more than twice in a month.
- Oral antihistamine helps itching that may persist up to one month after treatment.

FOLLOW-UP:
- Assess each day or two after first treatment.
- Watch for new lesions. A second treatment may be necessary.
- Watch for secondary infection and refer accordingly.
- Check siblings in school.
- Educate staff about scabies and transmission.

POTENTIAL COMPLICATIONS:
Vigorous scratching can cause breaks in the skin, potentially leading to secondary bacterial infections.

NOTES:
May be asymptomatic the first two to six weeks of an **initial** infection of scabies. However, even though the person is asymptomatic, they remain contagious during this time period.

SCABIES *(continued from previous page)*

Reference

American Academy of Dermatology. (n.d.). *Scabies.* Retrieved from http://www.aad.org/dermatology-a-to-z/diseases-and-treatments/q---t/scabies

American Academy of Pediatrics. (2013). Scabies. In S. Aronson, & T. Shope (Eds.), *Managing infectious diseases in child care and schools (2nd ed.)* (p. 151). Elk Grove Village, IL: American Academy of Pediatrics.

American Academy of Pediatrics. (2009). Summaries of infectious disease – scabies. In L.K. Pickering, C.J. Baker, D.W. Kimberlin, & S.S. Long (Eds.), *Red Book: 2009 report of the committee on infectious diseases (28th ed.)* (p. 589-591). Elk Grove Village, IL:American Academy of Pediatrics.

Ball, J., Binder, R., & Cowen, K. (Eds.). (2012). Alterations in skin integrity. *Principles of Pediatric Nursing: Caring for Children (5th ed.)* (p. 1052). Upper Saddle River, NJ: Pearson Education, Inc.

Center for Disease Control and Prevention. (2010). *Scabies.* Retrieved from http://www.cdc.gov/parasites/scabies/

Mayo Clinic. (2012). *Scabies.* Retrieved from http://www.mayoclinic.com/health/scabies/DS00451

Medline Plus, U.S. National Library of Medicine. (2013). *Scabies.* Retrieved from http://www.nlm.nih.gov/medlineplus/scabies.html

Merck Manual, Professional Edition. *Scabies.* (2013). Retrieved from http://www.merckmanuals.com/professional/dermatologic_disorders/parasitic_skin_infections/scabies.html?qt=scabies&alt=sh

Vernon, P., Brady, M. & Starr, N.B. (2008). Dermatologic diseases. In C. Burns, M. Brady, A. Dunn, N.B. Starr, & C. Blosser (Eds.), *Pediatric primary care, (4th ed.)* (pp. 969-9970). St. Louis, MO: Saunders Elsevier.

SCHOOL SPONSORED TRIPS

DEFINITION:
School sponsored trips are excursion(s) organized by school personnel. School sponsored trips may or may not occur during school time. School sponsored trips may occur locally, within the state, out of state or internationally. While on a school sponsored trip, students may require medications, treatments, and/or specific medical procedures. These health needs must be met. Legally, school districts are responsible for providing necessary accommodations so that all children can participate in school-related activities.

DESCRIPTION:
All students, even students with special health needs, have the legal right to fully participate in school-related activities including school sponsored trips. There are 3 federal laws that protect a student with special healthcare needs/disabilities.

- Americans with Disabilities Act (ADA) of 1990 – bars discrimination against individuals with disabilities
- Individuals with Disabilities Education Improvement Act (IDEIA), reauthorized in 2004 – mandates a free and appropriate education for students who qualify for special education services in a least restrictive environment
- Section 504 of the Rehabilitation Act (1973) – protects the rights of students with disabilities

There may also be state specific laws regarding discrimination against students with disabilities. It is important for the school nurse to know their state specific laws.

MANAGEMENT/PLANNING PROCESS:
School nurses must be actively involved in the planning process of school sponsored trips (especially out of state/international excursions). Depending on student's medical needs, it may be necessary for the school nurse who is familiar with the student, to attend certain school sponsored trips to provide necessary medical support if the school nurse determines that medical care cannot legally or safely be delegated, and an additional school nurse cover the school health office. The school nurse needs to review the following best practices in order to be prepared for a successful school sponsored trip well in advance of the trip.

1. Identify student specific needs by reviewing Individual Healthcare Plans (IHPs) and/or emergency cards.
2. Consider inviting the parent/guardian to attend the trip.
   a. The parent/guardian cannot be mandated to attend the trip
   b. Students cannot be excluded from school sponsored activities
   c. Denying the student the right to participate in a school sponsored trip due to their healthcare needs is discrimination against that student

SCHOOL SPONSORED TRIPS *(continued from previous page)*

    d. School districts must make accommodations to meet all necessary healthcare needs
3. Delegate tasks and procedures appropriately; when in doubt – don't delegate! This may mean that the school nurse must attend the trip to provide necessary medical care.
4. Adequately train school staff to respond appropriately to student health needs.
5. Prepare medications according to state law and school district policy.

Out of state trips:
Complete the above steps. In addition:

1. Review the state nurse practice act in the state in which the school sponsored trip will take place.
   a. Nurse practice acts vary from state to state.
   b. School nurses must know the scope of nursing practice in their home state and the state in which they will be visiting.
   c. The school nurse is responsible for knowing the scope of practice as it relates to delegation, medication administration, and emergency care.
   d. Is delegation to unlicensed school personnel permitted in the state that is being visited?
2. Contact the board of nursing in the state that you will be traveling. The school nurse may need to obtain a nursing license in that state.
   a. Some states participate in the nurse licensure compact (NLC).
   b. The NLC permits nurses to practice in both their home state and have a multistate license so that they can practice in another compact state.

FOLLOW UP:
For quality assurance, review healthcare services that were provided on the school sponsored trip. What needs to be done to improve the school sponsored trip process (earlier planning, more staff training, develop trip checklist, etc.)?

POTENTIAL COMPLICATIONS:
Health emergencies can happen anywhere – be prepared!
- Know the layout of the school sponsored trip site
- Identify location(s) of local urgent care or hospital

SCHOOL SPONSORED TRIPS *(continued from previous page)*

NOTES:

Preparing for school sponsored trips can be a complicated process. To safeguard the health and safety of children with special healthcare needs, it is recommended that the school nurse be involved in the planning process for all school sponsored trips, especially out of state and international trips.

References

Erwin, K. (2013, June 29). *Providing care for students with special healthcare needs on out-of-state field trips*. PowerPoint lecture presented at NASN 45th Annual Conference.

Foley, M. (2013). Health services management. In J. Selekman (Ed.), *School nursing: A comprehensive text* (2nd ed.) (pp. 1190- 1215). Philadelphia, PA: FA Davis Company.

Lechtenberg, J. (2009). *Legal aspects of school nursing.* School Health Alert. Retrieved from http://www.schoolnurse.com/public/images/Legal%20Aspects%20of%20School%20Nursing%2004-2009.pdf

National Association of School Nurses [NASN]. (2013). *School sponsored trips, role of the school nurse: Position statement.* Retrieved from https://www.nasn.org/PolicyAdvocacy/PositionPapersandReports/NASNIssueBriefsFullView/tabid/445/smid/853/ArticleID/304/Default.aspx

National Council of State Boards of Nursing. (2011). *Nurse licensure compact (NLC): Fact sheet for licensees and nursing students.* Retrieved from https://www.ncsbn.org/2011_NLCA_factsheet_students_Rev_Jan_2011.pdf

SEIZURES - EPILEPSY

A seizure results from abnormal and excessive electrical activity in cerebral neurons that lead to a change of consciousness, motor activity, behavior, and/or sensation. Most seizures last a minute or two typically followed by confusion and sleepiness. Triggers include stress, sleep patterns, hormone changes, light sensitivity or drugs. A seizure can be a one-time episode from a fever or brain injury or occur with frequency.

People may have one or more types of seizures, but most people with epilepsy will have a similar pattern with each seizure. Seizures are divided into types; generalized seizures (absence, atonic, tonic-clonic, myoclonic), partial (simple and complex), nonepileptic and status epilepticus.

A seizure is not a diagnosis but a symptom of a diagnosis. Epilepsy is a seizure disorder and is a chronic condition of recurrent seizures without an identifiable cause.

SIGNS/SYMPTOMS:
ALL TYPES
- Signs and symptoms are dependent on where the problem in the brain is located
- Distinct beginning and rapid cessation
- Amnesia of seizure, sometimes including events that occurred a few seconds to minutes prior to seizure (retrograde amnesia)
- EEG not always abnormal

GENERALIZED: ABSENCE (PETIT MAL)
- Very brief (10-20 seconds) period of cessation of motion
- Brief loss of consciousness
- May drop glass or pencil
- Occasional brief muscular twitches
- May chew or blink
- Usual onset between 5-12 years of age, may occur several times a day
- Lack of attention (e.g., staring out the window) often mistaken for petit mal

GENERALIZED
- Generalized, violent muscle contractions
- Affects most of the body
- Loss of consciousness
- Incontinence of urine/stool
- Tongue or cheek biting
- Sometimes seizure is preceded by aura of light, noise or odor

SEIZURES - EPILEPSY *(continued from previous page)*

- Post-convulsive state; drowsy to deep sleep
- Awakened to confusion, headache or speech difficulty
- Frequency varies from daily, to monthly, to annually

FOCAL PARTIAL

- Seizure of one part of body, usually on one side only; hand, arm, face, tongue, foot, or leg
- May "spread" to other muscle groups
- Usually no loss of consciousness
- May have nausea, sweating, or dilated pupils

COMPLEX PARTIAL: (PSYCHOMOTOR)

- Purposeful but inappropriate motor acts, often repetitive; running
- Arm extension with slow turn of body
- Usually no tonic or clonic activity
- Consciousness is impaired
- May be disorientated or confused
- Often sleepy after seizure

PARTIAL: SOMATOSENSORY

- Numbness, tingling, or pain that may originate in one part of body and spread
- Visual images or sensations
- Sudden tastes or smells

PARTIAL: EPILEPTIC EQUIVALENTS

- Symptoms of headache, stomachache, vomiting, diarrhea, uncontrollable laugh and other symptoms associated with autonomic nervous system
- Behavior disorders and learning problems
- Thought to be due to abnormal cerebral cortical discharges
- The existence of this category of epilepsy is questioned: attributed to psychological origin

NON-EPILEPTIC (PSEUDOEPILEPSY)

- Rarely injures self
- Incontinence rare
- Consciousness regained quickly
- Often preceded by anxiety
- Cyanosis absent or momentary

SEIZURES - EPILEPSY *(continued from previous page)*

STATUS EPILEPTICUS
- Definition: Seizure lasting 30 minutes or a 30 minute period of serial seizures without regaining consciousness
- Follow medical order and the individual healthcare plans for students with a history of seizures

MANAGEMENT/TREATMENT:
PHARMCOLOGICAL TREATMENT
- Antiepileptic drugs are the most common treatment for epilepsy
- Drug treatment varies with the type of seizure, age of person, and effectiveness
- Medication must be taken consistently
- Midazolam (rectal, buccal and intranasal) can be administered according to the healthcare provider instructions, state nursing practice guidelines and school district policy

NON-PHARMACEUTICAL TREATMENTS
KETOGENIC DIET
- High fat (80%) diet that works by burning stored fat versus glucose for energy.
- Ketosis prevents seizures.
- Important side effects include dehydration, constipation, kidney or gall stones, menstrual irregularities, pancreatitis, and decreased bone density.
- OTC medication may interfere with diet, check with healthcare provider for sugar free medication substitutes.

VAGAL NERVE STIMULATOR (VNS)
- Currently approved for people over age 12.
- Battery-operated device (similar in concept to a pacemaker), about the size of a silver dollar, that is implanted in the chest wall or sometimes in the lower abdominal area.
- Small wires are threaded under the skin and wound around the vagus nerve in the neck.
- The device works by sending regular small pulses of electrical energy to the brain.
- When a person feels a seizure coming on, they can activate the discharge of electrical energy by passing a small magnet over the battery to stop the seizure.
- It is also possible to turn the device off by holding the magnet over it.
- Side effects include hoarseness, voice alteration, coughing and increased salivation.

SURGICAL INTERVENTION
- Removes affected area of the brain
- Is done when other options are not successful
- Can significantly reduce or stop seizures
- Can result in personality or cognitive changes

SEIZURES - EPILEPSY *(continued from previous page)*

FIRST AID FOR SEIZURE
- Keep calm and reassure other people who may be nearby
- Do not hold person down or try to stop movements
- Time the seizure
- Gently lower person to the floor
- Position on side with mouth toward floor to prevent aspiration of salvia or vomitus
- Clear area around person of sharp objects or items that may lead to secondary injury
- Loosen anything around neck that may interfere with breathing
- Place something soft under the head
- DO NOT stimulate by rubbing chest, face, or arms or loosening clothing on body
- DO NOT try to force mouth open; DO NOT insert any padded object into the mouth
- Reassure person as consciousness returns
- Allow to rest following seizure
- Remain with student until entirely awake

FIRST AID FOR SEIZURE IN A WHEELCHAIR
- Do not remove the person from the wheelchair unless totally necessary
- Secure the wheelchair to prevent movement
- Loosely fasten the seatbelt
- Protect the head
- Pad the wheelchair to prevent injuries to the limbs

WHEN TO SEEK IMMEDIATE MEDICAL ATTENTION:
- First time seizure
- Generalized tonic-clonic seizures lasting more than 5 minutes unless otherwise instructed by physician
- Repeated seizures without regaining consciousness between seizures
- A change in seizure pattern or an increase in seizures
- Seizure in the water
- Injury occurs during seizure
- Some students will have a healthcare provider order for rectal valium for a seizure lasting a specific amount of time (this may vary for individuals, but often it is ordered given for seizures lasting over 3-5 minutes).
- Seek medical attention if person has:
  - Diabetes (follow emergency health plan)
  - Brain infection
  - Heat exhaustion
  - Pregnancy
  - Poisoning
  - Head injury

SEIZURES - EPILEPSY *(continued from previous page)*

FOLLOW UP:
- Obtain accurate detailed history
- Develop an Individualized Healthcare Plan
- Emergency plan should be available for classroom and EMS personnel
- Assess school environment for triggers
- Monitor medication
- Obtain necessary releases of information
- Educate all staff including bus drivers on all aspects of seizures
- Record current body weight, medications and typical seizure episodes
- Become familiar with quality of life issues; emotional issues, driving, cognitive abilities and employment

NOTES:
- Most seizures are not considered medical emergencies
- The most frequent cause of breakthrough is failure to take prescribed seizure medication
- Febrile seizures are common in young children
- About 70% of children using one or more treatment mentioned above become seizure free
- Some individuals are able to stop medication after a lengthy time and remain seizure free
- Epilepsy can be prevented by wearing safety equipment (helmets) and using a car seat to prevent trauma to the brain

Resources
Epilepsy Foundation, 2012. School Nurse Program: Managing Students with Seizures at http://www.epilepsyfoundation.org/livingwithepilepsy/educators/socialissues/schoolnurseprogram/

References
Blair, J. (2013). Seizures and epilepsy. In J. Selekman (Ed.), *School nursing: A comprehensive text (2nd ed.)*(pp. 1003-1027). Philadelphia, PA: F.A. Davis.

Epilepsy Foundation. (2012). *What is epilepsy?* Retrieved from http://www.epilepsyfoundation.org/aboutepilepsy/whatisepilepsy/index.cfm

Epilepsy Foundation. (2012). *Fact sheets on epilepsy*. Retrieved from http://www.epilepsyfoundation.org/livingwithepilepsy/educators/socialissues/schoolnurseprogram/fact-sheet-on-epilepsy.cfm

National Institute of Neurological Disorders and Stroke. (2013). *Seizures and epilepsy: Hope through research*. Retrieved from http://www.ninds.nih.gov/disorders/epilepsy/detail_epilepsy.htm

Medline Plus. U.S. National Library of Medicine. (2013). *Seizures*. Retrieved from http://www.nlm.nih.gov/medlineplus/seizures.html#skip

SELF-INJURIOUS/SELF-MUTILATION BEHAVIOR

DEFINITION/ETIOLOGY:
Self-injurious or self-mutilation behavior is a deliberate, secretive act that is the used as a means of coping with stress, emotional pain, anger or frustration. The person who engages in self injurious behavior often has a different intent than a person engaging in suicidal behaviors. The onset is usually in middle to later adolescence. Most often the action is cutting forearms or wrists with razor blades. Other forms of self- mutilation or self-inflicted injury includes biting, hitting, head banging or bruising oneself; picking or pulling at skin or hair; burning oneself with lighted cigarettes; or amputating parts of the body.

CAUSES:
Self-mutilation tends to be more common in females than males, and tends to begin in adolescence and early adulthood. There is no single cause but may be related to lack of personal identity and difficulty in expressing or feeling emotions. Various theories related to the causes of self-mutilation include:
- History of childhood sexual or physical abuse
- Emotional neglect
- Insecure attachment
- Prolonged separation from caregivers
- Psychological problems (dissociation, personality disorder, substance abuse, eating disorders)
- Antisocial personality

SIGNS/SYMPTOMS:
(Nursing assessment begins with establishing a trusting relationship with the student.)

- The most common sites are arms, wrists, ankles, and lower legs
- Hidden sites may include axilla, abdomen, inner thighs, feet, and under the breasts
- Broken bones
- Scars may be noted; they are usually superficial, faint, pink, with well demarcated lines and may have a specific pattern, design, symbol, word, or single, large repeatedly scarred line in the skin
- Burns

Common features among self-mutilators include:
- Wearing long sleeves or baggy clothing (even in hot weather)
- Unusual need for privacy
- Disappointment in self
- Perception of an interpersonal loss

SELF-INJURIOUS/SELF-MUTILATION BEHAVIOR *(continued from previous page)*

- Responds with deep emotional distress (tense, anxious, angry, fearful)
- Feels threatened with a loss of identity
- Lacks ability to verbalize emotions and may isolate self from others prior to self-mutilation an
- Impulsivity
- Feelings of hopelessness and helplessness
- May suffer from serious psychological problems or develop a borderline personality
- Keeping sharp objects on hands
- Offers excuses for frequent injuries

Many adolescents report self-injury as an attempt to feel better. Some report relief, feeling less tense or angry, after self-harm but then often feel guilt or shame if noticed by others.

MANAGEMENT/TREATMENT:

1. School nurses may be the first adults to observe self-mutilation wounds. Unlike tattoos or extreme body art (decorative scars or branding) intended to make a statement, self-injurious behavior is not planned behavior and needs thoughtful referral for evaluation and counseling.

2. School nurses need to evaluate any injuries and provide medical care as necessary.

3. A screening for suicide ideation should be done by a staff member trained in suicide risk assessment.

4. Parents/guardians and school administrators should be notified.

5. Parents/guardians should be provided with contact information in the community for referrals.

6. First responses upon discovery of self-mutilation are important.
   - Keep negative reactions in check since showing shock, denial, disapproval, frustration or sympathy or making demands that he or she stop are not helpful. Self-injurious behavior is a coping method, used as a last effort to relieve distress, so one goal is to help the self-mutilator learn other means of expressing pain and anger.
   - Talking about self-injurious behavior is essential; asking about the action can dispel secrecy and shame, allows him or her to connect with another person, and shows your willingness to help him or her to talk about painful events and what s/he feels they need.

SELF-INJURIOUS/SELF-MUTILATION BEHAVIOR *(continued from previous page)*

Notes:

Although self- injury is not usually a suicide attempt, the emotional problems that trigger self-injury may increase the risk of suicide. If the students is having any suicide thoughts or ideation the student should not be left alone and the school protocol for managing suicidal students should be followed.

References

American Academy of Child and Adolescent Psychiatry. (2009). *Self-injury in adolescents*. Retrieved from
    http://www.aacap.org/AACAP/Families_and_Youth/Facts_for_Families/Facts_for_Families_Pages/
    Self_Injury_In_Adolescents_73.aspx

Mayo Clinic. (2012). *Self-injury/cutting* . Retrieved from
    http://www.mayoclinic.com/health/self-injury/DS00775/DSECTION=causes

Medline Plus. U.S. National Library of Medicine. (2013). *Self-harm*. Retrieved from
    http://www.nlm.nih.gov/medlineplus/selfharm.html

National Center for PTSD. (2011). *Self-harm and trauma*. Retrieved from http://www.ptsd.va.gov/public/pages/self-harm.asp

SEXUALLY TRANSMITTED DISEASES/INFECTIONS

DEFINITION/ETIOLOGY:
Sexually transmitted infections (STI), sometimes referred to as sexually transmitted diseases (STD) are infections acquired by sexual contact. STIs can be passed to a person anytime they have unprotected sex with a partner who is already infected. It can be spread during vaginal, anal or oral sex. The organisms that cause STIs may pass from person to person through blood, semen, or vaginal fluids. Over twenty (20) diseases are classified as sexually transmitted and are reportable to the local health department. Sexually transmitted diseases commonly seen in the adolescent population will be reviewed in this document.

Chlamydial Infections
Chlamydia is the most frequently reported infectious disease in the United States and prevalence is highest among those under 25 years of age. It is caused by the organism *C. trachomatis*. Annual screening of all sexually active adolescents is recommended.

Gonococcal Infections
Gonorrhea is the second most commonly reported bacterial STI and is caused by *N. gonorrhoeae*. Symptoms usually develop 2-21 days after having sex.

SIGNS AND SYMPTOMS:
- Asymptomatic infection is common
- Vaginal, penile and cervical discharge
- Pain/burning with urination, between periods or after sex
- Unusual vaginal bleeding
- Abdominal pain, sometimes with fever or nausea
- Enlarged inguinal or femoral lymph nodes
- Swollen testicles
- Rectal pain or discharge

Treatment/ Management:
- Students with possible chlamydial and gonococcal infections should be referred to a healthcare provider for testing and treatment.
- Chlamydial and gonococcal infections or suspected infections should be treated with antibiotics.
- Students should be re-tested in 3-4 months.
- Students should be instructed to refer their sex partners to a healthcare provider if they have had sexual contact within 60 days of onset of the symptoms.

SEXUALLY TRANSMITTED DISEASES/INFECTIONS *(continued from previous page)*

Genital Herpes Simplex Virus

Genital herpes is a chronic, life- long viral infection. Two types have been identified, HSV-*1* and *HSV-2.* Most cases of genital herpes are caused by *HSV- 1.* Many persons have mild or asymptomatic infection but shed the virus intermittently in the genital tract.

Signs and Symptoms:
- A flu-like feeling
- Small painful blisters on these organs or mouth
- Itching or burning before the symptoms occur
- Blisters may last 1-3 weeks
- Blisters may return

Treatment/Management:
- Anti-viral medication may be ordered by the healthcare provider for initial and episodic infections and for suppression.
- Warm baths may be helpful.
- Students should understand that although it can be treated herpes cannot be cured.
- Daily suppression therapy may also decrease the risks of transmission.

Genital Human Papillomavirus (HPV)

HPV is the most common sexually transmitted infection in the U.S today. Over half of sexually active women and men are infected at some point in their lives. More than 100 different types of HPV commonly affect the mucosal surfaces of the genital area. The virus is transmitted through skin-to-skin contact. It is associated with genital warts and cervical cancers although most infections do not result in cancer.

Signs and symptoms:
- Many people have no symptoms
- Genital warts in the genital area
- Warts may be alone or in groups, flat or rounded, pink or skin colored

Treatment/Management:
- Students with genital warts should be referred to their healthcare provider.
- Although there is no cure for genital warts, they can be treated.
- Genital warts may spontaneously resolve without treatment.
- Warts can be treated with ointments, surgical or laser removal.
- Warts may recur after treatment.
- Vaccines for the prevention of HPV are available and approved for both males and females 10-25 years.

272

SEXUALLY TRANSMITTED DISEASES/INFECTIONS *(continued from previous page)*

POTENTIAL COMPLICATIONS of untreated STIs:
- Infertility
- Neurological or cardiovascular problems occur with some infections
- Pelvic Inflammatory Disease (PID)
- Ectopic pregnancy
- Reactive arthritis (Reiter Syndrome) as a complication of chlamydia
- Many STIs may be transmitted to newborns during birth or have an adverse effect on pregnancy
- Epididymitis, prostatitis

If a student had sexual contact with someone who had or has any of the above symptoms related to STI, it is important to **see a qualified physician or nurse practitioner immediately**.

FOLLOW-UP:
- Encourage student to continue full course of prescribed treatment and obtain necessary tests.
- Abstinence from sexual activity for 7 days is encouraged following treatment.
- Encourage student to cooperate in locating sexual contacts.
- Educate students in regard to prevention, re-infection, and complications.
    - HIV is easier to acquire if one already has another sexually transmitted disease.
    - Many infections are asymptomatic in boys but may cause serious infection in girls (e.g. chlamydia).
- Latex condom use has been shown to prevent transmission of most bacterial infections and is helpful in limiting some transmission of HSV and HPV.
- Students should be aware that abstinence is the only way to prevent a STI with 100% accuracy.
- Most state laws permit treatment of a minor without parental consent or notification.
- Nurses should be aware of their own state laws and regulations regarding confidentiality.
- Students should be encouraged to involve a parent or responsible adult in the process.

NOTES:
According to the CDC (2010), the reporting of STIs in an accurate and timely manner is important for assessing morbidity trends, targeting limited resources, and assisting local health authorities in partner notification and treatment. Cases related to STI, HIV, and acquired immune deficiency syndrome (AIDS) should be reported in accordance with state and local statutory requirements. Additionally, Syphilis, Gonorrhea, Chlamydia, Chancroid, HIV infection, and AIDS are reportable diseases in every state. The reporting requirements for other STIs differ by state, thus clinicians should be familiar with state and local reporting requirements.

SEXUALLY TRANSMITTED DISEASES/INFECTIONS *(continued from previous page)*

The rates of STIs are highest among adolescents ages 15-19 (CDC, 2010). Minor consent laws may vary from state to state. With a few exceptions, all adolescents in the United States can legally consent to confidential diagnosis and treatment of STIs. In all 50 states and the District of Columbia, adolescents can receive medical care for STIs without parental consent or knowledge. Additionally, adolescents can consent to HIV counseling and testing in the majority of states. According to the CDC (2010), the consent laws for vaccination of adolescents differ by state. However, some states consider provision of vaccine similar to treatment of STI and provide vaccination services without parental consent. Healthcare providers should follow policies which provide confidentiality and comply with state laws for STI services.

The management of children with STIs requires the close cooperation clinicians, laboratory technicians, and child protective services authorities. Prompt initiation of official investigations is important when needed. Specific diseases, e.g. Gonorrhea, Syphilis, and Chlamydia, if acquired after the neonatal period, are indicative of sexual contact. Other diseases, e.g. HPV infections and vaginitis, do not have a clear association with sexual contact.

References

Centers for Disease Control and Prevention. (2010). Sexually transmitted diseases treatment guidelines, 2010. MMWR 2010, 59 (No. RR-12). Retrieved from http://www.cdc.gov/std/treatment/2010/std-treatment-2010-rr5912.pdf

Fisher, M., Alderman, E., Kreipe, R., & Rosenfeld, W. (Eds.). (2011). *Textbook of adolescent health care* (pp. 477-501). Elk Grove Village, IL: American Academy of Pediatrics.

Gerlt, T. & Starr, N.B. (2008). Gynecologic conditions. In C. Burns, M. Brady, A. Dunn, N.B. Starr, C. Blosser (Eds.). *Pediatric primary care, (4th ed.)* (pp. 933-937). St. Louis, MO: Saunders Elsevier.

Mayo Clinic. (2013). *Sexually transmitted diseases (STDs)*. Retrieved from http://www.mayoclinic.com/health/sexually-transmitted-diseases-stds/DS01123

SICKLE CELL DISEASE

DEFINITION/ETIOLOGY:

Sickle cell disease is a hereditary disorder present at birth that affects the red blood cells. The term *sickle cell disease* refers to a group of genetic disorders where Hemoglobin S is more prevalent than the normal Hemoglobin A in the blood. The red blood cells take on a sickle shape, become sticky and hard, and fail to function well. The sickle cells die early causing chronic anemia. As they travel through small blood vessels, they often get stuck due to their sticky composition. The blocked flow of blood is called vaso-occlusive crisis (VOC). If the student develops a fever or dehydration or a decreased oxygen level, the sickling will become enhanced.

There are several types of sickle cell disease but the most severe form is sickle cell anemia and when the sickle cell gene is inherited from both parents.

Sickle cell disease is most common among those of African descent but also affects children from Central America, the Mediterranean, South America, and the Caribbean. It rarely affects white children.

SIGNS AND SYMPTOMS:
- Hand and foot syndrome, swelling of the hands and feet (may be the first sign)
- Pain episode or "crisis" caused by the sickle cells obstructing the circulation (the hallmark sign). Pain may be severe and include joint pain, chest pain, headache, abdominal pain, nausea or vomiting
- Frequently occurring infections
- Anemia
  - Fatigue
  - Pallor
  - Tachycardia
  - Delayed growth
  - Irritability
- Leg ulcers
- Vision loss
- Hematuria

MANAGEMENT/TREATMENT:
1. Treatment measures for the pain crisis should include prevention of an episode with plenty of fluids, avoiding hot and cold temperatures, avoiding high altitudes or extreme exercising.
2. Pain management with strong narcotic analgesics may be necessary to provide relief during an acute episode.

SICKLE CELL DISEASE (continued from previous page)

3. Fluid therapy is initiated during a crisis to restore circulating blood volume.
4. At the first sign of an infection, it is important for children to see a doctor.
5. Prophylactic antibiotics are often given to prevent infection.
6. Blood transfusions are sometimes needed for severe anemia.
7. During the school day, the child should receive extra fluids and rest periods during times of physical activity.
8. Children who have experienced splenic sequestration may subsequently have an elective splenectomy.

POTENTIAL COMPLICATIONS

- Acute Splenic Sequestration: Because the sickle cells are trapped, a large amount of blood accumulates in the spleen. This usually occurs in the young child as the spleen commonly stops functioning in early childhood.
- Aplastic Crisis: Episodes of bone marrow suppression that cause the red blood cell production to be decreased. Often occurs after a viral or bacterial infection including *parvovirus B19*.
- High risk for sepsis, meningitis, pneumonia, and other severe infections.
- Possible damage to internal organs.
- Acute chest syndrome: Similar to pneumonia, can cause chest pain, difficulty breathing and fever. It should be treated in the hospital.
- Cerebral stroke: Can occur in 10% of children with SCD due to the clogged blood flow to the brain.

FOLLOW UP:

- The child with SCD should be managed by an interdisciplinary medical team with ongoing maintenance and regular visits to the healthcare provider.

NOTES:

- Newborn screening for sickle cell is mandated in the United States. All infants should undergo testing between 24 and 72 hours of age. If sickle cell is suspected in an older child, hemoglobin electrophoresis is used to confirm the diagnosis.
- Children with SCD should have their eyes examined yearly to check for retinal damages.
- The school nurse can assist the child and family by providing information to the staff about the child and the condition. The staff should be aware of the need for prompt medical care in the event of a "crisis" or infection.
- An Individualized Healthcare Plan (IHP) should be developed for the child with sickle cell disease.

SICKLE CELL DISEASE (continued from previous page)

References

Bowden, V. Greenberb, C. (Eds.).(2010). The child with altered hematologic status. In *Children and their families: The continuum of care (2ⁿᵈ edition) (pp.* 1208-1215). Philadelphia, PA: Lippincott Williams and Wilkins.

Cosby, M.F., Miller, N.B., & Youngman, K. (2013). Acute measures for emergent problems. In J. Selekman (Ed.), School *nursing: A comprehensive text (2ⁿᵈ ed.)* (pp. 548-549). Philadelphia, PA: F.A. Davis.

Centers for Disease Control and Prevention (CDC), National Center for Infectious Diseases. (2011). Sickle *cell disease (SCD).* Retrieved from http://www.cdc.gov/ncbddd/sicklecell/treatments.html

Selekman, J., Bochenek, J. & Lukens, M. (2013). Children with chronic conditions. In J. Selekman (Ed.), School *nursing: A comprehensive text (2ⁿᵈ ed.)* (pp.734-737). Philadelphia, PA: F.A. Davis.

SINUSITIS

DEFINITION/ETIOLOGY:
Sinusitis is inflammation of the mucous membranes that line the paranasal sinuses, and is commonly referred to as **rhino-sinusitis.**

<u>Acute sinusitis</u>: abrupt onset of infection of one or more of the paranasal sinuses with resolution following therapy usually within 30 days.

<u>Subacute bacterial sinusitis</u>: persistent occurrence of purulent nasal discharge, despite treatment with symptoms lasting less than 3 months.

<u>Chronic sinusitis</u>: episodes of prolonged inflammation or may be repeated acute infection. Clinical symptoms last more than 90 days.

<u>Recurrent acute bacterial sinusitis</u>: episode lasts less than 30 days, 3 episodes/six months, or episodes in a year with complete resolution in the interim.

CAUSES:
Predisposing factors for acute bacterial sinusitis:
Any condition that blocks the flow of secretions can lead to sinusitis. Mucous stasis creates a good environment for pathogens to grow.
- 80% associated with acute viral rhino-sinusitis.
- 20% from allergic inflammation.
- Other factors that increase risk of sinusitis include smoke exposure, swimming, gastroesophageal reflux, cystic fibrosis, immunodeficiency, ciliary dyskinesia, and anatomical abnormalities.
- Sinusitis is more commonly seen in adults or older children.

Common pathogens:
- *Streptococcus pneumoniae* (about 30% of cases)
- *Haemophilus influenzae* (about 20% of cases)
- *Moraxilla catarrhalis* (about 20% of cases)

SIGNS/SYMPTOMS:
- Cough (worsening at night)
- Fever
- Purulent Rhinorrhea (runny nose) usually yellow or green
- Postnasal secretions (purulent drainage)
- Halitosis (bad breath) or loss of smell
- Headache/face pain/toothache
- Head pain with bending over of sudden movements
- Snoring

SINUSITIS *(continued from previous page)*

- Earache
- Nasal speech
- Facial swelling

A clinical diagnosis is generally made after upper respiratory signs and symptoms are present for greater than 10-14 days and with symptoms such as facial swelling, facial pain and fever.

CLASSIFYING SEVERITY:
Mild persistent symptoms: Nasal or postnasal discharge and daytime cough (which may be worse at night); symptoms last longer than 10-14 days, but less than 30 days.
Severe symptoms include high temperature, at least 102° F (39°C); purulent nasal discharge for at least 3 to 4 consecutive days.

MANAGEMENT/TREATMENT:
1. If student has fever or looks ill, notify parent/guardian(s) and refer to physician/ healthcare provider.
2. A cool compress on the forehead may make the student more comfortable.
3. Encourage fluids.
4. Students returning to school may be monitored for completing antibiotics and any side effects.
5. Many physicians/healthcare providers recommend normal saline nose drops to assist with drainage and ventilation that can be done both at home and at school.
6. Monitor for complications such as orbital cellulitis, exacerbation of asthma, cavernous sinus thrombosis and optic neuritis.
7. Prevention: avoid allergens and treat allergies when appropriate.

FOLLOW UP:
Sinus infections are usually curable with medical treatment and self-care measures. Recurrent sinus attacks require follow up with a healthcare provider to assess for underlying causes such as nasal polyps or allergies.

School nurses can help with prevention by encouraging hand washing, use and disposal of tissues and cough etiquette.

NOTES:
Risk factors include:
1) attendance at day care,
2) antimicrobial treatment within past 90 days, and
3) under 2 years of age.

SINUSITIS *(continued from previous page)*

References

Hogate, S., Giel, J. & Selekman, J. (2013). Allergy. In J. Selekman (Ed.), *School nursing: A comprehensive text* (2nd ed.) (p. 798). Philadelphia, PA: F.A. Davis.

Mayo Clinic. (2013). *Chronic sinusitis*. Retrieved from http://www.mayoclinic.com/health/chronic-sinusitis/DS00232

Medline Plus. (2012). U.S. National Library of Medicine. (2013). *Sinusitis*. Retrieved from http://www.nlm.nih.gov/medlineplus/ency/article/000647.htm

SKIN AND SOFT TISSUE INFECTION (Cellulitis, Lymphangitis, and MRSA)

DEFINITIONS/ETIOLOGY:

Acute infection of the skin and soft tissues (subcutaneous tissue, fascia, and muscles). The infection may occur secondary to a wound, abrasion, bug bite, impetigo, pustule, furuncle and/or carbuncle. Skin and soft tissue infections are classified as uncomplicated or complicated. Uncomplicated skin and soft tissue infections respond well to oral antibiotics and local wound care. Uncomplicated skin infections can become a complicated skin infection. Complicated skin and wound infections do not respond to conventional antibiotic therapy. A complicated skin and wound infection typically involves deeper tissue (subcutaneous tissue, fascia, and/or muscle). Complicated skin infections may require multiple antibiotics and surgical intervention.

Types of skin and soft tissue infections include:

Cellulitis – acute infection of skin and soft (subcutaneous) tissue. Cellulitis indicates an acute spreading infection of the dermis and subcutaneous tissues. *Staphylococcal aureus* and *Group A Streptococus* are the most common causes of cellulitis.

Lymphangitis is a bacterial infection in the lymphatic vessels. Most often results from *Group A Streptococus* infection of the skin, less frequently from *Staphylococcal aureus*. Lymphangitis may be an indication that a skin infection is worsening. This should raise concern that bacteria may have spread into the bloodstream which can cause life-threatening problems.

Methicillin-resistant *Staphylococcus aureus* (MRSA) is a type of *staphylococcus aureus* (staph) infection that is resistant to beta-lactams antibiotics (such as methicillin, penicillin, and amoxicillin). MRSA is usually transmitted by direct skin-to-skin contact or contact with shared items or surfaces that have come into contact with someone else's infection (e.g., towels, used bandages). MRSA skin infections can occur anywhere.

SIGNS AND SYMPTOMS:

Cellulitis
- First appears as a tiny edge of redness encircling a primary lesion
- Redness spreads in circular fashion, indicating that local body defenses are not limiting the infection. There is pain or tenderness, redness, warmth, and/or swelling at the site
- The sore or rash (macule) appears suddenly, grows quickly in the first 24 hr., and usually has sharp borders
- If the infection is around a skin wound, there may be swelling and drainage
- There may be enlarged lymph nodes near the cellulitis
- May be seen in children on the face, genital area or involving a joint or an extremity

SKIN & SOFT TISSUE INFECTION (Cellulitis, Lymphangitis, & MRSA) *(continued from previous page)*

Lymphangitis
- Painful, red streak below the skin surface leading away from primary lesion to the axilla or to the groin
- Lymph nodes or red streaks above the area (elbow, axilla, or groin) may be enlarged or painful
- May have chills, fever (100°-104°), and malaise

MRSA
- Abscess, pimple, boil, or area on skin
- Redness/swelling around lesion
- Painful around lesion
- Warm to touch
- Lesion may be full of pus or other drainage
- Fever

MANAGEMENT/TREATMENT:
1. Gentle skin cleansing of new wounds.
2. May apply warm, moist compresses to reduce inflammation and discomfort.
3. Refer to healthcare provider if no improvement after FIRST day.
4. Refer to physician/healthcare provider immediately if circle or redness is 1/2 cm (dime size) or larger, over a joint, or on the face.
5. Physician/healthcare provider may prescribe oral antibiotics for the infection and an analgesic for pain.
   - If antibiotic is prescribed, contact physician/healthcare provider if condition worsens or there is no improvement after 3 days on antibiotic.
   - **Cellulitis – if no improvement or condition worsens may need hospitalization and intravenous antibiotic therapy; refer to physician/healthcare provider for immediate follow-up.**
6. **Refer suspected lymphangitis to physician/healthcare provider for emergency care immediately.**
   - Prompt treatment with antibiotics typically result in complete recovery
7. **Contact physician/healthcare provider immediately if suspect MRSA.**
   - Most MRSA infections are treated with oral antibiotics.
   - May be treated by draining the abscess or boil; this is done by a healthcare professional.
   - If indicated, provide wound care per physician/healthcare provider's orders (may include topical antibiotic).
   - Cover the wound with an appropriate bandage.
   - MRSA infections may reoccur.
     - Prevention steps are necessary to avoid reoccurrence of infection (avoid sharing towels or athletic gear, etc.)

SKIN & SOFT TISSUE INFECTION (Cellulitis, Lymphangitis, & MRSA) *(continued from previous page)*

FOLLOW UP:
- MONITOR CAREFULLY!
- If antibiotic is prescribed, all doses must be completed unless otherwise directed by the physician/healthcare provider to stop medication.
- MRSA – the decision to close a school for any communicable disease should be made by school officials in consultation with local and/or state public health officials.
  - In most cases, it is not necessary to close schools because of a MRSA infection in a student.

POTENTIAL COMPLICATIONS:
- Methicillin-resistant *Staphylococcus aureus* (MRSA)
- Lymphangitis (abscess, cellulitis, sepsis)
- Meningitis (if cellulitis is on the face)
- Gangrene
- Sepsis

NOTES:
Prevention
- Keep skin clean and hydrated (use lotions) to prevent cracking.
- Give meticulous attention to cuts and wounds (cleaning, bandaging, and observing for signs of infection).
- Give special attention to foot care (trimming nails and wear properly fitted shoes).
- Wear protective clothing for work and sports.
- MRSA transmission can be prevented by simple habitual measures such as good handwashing hygiene, avoid sharing of personal items, and athletic gear.

References

Center for Disease Control. (2013). *Methicillin-resistant* Staphylococcus Aureus *(MRSA) infections.* Retrieved from http://www.cdc.gov/mrsa/

Center for Disease Control. (2010). *Personal prevention of MRSA skin infections.* Retrieved from http://www.cdc.gov/mrsa/prevent/personal.html

Mayo Clinic. (2012). *Cellulitis.* Retrieved from http://www.mayoclinic.com/print/cellulitis/DS00450/DSECTION=all&METHOD=print

Merck Manual for Health Care Professionals. (2013). *Cellulitis.* Retrieved from http://www.merckmanuals.com/professional/dermatologic_disorders/bacterial_skin_infections/cellulitis.html?qt=mrsa&alt=sh

Merck Manual for Health Care Professionals. (2013). *Overview of bacterial infections.* Retrieved from http://www.merckmanuals.com/professional/dermatologic_disorders/bacterial_skin_infections/overview_of_bacterial_skin_infections.html

Ross, L. & Graham, M. (2013). Skin disorders. In J. Selekman (Ed.), *School nursing: A comprehensive text* (2nd ed.) (pp. 578-697). Philadelphia, PA: F. A. Davis.

Singhal, H. (2012). *Skin and soft tissue infections - incision, drainage, and debridement.* Retrieved from http://emedicine.medscape.com/article/1830144-overview

Sloand. E. *(2012). How should MRSA skin infections be managed in children?* Retrieved from http://www.medscape.com/viewarticle/758307

SORE THROAT (PHARYNGITIS) (including Streptococcal Infection)

DEFINITION/ETIOLOGY:
Pharyngitis is defined as inflammation of the pharynx and the surrounding lymph tissue which is often caused by a viral (influenza or common cold) or bacterial (streptococcus) infection, and/or non- infectious causes such as an irritation (air pollution, allergens, sinus drainage). The most common causes are viruses that cause upper respiratory infections.

SIGNS AND SYMPTOMS OF VIRAL PHARYNGITIS:
- Dry, scratchy throat
- Complaints of pain with swallowing
- Frequent swallowing and sniffing (from sinus drainage)
- Presence/absence of fever and signs of systemic illness
- Appearance of tonsils and tympanic membrane
- Irritability in the younger child
- Increased drooling
- Symptoms associated with the common cold such as runny nose , cough, and congestion

SIGNS AND SYPMTOMS OF STREP THROAT:
"Strep" throat is due to *Group A Streptococcus*.
- Sudden onset of sore throat
- Fever (often > 101 F)
- Headache, nausea, abdominal pain, occasionally vomiting
- Marked inflammation of throat and tonsils; bright red tonsils may have thin white exudate
- Enlarged cervical lymph nodes
- Absence of diarrhea or coryza, cough, and conjunctivitis
- Does not usually result in a cough or runny nose

Scarlet Fever is a vascular response usually associated with streptococcal pharyngitis.

UNIQUE FINDINGS OF SCARLET FEVER:
- Diffuse redness of cheeks and upper chest on "goose flesh" skin, the sensation of fine sandpaper.
- The rash spreads and, in 5-10 days, skin peels. Most cases are mild, lasting a few days, but severe cases occur.
- Two major complications: acute rheumatic fever (joints, heart) occurs in 1% of Group A strep cases, and acute self-limiting glomerulonephritis (kidney disease) can be serious.

SORE THROAT (PHARYNGITIS) (including Streptococcal Infection) *(continued from previous page)*

MANAGEMENT/TREATMENT OF MINOR, VIRAL, AFEBRILE SORE THROAT:
1. Warm, salty (1/2 teaspoon to 1 glass water) gargles
2. Warm fluids (broth; hot water with melted lemon drop or warm lemonade)
3. Over-the-counter lozenges (some do not advise lozenges or drops at school for safety reasons)
4. Analgesics such as Tylenol® or Advil®
5. May attend school if feeling well enough unless other exclusion criteria are present such as fever

MANAGEMENT/TREATMENT (Streptococcal Infection):
1. Refer for diagnosis by rapid strep test and culture. Some school clinics are equipped to provide the rapid strep test. If positive, it confirms Group A strep infection. If the test result is negative, a regular culture (read in 12-24 hours) is still required to rule out strep, so many prefer to refer all suspected cases directly.
2. Encourage adequate fluid to keep mucus thin.
3. Treatment of choice is penicillin; untreated cases (milder sore throat, low fever) treated symptomatically risk complications. Treatment is aimed at preventing complications such as Rheumatic fever.
4. Return to school after 24 hours on antibiotic treatment and fever-free. For many children, 3-5 days absence may occur.
5. Treatment of scarlet fever is no different from the treatment of streptococcal infection

FOLLOW-UP (Strep and Scarlet Fever):
- Monitor for a completed course of antibiotic therapy to prevent complications and carrier state.
- Encourage student to replace toothbrush.
- Monitor for complications (high fever, joint pain, blood in the urine) and refer immediately.

POTENTIAL COMPLICATIONS:
- Ear infection
- Glomerulonephritis
- Rheumatic fever
- Sinusitis
- Tonsillitis
- Peritonsillar abscess

NOTE:
Avoid giving aspirin under the age of eighteen. Aspirin can play a role in causing Reye's Syndrome.

SORE THROAT (PHARYNGITIS) (including Streptococcal Infection) *(continued from previous page)*

References

American Academy of Pediatrics. (2013). Strep throat (streptococcal pharyngitis). In S. Aronson, & T. Shope (Eds.), *Managing infectious diseases in child care and schools (2nd ed.)* (p.p. 157-158). Elk Grove Village, IL: American Academy of Pediatrics.

Mayo Clinic. (2013). *Sore throat.* http://www.mayoclinic.com/health/sore-throat/DS00526

Medline Plus, U.S. National Library of Medicine. (2013). *Sore throat.* Retrieved from http://www.nlm.nih.gov/medlineplus/sorethroat.html

John, R. & Chewey, L. (2013). Common complaints. In J. Selekman (Ed.), *School nursing: A comprehensive text* (2nd ed.) (pp. 578-640). Philadelphia, PA: F.A. Davis.

SPIDER BITE (Brown Recluse, Black Widow, and Hobo)

DEFINITION/ETIOLOGY:
Brown Recluse spider bites produce poisonous venom that contains both a toxin and an enzyme that spreads the toxin through tissue. Ten species, six of which are poisonous, live in the United States. The spiders are non-hairy, yellowish-tan to dark brown, and have a violin pattern on their back. They prefer dark, dry spaces (under porches, attic, closet, woodpiles). They are not aggressive but bite defensively.

Black Widow spiders produce potent, protein venom that attacks the central nervous system. The Southern species are about ½-inch long, shiny, black, globular shape with distinctive red hourglass shape on the underside. The Northern species have a row of red spots down the middle of the upper surface of the abdomen and 2 cross bars on the underside. The Black Widow spider is nocturnal, prefers dark corners and crevices, and bites defensively.

Hobo spider bites may go unnoticed until a moderate to severe, slow healing wound develops. Hobo spiders do not have banded legs and have distinct, yellow markings on their under-belly. The Hobo builds funnel shaped webs in which to trap their prey and therefore are found outdoors and indoors around structural areas, stacked materials and storage areas. The Hobo spider, unlike other spiders, does not climb, but they are fast runners. Threatened or provoked they are likely to attack. Hobo spiders are found throughout the Pacific Northwest.

SIGNS AND SYMPTOMS:
Brown Recluse
- Immediate local stinging or burning pain that may become severe after 4 hrs.
- Initially, the lesion is red and swollen or blanched, and may develop a blue-gray halo around the puncture (due to hemolysis and vasospasm). The lesion may change to bluish pustules or large blistering surrounded by purpura discoloration.
- Within 12 hours, fever, chills, nausea/vomiting, scarlatiniform rash, arthralgia, diarrhea and weakness may develop. Rarely, in children, renal failure, or hemoglobinuria and shock coagulation occur.
- Centrally, necrosis or a "sinking center" develops. The ulcer may take weeks to months to heal.

Black Widow
- Symptomatic within 20 minutes to 1 hour after bite.
- Localized to generalized severe muscle cramps, abdominal pain, weakness, and tremor may occur.
- Nausea and vomiting, dizziness, chest pain, and respiratory difficulty may follow.

SPIDER BITE (Brown Recluse and Black Widow) *(continued from previous page)*

<u>Hobo</u>
- The bite may go unnoticed; however, a moderate to severe, slow healing wound will appear. Symptoms can be mild to severe.
- Localized to general itching, rash, pain radiating from the site, muscle pain or cramping, and redness to purple tinge at the site may occur.
- Sweating, difficulty breathing, headache, nausea and vomiting, fever, chills, anxiety and restlessness, and elevated blood pressure may follow.

MANAGEMENT/TREATMENT:
<u>Brown Recluse</u>
1. Ask about description of spider and presence of general reaction symptoms.
2. Apply ice, elevate, and seek immediate medical attention.
3. Immobilize affected area and avoid vigorous activity.
4. OTC analgesics for pain management.
5. Primary healthcare provider may begin antibiotic therapy.

<u>Black Widow</u>
1. Ask about description of spider and presence of general reaction symptoms.
2. Apply ice, elevate, and seek *emergency* medical attention.
3. Immobilize affected area and avoid vigorous activity.

<u>Hobo</u>
1. Ask about description of spider and presence of general reaction symptoms.
2. Wash area with soap and water.
3. Apply cold compress or ice (covered) to site.
4. Elevate affected area.
5. <u>DO NOT</u> attempt to remove venom.
6. Seek immediate medical attention.

FOLLOW UP:
- Re-assess in 48 hours; may need referral for debridement.
- Continue to monitor. Wound may need skin grafting.
- Educate regarding poisonous spider recognition:
  - <u>Brown Recluse:</u> About one inch long, non-hairy, yellowish-tan to dark brown, and have a violin pattern on their back. They prefer dark, dry spaces (under porches, attic, closet, woodpiles. They are not aggressive but bite defensively.
  - <u>Black Widow</u>: The Southern species are about ½-inch long, shiny, black, globular shape with distinctive red hourglass shape on the underside. The Northern species have a row of red spots down the middle of the upper surface of the abdomen and 2 cross bars on the underside. The Black Widow spider is nocturnal, prefers dark corners and crevices, and bites defensively.

288

SPIDER BITE (Brown Recluse and Black Widow) *(continued from previous page)*

o <u>Hobo</u>: Hobo spiders do not have banded legs and have distinct, yellow markings on their under-belly. The Hobo builds funnel shaped webs in which to trap their prey and therefore are found outdoors and indoors around structural areas, stacked materials and storage areas. Hobo spiders do not climb, but they are fast runners. Threatened or provoked they are likely to attack. Hobo spiders are found throughout the Pacific Northwest.

References

Balentine, J. R. (2008). *Black widow spider bite*. E Medicine Health. Retrieved from http://www.emedicinehealth.com/black_widow_spider_bite/article_em.htm

Balentine, J. R. (2012). *Brown recluse spider bite*. **E medicine Health Retrieved from** http://www.emedicinehealth.com/spider_bite_brown_recluse_spider_bite/article_em.htm

Brehm, C. (2008). Common injuries. In C. Burns, M. Brady, A. Dunn, N.B. Starr, C. Blosser (Eds.), *Pediatric primary care* (4th ed.) (pp. 1101-1102). St. Louis, MO: Saunders Elsevier.

Centers for Disease Control. *(2013). NIOSH safety and health topic: Venomous spiders*. Retrieved from http://www.cdc.gov/niosh/topics/spiders/

Mayo Clinic. (2012). *Spider bites: First aid*. **Retrieved from** http://www.mayoclinic.com/health/first-aid-spider-bites/FA00048

Medline Plus, U.S. National Library of Medicine. (2009). *Brown recluse spider*. Retrieved from http://www.nlm.nih.gov/medlineplus/ency/article/002859.htm

Merck Manual, Professional Edition. *Spider bites*. (2013). Retrieved from http://www.merckmanuals.com/professional/injuries_poisoning/bites_and_stings/spider_bites.html?qt=spider%20bites&alt=sh

SPRAIN OF ANKLE OR KNEE

DEFINITION:

A sprain is a stretched or torn ligament (fibrous tissue that connects bones to other bones). The injury can range from a stretch to a tiny tear to a complete severing of the ligament. They are often a common athletic injury of children. A strain results from pulling or overexerting a muscle or tendon (tough band of fibrous connective tissue that connects muscle to bone).

SIGNS AND SYMPTOMS:

- History of trauma (for example, person steps down on the outside of the foot and twists the foot)
- During trauma, persons may feel a flash of heat or may describe hearing a "snap" or "pop"
- History of prior injury to same joint
- Pain/tenderness at site of injury
- Variable swelling, and/or bruising
- Limited ability to move affected part

MANAGEMENT/TREATMENT:

1. Take careful detailed history of injury, including what happened, what person felt, what person heard.
2. Assess pulse quality and capillary refill below the injured site.
3. Check range of motion and sensation (compare with corresponding area on opposite extremity).
4. Institute RICE principle:

Rest of the injured area for 48 hours	• Weight bearing may increase injury. If uncomfortable to walk, use crutches. • Review safe crutch walking technique. • Get permit to use elevator (if any). • If hall traffic is unmanageable on crutches, get permit to leave class a few minutes early. • Arrange for help to carry books.
Ice placed on the injured area for 20 minutes every 2 -3 hours while awake for first 24 hours	Ice cubes or frozen wet sponges can be placed in a plastic bag, wrapped in a light cloth, and applied to the painful area. Remove compression bandage while using ice.

SPRAIN OF ANKLE OR KNEE *(continued from previous page)*

Compression with elastic bandages or if authorized, splints	• A pressure bandage may reduce swelling. Use a compression bandage, especially when the ankle is not elevated while crutch walking. • A 3" elastic ACE wrap is generally used. A more convenient material is elastic tubular bandage, a surgical dressing available from a medical or athletic supply store.
Elevate injured part	Keep the foot higher than the hip when not mobile at least 24 hours following injury.

WHEN TO REFER TO PHYSICIAN:
- All injuries associated with severe pain or immediate swelling /or injured area is misshapen (may indicate fracture)
- If there are signs that circulation beyond the injured area is impaired
- Inability to bear weight
- All suspected fractures

FOLLOW UP:
- Monitor for blood flow above and below injured area; if a splint/wrap/cast has been applied, watch fingers and toes for cyanosis and coldness.
- For mild to moderate pain, a non-steroidal anti-inflammatory analgesic (ibuprofen) taken with food to limit stomach upset may be administered (if medically approved or with parent/guardian approval and per policy).
- ROM or physical therapy to retain full use of injured part.
- Advise student to not engage in physical activity until pain has subsided.

POTENTIAL COMPLICATIONS:
- Swelling may decrease blood flow to area below sprain.
- Unrecognized and inappropriately managed injury can lead to more long-term functional disability.

NOTES:
Once an ankle has been sprained, it may be susceptible to recurring sprains because of instability in the joint. The following suggestions to avoid re-injury:

- Avoid activities (exercising or sports) when tired or in pain.
- Correctly fitted shoes and equipment.
- Warm-up and stretch before participating in exercises or sports.

SPRAIN OF ANKLE OR KNEE *(continued from previous page)*

References

Brehm, C . (2008). Common injuries. In C. Burns, M. Brady, A. Dunn, N.B. Starr, C. Blosser (Eds.), *Pediatric primary care* (4th ed.) (pp. 1090-1093). St. Louis, MO: Saunders Elsevier.

Mayo Clinic. (2011). *Sprains and strains*. Retrieved from http://www.mayoclinic.com/health/sprains-and-strains/DS00343

Merck Manual, Professional Edition. (2012). *Sprains, strains, & tendon tears.* Retrieved from http://www.merckmanuals.com/professional/injuries_poisoning/fractures_dislocations_and_sprains/ sprains_strains_and_tendon_tears.html?qt=sprains&alt=sh

Subbarao, I., Lyznicki, J., & James, J. (Eds.). (2009). *AMA Handbook of First Aid and Emergency Care.* New York, NY: Random House.

WebMD. (2012).*Ankle injuries: Causes and treatment.* Retrieved from http://www.webmd.com/fitness-exercise/ankle-injuries-causes-and-treatments

STOMATITIS (ORAL LESION)

DEFINITION/ETIOLOGY:
Stomatitis is an inflammation of the oral mucous membrane. Lesions can occur anywhere in the mouth including the cheeks, gums, soft and hard palate, and on the tongue and/or lips. Oral lesions may be caused by trauma, viral, bacterial and fungal infections, poor dental hygiene and chewing (smokeless) tobacco. Mouth sores may occur after dental work, with braces or from accidental biting of the inside of the mouth. Certain autoimmune diseases such as Crohn's disease can affect the mucous membranes of the mouth. Mouth ulcers are also a common side effect of chemotherapy.

SIGNS AND SYMPTOMS:
Symptoms are dependent on the etiology of the oral lesion. General symptoms include:
- Oral ulcers
- Pain in the mouth

Aphthous Ulcer (canker sore)
- Small, oval, indurated papules with surrounding redness and a white, gray or yellow center
- Often preceded by a "burning" sensation that progresses into an ulcer with surrounding redness
- Usually a single lesion but may occur in a cluster of 4-5
- May experience enlarged lymph nodes

Herpes simplex virus (cold sore, fever blister)
- Vesicular lesion
- Lesions are generally located on or around the outer lips
- Sore crust over with scab

Autoimmune diseases
- Crohn's – inflammatory bowel disease that commonly affects the small intestines; may also exhibit ulcerative lesions in the mouth

Oral candidiasis (thrush) – fungal (yeast) infection that occurs when there is overgrowth of *Candida*. Thrush may occur after a course of antibiotics or in immunocompromised individuals. Typically not seen in healthy youth.
- White patches on tongue and oral mucous membrane
- Lesions may bleed when gently scraped

STOMATITIS (*continued from previous page*)

MANAGEMENT/TREATMENT:
- Do not exclude from school since the condition is not considered contagious
- Treatment is focused on relieving symptoms
- Rinse with salt water
- Avoid irritating foods/liquids (spicy, salty or acidic).
- Advise careful tooth brushing to avoid the lesion(s)

FOLLOW UP:
Oral lesions may be an indication of a compromised immune system.
- Refer to healthcare provider if oral lesions are not healed in 2-3 weeks or if lesions are severe
- Physician may consider performing a biopsy on a lesion that does not heal properly

POTENTIAL COMPLICATIONS:
- Dehydration – encourage non-acidic fluids
- Oral cellulitis – secondary from bacterial infection
- Oral cancer

NOTES:
- If prone to mouth sores, avoid acidic and/or spicy foods
- Practice good oral hygiene. Brush teeth (with soft bristle toothbrush) after meals/bedtime and floss daily; change toothbrush at least 2 times per year
- Ulcers in the mouth occur with some childhood infections including:
  - Hand, foot and mouth disease
  - Herpangina (typically caused by Coxsackie group A virus)
- Sexually Transmitted Diseases
  - Syphilis chancres may be present with primary syphilis
  - Syphilis and Gonorrhea can also be transmitted during oral sex
  - **Syphilis**
    - Lesion is located at point of syphilis entry
    - Syphilis ulcer is firm, round and painless
    - Syphilis lesion may last 3-6 weeks
  - **Oral gonorrhea** (rare) may have redness and/or ulcerative lesions on gingiva and tongue.
    - Inquire about history of engaging in oral sex
    - Refer to physician for appropriate treatment
    - Depending on school district policy – consider educating adolescent on appropriate barrier protection

STOMATITIS (*continued from previous page*)

References

Centers for Disease Control and Prevention (CDC). (2013). *Syphilis – CDC fact sheet.* Retrieved from http://www.cdc.gov/std/syphilis/STDFact-Syphilis.htm

John, R. & Chewey, L. (2013). Common complaints. In J. Selekman (Ed.), *School nursing: A comprehensive text* (2nd ed.) (pp. 578-640). Philadelphia, PA: F. A. Davis.

Mayo Clinic. (2012). *Canker sore.* Retrieved from http://www.mayoclinic.com/health/canker-sore/DS00354

Mayo Clinic. (2011). *Crohn's disease.* Retrieved from http://www.mayoclinic.com/health/crohns-disease/DS00104

Medline Plus, U.S. National Library of Medicine. (2011). *Canker sore.* Retrieved from http://www.nlm.nih.gov/medlineplus/ency/article/000998.htm

Medline Plus, U.S. National Library of Medicine. (2013). *Mouth ulcers.* Retrieved from http://www.nlm.nih.gov/medlineplus/ency/article/001448.htm

Merck Manual. (2012). *Stomatitis.* Retrieved from http://www.merckmanuals.com/professional/dental_disorders/symptoms_of_dental_and_oral_disorders/stomatitis.html?qt=oral%20lesions&alt=sh

WebMD. (2012). *Stomatitis.* Retrieved from http://www.webmd.com/oral-health/guide/stomatitis-causes-treatment

STRESS DISORDER/POST-TRAUMATIC

DEFINITION/ETIOLOGY:
Stress is the body's reaction to a change that requires a physical, mental, or emotional adjustment or response to a stressor. Stress includes cognitive, emotional, behavioral, and somatic symptoms due to intense fear or feelings of helplessness. Most reactions are normal responses to a serious event.

Post-traumatic disorder (PTSD):
If symptoms and behavioral problems associated with acute stress disorder continue for more than a month, and if these characteristics are associated with functional impairment or significant distress to the sufferer, the diagnosis is changed to post-traumatic stress disorder (PTSD). Symptoms of PTSD typically begin within 3 months of the traumatic incident but may not occur until years after the event.

An individual child's response to a tragedy or disaster is related to age/development, parent/guardians' responses, separation from parent/guardian(s) or peers, and disruption of routines. The severity of anxiety is usually related to proximity to the event, significant losses, and changes in lifestyle and relationships.

CAUSES:
Personal life events (parental death, fires, assault) or sudden natural disasters (tornado, hurricane, earthquake, flood).

SIGNS AND SYMPTOMS:
Symptoms vary from person to person. General signs and symptoms associated with PTSD include:
- Intrusive memories – flashbacks (reliving the traumatic event); upsetting dreams about the disturbing event
- Avoidance and numbing – tries to avoid talking/thinking about the event, feels helpless/hopeless, avoids activities that they once enjoyed, avoids to the point of developing a phobia of person/place that reminds them of the traumatic incident
- Increased anxiety – easily startled or frightened, difficulty sleeping, irritability, anger, has trouble concentrating/focusing, guilt/shame surrounding the event

Common somatic symptoms often reported by those experiencing extreme stress include:
- Sleep disturbances
- Muscle tension
- Headache
- Gastrointestinal disturbances
- Fatigue

STRESS DISORDER/POST-TRAUMATIC *(continued from previous page)*

Preschoolers and young elementary children use "magical thinking" to explain the event. Responses may include:
- Crying/sadness
- Confusion, regression to toddler behaviors (thumb sucking, clinging, enuresis)
- Sleep disorder
- Hyperactivity or withdrawal from everyday activities

Adolescents – responses to stress may include:
- Irritable/moody
- Difficulty sleeping
- Changes in eating patterns
- Anxiety/depression
- Acting out/behavior problems
- Poor school performance/trouble concentrating

MANAGEMENT/TREATMENT:
General management/treatment for stress
1. Get regular exercise
2. Encourage student to share thoughts and worries
3. Encourage student to eat a healthy, balanced diet; drink less caffeine
4. Utilize relaxation techniques
5. Encourage adequate sleep
6. Help student set realistic goals
7. Encourage student to talk to parent/guardian/school nurse/teacher/friend when they are feeling stressed
8. Refer to physician (for possible medication/counseling) if above suggestions do not alleviate student's stress

PTSD treatment includes:
1. **Medication** – antidepressants can help symptoms of depression and anxiety, help improve sleep problems, and improve concentration. Anti-anxiety medications also can improve feelings of anxiety and stress.
2. **Psychotherapy**
   - Cognitive therapy – helps person identify and change self-destructive thoughts
   - Exposure therapy – behavioral therapy technique that safely confronts the stressor that the person finds upsetting or disturbing so that they can learn to cope effectively

STRESS DISORDER/POST-TRAUMATIC *(continued from previous page)*

3. Management during a crisis
- The child must perceive the environment as safe
- Create/implement (mock drills) a crisis plan at school to deal with student tragedies or natural disasters
- Restore contact with parent as soon as possible; for adolescents contact with close friends is equally important during a crisis
- Provide simple, honest explanations to correct distorted perceptions of what occurred
- Re-establish routines as soon as possible
- Help the child gain control of fear by choosing how to express the event in role play, pictures and games
- Facilitate group activities to help children tell their stories (disasters, school tragedy)
- Class projects related to the event/disaster may help children take control of information (cognitive coping) and recognize that their feelings are normal and shared

FOLLOW UP:
Professional intervention is indicated when reactions interfere with usual daily activities.
- Continuing sleep disturbance
- Prolonged separation anxiety or clinging
- Fears about stimuli that remind the child of the event
- Acting out behaviors
- Withdrawal and expressions of declining self-worth

POTENTIAL COMPLICATIONS:
- Increased vulnerability to infections
- Increased risk of accidents
- Self destructive behaviors
- Substance/alcohol abuse

NOTES:
- In disasters, include children in efforts to help others more affected; helping others assists the child in regaining a sense of normalcy.

STRESS DISORDER/POST-TRAUMATIC *(continued from previous page)*

References

Cory, A., & Jovanovic, J. (2013). The student's family. In J. Selekman (Ed.), *School nursing: A comprehensive text* (2nd ed.) (pp. 383-406). Philadelphia, PA: F.A. Davis Company.

Mayo Clinic. (2011). *Post traumatic stress disorder.* Retrieved from http://www.mayoclinic.com/health/post-traumatic-stress-disorder/DS00246/DSECTION=symptoms

Merck Manual. (2012). *Anxiety disorders in children and adolescents.* Retrieved from http://www.merckmanuals.com/professional/pediatrics/mental_disorders_in_children_and_adolescents/anxiety_disorders_in_children_and_adolescents.html?qt=post%20traumatic%20stress%20disorder&alt=sh

National Institute of Mental Health. (2011). *Post-traumatic stress disorder (PTSD).* Retrieved from http://www.nimh.nih.gov/health/topics/post-traumatic-stress-disorder-ptsd/index.shtml

PubMed Health. (2013). *Post-traumatic stress disorder.* Retrieved from http://www.ncbi.nlm.nih.gov/pubmedhealth/PMH0001923

STY or STYE (Hordeolum and Chalazion)

DEFINITION/ETIOLGY:

A **hordeolum** is a sudden onset, localized, staphylococcal infection of the eyelash follicle at the margin of the eyelid or associated sebaceous or sweat gland. A **chalazion** is an inflammatory/ noninfectious nodule due to an occluded meibomian gland duct. The nodule is painful and localizes to an eyelid margin With time, a chalazion becomes a small non-tender nodule in the eyelid center. Both conditions initially cause eyelid hyperemia and edema, swelling, and pain. Both improve spontaneously.

Hordeolum

SIGNS AND SYMPTOMS:
- Tiny abscess (0.5-1.0 mm) on edge of eyelid
- Slight redness around abscess (may look like a pimple or boil)
- Local tenderness / pain over the affected area
- Eyelid swelling (this may make it difficult to see because eyelid can't open fully)
- Usually filled with pus
- Tearing
- Crusting around eyelids

MANAGEMENT/TREATMENT:
- Warm, moist compresses
- Improves spontaneously
- Instill ophthalmic antibiotic drops or ointment if prescribed by primary healthcare provider.
- DO NOT use bacitracin or other topical ointment
- DO NOT try to open (squeeze) the abscess
- Refer to primary healthcare provider if no improvement in 2-3 days or if redness or swelling extends beyond eyelid into face
- School exclusion not necessary

FOLLOW UP:
- Watch for unusual spread; should heal in 3-5 days.
- If infection continues or a hordeolum (cyst) develops, refer to an ophthalmologist.

POTENTIAL COMPLICATIONS:
- Cross-contamination - avoid rubbing eyes. This can cause development of another sty.
- Seek medical advice if vision is impaired.

STY (STYE) *(continued from previous page)*

NOTES:
Education:
- Encourage frequent hand washing .
- Person should keep hands away from face.
- Avoid wearing eye make-up.
- Discard all used and outdated eye make-up.
- Wash hands thoroughly before handling, cleaning or inserting/removing contact lens.

Chalazion

SIGNS AND SYMPTOMS:
- Hard, non-tender nodule
- If infected, there is painfully swollen eyelid

MANAGEMENT/TREATMENT:
- Small chalazion disappears without intervention
- Warm, moist compresses (15-minute duration).
- Physician/healthcare provider may order antibiotic ointment if there is secondary infection

FOLLOW UP: Recheck large chalazion in 2-3 weeks for resolution.

References

American Academy of Pediatrics. (2009). Summaries of infectious disease – staphylococcal infections. In L.K. Pickering, C.J. Baker, D.W. Kimberlin, & S.S. Long (Eds.), *Red Book: 2009 Report of the Committee on Infectious Diseases*. 28th ed. (pp. 601). American Academy of Pediatrics: Elk Grove Village, IL.

American Academy of Pediatrics. (2013). Sty. In S. Aronson, & T. Shope (Eds.), *Managing infectious diseases in child care and schools (2nd ed.)* (p. 159). Elk Grove Village, IL: American Academy of Pediatrics.

Children's Hospital of Boston. (n.d.). *Stye (hordeolum).* Retrieved from http://childrenshospital.org/az/Site1050/mainpageS1050P0.html

The Merck Manual, Professional Edition. (2012). *Chalazion & hordeolum (stye).* Retrieved from http://www.merckmanuals.com/home/eye_disorders/eyelid_and_tearing_disorders/chalazion_and_stye_hordeolum.htmlAgile

Mayo Clinic. (2012). *Sty.* Retrieved from http://www.mayoclinic.com/health/sty/DS00257

SUBSTANCE ABUSE

School nurses are often asked to determine whether a student is under the influence of an illicit substance or chemical. School health services programs may need to have a policy in place for identifying students who may be under the influence of an illicit substance or chemical. The school's legal counsel or attorney should review the policy prior to approval of the policy by the school board. Additionally, school nurses may need specialized training and orientation for completing a student assessment for substance and chemical abuse.

DEFINITION/ETIOLOGY:
The use of illegal substances or the misuse of prescription or over-the-counter drugs constitutes drug abuse. Additionally, the repeated use of drugs to produce pleasure, to alleviate stress, or to alter or avoid reality (or all three) constitutes drug abuse.

CAUSES:
Most drug abuse results from a combination of experimentation, peer pressure, and external and internal stressors. If a young person's environment causes anxiety and an illicit drug eases the pain, the gateway for abuse has been opened. Risk factors and protective factors are important in substance abuse among youth and adolescents. According to the National Institute of Drug Abuse (NIDA) (2013), risk factors can increase a person's chances for drug abuse while protective factors can reduce the risk. It is important to note that most people at risk for drug abuse do not start using drugs or become addicted to drugs. In addition, a risk factor for one person may not be the same for another person. Risk factors and protective factors can occur at different stages of children's lives. However, risks that occur at early stages can be change by prevention interventions.

Alcohol is still the number one drug of abuse among young people in the United States compared to tobacco or illicit drugs (Monitoring the Future, 2012). Driving while intoxicated results in the largest number of deaths in the adolescent age group.

SIGNS AND SYMPTOMS:
Specific symptoms:
- Stimulants: dilated pupils, rapid pulse, talkativeness and sometimes elevated blood pressure; very high doses may cause psychotic symptoms.
- Depressants: pupils normal to small, drowsiness and slurred speech (in the absence of an alcohol odor).

SUBSTANCE ABUSE *(continued from previous page)*

General signs and symptoms/behaviors of possible substance abuse include the following[1]:

- Sudden personality changes that include abrupt changes in work or school attendance, quality of work, work output, grades, discipline
- Unusual flare-ups or outbreaks of temper
- Withdrawal from responsibility
- General changes in overall attitude
- Loss of interest in what were once favorite hobbies and pursuits
- Changes in friends and reluctance to have friends visit or talk about them
- Difficulty in concentration, paying attention
- Sudden jitteriness, nervousness, or aggression
- Increased secretiveness
- Deterioration of physical appearance and grooming
- Wearing of sunglasses at inappropriate times
- Continual wearing of long-sleeved garments particularly in hot weather or reluctance to wear short-sleeved attire when appropriate
- Association with known substance abusers
- Unusual borrowing of money from friends, co-workers or parents
- Stealing small items from employer, home or school
- Secretive behavior regarding actions and possessions; poorly concealed attempts to avoid attention and suspicion such as frequent trips to storage rooms, restroom, basement, etc.
- Change, sometimes radical, in behavior
- Slurred speech
- Memory impairment
- Impaired coordination

MANAGEMENT AND TREATMENT:

1. Behavior and physical findings will dictate urgency of medical referral.
2. Notify parents (and police if an illicit substance is suspected).
3. Call 911 if condition deteriorates.

FOLLOW UP:

Once the drug of abuse is identified, a treatment plan can be developed. Polydrug use (alcohol plus marijuana, etc.) is hardest to treat. Many school systems have drug prevention/substance abuse programs in place and collaborate with local health departments/mental health agencies to assist, youth, adolescents, and families.

---

1 *Teenage Substance Abuse*, National Youth Network, http://www.nationalyouth.com/substanceabuse.html

SUBSTANCE ABUSE *(continued from previous page)*

POTENTIAL COMPLICATIONS:

The following table defines the five stages of substance abuse and serves as a guide for referral in non-acute cases[2].

Stage	Description
1	*Potential for abuse* Decreased impulse control Need for immediate gratification Availability of drugs, alcohol, inhalants Need for peer acceptance
2	*Experimentation: learning the euphoria* Use of inhalants, marijuana, and alcohol with friends Few, if any, consequences May increase to regular weekend use Little change in behavior
3	*Regular use: seeking the euphoria* Use of other drugs, e.g., stimulants, LSD, sedatives Behavioral changes and some consequences Increased frequency of use; use alone Buying or stealing drugs or money for drugs
4	*Regular use: preoccupation with the "high"* Daily use of drugs Loss of control Multiple consequences and risk-taking Estrangement from family and "straight" friends
5	*Burnout: use of drugs to feel normal* Use of multiple substances Guilt, withdrawal, remorse, depression Physical and mental deterioration Increased risk-taking, self-destructive behavior

NOTES:

Prevention - According to the National Institute of Drug Abuse (NIDA), drug abuse is preventable. Research conducted by NIDA indicates prevention programs that involve family, schools, communities, and the media are effective in reducing drug abuse. Youth who experience a positive connection to school, family, and community are less likely to engage in risky behaviors, including alcohol and drug abuse.

---

2 American Academy of Pediatrics, Committee on Substance Abuse. Indications for Management and Referral of Patients Involved in Substance Abuse. *Pediatrics.* 2000;106 (1):143-148.

SUBSTANCE ABUSE (continued from previous page)

References

Centers for Disease Prevention. (2012). Youth risk behavior surveillance-United States 2011. *Morbidity & Mortality Weekly Report,* 64 (4). Retrieved from http://www.cdc.gov/mmwr/pdf/ss/ss6104.pdf

Gottesman, M.M. & Houck, G. (2008). Coping and stress tolerance: Mental health problems. In C. Burns, M. Brady, A. Dunn, N.B. Starr, C. Blosser (Eds.), *Pediatric primary care*, 4th ed. (pp. 435-437). St. Louis, MO: Saunders Elsevier.

National Institute of Drug Abuse (NIDA). (2013). *NIDA for teens*. Retrieved from http://teens.drugabuse.gov

National Institute of Drug Abuse (NIDA). *Preventing drug abuse among children and adolescents – Risk factors and protective factors (2nd ed.)*. Retrieved from http://www.nida.nih.gov/Prevention/risk.html

Substance Abuse and Mental Health Service Administration (SAMSHA). (2013).*Talk – They hear you. Underage drinking prevention national media campaign.* Retrieved from http://www.samhsa.gov/underagedrinking/

U.S. Department of Health and Human Services. (2007). *The surgeon general's call to action to prevent and reduce underage drinking*. U.S. DHHS, Office of the Surgeon General. Retrieved from http://www.surgeongeneral.gov/library/calls/underagedrinking/index.html

U.S. Department of Health and Human Services, National Institutes of Health, National Institute of Drug Abuse. (2013). *Monitoring the future – overview of key findings 2012*. Retrieved from http://www.monitoringthefuture.org//pubs/monographs/mtf-overview2012.pdf

SUBSTANCE ABUSE *(continued from previous page)*

Appendix A – Drugs of Potential Abuse Among Youth and Adolescents
(Adopted from the 2012 Monitoring the Future Survey)

Monitoring the Future (MTF) is a long-term study of American adolescents, college students, and adults through age 50. The study is conducted annually by the University of Michigan's Institute for Social Research since its inception in 1975 and is supported by grants from the National Institute of Drug Abuse (NIDA). Substance abuse among American youth is rapidly changing and requires frequent assessments and reassessments. Alcohol, cigarettes (any use), and illicit drugs are the leading causes of morbidity and mortality during adolescence and adulthood. The following list summarizes drugs of potential abuse among youth and adolescents in the United States as of 2009 to 2012.

<u>Name of Drug</u>

Alcohol
Cigarettes (any use)
Smokeless Tobacco
Illicit Drugs
Cocaine
Crack Cocaine
Gamma-hydroxybutyrate (GHB)
Hallucinogens
Lysergic Acid (LSD)
MDMA (Ecstasy)
Heroin
Inhalants
Ketamine
Marijuana/Hashish
Methamphetamine
PCP
Any Prescription Drug
Rohypnol
Salvia
Steroids

(Adopted from Monitoring the Future Study: Trends in Prevalence of Various Drugs website link http://www.drugabuse.gov/related-topics/trends-statistics/monitoring-future/trends-in-prevalence-various-drugs)

SUICIDE IDEATION/THREATS

DEFINITION/ETIOLOGY:
Suicidal ideation is the reoccurring thoughts of committing suicide. In 2010, in the United States, suicide was rated the second leading cause of death in 12-17 year olds (CDC, 2013a). Culture and family factors influence the possibility that youth consider suicide as an option for handling distress, depression or hopeless feelings. There are many contributing factors linked to suicidal ideation. Aggravating factors may include:

- History of mental disorder, including depression
- Chronic medical condition such as seizure disorder or diabetes
- Fewer social and personal supports than peers
- Youth who attempt suicide report more negative life events (disappointments and losses)
- May have experienced a significant loss: relationship breakup, death of someone close, physical disability, or loss of status/perceived humiliation (losing a competitive event or admission to a group/school)
- Family history of psychiatric disorder or suicide

SIGNS AND SYMPTOMS:
WARNING SIGNS OF SUICIDE
- Changed eating and sleeping habits
- Withdrawal from friends, family and everyday routine
- Personality changes
- Acting out, rebellion, running away
- Violent behavior / explosive rage
- Substance/alcohol use
- Difficulty focusing/concentrating
- Hinting that "nothing matters" and "I won't be a problem much longer"
- Preoccupation with death/dying
- Throwing or giving personal items away
- Sense of hopelessness or dramatically upbeat following a period of depression
- Talking about suicide ("I wish I was never born" and "I wish I was dead")
- Existence of specific suicide plan

MANAGEMENT/TREATMENT:
1. **Emergency situations**
   - Refer immediately for crisis intervention
   - Suicidal attempts necessitate an immediate psychological evaluation
   - Address the need for a safe environment (this may mean psychiatric hospitalization)
   - Medical treatment for underlying mental health conditions (depression, bipolar disease, schizophrenia)

SUICIDE *(continued from previous page)*

2. Nonemergency situations
- Psychotherapy (counseling)
- Medications – antidepressants, antipsychotic medications, anti-anxiety medications
- Treatment for underlying mental health conditions

3. General guidelines
- Recognize and approach the student directly; *talking about suicide does not increase the risk.*
- Encourage verbalizing feelings (rather than internalizing); provide support.
- Suspend judgments, arguments and moral views of suicide; listen for immediate risk
- Inquire about a plan and means (drug, weapon, and/or car).
- If present, **act immediately;** provide constant supervision, set a contract, and call for local crisis assistance, notify parent/guardian(s).
- Be aware of others likely to identify with a student who is known to have attempted suicide and who may imitate the action; a trained school person should check their well-being.

FOLLOW UP:
- Participate in interdisciplinary team so that the student has a plan for support and successful return to school.
- Review crisis plan to address the needs of any student who indicates intent to commit suicide.
- Provide general health education for all students about mental health, including depression and related risk and protective factors for suicide.

POTENTIAL COMPLICATIONS:
- Consumed by suicidal thoughts – may not be able to function in daily activities
- Unsuccessful suicide attempt may leave person with permanent and/or debilitating injuries such as organ failure or brain damage
- Death

NOTES:
- About a third of those who attempt suicide have additional problems such as mood disorders, delinquent behavior, concern about sexual orientation, or substance abuse.
- Many people who commit suicide have had at least one previous attempt, and half had prior contact with a mental health professional.
- Educate staff/parents on the warning signs of suicide.

SUICIDE *(continued from previous page)*

References

Center for Disease Control. (2013a). *Mental health surveillance among children – United States, 2005—2011.*
http://www.cdc.gov/mmwr/preview/mmwrhtml/su6202a1.htm?s_cid=su6202a1_w

Center for Disease Control. (2013b). *Suicide prevention.* Retrieved from
http://www.cdc.gov/ViolencePrevention/suicide/index.html

Mayo Clinic. (2012). *Suicide and suicidal thoughts.* Retrieved from http://www.mayoclinic.com/health/suicide/MH00058

Merck Manual. (2013). *Suicidal behavior.* Retrieved from http://www.merckmanuals.com/professional/psychiatric_disorders/suicidal_behavior/suicidal_behavior.html?qt=suicide&alt=sh

Selekman, J., Diefenbeck, C. & Guthrie, S. (2013). *Mental health concerns.* In J. Selekman (Ed.), *School nursing: A comprehensive text* (2nd ed.) (pp. 927-969). Philadelphia, PA: F. A. Davis Company.

TATTOO/BODY PIERCING

DEFINITION/ETIOLOGY:
Tattoos and body piercing are forms of body art that have been practiced for years by various cultures. The English word tattoo derived from the Polynesian word *tatau* that means, "to mark". Tattooing became a trendy fashion statement in the U.S. in the 1990s. Tattoos and body piercing can express individuality, rebellion or group membership. It may signify spiritual meaning or a life milestone, such as a new love. While most states prohibit tattooing of minors, school nurses see students with tattoos or piercings, often done outside of commercial establishments and by peers.

As a result of 2009 U.S. Senate Bill 5391, the definitions of "tattoo" and "body art" have changed. Tattoo is "to pierce or puncture the human skin with a needle or other instrument for the purpose of implanting an indelible mark, or pigment, into the skin". Body art is "the practice of invasive cosmetic adornment."

SIGNS/SYMPTOMS:
- Inflammation of the pierced or tattooed area
- Allergic reaction includes swelling, redness, and itching
- Scars
- Severe allergic reaction can lead to anaphylactic shock

MANAGEMENT/TREATMENT:
1. Treatment for local infection may include warm compresses, and antibacterial ointment for local infection, to a course of oral antibiotics.
2. Tattoos are considered permanent; removal can be both painful and expensive. The methods of tattoo removal include the following:
   - Surgical removal – cutting the tattoo away
   - Dermabrasion – sanding the skin (epidermis and dermis)
   - Salabrasion – using a salt solution to soak the tattooed skin
   - Scarification – removing the tattoo with an acid solution and creating a scar in its place
   - Laser therapy as regulated by the Food and Drug Administration (FDA) may also be used as a method of tattoo removal

FOLLOW UP:
- Youth are a population at risk and influenced by media, peers, and "heroes". Most tattoos are done on a whim, so youth may not consider the long-term health risks of receiving a tattoo or the permanent marking of the skin. School personnel such as health educators and school nurses can educate students in making informed decisions about tattoos.

TATTOO/BODY PIERCING *(continued from previous page)*

- Infection control may depend on certification of artists and shop inspections. If a student intends to get a tattoo or piercing, the Alliance of Professional Tattooists suggests safety measures: ask about or look for autoclaving instruments, one-time needle and pigment use, and how the work space is cleaned. (Christensen, 2000)

COMPLICATIONS:

Tattoos and body piercings may be popular but pose definite health risks. When proper sterilization and safety procedures are not exquisitely followed, tattooing can transmit blood-borne pathogens including Hepatitis B and C, and HIV. Body piercing can also present the risk of scarring, infection, (e.g., Hepatitis B and C, Tetanus), and skin allergies.

Black henna tattoos can cause allergic reactions to those sensitive to the ingredients of henna.

REFERENCES:

Brown K.M., Perlmutter, P., & McDermott, R.J. (2000). Youth and tattoos: What school health personnel should know. *Journal of School Health*, *70*(9), 355-360. doi:10.1111/j.1746-1561.2000.tb07273.x

Centers for Disease Control and Prevention. (2013). *Body art – Follow regulations*. Retrieved from http://www.cdc.gov/niosh/topics/body_art/stateRegs.html

Mayo Clinic. (2013). *Tattoos: Understanding risks and precautions*. Retrieved from http://www.mayoclinic.com/health/tattoos-and-piercings/MC00020

Senate Bill 5391. (2009). *Regulating tattooing and body piercing*. Retrieved from http://www.washingtonvotes.org/2009-SB-5391

Vernon, P., Brady, M. & Starr, N.B. (2008). Dermatologic diseases. In C. Burns, M. Brady, A. Dunn, N.B. Starr, C. Blosser (Eds.), *Pediatric primary care* (4th ed.) (pp. 996-998). St. Louis, MO: Saunders Elsevier.

TEEN PREGNANCY/PREGNANCY PREVENTION

DEFINITION/ETIOLOGY:

The Center for Disease Control and Prevention (CDC) reports that in 2011, 329,797 babies were born to teenagers 15-19. This is a record low for the U.S. Although the vast majority of teen pregnancies are unplanned, the number of adolescents engaging in sexual activity has declined, and more adolescents are using birth control, the U.S. rates of teen pregnancy remains than in most developing countries. Teen pregnancy and childbearing brings great social and economic costs to teen parents and their children with only 40% of teen mothers finishing high school. Teen birth rates are especially high among black and Hispanic teens compared to white teens (CDC, 2011).

The National Association of School Nurses (NASN) believes that the school nurse is in a prime position to support the health and wellbeing of pregnant and parenting students and contribute to their lifelong success by linking them to resources and advocating for policies and practices that promote high school graduation. It is the position of NASN that school nurses have a vital role in the development and implementation of evidenced-based policies, nursing care procedures, educational programs and materials for students and their parents relating to pregnancy prevention, teen parenting and school completion. School nurses track pregnancy trends, review the school's human growth and development curriculum, assist in the selection of high-quality educational materials and programs based on the age, culture, and level of risk of the target population, and evaluate the short-term and long-term outcomes of the school's programs (NASN, 2011).

Pregnant and parenting students in public schools are protected against discrimination by law and are eligible for a free and appropriate education in the least restrictive environment.

It is important that the school nurse follow state and federal laws regarding adolescent reproductive health issues, confidentiality rights, and consent. Additionally the school nurse must be knowledgeable about child protection laws concerning minors' suspected sexual abuse and pregnancy (some states have mandates that require reporting to Child Protective Services should a girl of a specific age or younger be suspected of being pregnant).

SIGNS AND SYMPTOMS:

Pregnancy

If the youth has had sexual intercourse and experience the following symptoms:
- Missed period
- Short, scant period
- Sore, tender or swollen breasts
- Nausea and/or vomiting
- Fatigue
- Frequent urge to urinate
- Mood swings

TEEN PREGNANCY/PREGNANCY PREVENTION *(continued from previous page)*

RISK FACTORS ASSOCIATED FOR TEEN PREGNANCY:

- Poverty
- Not living with biological parent
- Growing up in a single family home
- Poor self-esteem
- School failure
- No future plans
- Minority race/ethnicity
- Childhood victimization
- Depression/ Stress

MANAGEMENT/TREATMENT:

1. Be non-judgmental when asking questions about sexual activity or exploitation in order to be effective in encouraging the student to share concerns and behaviors.
2. Develop supportive relationships with students and student parents.
3. Provide the student with local and community resources as necessary.
4. Support student's achievement; attendance and involvement can help in pregnancy prevention.
5. Maintain student confidentiality as appropriate.
6. Encourage students to involve parents/guardians or another responsible adult in pregnancy.
7. Encourage youth to seek pregnancy testing and counseling services.
8. If confirmed pregnancy, inform students of legal options (following laws and policies in your state) and encourage youth to seek prenatal care/counseling.
9. Encourage testing for STIs.
10. Work with the multidisciplinary school team to provide necessary accommodations to support the student, the pregnancy in the school setting, and plan for re-entry into school after pregnancy.
11. Be alert to signs of emotional and psychological reactions to the pregnancy.
12. Provide educational programs to pregnant teens including fathers, to promote positive parenting.

PREVENTION

The school nurse plays a role in teen pregnancy prevention along with school health educators and school counselors.

Effective reproductive health education has been shown to delay sexual activity and increase the use of condoms and other contraception for sexually active adolescents (NASN, 2012). *School nurses are challenged to examine their communication skills and views of youth behavior to determine how they can best contribute to teen pregnancy prevention efforts.*

TEEN PREGNANCY/PREGNANCY PREVENTION *(continued from previous page)*

POTENTIAL COMPLICATIONS:

1. Pregnant teens and their babies are at higher risk of health problems. Possible complications for low-income pregnant teens, especially those younger than age 15, include:
    - Premature labor
    - Anemia
    - High blood pressure

    Possible complications for a baby born to a teen mother include:
    - Premature birth
    - Low birth weight

2. Childbearing during early adolescence has been associated with decreased likelihood of completing school, advancing education, and being employed and increased dependence on public assistance. In addition many adolescent mothers have a second pregnancy. Recent studies suggest that background factors such as economic status, lifetime adversities and family support or conflict/violence are more influential on maternal and child outcomes than maternal age alone (SmithBattle, 2009).

NOTES:

Some teens may be prescribed contraceptives by a healthcare professional.

CONTRACEPTIVE METHODS:

- *Sexual abstinence* (practice of refraining from some or all aspects of sexual activity)
- *Condoms* (male and female) - latex, polyurethane, and silicone rubber (some with spermicidal agents).
- *Oral Contraceptives* – (hormonal methods).
- *Depo-Provera* - (medroxyprogesterone) - a progestin-only injectable given every three months; like the pill, it suppresses ovulation.
- *Norplant* - a subdermal implant of six sustained-release silastic capsules containing levonorgestrel; provides protection for five years. Failure rates similar to Depo-Provera, <1%.
- *Spermicides* - (nonoxynol-9); also provides some protection against HIV; spermicides increase the contraceptive efficacy of condoms significantly.
- *Emergency contraception (E.C.)* -also known as oral postcoital contraception, uses high doses of levonogestrel (Plan B®) (within 72 hours of unprotected intercourse). Because implantation defines an established pregnancy and because EC is used before implantation occurs, it should be considered contraception and not an abortifacient.
- *Contraceptive vaginal ring* (Nuvaring*). A soft plastic vaginal ring worn for 3 weeks and taken out for 1 week to allow menses.
- *Transdermal contraceptive patch* (ortho evra). A patch worn for 3 weeks and removed for one week to allow for menses.

TEEN PREGNANCY/PREGNANCY PREVENTION *(continued from previous page)*

- *Other methods* -IUD, diaphragm and cervical cups, sponge. IUD candidates should be multiparous because the uterine cavity is larger and accommodates the IUD better.

References

America's Promise Alliance /National Campaign to Prevent Teen and Unplanned Pregnancy (NCPTP). (2010). *Policy brief: Preventing teen pregnancy is critical to school completion.* Retrieved from http://www.thenationalcampaign.org/resources/pdf/Briefly_PolicyBrief_School_Completion.pdf

Centers for Disease Control and Prevention. (2013). *Teen pregnancy.* Retrieved from http://www.cdc.gov/teenpregnancy/

Fisher, M., Alderman, E., Kreipe, R., & Rosenfeld, W. (Eds.). (2011). *Textbook of adolescent health care* (pp. 453-473). Elk Grove Village, IL: American Academy of Pediatrics.

Kaiser Family Foundation. *(2013). Sexual health of adolescents and young adults in the United States.* Retrieved from http://www.kff.org/womenshealth/3040.cfm

Mayo Health Clinic. (2011). Tween and teen health: Teenage pregnancy: Consider the options. Retrieved from http://www.mayoclinic.com/health/teen-pregnancy/MY00820

National Association of School Nurses [NASN] (2011). *Pregnant and parenting students, the role of the school nurse: Position Paper.* Retrieved from *http://www.nasn.org/PolicyAdvocacy/PositionPapersandReports/NASNPositionStatementsFullView/tabid/462/smid/824/ArticleID/120/Default.aspx*

National Association of School Nurses [NASN] (2011). *School health education about human sexuality: Position Paper.* Retrieved from *http://www.nasn.org/PolicyAdvocacy/PositionPapersandReports/NASNPositionStatementsFullView/tabid/462/ArticleId/43/School-Health-Education-about-Human-Sexuality-Revised-2012*

SmithBattle L. (2009). Reframing the risks and losses of teen mothers. *Maternal Child Nursing,* 34(2), 123-128. doi: 10.1097/01.NMC.0000347307.93079.7d

TICK-BORNE DISEASES (Rocky Mountain Spotted Fever [RMSF] and Lyme Disease) AND TICK REMOVAL

DEFINITION/ETIOLOGY:

A tick is a small, blood-sucking, parasitic arachnid that lives in moist or humid environments, particularly in or near wooded or grassy areas. Ticks live on the blood of large animals such as deer, but can also attach to humans. Once a tick attaches to a host, it will move to a warm, moist location such as the armpit, groin, or hair. Ticks vary in size, can range from very large to very small, and are almost impossible to see.

Tick bites in humans may be caused as one moves by bushes, plants, or grass in tall wooded areas or fields. Ticks can cause a variety of health conditions ranging from harmless to serious. While most ticks are harmless and do not carry disease, some ticks can carry bacteria which can lead to diseases such as Colorado tick fever, Lyme disease, Rocky Mountain spotted fever, and Tularemia.

Tick-borne Diseases		
Disease	**Lyme Disease***	**Rocky Mountain Spotted Fever***
Cause	Spirochete (Borrelia burgdorferi)	Rickettsia rickettsii
Transmission	Wild rodents (nymph stage) and deer tick (adult stage)	Various species (dog, wood ticks)
Exposure risk	Bite 12 hours or more	Bite 4-6 hours; crushing with fingers
Incubation	1-32 days	2-14 days
Early signs	Skin lesion, starting as red maculae or papule, enlarging to a "bull's eye" at least 5 cm	Sudden onset of fever, lasting 2-3 weeks, severe headache, nausea, muscle pain
Other signs	"flu-like" fatigue, chills, muscle and joint pain, swollen lymph nodes	May have a maculopapular rash on limbs by day 3 which spreads to trunk/face; may have petechiae
Complications	Arthritis, encephalitis, Bell's palsy, Cardiac arrhythmia	Multisystem involvement, shock, 15% fatality if untreated

SIGNS AND SYMPTOMS:

Initially, the tick bite is usually painless and remains that way after the tick stops the blood meal and falls off the skin. Later, the following signs and symptoms may develop at the site of the tick bite:

- Itching
- Burning
- Redness
- Localized pain in some individuals

316

TICK-BORNE DISEASES (Rocky Mountain Spotted Fever [RMSF] and Lyme Disease) AND TICK REMOVAL *(continued from previous page)*

Some individuals develop sensitivity or an allergic reaction to tick bites and may experience:
- Rash
- Shortness of breath
- Swelling
- Numbness
- Paralysis

Other symptoms may be rare or infrequent immediately after or during a tick bite and require **immediate medical attention**. These symptoms include:
- Fever
- Shortness of breath
- Weakness
- Vomiting
- Swelling
- Weakness or Paralysis
- Headache
- Confusion
- Palpitations

MANAGEMENT/TREATMENT:
1. Try to establish source and duration of tick adherence. Be familiar with the types of ticks in the area that carry disease.
2. Cleanse the site and then remove the tick with a small, fine-tipped forceps or tweezers grasp the tick as close to the skin as possible, pulling upward with a firm, steady pressure to keep the tick intact.
3. Re-cleanse the site.
4. Place tick in small vial or plastic bag and mark with victim's name, address, date, site of attachment. Have the tick identified by lab, health department, or veterinarian. If unable to retain the tick for identification, flush the tick in toilet; do not burn or dispose of in waste can.
5. Inform parent/guardian of signs that need a physician's attention following a tick bite.
6. Monitor student for signs of illness for up to one month.

*May be reportable to the health department

FOLLOW-UP:
Educate about tick avoidance (clothing, DEET repellents, and pet protection), frequent checks, and careful removal.

TICK-BORNE DISEASES (Rocky Mountain Spotted Fever [RMSF] and Lyme Disease) AND TICK REMOVAL *(continued from previous page)*

NOTES:

- Children should be taught to seek the help of an adult for tick removal.
- If the tick must be removed using your fingers, use a barrier such as a tissue or leaf to avoid contact with possible infected fluids.
- Do not pick, crush, or burn the tick as it may release infected tissues or fluids.
- Do not attempt to smother the tick with substances such as petroleum jelly or nail polish. Smothering is not an effective technique for tick removal as the tick has enough oxygen to complete the feeding (adopted from Lyme Disease Foundation, Inc.).

Check state and local health department websites for details pertinent to the occurrence and types of ticks in your school's location.

References

American Academy of Pediatrics. (2013). Lyme disease (and other tick-borne diseases). Scabies. In S. Aronson, & T. Shope (Eds.), *Managing infectious diseases in child care and schools (2nd ed.)* (p. 115-116). Elk Grove Village, IL: American Academy of Pediatrics.

American Academy of Pediatrics. (2009). Summaries of infectious disease- lyme disease and rocky mountain spotted fever. . In L.K. Pickering, C.J. Baker, D.W. Kimberlin, & S.S. Long (Eds.), *Red Book: 2009 report of the committee on infectious diseases* (28th ed.) (pp. 430-435 and 573-575). Elk Grove Village, IL: American Academy of Pediatrics.

Centers for Disease Control and Prevention (CDC), National Center for Zoonotic, Vector-Borne, and Enteric Diseases, Division of Vector-borne Infectious Diseases. (2013). *DEET, showers, and tick checks can stop ticks.* Retrieved from *http://www.cdc.gov/features/stopticks/*

Centers for Disease Control and Prevention(CDC). (2013). *Ticks.* Retrieved from *http://www.cdc.gov/ticks/index.html*

Centers for Disease Control and Prevention(CDC). (2013). *Rocky mountain spotted fever (RMSF).* Retrieved from *http://www.cdc.gov/rmsf/*

Centers for Disease Control and Prevention(CDC). (2011). *Lyme disease.* Retrieved from http://www.cdc.gov/lyme/

Davis, Charles. (2012). *Ticks.* Retrieved from *http://www.medicinenet.com/ticks/article.htm*

Lyme Disease Foundation, Inc. (LDF). (2012). *Tick removal .* Retrieved from *http://www.lyme.org/ticks/removal.html*

Medline Plus, U.S. National Library of Medicine. (2013). *Tick removal.* Retrieved from *http://www.nlm.nih.gov/medlineplus/ency/article/007211.htm*

University of Maryland Medical Center. (2013). *Tick bite – overview.* Retrieved from *http://www.umm.edu/ency/article/002856.htm*.

TIC DISORDERS AND TOURETTE SYNDROME

DEFINITIONS/ETIOLOGY:
A *tic* is a sudden, rapid, recurrent, non-rhythmic, stereotyped motor movement or vocalization. Any part of the body can be involved—face, neck, hands, legs. The person can hold a tic back for a little while but the condition is involuntary. Many children have mild tics that disappear over time without intervention.

- *Tourette Syndrome* is an inherited, neurological disorder characterized by repeated, involuntary body movements and vocal sounds. It may be accompanied by obsessions, attention problems, learning disabilities and impulsivity. The onset is before age 18, usually between 2 and 12 years with an average onset of 7 years of age. The cause of Tourette syndrome is unknown, but research suggests that it is very complex.

TICS
Tics are classified as **transient or chronic** (Tourette Syndrome) and are most common during adolescence.

TRANSIENT
- The essential feature of Transient Tic Disorder is the presence of single or multiple motor tics and/or vocal tics using limited muscle groups. The tics occur many times a day, nearly every day for at least 4 weeks, but for no longer than 12 consecutive months.

TOURETTE
The full name of the disorder is Gilles de la Tourette Syndrome (GTS). The essential features of Tourette Syndrome are:
- Multiple motor tics and one or more vocal tics involving several muscle groups appear simultaneously or at different periods.
- Tics occur many times a day (usually in bouts), nearly every day or intermittently for a period of more than one year, and during this period, there is never a tic-free period of more than 3 consecutive months.
- The disorder is not due to direct physiological effects of a substance (e.g., a stimulant) or a general medical condition (e.g., post-viral encephalitis).
- It causes marked distress or significant impairment in social, occupational, or other important areas of functioning.

The type, number, frequency, complexity and severity of tics change over time. Motor tics typically involve the head and frequently, other parts of the body (torso, upper and lower limbs). Vocal tics include words or sounds, such as clicks, grunts, yelps, barks, sniffs, snorts and coughs. Complex sounds such as obscenities occur in only 10% of cases.

TIC DISORDERS AND TOURETTE SYNDROME *(continued from previous page)*

SIGNS AND SYMPTOMS:
Tics vary greatly between and within individuals. Some clinical features include:
- Simple motor tics with brief, sudden, and meaningless muscle movements, e.g. eye blinking, nose twitching, or shoulder shrugging (usually the first to appear)
- May only appear when tired, stressed or anxious and have 30-100 tics per minute
- Complex motor tics are more purposeful and involve several muscle groups, e.g. touching other people or objects, retracing steps when walking, and various complex hand gestures
- Vocal tics may be simple or complex and range from meaningless sounds (clearing throat, sniffling, or barking) to sudden utterance of words, phrases, and complete sentences (echolalia or coprolalia)
- Tic intensity can vary from barely visible and audible tics to extremely forceful and loud expressions
- Tics may severely interfere with everyday activities including social relationships and school performance

MANAGEMENT/TREATMENT:
1. Identification and careful diagnosis of the disruptive effects of tics
2. Minimize stress and teach relaxation techniques
3. Rewards and punishments are not indicated or helpful
4. Educate staff and student to understand the disorder. GTS does not diminish intellect.
5. Support groups and education: Tourette Syndrome Assn. (New York) website is www.tsa-usa.org.
6. Medications are used when tics significantly interfere with functioning and for co-morbid conditions (e.g., ADHD, obsessive-compulsive disorder, anxiety)
7. Medication side effects include tremors, depression, weight gain, decreased cognitive abilities and heart problems
8. Severe tics lasting for more than a year may need intervention from a mental healthcare provider

SCHOOL NURSE FOLLOW UP:
- Communicate with parents/guardians regarding health needs and special accommodations during school (may need a 504 plan).
- Participate as a member of the multidisciplinary team to promote health and academic success.
- Provide information and educate school staff.
- Follow up on individualized healthcare plans, emergency plans, and health goals are necessary for continuity of care in school and at home.

TIC DISORDERS AND TOURETTE SYNDROME *(continued from previous page)*

- Provide support and try to build self- esteem in student.
- Provide an emotionally and physically safe environment.
- Monitor symptoms in various situations and report to licensed healthcare provider.

RESOURCES

National Tourette Syndrome Association, Tourette Syndrome in the Classroom School & Community at http://www.tsa-usa.org/news/ED_DVD_TSA_Free_Offer.html

References

Ball, J., Binder, R., & Cowen, K. (Eds.). (2012). Alterations in mental health and cognition. *Principles of Pediatric Nursing: Caring for Children (5th Ed.)* (pp. 931-932). Upper Saddle River, NJ: Pearson Education, Inc.

Mayo Clinic. (2013). *Tourette syndrome*. Retrieved from http://www.mayoclinic.com/health/tourette-syndrome/DS00541

Selekman, J., Diefenbeck, C., Guthrie, S. (2013).Mental health concerns. In J. Selekman (Ed.), *School nursing: A comprehensive text* (2nd ed.) (pp.952-954). Philadelphia, PA: F.A. Davis.

National Institute of Neurological Disorders and Stroke. (2012). *Tourette syndrome fact sheet.* Retrieved from http://www.ninds.nih.gov/disorders/tourette/detail_tourette.htm#220493231

Tourette Syndrome Association, Inc. (n.d.). *Getting help at school*. Retrieved from http://www.tsa-usa.org/aeduc_advoc/getting_help_at_school.htm

TRACHEOSTOMY CARE

DEFINITION/ETIOLOGY:
A tracheostomy is a surgical opening into the trachea. It is often referred to as a "trach". The opening is called a stoma, and a tracheostomy tube is inserted into the stoma. The trach tubes are primarily made of specialized plastic, and come in a variety of brands and sizes. Tracheostomies may be temporary or long term. Common indications for tracheostomies include: bronchopulmonary dysplasia (BPD, which can be a sequalae of severe prematurity), central hypoventilation syndrome, chronic pulmonary diseases, congenital anomalies, degenerative neuromuscular diseases (such as Muscular Dystrophy), and spinal cord injuries. Many children with tracheostomies also require support from a ventilator, either all of the time or for parts of the day.

When planning for the care of the medically fragile child in the school setting, it is essential that the school nurse bear in mind child development and family needs along with legal, clinical, and policy and procedural considerations.

LEGAL CONSIDERATIONS:
The major law that affords students with disabilities to attend school is the Individuals with Disabilities Education Improvement Act (IDEIA). Landmark cases interpreting IDEIA have centered on students requiring skilled medical care, including the maintenance of tracheotomies and ventilators. Possibly the most widely recognized court case regarding technology dependent students is the 1999 United States Supreme Court case Cedar Rapids Community District v. Garret F. It was decided by courts that the school district must provide educational and health services to the student. Additionally, delegation of trach care to unlicensed support staff is dependent on the Nurse Practice Act of each individual state.

MANAGEMENT/TREATMENT:

TRACHEOSTOMY CARE:
The primary goal is airway maintenance. Respiratory assessment, assessment of stoma site, tracheal suctioning, and trach tube replacement are components of care. The school nurse should develop an Individualized Healthcare Plan (IHP) outlining the procedure, along with emergency interventions.

I. **RESPIRATORY ASSESSMENT. Tracheostomy may need to be suctioned if you observe the following after checking placement of trach tube:**
   - Increased respiratory rate
   - Trouble breathing
   - Noisy respirations
   - Visible mucus

TRACHEOSTOMY CARE *(continued from previous page)*

- Restlessness
- "Wet" sounding breathing
- Color change, particularly blue or pale around the mucous membranes and nail beds
- Increased heart rate
- Skin feels moist or "clammy" to the touch

II. **ASSESSMENT OF THE STOMA SITE:** Assessment of the site may be done as you carry out routine trach care. Incorporate the type of care recommended by the provider (i.e. cleaning with soap and water vs. half strength hydrogen peroxide) into the school health plan. The area around the stoma should be kept clean and dry. Many children use a trach dressing and the dressing should be changed when it becomes moist. Notify parent/guardian if there is an increased need for dressing changed secondary to increased drainage, redness at the stoma site, "crusting" at the site or any type of skin breakdown or signs/symptoms of infection.

III. **SUCTIONING:**
- Clean technique is recommended for home/school
- Equipment needed: suction machine, catheter or Yankauer, gloves, water/normal saline, mask if needed.
- Shallow suctioning: this method is used when mucus is visible at the opening of the trach. This may occur after the child coughs. A Yankauer catheter or even a bulb syringe may be used to remove the mucus.
- Premeasured depth suctioning: Measure the length of the trach tube and add ¼ inch. Make a note of this on the child's Individualized School Health Plan. When suctioning, only advance the catheter as far as the premeasured length. It is beneficial to use pre-marked suction catheters.
- Deep suctioning: The catheter is advanced beyond the tip of the tracheal tube until resistance is felt. This procedure usually is not needed in the school setting and requires specific orders from the licensed healthcare provider. If deep suctioning necessary, it should be performed only by a licensed nurse.

TRACHEOSTOMY CARE *(continued from previous page)*

> **PROCEDURE**
> 1. Wash hands.
> 2. Glove.
> 3. Set up equipment.
> 4. Turn on suction machine, check by tip of catheter into cup of NS/water.
> 5. Advance the catheter to pre-measured length into trach tube.
> 6. Cover the air vent with your thumb to apply suction, gently twirl the catheter as you withdraw the catheter from the trach tube. This should take 5 seconds or less.
> 7. Allow student to rest for approximately 30 seconds between suctioning.
> 8. After each suction pass, rinse the tubing in the cup of sterile water/saline.
> 9. Notify parent/guardian if: increased need for suctioning, a color change in the mucus such as green or yellow, bleeding from the trach .
> 10. Replace artificial nose after suctioning.
>
> Note: If oral suctioning is also required, the oral cavity may be suctioned with the trach catheter, but a catheter used in the oral cavity cannot be used to suction the trach.

III. TRACHESTOMY TUBE CHANGE:

- Indications for trach change or replacement should be written into the school health plan.
- Ideally, a member of the child's healthcare team should provide training for school staff.
- Maintain a "go bag" containing emergency supplies for trach change. This bag should travel with the child and must be checked daily upon arrival to school. It is recommended that a checklist be developed for documentation. Following is a list of basic components for the "go bag":
  - ✓ Extra trach tube, with obturator placed inside
  - ✓ Additional extra trach tube, one size smaller than normal, with obturator placed inside
  - ✓ Clean trach ties
  - ✓ Scissors
  - ✓ Water-soluble jelly or lubricant
  - ✓ Suction equipment with correct size catheters
  - ✓ Ambu bag and mask.
  - ✓ Oxygen (if part of school health plan)
  - ✓ Gloves
  - ✓ Trach dressing
  - ✓ Delee mucus trap
  - ✓ Bulb syringe
  - ✓ Artificial noses

Immediately replace any supplies used after child is stabilized.

TRACHEOSTOMY CARE *(continued from previous page)*

SCHOOL NURSE'S ROLE:
- Child and family advocate
- Assess and plan for routine and emergency care including disaster planning
- Collaborate with the physician, parents/guardians and other members of the school health team to develop the Individualized School Health Plan
- Assemble and lead the schoolchild care team
- Case management
- Staff development/in-service
- Monitor respiratory status
- Coordinate care with private duty nurse, if applicable
- Participate in Individualized Education Plan (IEP)meetings

RECOMMENDED GUIDELINES FOR CAREGIVER TRAINING:
- CPR/Tracheostomy CPR certification
- Recognize signs and symptoms of respiratory distress
- Understanding of emergency plan
- RN or licensed respiratory therapist (unless state medical and nursing practice acts state otherwise)
- Training individualized to the child
- Caregivers trained in care and replacement of the trach tube
- Caregivers trained in procedures and problem management
- Evaluate need for 1:1 caregiver
- If unlicensed caregiver, school nurse in building at all times

TRANSPORTATION CONSIDERATIONS:
- Attendant on bus to monitor student
- Emergency plan in place addressing response to potential emergencies on the bus
- Transportation staff trained in emergency trach management
- Transportation staff to check "go bag" and ensure contents are compete before transporting student to school (see suggested contents in previous section)
- Copy of emergency plan in "go bag"
- Transportation staff to check equipment: ensure that suction machine is working properly and all necessary suction equipment in place prior to transporting student to school
- Transportation plan should indicate any other special needs necessary to transport student safely, i.e. oxygen, wheelchair restraints, etc.
- It is recommended that a daily checklist be developed for efficiency and documentation (i.e. "go bag" contents checked, etc.)
- Substitute transportation must also be trained

TRACHEOSTOMY CARE *(continued from previous page)*

Resources
Easy to understand, downloadable trach care guides are available at:
- http://www.cookchildrens.org/SiteCollectionDocuments/HomeHealth/Education/ RespiratoryTherapy/Tracheostomy/ CCHH_Trach_PediatricTracheostomyHomeCareGuide.pdf
- http://www.cincinnatichildrens.org/assets/0/78/1067/1395/1957/1959/1961/ 98555d88-d30c-4fda-a8a7-b2f3df74b762.pdf

References

American Thoracic Society. (2000). Care of the child with a chronic tracheostomy. *American Journal of Respiratory and Critical Care Medicine, 161*, 297-308. doi: 10.1164/ajrccm.161.1.ats1-00

Bassham, B. S., Kane, I., MacKeil-White, K., Fischer, J., Arnold, D., Whatley, V., & Walsh. M. (2012). Technology: Respiratory treatment of the special needs child http://www.mc.vanderbilt.edu/documents/vanderbiltnursing/files/ PEM_13_2_1st_revises%20(1).pdf

Brubaker, C. & Selekman, J. (2013). Skills needed by children who are technology dependent. In J. Selekman (Ed.), School nursing: A comprehensive text (2nd ed.) (pp. 1028-1032, 1047-1053). Philadelphia, PA: F.A. Davis.

Cincinnati Children's Hospital Medical Center. (2011). Best evidence statement (BESt): Basic pediatric tracheostomy care. Retrieved from www.cincinnatichildrens.org/workarea/linkit.aspx?linkidentifier=id&itemid=88057&libid=87745

Golinker, L. (1999). *Tatro to Detsel to Garret F.: a personal reflection on the evolution of the IDEA "school health services" provisions.* Retrieved from http://www.nls.org/golinker.htm

Heller, K.W., Fredrick, L.D., Best, S., Dykes, M.K., & Cohen, E.T. (2000). Specialized health care procedures in schools: Training and service delivery. *Exceptional Children, 66*(2), 173-186.

Overgaard, P.M. (2005). Keys to safely transporting students with tracheostomies. *School Bus Fleet.* Retrieved from http://www.schoolbusfleet.com/Channel/Special-Needs/Articles/Print/Story/2005/02/ Keys-to-safely-transporting-students-with-tracheostomies.aspx

Raymond, J.A. (2009). The integration of children dependent on medical technology into public schools. *The Journal of School Nursing, 25*(3), 186-193.

Rehm, R.S. (2002). Creating a context of safety and achievement at school for children who are medically fragile/technology dependent. *Advances in Nursing Science, 24*(3), 71-84.

Selekman, J., Bochenek, J., & Lukens, M. (2013). Children with chronic conditions. In J. Selekman (Ed.), *School nursing: A comprehensive text (2nd ed.)* (pp. 700-783). Philadelphia, PA: F.A. Davis.

Turnball, H.R. (2005). Individuals with Disabilities Education Act reauthorization: Accountability and personal responsibility. *Remedial and Special Education, 26*(6), 320-326.

TUBERCULOSIS (PRIMARY OR CHILDHOOD)

DEFINITIONS/ETIOLOGY:
Tuberculosis (TB) is caused by *Mycobacterium tuberculosis*, an acid-fast bacillus (AFB). Mycobacterium are usually slow growing and have waxy cell wall that are resistant to digestion. Many mycobacterium are intracellular parasites. Additional information related to TB definitions and etiology includes the following:

- **Childhood or Primary TB** is *M. tuberculosis* infection in older infants and children, contracted from prolonged household case contact. It is usually an asymptomatic infection. The diagnosis is confirmed only by a positive tuberculin skin test (TST).
- **Tuberculin Skin Test** also known at the Mantoux test or purified protein derivative (PDD) is the standard for identifying infected persons. The Mantoux test is read 48-72 hours after being placed.
- **Positive tuberculin skin test**: The classifications of reactions (measuring *induration*, not redness) are:
    - Induration ≥ 5mm: Positive if patient is at high risk, such as household contact with TB disease, clinical evidence of TB, abnormal chest radiograph, or HIV+.
    - Induration ≥ 10 mm: Positive if patient is at moderate risk, e.g., children < 4 years of age, or born in high-prevalence regions, or those who travel to these regions.
    - Induration ≥ 15mm: Positive if patient is 4 years of age or older without any risk factor.
- **Latent tuberculosis infection (LTBI)** is defined as TB infection in a person who has a positive TST result but no physical finding of TB disease; chest radiograph findings are normal or reveal evidence of healing infection.
- **Tuberculosis disease** is defined as disease in a person with TB infection having symptoms, signs, or radiographic manifestations.

CAUSES:
All cases of TB are passed from person to person through airborne transmission of droplets. Inhalation of droplets can occur from an adult or adolescent with contagious, cavity, pulmonary tuberculosis. When a person with TB infection coughs, sneezes, or talks, tiny droplets of saliva or mucus are expelled in the air and can be transmitted through inhalation by another person.
- The incubation period from infection to development of a positive TST is 2-10 weeks. The risk of developing of TB disease is highest during the 6 months after infection and remains high for 2 years.
- Once the infectious particles are inhaled and reach the alveoli, small sac-like structures develop in the air spaces in the lungs and the macrophage cell engulfs the TB bacteria.
- The TB bacteria are then transmitted to the lymphatic system and bloodstream and the spread to other organs occurs.

TUBERCULOSIS (PRIMARY OR CHILDHOOD) *(continued from previous page)*

- The TB bacteria begin to multiply in organs with high oxygen pressures, e.g. the upper lobes of the lungs, kidneys, bone marrow, and meninges.
- TB disease occurs when the bacteria cause clinically detectable disease.
- Persons who have inhaled the TB bacterium but show no signs of clinically detectable disease are referred to as infected. Persons infected with TB have no symptoms of disease because the immune system has walled off the organism in an inflammatory focus known as a granuloma.
- The skin test for TB will often be positive in people infected with TB, but the disease cannot be transmitted to others while in the latent phase of TB infection.

EVIDENCE-BASED RECOMMENDATIONS FOR SCREENING FOR CHILDREN AND ADOLESCENTS
- Screen for risk factors of TB and LTBI.
- Test with a TST only if more than 1 risk factor is present.

RISK FACTORS
- Contact with adult with active TB disease
- Foreign birth
- Travel to a country with high prevalence of infection
- Household member with latent tuberculosis infection (LTBI)

SIGNS/SYMPTOMS:
- Common symptoms of TB may include fever, cough, chest x-ray abnormalities, loss of appetite, weight loss, and night sweats.
- Most children and adolescents with tuberculosis infection have no symptoms (asymptomatic).
- Children and adolescents with continued exposure or weakened immunity can develop symptoms such as fatigue, malaise, low-grade fever, and symptoms resulting from lymph node enlargement, especially in the center of the chest (hilar node).
- In 6-8 weeks, the body's defenses wall off the infection with scar tissue. There are no further consequences other than positive TST. This is the typical course of childhood or primary TB.
- About 5% of children with a delayed diagnosis or no treatment can develop a serious form of TB.

TUBERCULOSIS (PRIMARY OR CHILDHOOD) *(continued from previous page)*

MANAGEMENT/TREATMENT:
Medical treatment of TB includes the following recommendations:
1. Treatment is recommended for all children and adolescents diagnosed with LTBI, because young children are at higher risk for progression to TB disease.
2. Treatment is with multiple antimicrobial drugs.
3. First line drugs are isoniazide (INH), rifampin (RIF), pyrazinamide (PZA), and ethambutol (EMB).
4. Children are usually treated with isoniazid (INH), daily by mouth for 9 months.
5. For children < 4 years of age with a close contact, INH should be initiated, even if the TST result is first negative. TST should be retested 12 weeks after the last contact. If the result is negative, INH may be discontinued.
6. Second line drugs include both the aminlglycosides (streptomycin, kanamkin, amikacin, and capreomycin) and fluroquinolones (levofloxacin, moxifloxacin).

Management for schools of TB includes the following recommendations:
1. Suspected or known tuberculosis must be reported to the Public Health Department immediately, because early reporting may help minimize the spread of TB.
2. **With rare exception, primary TB is non-contagious; student may remain in school, even though a person at home has active TB.**
3. Children with LTBI can participate in all activities whether they are receiving treatment or not.
4. Educate faculty and staff to understand relative risk.
5. Cooperate with the Public Health Department or the school physician to assist students with skin testing and/or x-rays of students and staff when these tests are recommended.

FOLLOW UP:
- Promote and monitor adherence to treatment of LTBI in all students.
- Provide education about the importance of adhering to completing treatment and the potential side effects of INH. These include hepatitis, gastrointestinal disturbances, and peripheral neuropathy.
- If a student demonstrates any symptom of liver toxicity, stop treatment immediately and refer the student to the primary care provider for assessment.

NOTES:
- TB is preventable through effective management and treatment. Treatment of TB in a single person prevents latent infection from becoming active disease. Treatment is also effective in controlling the spread of disease among large populations.
- The TB vaccine, bacilli Calmette-Guerin (BCG), may often be used in foreign countries to prevent the spread of disease among children. However, the vaccine does not protect against pulmonary tuberculosis and often results in a false positive TST.

329

TUBERCULOSIS (PRIMARY OR CHILDHOOD) *(continued from previous page)*

References

American Academy of Pediatrics. (2013). *Tuberculosis (tb)*. In S. Aronson, & T. Shope (Eds.), *Managing infectious diseases in child care and schools (2nd ed.)* (p. 163-164). Elk Grove Village, IL: American Academy of Pediatrics.

Batra, V. (2012*). Pediatric tuberculosis*. Retrieved from http://emedicine.medscape.com/article/969401-overview

Blosser, C.G., Brady, M. & Muller, W. (2008). Infectious diseases and immunizations. In C. Burns, M. Brady, A. Dunn, N.B. Starr, C. Blosser (Eds.), *Pediatric primary care (*4th ed.) (pp. 535-539). St. Louis, MO: Saunders Elsevier.

Centers for Disease Control and Prevention (CDC). (2012). *Tuberculosis*. Retrieved from http://www.cdc.gov/tb/?404; http://www.cdc.gov:80/tb/publications/factsheets/testing/skintest.htm

Emedicine Health. (2010). *Tuberculosis*. Retrieved from http://www.emedicine.com/tuberculosis/page12_em.htm

Merck Manual, Professional Edition. (2012). Tuberculosis. Retrieved from http://www.merckmanuals.com/professional/infectious_diseases/mycobacteria/tuberculosis_tb.html

UPPER RESPIRATORY INFECTION or "COMMON COLD"

DEFINITION/ETIOLOGY:
Common cold – viral infection of the upper respiratory tract (affects the nose, throat, ears and eyes). More than 200 viruses can cause a cold. The rhinovirus is the most common pathogen that causes upper respiratory infections. Incubation period is 2 – 14 days. Symptoms typically last 7 – 10 days. The virus is spread by airborne droplets, hand to hand contact or by sharing contaminated objects.

SIGNS AND SYMPTOMS:
- Runny nose – nasal drainage initially clear; after few days mucous becomes whitish or yellowish in color; as the cold progresses the mucous may change to a greenish color (this is normal)
- Sneezing
- Watery eyes
- Sore (or scratchy/itchy) throat
- Cough
- Mild headache
- Mild joint pain
- Earache (may result from the URI virus or from a secondary bacterial infection)
- May have a low grade fever

MANAGEMENT/TREATMENT:
There is no cure for an upper respiratory infection. Treatment is supportive.
1. Limit exercise if cough is troublesome. Coordinate with PE teacher.
2. Exclude from school if student has severe cough.
3. Educate about hygienic use and disposal of tissues and thorough hand washing.
4. Educate to not pick at nose and to blow nose gently.
5. Encourage fluids.
6. Diet as tolerated.
7. Do not use aspirin under age 18. Aspirin can play a role in causing Reye's Syndrome.
8. If giving acetaminophen, follow medication orders.
9. Nasal antihistamines/decongestants may provide nasal relief. Parent/guardian(s) should follow physician/pharmacist's guidelines.
10. Watch for adverse side effects even with over-the-counter medicines taken at home; antihistamines can cause drowsiness; decongestants can cause excitability.
11. Refer to physician if temperature is > 100.4
12. If lasts more than 10-14 days, another diagnosis may be explored by the physician/ healthcare provider.

UPPER RESPIRATORY INFECTION or "Common Cold" *(continued from previous page)*

FOLLOW UP:
- Refer to physician for persistent cough or complications: earache, fever, vomiting, headache, loss of appetite, sore throat, dehydration, etc.

POTENTIAL COMPLICATIONS:
Complications are rare. Potential complications include:
- Sinus infection
- Ear infection
- Bronchitis
- Wheezing – colds may exacerbate asthma

NOTES:
Educate parent/guardians and staff regarding the importance of:
- Good handwashing
- Covering nose and mouth with a tissue when coughing or sneezing, and proper disposal of tissues; wash hands or use alcohol-based hand sanitizer after blowing nose or touching nasal secretions
- To prevent the spread of germs, teach children to cough or sneeze into their shoulder or elbow if a tissue is not available
- Keep fingers away from eyes and nose – spreads the virus
- Educate parent/guardian that antibiotics will not cure the common cold; a cold is caused by a virus; an antibiotic may be needed for secondary bacterial infections (ear infection, etc.)
- Exposure to cold temperature (outdoor recess, etc.) does not make a person more susceptibility to an upper respiratory infection

References

American Academy of Pediatrics. (2013). Upper respiratory infection (common cold). In S. Aronson, & T. Shope (Eds.), *Managing infectious diseases in child care and schools (2nd ed.)* (pp. 165-166). Elk Grove Village, IL: American Academy of Pediatrics.

Centers for Disease Control and Prevention. (2012). *Common cold and runny nose.* Retrieved from http://www.cdc.gov/getsmart/antibiotic-use/URI/colds.html

John, R., & Chewey, L. (2013). *Common complaints.* In J. Selekman (Ed.), *School nursing: A comprehensive text* (2nd ed.) (pp.578-640). Philadelphia, PA: F. A. Davis.

Mayo Clinic. *(2013). Common cold.* Retrieved from *http://www.mayoclinic.com/health/common-cold/DS00056*

Merck Manual. (2012). *Common cold.* Retrieved from http://www.merckmanuals.com/professional/infectious_diseases/respiratory_viruses/common_cold.html?qt=UpperRespiratory Infection&alt=sh

Warts (Verrucae Vulgaris)

DEFINITIONS/ETIOLOGY:
Warts are non-cancerous epidermal skin growths caused by the *Human Papillomavirus* (HPV). There are many different types of warts. Types include: common, flat, plantar and genital. Warts affect all age groups, but are common in children. Most warts are asymptomatic.

SIGNS AND SYMPTOMS

Type	Location	Symptoms
Common warts	Often appear on hands and/or fingers	• Small, grainy flesh-colored, white, tan or pink lesions • Lesions may be rough to touch
Flat	Appear in areas you shave – difficult to treat	• Flat topped, slightly raised lesions • Darker than skin pigment
Plantar	Found on soles and balls of feet	• Small, fleshy colored lesion • Callus on the balls of feet or soles of feet (wart has grown inward) • May have black "seeds" • May have mild pain
Genital	• Sexually transmitted disease; lesions grow on penis (tip or shaft), exterior female genitals, vulva, walls of vagina, anus, and cervix; genital warts can grow in the mouth. • Transmitted during sexual intercourse and/or skin to skin contact • Can be transmitted by asymptomatic infected persons	• More common in women • Itching, burning and/or pain around lesions • Small and flat (may be so small that they are not visible) • Left untreated, may grow into large clusters

MANAGEMENT/TREATMENT:
Most warts resolve spontaneously. If treatment is indicated:
- Over-the-counter (OTC) medication (salicylic acid)
  - OTC medication is effective if the individual is motivated to adhere to treatment
  - Can take several weeks for the medication to be effective
  - Can erroneously mistake cancerous lesion for wart
- Cryosurgery (freezing) – may take several treatments
- Excision – virus may remain in tissue even though the lesion has been removed
- Laser surgery

WARTS *(continued from previous page)*

FOLLOW UP:
- See physician or healthcare provider if wart if located on face or genitals.
- To avoid the spread of warts, educate child/youth to avoid picking at own wart (autoinoculation); avoid touching someone's wart.
- If district allows; educate teens on avoiding risky sexual behaviors.
- Refer diabetic students with plantar warts to a physician or healthcare practitioner for treatment – poor healing could lead to nerve damage.

POTENTIAL COMPLICATIONS:
- Autoinoculation
- May spread to other people
- Cervical cancer is linked to genital warts

NOTES:
- Monitor wart lesions – skin cancer may look like a wart.
- Educate students and staff to wear flip-flops in public showers, locker rooms and on pool decks.
- Prevention – Gardasil vaccine is available to protect from certain strains of HPV that cause genital warts.

References

American Academy of Dermatology. (2013). *Warts. Tips for management.* Retrieved from http://www.aad.org/dermatology-a-to-z/diseases-and-treatments/u---w/warts/tips/warts-tips-for-managing

Mayo Clinic. (2012a). *Common warts.* Retrieved from http://www.mayoclinic.com/health/common-warts/DS00370

Mayo Clinic. (2012b). *Genital warts.* Retrieved from http://www.mayoclinic.com/health/genital-warts/DS00087

Mayo Clinic. (2011). *Plantar warts.* Retrieved from http://www.mayoclinic.com/health/plantar-warts/DS00509

Medlineplus. U.S. National Library of Medicine. (2013). *Warts.* Retrieved from http://www.nlm.nih.gov/medlineplus/warts.html

Merck Manual. (2012). *Warts.* Retrieved from http://www.merckmanuals.com/professional/dermatologic_disorders/viral_skin_diseases/warts.html

Selekman, J. & Kahn, P. (2013). High-risk behaviors. In J. Selekman (Ed.), *School nursing: A comprehensive text* (2nd ed.) (pp. 1118-1154). Philadelphia, PA: F. A. Davis.

CPSIA information can be obtained
at www.ICGtesting.com
Printed in the USA
BVOW09s2123261116

468725BV00002BA/8/P

9 780979 249747